Begin to Code Building apps and games in the cloud

Rob Miles

ISBN-13: 978-0-13-806540-9
ISBN-10: 0-13-806540-3

Library of Congress Control Number: 2023935868

1 2023

TRADEMARKS
Microsoft and the trademarks listed at http://www.microsoft.com on the "Trademarks" webpage are trademarks of the Microsoft group of companies. All other marks are property of their respective owners.

WARNING AND DISCLAIMER
Every effort has been made to make this book as complete and as accurate as possible, but no warranty or fitness is implied. The information provided is on an "as is" basis. The author, the publisher, and Microsoft Corporation shall have neither liability nor responsibility to any person or entity with respect to any loss or damages arising from the information contained in this book or from the use of the programs accompanying it.

SPECIAL SALES
For information about buying this title in bulk quantities, or for special sales opportunities (which may include electronic versions; custom cover designs; and content particular to your business, training goals, marketing focus, or branding interests), please contact our corporate sales department at corpsales@pearsoned.com or (800) 382-3419.

For government sales inquiries, please contact governmentsales@pearsoned.com.

For questions about sales outside the U.S., please contact intlcs@pearson.com.

Editor-in-Chief
Brett Bartow

Executive Editor
Loretta Yates

Development Editor
Rick Kughen

Managing Editor
Sandra Schroeder

Senior Project Editor
Tracey Croom

Project Editor
Charlotte Kughen

Copy Editor
Rick Kughen

Indexer
Cheryl Lenser

Proofreader
Charlotte Kughen

Technical Editor
John Ray

Editorial Assistant
Cindy Teeters

Cover Designer
Twist Creative, Seattle

Compositor
Bronkella Publishing, LLC

Graphics
TJ Graham Art

Credits
Cover: 32 pixels/Shutterstock, Chapter 04, Screenshot of OpenJS website: OpenJS Foundation

Chapters 7 and 11: Screenshots of MongoDB UI: MongoDB, Inc.

Chapter 11: Screenshots of JWT.io UI: Okta, Inc.

Chapter 12: Screenshots of Raspberry Pi UI: Raspberry Pi Ltd; screenshots of HiveMQ website: HiveMQ GmbH; screenshots of Connected Little Boxes website: Connected Humber CIC

To Mary

About the author

Rob Miles spent more than 30 years teaching programming at the University of Hull in the United Kingdom. He's a Microsoft MVP with a passion for programming and creating new things. He runs a tiny company promoting the use of software and devices in the community and loves building things and putting code into them. He reckons that programming is the most creative thing you can learn how to do. He claims to know a lot of really good jokes, but nobody has ever heard him tell one.

If you want an insight into the Wacky World™ of Rob Miles, you can read his blog at *www.robmiles.com* and follow him on Twitter as @RobMiles.

Contents at a glance

Contents

Part 1: The cloud

Part 2: Make a cloud-based application

8 Build an application 298

Part 3: Building with cloud technologies

Introduction

The fundamentals of what a program does have not changed since the invention of the first computer more than 80 years ago. Programs still take data in, do something with it, and then send data out. However, how programs are created, deployed, and consumed has changed massively, from central mainframes to personal computers to the cloud.

The cloud takes your programs and gives them wings. The cloud enables you to turn your ideas into solutions that anyone in the world can use. This book gives you a handle on cloud development. It explains the evolution of the cloud, identifies its challenges, and sets you on the road to becoming an accomplished cloud developer. You will learn how to code for the cloud, how to use cloud technology on your local machine, where code and data can be hosted, and how applications are built from cooperating software components.

It won't always be an easy journey. Things worth doing tend to involve effort, and learning how to code for the cloud is one of them. Not everything will make sense when you first see it. Cloud solutions may contain multiple moving parts, which must all fit together to work correctly. In addition, there are people out there who will make it their business to try to undermine, overload, break, or steal your work, so you need to be prepared for this. You will have to learn how the cloud enables both bad and good behaviors. However, if you stay the course, you'll be rewarded with skills you can use to take your ideas and bring them to life across the world.

How this book fits together

I've organized this book into three parts. Each part builds on the previous one to turn you into a successful cloud developer.

Part 1: The cloud

We start by considering where the cloud came from and the drivers behind its development. Then we begin making applications using JavaScript, learning language features and application libraries as we go. By the end of this part, we'll have built applications running in the browser and also created server code that can run in the cloud.

Part 2: Make a cloud-based application

First we investigate the HTML Document Object Model in the browser and use it to create a playable game. Then we deploy the game into the cloud for anyone in the world to access. Next we move on to make our game a shared user experience powered by connected code running in both browser and server. We finish with an application design and build exercise, starting with an idea and ending with a cloud-ready application.

Part 3: Building with cloud technologies

This part starts by introducing techniques and tools to improve the quality of your applications. Then we move on to consider how to store application data in files and database documents. Next we discover how to create logins and implement role-based security for users of an application. Finally we take a look at a host of exciting JavaScript-powered technologies, including creating your own servers to build your own personal cloud, connecting hardware lights and buttons to servers, linking applications to Internet Of Things devices, and making a fast-moving sprite-based game.

Online glossary

To help you learn the basic terminology of cloud application programming, I've created an expansive glossary. It contains definitions of terms you might not have seen before, or have seen in a different context. You can find the glossary at *https://begintocodecloud.com/glossary.html*.

How to use this text

A good way to use the text is to read through a section away from the computer, perhaps on the bus (unless you are driving it), and then go back and work through the examples and exercises when you are sitting next to a computer. This way, you can pick up on the theory and context without feeling forced to do anything with it, and then you can reinforce your understanding by applying it later. Each chapter starts by setting out what you will learn and finishes with questions that help you validate your understanding and give you thoughts to ponder.

Everything will be described in a strong context. You might not initially understand how something works, but you should understand the problem it is being used to solve. Eventually, you will start to see other contexts in which the tool or technique is used, at which point you can call yourself a proper developer.

The text is sprinkled with coding and debugging exercises to try, along with suggestions of how the examples can be applied and extended. If you get stuck, you can watch a video walkthrough of the exercise.

Like learning to ride a bicycle, you'll learn by *doing*. You must put in the time and practice to learn how to code. But this book will give you the knowledge and confidence to try your hand at programming, and it will also be around to help you if your programming doesn't turn out as you expected. The following are some elements in the book that will help you learn by doing.

MAKE SOMETHING HAPPEN

Yes, the best way to learn things is by doing, so you'll find Make Something Happen elements throughout the text. These elements offer ways for you to practice your programming skills. Each starts with an example and then introduces some steps you can try on your own. Everything you create will run on Windows, macOS, or Linux.

Also, each Make Something Happen includes a QR code like this one. Simply scan it with your mobile device to be taken to a video I've created, which takes you through the exercise. You can also see the video by visiting *https://www.youtube.com/watch?v=LQJOm9zFfNk*.

CODE ANALYSIS

A great way to learn how to program is by looking at code written by others and working out what it does (and sometimes why it doesn't do what it should). You'll find Code Analysis sections at regular intervals in the text. There are also a few debugging exercises that teach you how to view your code as it runs.

Colorful code

You'll already have noticed that the book is presented in bright colors, with eye-catching illustrations here and there. The code samples use color highlighting to help you navigate programs:

- In JavaScript samples, code keywords (parts of the language) are **blue**, strings of text are **red**, and numeric values and comments are green

- In HTML samples, elements and delimiters are brown, attribute names are **red** and attribute values are **blue**.

Delimiters are color matched. In other words, a **blue** open brace { will be matched with a corresponding blue close brace }, as green will be paired with green, brown with brown, and so on. This might not make a lot of sense right now, but it will really help you find your way around the sample code. The color schemes are based on ones used by the Visual Studio Code editor.

What you will need

You'll need a computer and some software to work with the programs in this book. I'm afraid I can't provide you with a computer, but in the first chapter, you'll find out how you can get started with nothing more than a computer and a web browser. The book examples use the Edge browser, but you can use any browser you like, such as Chrome, FireFox, or Safari. Later, you'll discover how to use the Visual Studio Code development environment to create and debug JavaScript programs.

As you work through the book, you will create and use cloud services that will be hosted on systems in the cloud. You might think that this would be expensive, but all the example applications are based on technologies that are free for personal use. You will have to register for some of them, but they will not cost any money.

Using a PC or laptop

You can use Windows, macOS, or Linux to create and run the programs in the text. Your PC doesn't have to be particularly powerful, but these are the minimum specifications I'd recommend:

- A 1 GHz or faster processor, preferably an Intel i5 or better.

- At least 4 gigabytes (GB) of memory (RAM), but preferably 8 GB or more.

- 256 GB hard drive space. (The JavaScript frameworks and Visual Studio Code installations take about 1 GB of hard drive space.)

There are no specific requirements for the graphics display on your machine, although a higher-resolution screen will enable you to see more when writing your programs.

Programming experience

This book will not tell you what programs do or the fundamentals of program creation. You need to know a bit about programming, ideally with JavaScript. The book will put lots of programming techniques into a cloud context. There are many examples you can use as jumping-off points for your own ideas, and we will use the cloud in many different scenarios, from useful applications to turning lights on and off in your house with the Internet of Things devices to creating compelling shared experiences.

You can write cloud applications in any programming language. But the JavaScript language has been associated with the cloud ever since the language was first built into early web browsers. JavaScript lends itself very well to cloud development, not least because of the huge number of libraries built around it and the ease with which these can be used to develop solutions.

If you have a lot of wonderful JavaScript experience, you'll be able to get the most from the content immediately. However, if you've programmed in any language, you should be able to get the hang of what the sample code is doing. Programming is a universal skill; the programming language is just how you present your program instructions to the computer. So don't be afraid to have a go just because your background is in C, C++, Java, or Python (to name a few). To make this easier for you, I've added an expansive glossary. It contains definitions of terms you might not have seen before, or have seen in a different context. You can find the glossary at *https://begintocodecloud.com/glossary.html*.

Book Resources

The book content includes 52 code examples, 25 sample applications, and 67 Make Something Happen screencast videos. In the first chapters of the book, you will work with code hosted at the book website at *https://begintocodecloud.com/*. Later, you will make your own copies of the book resources, which are held on GitHub at *https://github.com/Building-Apps-and-Games-in-the-Cloud*. Full instructions are in the text.

Errata, updates, and book support

We've made every effort to ensure the accuracy of this book and its companion content. You can access updates to this book—in the form of a list of submitted errata and their related corrections—at

MicrosoftPressStore.com/CodeAppsGames/errata

If you discover an error not already listed, please submit it to us at the same page.

If you need additional support, please visit

MicrosoftPressStore.com/Support

Please note that product support for Microsoft software and hardware is not offered through the previous addresses. For help with Microsoft software or hardware, go to

http://support.microsoft.com

Stay in touch

Let's keep the conversation going! We're on Twitter: *http://twitter.com/MicrosoftPress*.

Pearson's Commitment to Diversity, Equity, and Inclusion

Pearson is dedicated to creating bias-free content that reflects the diversity of all learners. We embrace the many dimensions of diversity, including but not limited to race, ethnicity, gender, socioeconomic status, ability, age, sexual orientation, and religious or political beliefs.

Education is a powerful force for equity and change in our world. It has the potential to deliver opportunities that improve lives and enable economic mobility. As we work with authors to create content for every product and service, we acknowledge our responsibility to demonstrate inclusivity and incorporate diverse scholarship so that everyone can achieve their potential through learning. As the world's leading learning company, we have a duty to help drive change and live up to our purpose to help more people create a better life for themselves and to create a better world.

Our ambition is to purposefully contribute to a world where

- Everyone has an equitable and lifelong opportunity to succeed through learning.

- Our educational products and services are inclusive and represent the rich diversity of learners.

- Our educational content accurately reflects the histories and experiences of the learners we serve.

- Our educational content prompts deeper discussions with learners and motivates them to expand their own learning (and worldview).

While we work hard to present unbiased content, we want to hear from you about any concerns or needs with this Pearson product so that we can investigate and address them.

Please contact us with concerns about any potential bias at
https://www.pearson.com/report-bias.html.

Part 1

The cloud

We start by considering where the cloud came from and the drivers behind its development. Then we begin making applications using JavaScript, learning language features and application libraries as we go. By the end of this part, we'll have built applications running in the browser and also created server code that can run in the cloud.

1

Code and the cloud

What you will learn

In this chapter, we will investigate the fundamentals of cloud computing and discover what makes an application "cloud-based." We will also start our journey with the JavaScript language by exploring how JavaScript functions allow code running in the browser to interact with the JavaScript environment. We'll see how programs run inside a web browser and how we can interact directly with code running in the browser via the Developer Tools, allowing us to view inside our programs as they run.

I'm assuming you are familiar with programming, but just in case there are things that you don't know (or I have a different understanding), I've added a glossary at the end of this book. Whenever you see a word formatted in *italic*, it means that the word is defined in the glossary. If something doesn't make sense to you, go to the online glossary at *https://begintocodecloud.com/glossary.html* to see the definition I'm using.

What is the cloud?

The Internet now underpins many of our daily activities. Things like booking a table at a restaurant, buying a book, or keeping in touch with our friends are now performed using networked services. Nowadays, we refer to these services as "in the cloud." But what is the cloud? What does it do? And how can we use it? Let's start with a look at how things were done before we had the cloud.

The World Wide Web

The *world wide web* and the *Internet* are different things. The Internet was invented to make it easy to connect software over long distances. Email is one of the first major Internet apps. Internet-connected computers acting as "mail servers" managed mailboxes for users, replacing paper messages with digital ones.

The world wide web was created some years after the Internet to make it easier to work with documents. Rather than having to fetch and read a paper document, you use a *browser* program to load an electronic copy from a web *server*. Documents can contain links to other documents, allowing you to follow a reference without fetching another physical document.

Figure 1-1 shows how the web works. The user sits at the browser and sends the web server computer requests for documents that are then sent back to the browser to be read. Later versions of the web added graphics, allowing documents to contain pictures.

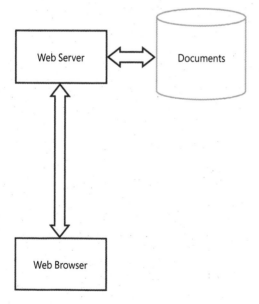

Figure 1-1 Browser and server

Putting the web in the cloud

If you wanted a website in the early days of the Internet, you would set up your own *server* computer. If your site became popular, you had to increase the power of your server (or get extra ones) to handle the load. Then you might find that all your capacity was only used at times of peak demand. The rest of the time, your expensive hardware was left sitting, twiddling its digital thumbs.

The cloud addresses this problem by turning computing resources into a commodity that can be bought and sold. Rather than setting up your own server, you now rent space in the cloud and pay someone else to host your site. The amount you spend on computer resources is proportional to the demand for your service. You never have to pay for resources that you don't use. What's more, the cloud makes it possible to create and deploy new services without having to set up expensive servers to make the service available. Most popular cloud suppliers even have pricing plans that provide free tariffs to help you get started.

So, the server you connect to when using a network service (including the world wide web) might be owned by the service provider. (Facebook has invested considerable sums in setting up its own servers.) However, it's just as likely that you will be connected to a system hosted by a cloud provider. Later in the book, we will discover how to create an account on a cloud provider and set up a service in the cloud.

Figure 1-2 shows how a web server works. The web server and the documents are hosted in the cloud. Note that you could use a mix of different service providers, hosting the documents in one place and the server elsewhere. From the service user's perspective, a cloud-based website works the same as a server-based one.

Figure 1-3 shows a service we will be creating in Chapter 8 that performs tiny surveys. My version of the service is at *https://tinysurvey.azurewebsites.net/.* If you enter that address into your browser, you will be connected to a process in the cloud hosting this website. If you enter the **robspizza** topic and click **Open**, you can help me choose what I'm having for tea.

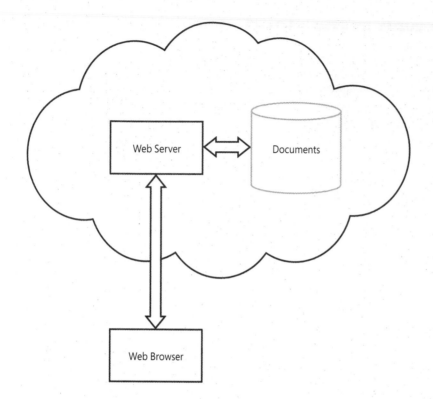

Figure 1-2 HTML browser in the cloud

Figure 1-3 Cloud application

You can manage your cloud services from the web. **Figure 1-4** shows the overview page on the Azure Portal for the service shown previously in **Figure 1-3**. This figure shows the amount of traffic the page receives and the time it takes to respond. There are also lots of options for service management and diagnostics. You can also use this page to increase the service provision to support many thousands of users. Currently, this service uses a free service level that supports enough users to allow demonstration and testing.

Figure 1-4 Cloud management

The cloud is a means by which companies can provide computing resources as a service. It hides the *physical* location of computing resources behind a *logical* address to which users connect. We can use the cloud to host our own services and make them available for others to use via web addresses. A cloud service provider will provide a management interface for each service it hosts. Now, let's move on to take a look at the JavaScript language.

PROGRAMMER'S POINT

The cloud makes it a great time to be a developer

When I was learning to program, it was very nearly impossible to show people what I had done. I could send them my punched cards (each card was punched with holes containing the text for one line of my code), but the program would be unlikely to run on the recipient's computer. Today, you can invent something and make it available to the whole world by writing some JavaScript and hosting it in the cloud for free. This is tremendously empowering.

Nowadays, the hard part is not making your service available but making people aware that it exists. Take a look at the Programmer's Points in Chapter 2, "Open-source projects are a great place to start your career," and "GitHub is also a social network," for hints on how to do this.

JavaScript

We now know what the cloud does. It provides a means of buying (or even getting for free) space on the Internet where we can host our services. JavaScript has been described as "the programming language for the cloud." Let's look at what this means.

Originally the browser just displayed information that had been received from the server. Then it was decided that it would be useful if the browser could run programs loaded from websites. Putting a program inside a web page makes the page interactive without increasing the traffic to and from the web server. The user can interact with a program running in the browser without the server having to do anything. The program in the browser can animate the display or check user input to make sure it is correct before sending it to the server.

The language developed to run inside the browser was JavaScript. There have been several different versions of the language. Early ones suffered from a lack of standardization. Browsers from different companies provided different sets of features that were accessed differently. But this has now settled down. The language specification is now based on a worldwide standard managed by a standards organization called ECMA. We are going to be using version ES6 of the language.

Figure 1-5 shows how a modern, JavaScript-enabled browser and server work together. The web pages and the server program both contain JavaScript elements, and the document store has been replaced with a range of resources that can also contain JavaScript code.

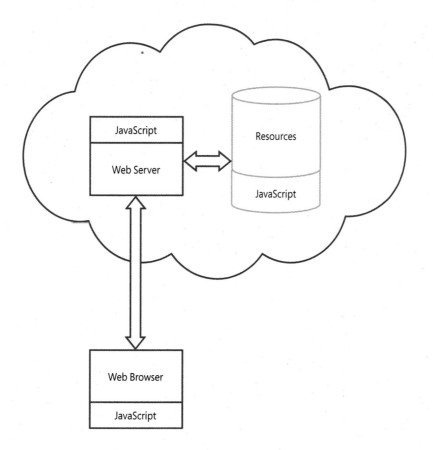

Figure 1-5 JavaScript-powered web

JavaScript has become extremely popular. You will almost certainly run JavaScript code when you visit a website. JavaScript has also become very popular on web servers (the machines on the Internet that deliver the information the browser requests). A technology called *node.js* allows JavaScript programs to run on a server to respond to requests from browsers. The web page shown in **Figure 1-3** is produced by a JavaScript program running in the cloud using node.js. We'll discover how to do this later. In the remainder of this chapter, we will be running JavaScript in the web browser. We'll start by looking at a JavaScript hero, the JavaScript function.

JavaScript heroes: functions

This is the first of our "JavaScript heroes." JavaScript heroes are features of the language that make it super useful for creating cloud applications. A cloud application is all about events. Events happen when the user clicks the mouse button, when a message arrives from a server, and when a timer ticks. In all these situations, you need a way to connect a behavior to what has just happened. As we shall see, functions in JavaScript simplify the process of connecting code to events. You might think you already know about functions in a programming language. However, I'd advise you to work through this section carefully. I'm sure there will be at least one thing here that you didn't know about functions in JavaScript. This is because JavaScript has a very interesting function implementation that sets it apart from other programming languages. Let's start with an overview of functions and then drill down into what makes them special in JavaScript.

The JavaScript function object

A JavaScript function is an object that contains a "body" made up of JavaScript statements that are performed when the function is called. A function object contains a name property, which gives the name of that function. Functions can be called by their names, at which point the program execution is transferred into the statements that make up the function body. When the function completes, the execution returns to the statement after the one that called the function. Functions can be made to accept values to work on and can also return a result value.

The following code defines a function with the name doAddition. The definition comprises the header (the part with the name of the function and the parameters it accepts) and the body (the block of two statements obeyed when the function is called). This function calculates the sum of two values and displays the result in an alert box. The alert function is one of many "built-in" functions provided by the browser Application Programming Interface or API. Learning how to use the facilities provided by the API in a system is a huge part of learning how to be an effective developer.

```javascript
function doAddition(p1, p2) {
    let result = p1 + p2;
    alert("Result:" + result);
}
```

We call the `doAddition` function as shown below. The values 3 and 4 are called the *arguments*. Argument values are mapped onto the parameters in the function. When the `doAddition` call starts to run, the `p1` parameter will hold the value 3, and the `p2` parameter will hold the value 4. This leads to the display of an alert box that displays the value 7.

```
doAddition(3,4);
```

Figure 1-6 shows the alert box that is displayed when the function runs. An alert box always has the name of the originator at the top. In this case, the function was running on a page on a website located at *begintocodecloud.com*. The `alert` function is the first JavaScript function that we have seen. It asks the browser to display a message and then waits for the user to click the OK button. From an API point of view, we can say the `alert` function accepts a string of text and displays it.

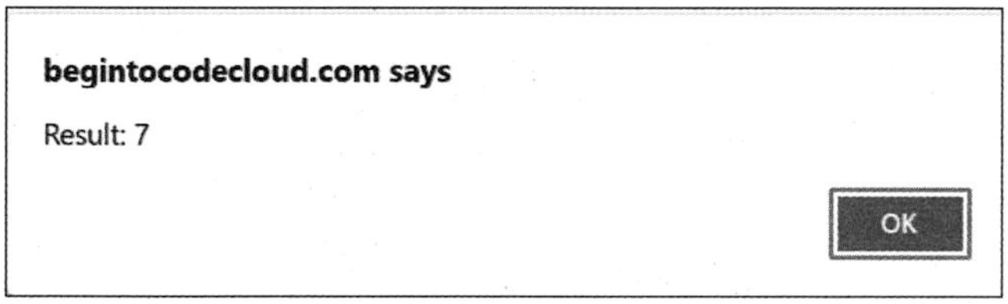

begintocodecloud.com says

Result: 7

OK

Figure 1-6 Alert box

Lifting the lid on JavaScript

Wouldn't it be nice if we could watch the `doAddition` function run? It turns out that we can. Modern browsers contain **Developer Tools**, which let you view the contents of a web page, step through program code, and run individual JavaScript statements. How you start the tools depends on the browser you are using.

Table 1-1 shows the shortcut keys for different browsers and operating systems. Note that the console will look slightly different on each browser, but the views we will use are present on all of them. Let's do our first Make Something Happen and use the **Developer Tools** to explore functions from our web browser.

Table 1-1   Shortcut keys

OPERATING SYSTEM	BROWSER	SEQUENCE	NOTES
Windows	Edge	F12 or CTRL+SHIFT+J	The first time you do this, you will be asked to confirm the action.
Windows	Chrome	F12 or CTRL+SHIFT+J	
Windows	Firefox	F12 or CTRL+SHIFT+J	
Windows	Opera	CTRL+SHIFT+J	
Macintosh	Safari	CMD+OPTION+C	Choose **Preferences->Advanced** and select **Show Develop Menu In Menu Bar** to enable it.
Macintosh	Edge	F12 or CTRL+SHIFT+J	
Macintosh	Chrome	CMD+OPTION+J	
Macintosh	Firefox	CMD+SHIFT+J	
Macintosh	Opera	CMD+SHIFT+J	
Linux	Chrome	F12 or CTRL+SHIFT+J	This also works with the Chromium browser on the Raspberry Pi.

MAKE SOMETHING HAPPEN 1

Scan the QR code or visit *https://www.youtube.com/watch?v=Aa2xfBSlHz8* for a video walk-through of this Make Something Happen.

Explore functions in the console

In this Make Something Happen, we will open the Developer Tools view in the browser and use the console to run JavaScript code that calls the functions we have just created. All the example code for this book is available in the cloud, of course. You can find the sample pages at *begintocodecloud.com*. Open this website and scroll down to the **Sample Code** section.

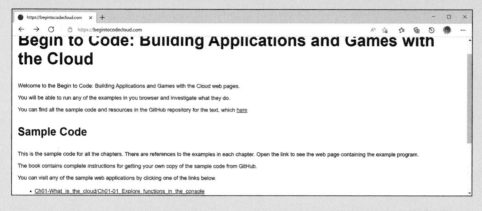

The sample code is presented as a list of links to each sample page. For this first example, click **Ch01-What_is_the_cloud/Ch01-01_Explore_functions_in_the_console.**

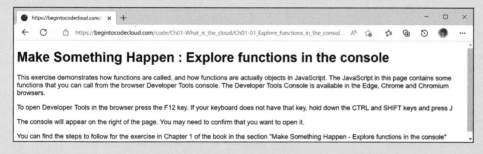

The web page for this exercise appears. Press the appropriate key sequence (see Table 1-1) to open the Developer Tools in your browser. The screenshots for this section are from the Edge browser running in Windows.

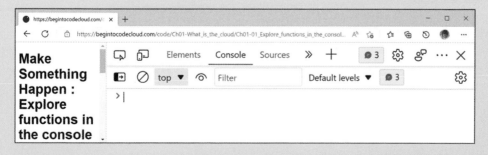

The **Developer Tools** will open on the right-hand side of your page. You can make the tools area larger by clicking the line separating the sample code from the tools and dragging it to the left. The web page will automatically resize. The Developer Tools contain several different tabs. We will look at the Elements and Sources tabs later. For now, click the **Console** tab to open the console.

When we type JavaScript statements into the console and press **Enter**, they will be performed immediately. The console provides a > prompt where you type the statements. Click the console, start typing **doAddition**, and watch what happens.

As you type text, the console presents you with a menu of possibilities; simply select one option from the menu, saving you from typing everything. Also, choosing from this menu makes it less likely that you will mistype something. You can move up and down the menu of items by using the arrow keys or mouse. Click doAddition in the list or highlight the item and press the tab key. Now fill in the rest of the function call by adding the two arguments, 3 and 4:

When you have finished, the console should look like the above. Now press **Enter** to run the function.

The alert function has control and is displaying the alert box containing the result. Note that you can't enter new statements into the console at this point. The only thing you can do is clear the alert by clicking **OK.**

When you click **OK**, the alert box disappears, and the doAddition function completes. You can now enter further commands in the console.

CODE ANALYSIS

Calling functions

A code analysis section is where we examine something that we have just seen and answer some questions you might have about it. There are a few questions you might have about calling functions in JavaScript. Keep the browser open with the console displayed.

Question: What does the undefined message mean in the console after doAdditon has completed running?

> **Answer:** The console takes a JavaScript statement, executes it, and displays the value generated by the statement. If the statement calculates a result, the statement will have the value of that result. This means you can use the console as a calculator. If you type in 2+2 the console will display 4.

```
> 2+2
< 4
```

The 2+2 expression is a valid JavaScript statement that returns the value of the calculation result. So, the console displays 4.

However, the doAddition function does not deliver a result. It has no value to return, so it returns a special JavaScript value called undefined. Later we will discover JavaScript functions that do return a value.

Question: What happens if I try to call an unavailable function?

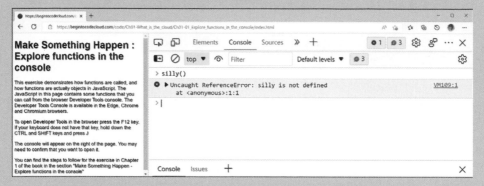

Answer: Above, you can see what happened when I tried to call a function called silly. JavaScript told me that the function is not defined.

Question: What would happen if I added two strings together?

Answer: In JavaScript, you can express a *string* of text by enclosing it in double or single quotes.

```
> doAddition("hello","world");
```

The doAddition call above has two string arguments. When the function runs, the p1 value is set to hello, and the value of p2 is set to world. The function applies the + operator between the parameters to get the result.

```
let result = p1 + p2;
```

Above, you can see the statement in the doAddition function that calculates the value of the result of the function. The statement defines a variable called result, which is then set to the sum of the two parameters. We will look at the let keyword in Chapter 3. (Also, you can find let in the glossary.) The JavaScript selects a + operator to use according to the *context* of the addition. For example, if p1 and p2 are numbers, JavaScript will use the numeric version of +.

If p1 and p2 are strings of text, JavaScript will use the string version of + and set the value of `result` to a string containing the text `helloworld`. You might find it interesting to try adding strings to numbers and watching what JavaScript does. If you look in the `doAddition` function itself, you will find a statement that does this.

Question: What happens if I subtract one string from another?

   Answer: Adding two strings together makes sense, but subtracting one string from another is not sensible. We can investigate what happens if we do this because the web page for this exercise contains a function called `doSubtraction`. Normally, you would give this function numeric arguments. Let's discover what happens if we use text.

```
> doSubtraction("hello","world");
```

If you make the above `doSubtraction` call, the following message is displayed by the alert:

```
Result: NaN
```

The NaN value means "not a number." There is only one version of the – operator—the numeric one. However, this can't produce a number as a result because it is meaningless to subtract one string from another. So, the result of the operation is to set the value of result to a "special" value NaN to indicate that the result is not a number. You can read more about NaN in the glossary.

Question: Why do some strings have " around them and some have '.

   Answer: When the debug console shows you a string value, it will enclose the string in single quotation characters. However, in some parts of the program, strings are delimited by double quotation characters. In JavaScript, you can use either double or single quotation marks to identify a string's start and end.

Question: Where do these functions come from?

   Answer: That's a good question. The function statements are on the web page loaded by the browser from the *begintocodecloud.com* server. To use the Developer Tools to view this file, we must change the view from **Console** to **Sources**. Click the **Sources** tab next to the **Console** tab in the top row.

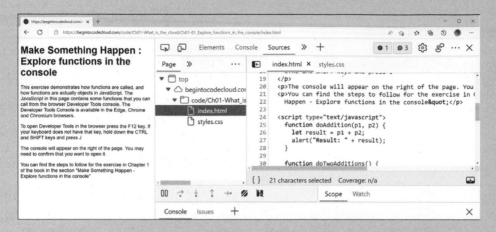

The **Sources** view shows you all the files behind the website you are visiting. This site has two files:

- A `styles.css` file that contains style definitions (discussed in more detail in Chapter 2)

- An `index.html` file that contains the text of the web page, along with the JavaScript programs.

If you select the `index.html` file as shown above, you will see the file's contents, including the JavaScript for `doAddition`. There is another function called `doTwoAdditions` which calls `doAddition` twice.

Question: Can we watch the JavaScript run?

Answer: Yes. We can set a "breakpoint" at a statement, and when that statement is reached, the program will pause, so we can go through it one step at a time. This is a wonderful way to see what a program is doing. Put a breakpoint at the first `doTwoAddi-tions` statement by clicking in the margin to the left of the line number:

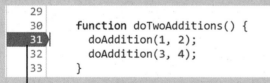

```
29
30      function doTwoAdditions() {
31          doAddition(1, 2);
32          doAddition(3, 4);
33      }
```

Click here

The breakpoint is indicated by the arrow highlighting the line number. It will cause the program to pause when it reaches line 31. Now we need to call the `doTwoAdditions` function. Select the **Console** tab, type in the following code, and press **Enter**:

```
> doTwoAdditions();
```

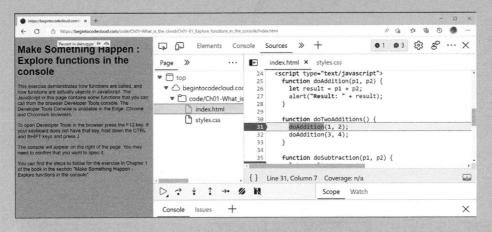

Above, you can see what happens when a breakpoint is hit. The browser shows the program paused at the statement with the breakpoint. The control buttons toward the bottom of the page are the most interesting part of this view:

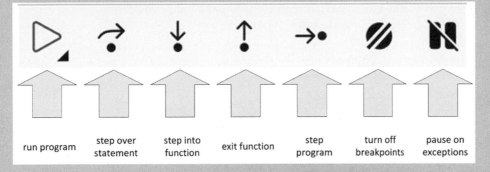

| run program | step over statement | step into function | exit function | step program | turn off breakpoints | pause on exceptions |

These controls might look a bit like cave paintings, but they are very useful. They control how the browser will work through your program. First, we will use the **Step Into Function** control. Each time you press this control, the browser will perform one statement in your program. The browser will step into the function if the statement is a function call. You can use the **Step Over Statement** control to step over function calls and the "exit function" to leave a function you just entered.

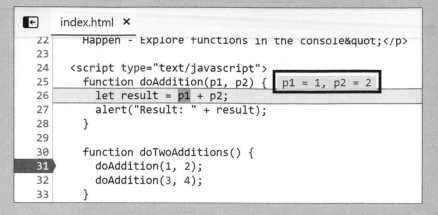

```
index.html ×
22      Happen - Explore functions in the console&quot;</p>
23
24      <script type="text/javascript">
25          function doAddition(p1, p2) {   p1 = 1, p2 = 2
26              let result = p1 + p2;
27              alert("Result: " + result);
28          }
29
30          function doTwoAdditions() {
31              doAddition(1, 2);
32              doAddition(3, 4);
33          }
```

The highlighted line has now moved to the first statement of the doAddition function. The debugger shows you the values in the parameters. If you keep pressing the **Step Into Function** button in the control panel, you can see each statement obeyed in turn. Note that you must click the alert's **OK** button when you perform the statement on line 27 that calls alert. If you get bored, you can press the **Run Program** button at the left of the program controls to run the program. You can clear the breakpoint at line 31 by clicking it.

You can add as many breakpoints as you like and use this technique on any web page you visit. It is interesting to see just how much complexity is behind a simple site. Leave the browser open on this page; we will make some more things happen in the following section.

References to JavaScript function objects

We have seen that a function in a JavaScript program is function is represented by a JavaScript function object. A JavaScript function *object* is managed by *reference*. Our programs can contain reference variables that can be made to refer to functions.

```
Function doAddition(p1, p2) {
    let result = p1 + p2;
    alert("Result:" + result);
}
```

We've seen the definition above before. It defines the doAddition function that sums the two parameters and displays the result. When JavaScript sees this, it creates a function object representing the function and a variable called doAddition that refers to the function object.

```
doAddition(1,2);
```

The statement above calls the doAddition function, which will display an alert containing a result of 3. JavaScript variables can contain references to objects, so you can write statements like this in your program:

```
let x = doAddition;
```

This statement creates a variable called x and makes it refer to the same object as the doAddition function.

```
x(5,6);
```

This statement calls whatever x refers to and passes the arguments 5 and 6 to it. This would call the same object that doAddition refers to (because that is what x is referring to), resulting in an alert with the Result:11 message displayed. We can make the variable x refer to a different function:

```
x = doSubtraction;
```

The above statement only works if we have previously declared a function called doSubtraction, which performs subtraction. This statement makes x refer to this function:

```
x(5,6);
```

When the statement above calls x, it will run the doSubtraction function and display a result value of –1 because that is the result when 6 is subtracted from 5. We can do evil things with function references. Consider the following statement:

```
doAddition = doSubtraction;
```

If you understand how evil this statement is, you can call yourself a "function reference ninja." It is completely legal JavaScript, meaning a doAddition call will run the doSubtraction function from now on. If I put this statement into your program you would find that when you thought your program was adding numbers together it was actually subtracting them because a call to doAddition would now run the code in doSubtraction.

Function expressions

You can create JavaScript functions in places where you might not expect you can because we are used to setting variables by assigning *expressions* to them:

```
let result=p1+p2;
```

The above statement assigns the expression p1+p2 to a variable called `result`. However, you can also assign a variable to a *function expression:*

```
let codeFunc = function (p1,p2){ let result=p1+p2; alert("Result: "+result);};
```

The above statement creates a function object that does the same thing as the doAddition function we have been using. I've put the entire function on a single line, but the statements are exactly the same. The function is referred to by a variable called codeFunc. We can call codeFunc in the same way as we used doAddition. The statement below calls the new function and would display a result of 17:

```
codeFunc(10,7);
```

Function references as function arguments

This is probably the most confusing section title so far. Sorry about that. We want to look at how you can pass function references into functions. In other words, a program can tell a function what function to call. Later in this chapter, we will tell a timer what function to call when the timer ticks. This is how it works.

An *argument* is something that is passed into a function when it is called. We have passed two arguments *(p1 and p2)* into the doAddition function each time we call it. (These are the items to be added.) We can also use references to functions as arguments to function calls:

```
function doFunctionCall(functionToCall, p1, p2){
   functionToCall(p1,p2);
}
```

The function doFunctionCall above has three parameters. The first (functionToCall) is a function to call, and the second (p1) and third (p2) are values to be passed into that function when it is called. All the `doFunctionCall` does is call the supplied function with the given arguments. It's not particularly useful, but it does show that you can make a function that accepts a function reference as a parameter. We could call `doFunctionCall` like this:

```
doFunctionCall(doAddition,1,7);
```

This statement calls the `doFunctionCall` function. The first argument is a reference to `doAddition`. The second argument is 1, and the third is 7. The result would be an alert that displayed "Result:8." We can get different behaviors by using `doFunctionCall` to call different functions.

We can take this further and use function expressions as arguments to function calls, as shown in the statement below, which defines a function used as an argument in a call to the `doFunctionCall` function. A function created as an argument has no name, so it is called an *anonymous function*.

```
doFunctionCall(function (p1,p2){ let result=p1+p2; alert("Result: "+result);},1,7);
```

MAKE SOMETHING HAPPEN 2

Scan the QR code or visit *https://www.youtube.com/watch?v=Jjblef-LaB8* for a video walk-through of this Make Something Happen.

Fun with function objects

Function objects can be confusing. Let's use our debugging skills to examine how they work. First, open this book's web page at *begintocodecloud.com* and select the **Ch01-What_is_the_cloud/Ch01-01_Explore_functions_in_the_console sample**. Then press F12 (or CTRL+SHIFT+J) to open **Developer Tools** and select the **Console**.

```
> let x = doAddition;
```

Now press **Enter**.

```
> let x = doAddition;
< undefined
```

The console shows the undefined value because the console always displays the value returned by a statement, and the act of assignment (which is what the program is doing) does not return a value. After this statement has been performed, the x variable now refers to the doAddition function. We can check this by looking at the name property of x. A function object has a name property, which is the name of the function. Type in x.name, press **Enter**, and look at what comes back:

```
> x.name;
< 'doAddition'
```

The console displays the value returned by the statement. In this case, the statement is accessing the name property of the variable x, which is the string doAddition string.

```
> x.name;
< 'doAddition'
```

Now, let's call x with some arguments Type in the following statement and press **Enter**.

```
> x(10,11);
```

Because x refers to doAddition, you will see an alert displaying the value 21. Next, we will feed the x function reference into a doFunctionCall call, but before we do that, we will set a breakpoint to watch the program run. Select the **Sources** tab and scroll down in the index. htm source file until you find the definition of doFunctionCall. Click the left margin near line 41 to set a breakpoint inside the function at statement 41.

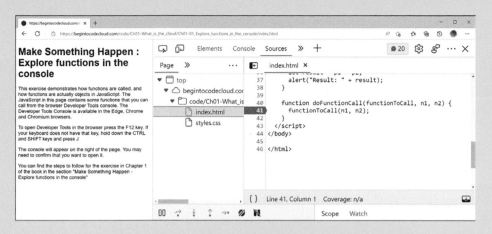

Now, return to the **Console** view, type the following statement, and press **Enter**.

```
> doFunctionCall(x,11,12);
```

When you press **Enter**, the console calls doFunctionCall. When it reaches the first state-ment in the function, it hits the breakpoint and pauses.

```
40        function doFunctionCall(functionToCall, n1, n2)
41        functionToCall(n1, n2);
42      }
43    </s
44  </boc
45
46  </htr
```

> ƒ **doAddition(p1, p2)**
>
> **arguments**: null
> **caller**: null
> **length**: 2
> **name**: "doAddition"
> ▶ **prototype**: {constructor: ƒ}
> [[FunctionLocation]]: index.html:25
> ▶ [[Prototype]]: ƒ ()
> ▶ [[Scopes]]: Scopes[2]

Above, you can see the program is paused. The doFunctionCall function has been entered, and the function's parameters have been set to the supplied arguments. If you hover the mouse pointer over functionToCall in line 41, you will see a full description of the parame-ter's value. The description shows that the parameter refers to the doAddition function.

A program statement is performed each time you press the **Step Into Function** in the control buttons. We can repeatedly press this button to step through the program and watch what it does. Repeatedly press the button to see the program go into the doAddition function, calculate the result, and display the result in an alert. Clear the alert by clicking **OK** in the alert message box. Now press the **Run Program** button on the left of the control buttons to complete this call. Finally, return to the console for the grand finale of this Make Something Happen.

In the grand finale, we will create an anonymous function and pass it into a call of doFunctionCall. The function will be defined as an argument to doFunctionCall. The statement we will type is a bit long, and you must get it exactly right for it to work. The good news is that the console will suggest sensible things to type. If you get an error, you can edit the text by pressing the up arrow key to go back up to the line and then typing the correct text.

```
> doFunctionCall(
      function (p1,p2){let result=p1+p2;alert("Result: "+result);},
      1,7)
```

Now press **Enter** to execute this statement. The program will hit the same breakpoint as before, but the display will be different:

```
40        function doFunctionCall(functionToCall, n1, n2)
41        functionToCall(n1, n2);
42     }
43   </s        ƒ (p1,p2)
44 </boo
45              arguments: null
46 </htm         caller: null
                 length: 2
                 name: ""
              ▶ prototype: {constructor: ƒ}
                 [[FunctionLocation]]: VM980:1
              ▶ [[Prototype]]: ƒ ()
              ▶ [[Scopes]]: Scopes[2]

{} Line 4
```

This time, the function's name property is an empty string, and the function is anonymous. Click the **Step Into Function** button to see what happens when an anonymous function is called.

```
⬌  index.html    VM980  ✕                                          ⮕
 1  doFunctionCall(function (p1,p2){ let result=p1+p2; alert("Result: "+result);},1,7);
```

The browser has created a temporary file—VM980—to hold the anonymous function while it is in the debugger. When you do this exercise, you might see a different name. We can step through the statements in this file using **Step Into Function**. If you just want to run the function to completion, you can press the **Run Program** button in the control buttons.

Anonymous functions are often used in JavaScript, particularly when calling API functions to perform tasks. An object from the JavaScript API will signal that something has happened by calling a function. The quickest and most convenient way to create the function to be called is to declare it as an anonymous function.

Returning values from function calls

Until now, we have just called functions that have not returned a value. Instead, they have returned the `undefined` value. Now we are going to investigate how a function can return a value and how a program can use the returned value.

```
function doAddSum(p1, p2) {
    let result = p1 + p2;
    return result;
}
```

The `doAddSum` function above shows how a function can return a value. The `return` keyword is followed by an expression that gives the value to be returned when the function is called.

```
let v = doAddSum(4,5);
```

The statement above creates a variable called `v` and sets the variable value to the result of the `doAddSum` call—in this case, the value 9 (the result of adding 4 to 5). The return from a function can be used anywhere you can use a value in a function.

```
let v = doAddSum(4,5) + doAddSum(6,7);
```

In the statement above, the `doAddSum` function would be called twice, and the value of v would be set to 22. We can also use function returns as arguments in function calls.

```
let v = doAddSum(doAddSum(4,5), doAddSum(6,7));
```

The code above looks a bit confusing, but JavaScript would not have a problem performing it. The outer call of `doAddSum` would be called first, and then the two further calls would run to calculate the values of the two arguments. Then, the outer call would run with these values.

Try to design your code to make it easy to debug and maintain

You will spend at least as much time debugging and maintaining code as you will writing it. Worse still, you will frequently be called on to debug and maintain programs that other people have written. Even worse, six months after you've written a piece of code, you become one of the "other people" who have written code that needs to be debugged. I've occasionally asked myself, "What idiot wrote this code?" only to find out it was me.

When you write a program, try to make sure that it will be easy to debug. Consider the implementation of doAddSum below.

```
function doAddSum(p1, p2) {
    let result = p1 + p2;
    return result;
}
```

You might think that it would be more efficient to return the result directly and get rid of the result variable:

```
function doAddSum(p1, p2) {
    return p1 + p2;
}
```

The above version of the function works fine. And it might even save a few millionths of a second when it runs (although I doubt this because browsers are very good at optimizing code). However, the second one will be harder to debug because you can't easily view the value of the result that it returns. With the original code, I can just look at the contents of the result variable. In the "improved" version, I'll have to mess around a bit to find out what value is being returned to the caller.

If the function just performs a task, a good trick is to make a function return a status code so that the caller knows exactly what has happened. I often use the convention in which an empty string means that the operation worked, whereas a string contains a reason for failing.

If the function is supposed to return a value, you can use the JavaScript values null and undefined to indicate something has not worked.

Oh, and if you find yourself thinking, "What idiot wrote this code?" don't be so hard on the "idiot." They were probably in a hurry, lacked your experience, or maybe, just maybe, there's a good reason for why they did it that way that you just don't know.

Returning multiple values from a function call

A problem with functions is that they can only return one value. However, sometimes we would like a function that returns multiple values. Perhaps we need a function to read information about a user. The function returns a name and address along with status, indicating whether the function has succeeded. If the status is an empty string, it means the function worked. Otherwise, the status string contains an error message:

```javascript
function readPerson() {
    let name = "Rob Miles";
    let address = "House of Rob in the city of Hull";
    let status = "";
}
```

Above is an implementation of a `readPerson` function that sets up some return values but doesn't return anything. We now want a means for the function to return these values to a caller.

Returning an array from a function call

```javascript
function readPersonArray() {
    let name = "Rob Miles";
    let address = "House of Rob in the city of Hull";
    let status = "";
    return [status, name, address];
}
```

The above code creates a function called `readPersonArray` that returns an array containing the status, name, and address values. We create an array in JavaScript by enclosing a list of values in brackets.

```javascript
let reply = readPersonArray();
```

The statement above shows how we would create a `reply` variable that holds the result of a `readPersonArray` call. We can now work with the values in the array by using an index value to specify which element we want to use in our program.

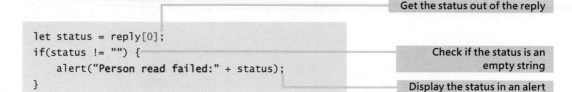

```
let status = reply[0];
if(status != "") {
    alert("Person read failed:" + status);
}
```

Get the status out of the reply

Check if the status is an empty string

Display the status in an alert

The above code puts the element at the start of the `reply` array into a variable called `status`. (JavaScript arrays are indexed starting at 0.) This should be the status value of the call that has just been made. If this element is not an empty string, the code displays an alert containing the status so the user can see something has gone wrong. If you look at the code for `readPersonArray`, you'll see that the element at the start of the array is the status value, so this code would display an alert if the `status` variable contains an error message.

This code works, but it is not perfect. The person making the `readPersonArray` call needs to know the order of the values returned by the function. For this reason, I don't think using an array in this context is a very good idea. Let's look at a better one.

PROGRAMMER'S POINT
Use extra variables to make code clearer

You might look at the code above and decide I've used a variable when I don't need to. I've created a variable called **status** that contains a copy of the value in `reply[0]`. I've done this because it makes the code that follows much clearer. The test of the status and the display in the alert make a lot more sense to the reader than they would if the code contained the variable `reply[0]`. This won't slow the program down or make it larger because the JavaScript engine is very good at optimizing statements like these.

Returning an object from a function call

```
function readPersonObject() {
  let name = "Rob Miles";
  let address = "House of Rob in the city of Hull";
  let status = "";
  return { status: status, name: name, address: address };
}
```

The above code creates a function called `readPersonObject` that returns an object containing `status`, `name`, and `address` properties.

```
let reply = readPersonObject();
if (reply.status != "") {
    alert(reply.status);
}
```

The code above shows how the `readPersonObject` function would be called and the status property tested and displayed. This time, we can specify the parts of the reply we want by using their names. If you want to experiment with these functions, you can find them in the example web page we have been using for this chapter: **Ch01-What_is_the_cloud/Ch01-01_Explore_functions_in_the_console.**

PROGRAMMER'S POINT

Make good use of object literals

This way of creating objects in JavaScript programs is called an *object literal*. I'm a big fan of object literals because they are a great way to create data structures that are easy to use and understand, right at the point you want to use them. You can also make an object literal to supply as an argument to a function call. I can do this if I want to supply name and address values to a function because a function can have multiple arguments.

```
function displayPersonDetails(name, address) {
    // do something with the name and address here
}
```

The `displayPersonDetails` function has two parameters to accept incoming information. However, I'd have to be careful when calling the function because I don't want to get the arguments the wrong way around:

```
displayPersonDetails("House of Rob", "Rob Miles");
```

This would display the details of someone called "House of Rob" living at "Rob Miles." A much better way would be to have the function accept an object that contains name and address properties:

```
function displayPersonDetails(person) {
    // do something with the person.name and person.address here
}
```

When I call the function, I create a object literal to deliver the parameters:

```
displayPersonDetails({ address:"House of Rob", name:"Rob Miles"});
```

This function call creates an argument that is an object literal containing the person's name and address information. Now, getting the properties the wrong way around in the function is impossible.

Make a console clock

We will now apply what we have learned to create a clock that we can start from the console. The clock will display the hours, minutes, and seconds on a web page. At the moment, we don't know how to display things on web pages (that is a topic for Chapter 2), so I've provided a helper function that we can use. You can use the **Developer Tools** to see how it works.

Getting the date and time

Our clock will need to know the date and time so it can display it. The JavaScript environment provides a Date object we can use to do this. When a program makes a new Date object, it is set to the current date and time.

```
let currentDate = new Date();
```

The statement above creates a new Date object and sets the currentDate variable to refer to it. The keyword new tells JavaScript to find the definition of the Date object and then construct one. We will look at objects in detail later in the text. Once we have our Date object, we can call *methods* on the object to make it do things for us.

```
function getTimeString() {
  let currentDate = new Date();
  let hours = currentDate.getHours();
  let mins = currentDate.getMinutes();
  let secs = currentDate.getSeconds();
  let timeString = hours + ":" + mins + ":" + secs;
  return timeString;
}
```

The `getTimeString` function above creates a `Date` object and then uses the `getHours`, `getMinutes`, and `getSeconds` methods to get those values out of it. The values are then assembled into a string returned by the function. We can use this function to get a time string for display.

MAKE SOMETHING HAPPEN 3

Scan the QR code or visit *https://www.youtube.com/watch?v=Ba9Gib_XgoU* for a video walk-through of this Make Something Happen.

Console clock

Open *begintocodecloud.com* and scroll down to the **Samples** section. **Click Ch01-What_is_the_cloud/Ch01-02_Console_Clock** to open the sample page. Then, open the **Developer Tools** and select the **Console** tab.

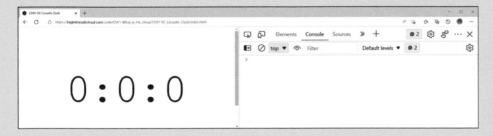

The page shows an "empty" clock display. Let's start by investigating the `Date` object. Type in the following:

```
> let currentDate = new Date();
```

Now press **Enter** to create the new `Date` object.

```
> let currentDate = new Date();
< undefined
```

This statement creates a new `Date` and sets the `currentDate` variable to refer to it. As we have seen before, the `let` statement doesn't return a value, so the console will display `undefined`. Now, we can call methods to extract values from the object. Type in the following statement:

```
> currentDate.getMinutes();
```

When you press **Enter**, the `getMinutes` method will be called, which returns the `Minutes` value for the current time. This value is displayed in the console:

```
> currentDate.getMinutes();
< 17
```

The code above was run at seventeen minutes past the hour, so the value returned by `get-Minutes` will be 17. Note that `currentDate` holds a "snapshot" of the time. You will have to make a new `Date` object to get an updated date. You can also call methods to set values in the date. The date contents will automatically update. You could use `setMinutes` to add `1000` to the `Minutes` value to see what the date would be 1,000 minutes in the future.

The clock's web page has the `getTimeString` function built in, so we can use it to get the current time as a string. Try this by entering a function call and pressing **Enter**:

```
> getTimeString();
< '13:18:17'
```

Above, you can see a function call and the exact time it returned. Now that we have our time, we need a way of displaying it. The page contains a function called `showMessage`, which displays a text string. Let's test it out by displaying a string. Type the statement below and press **Enter**:

```
> showMessage("hello");
```

The web page now displays the string that was entered. Now, we need a function that will display a clock tick. We can define this in the console window. Enter the following statement and press **Enter**:

```
> let tick = function(){showMessage(getTimeString());};
< undefined
```

Take a careful look at the contents of the function and see if you can work out what they do. If you're not clear about this, remember that we want to get a time string and display it. The getTimeString function delivers a time string, and the showMessage function displays a string. If we have typed it correctly, we should be able to display the time by calling the tick function. Type the following statement and press **Enter**:

```
> tick();
```

The time is displayed. The final thing we need for our ticking clock is a way of calling the tick function at regular intervals so that the clock keeps time. It turns out that JavaScript provides a function called setInterval that will do this for us. tick is the first parameter to setInterval and is a reference to the function to call. The second parameter, 1000, is the interval between calls in thousandths of a second. We want to call the tick function every second, so type in the statement below and press **Enter**.

```
> setInterval(tick,1000);
```

This should start the clock ticking. The `setInterval` function returns a value of 1, as you can see below:

```
> setInterval(tick,1000);
< 1
```

The return from `setInterval` is a value that identifies this timer. You can use multiple `setInterval` calls to set up several timers if you wish. You can use the `clearInterval` function to stop a particular timer:

```
> clearInterval(1);
```

If you perform the statement above, you will stop the clock ticking. You can make another call of `setInterval` to start the clock again. At the moment, we have to enter commands into the console to make the clock start. In the next chapter, we'll discover how to run JavaScript programs when a page is loaded so that we can make the clock start automatically.

Arrow functions

If you look at lots of popular cartoon figures, you will notice that some only have three fingers on each hand, not five. You might be wondering why this is. It is to reduce the "pencil miles" for the animators. The first cartoons were made from frames that were all hand-drawn by animators. They discovered that they could make their lives easier by reducing the number of fingers they had to draw. Fewer fingers meant fewer "pencil miles."

The JavaScript `arrow` function is a way of reducing the "keyboard miles" of a developer. The character sequence => provides a way to create a function without using the word `function` in the definition.

```
doAdditionArrow = (p1, p2) => {
  let result = p1 + p2;
  alert("Result: " + result);
}
```

The JavaScript above creates a function called doAdditionArrow, which is exactly the same as the original doAdditon. However, it is much quicker to type in. If the arrow function's body only contains one statement, you can leave off the braces marking the function body's start and end. And a single-statement arrow function returns the value of the statement, so you can leave off the return keyword, too. The code below creates a function called doSum, which returns the sum of the two arguments.

```
doSum = (p1,p2) => p1 + p2;
```

We could call the doSum function as we would any other:

```
let result = doSum(5,6);
```

This would set the value of result to 11. You see the true power of the arrow notation when you start using it to create functions to be used as arguments to function calls.

```
setInterval(()=>showMessage(getTimeString()),1000);
```

This innocent-looking statement is worth careful study. It makes our clock tick. In the preceding Make Something Happen, we used the setInterval function to make the clock tick. The setInterval function accepts two arguments, a function to call and the interval between each function call. I've implemented the function to call as an arrow function containing a single statement that is a call to showMessage. The showMessage function has a single argument: the message to be displayed, which is provided by a call to the getTimeString function.

PROGRAMMER'S POINT

Arrow functions can be confusing

JavaScript is not the first programming language that I've learned. It might not be your first language, either. When I was learning JavaScript, I found the arrow function to be one of the hardest things to understand. If you have seen C, C++, C#, or even Python programs before, you already know about functions, arguments, parameters, and return values. This means "traditional" JavaScript functions will be easy to grasp.

But you will not have seen arrow functions before because they are unique to JavaScript. And you can't easily work out what they do from seeing them in code. If you don't know what an arrow function does, you will find it quite tricky to understand what the creation of doSum above is doing. One way to deal with this would be to just regard arrow functions as a little extra feature provided by the language to make your life easier. If you don't mind doing the extra typing, you can create all your programs without using the arrow notation. However, I think you should spend extra time learning how they work so that you can understand other people's JavaScript.

When we started talking about JavaScript functions, we noted that they are used to attach JavaScript code to events. The `arrow` function makes this very easy to do.

What you have learned

At the end of each chapter, the "What you have learned" section sets out the major points covered in the chapter and poses some questions you can use to reinforce your understanding.

- A web browser is an application that requests data from a web server in the form of web pages. The Internet provides the connection between the two applications.

- Originally, web servers were single machines connected to the Internet that the site owner operated. The cloud transformed computing power into a resource that can be bought and sold. We can pay to have our websites hosted on the Internet. Page requests sent to our site's address will be processed on our service provider's machines.

- The JavaScript programming language was invented to allow a browser to run program code downloaded from a website. It has since developed into a language that can be used to create web servers and freestanding applications.

- A JavaScript function is a block of code and a header that specifies the function's name and any parameters it accepts. Within the function, the parameters are replaced by values that were supplied as arguments to the function call.

- When a running program calls a function, the statements in the function are performed, and then the running program continues from the statement after the function call. A function can return a value using the `return` keyword.

- When a JavaScript program runs inside the browser, it uses an Application Programming Interface (API) to interact with the browser's services. Many JavaScript functions provide the API.

- Operators in JavaScript statements act according to the context established by the operands they are working on. For example, adding two numbers will result in an arithmetic addition, but adding two strings will create a single string that contains one string added to the end of the other. If a numeric operation is attempted with incompatible operands, the result will be set to the `NaN` (not a number) value.

- Variables in JavaScript can hold values that indicate a specific variable state. A variable that has not been assigned a specific value has the `undefined` value. A calculated value that is not a number (for example, the result of adding a number to a string of text) will have the `NaN` value.

- Modern browsers provide a **Developer Tools** component containing a console that can execute JavaScript statements. The Developer Tools interface also lets you view the JavaScript being run inside the page and add breakpoints to stop the code. You can step through individual statements and view the contents of variables.

- A JavaScript function is represented by a function object. JavaScript manages these by reference so variables can contain references to functions. Function references can be assigned between variables, used as arguments to a function call, and returned by functions.

- Function expressions allow a function to be created and assigned to a reference at any point in a program. A function expression used as an argument to a function call is called an *anonymous function* because it is not associated with any name.

- The JavaScript API provides a `Date` object that can be used to determine the current date and time and also allows date and time manipulation. The API also provides the `setInterval` and `clearInteval` functions, which can trigger functions at regular intervals.

- Functions can be defined using "arrow notation," which is shorter than the normal function definition. This is especially useful when creating functions to be used as arguments for function calls.

To reinforce your understanding of this chapter, you might want to consider the following "profound questions" about the cloud and what we do with it.

Question: What is the difference between the Internet and the web?

Answer: The Internet is the technology that allows computers to communicate. The web is a service that uses the Internet to link web browsers and web servers.

Question: What is the difference between the cloud and the Internet?

Answer: The Internet is the networking technology that allows a program running on one computer to exchange data with a program running on another computer. We don't need the cloud to make an Internet-based application. We just need two computers with Internet connections. The cloud lets you replace a computer connected to the Internet with a service you purchased from a cloud service provider. The cloud-based server will have a network address that the cloud service provider uses to locate the required service.

Question: How does the cloud work?

Answer: A server hosted by a cloud service provider runs an operating system that allows it to switch between processes running services for different clients. At the front of the cloud service is a component that accepts requests and routes them to the process that provides the required service. The computing resources used by each process are monitored so that the services can be billed for the computer time they have used.

Question: What is the difference between a function and a method?

Answer: A function is declared outside any objects. We have created lots of functions in this chapter. A method is a function that is part of an object. A `Date` object provides a `GetMinutes` method that returns the `Minutes` value for a given date. This is called a method because it is part of the `Date` object. Methods themselves look like functions; they have parameters and can return values.

Question: What is the difference between a function and a procedure?

Answer: A function returns a value. A procedure does not.

Question: Can you store functions in arrays and objects?

Answer: Yes, you can. A function is an object and is manipulated by a reference. You can create arrays of references, and objects can contain references.

Question: What makes a function anonymous?

Answer: An anonymous function is one that is created in a context where it is not given a name. Let's take a look at the `tick` function we created for the clock:

```
let tick = function(){showMessage(getTimeString());};
```

You might think this function is anonymous. However, JavaScript can determine that the function is called "tick." If you look at the function's `name` property, you will find that it has been set to `tick`. But instead of creating a tick function, we might use a function expression as an argument to the `setInterval` call:

```
setInterval(()=>showMessage(getTimeString()),1000);
```

The statement above feeds a function expression into `setInterval`. The function expression does the same job as `tick`, but now it is an anonymous function. There is no name attached to the function. Note that this statement uses the `arrow` notation to define the function.

Question: Why do we make functions anonymous?

Answer: We don't have to use anonymous functions. We could create every function with a name and then use the name of that function. However, anonymous functions make life a lot easier. We can bind behaviors very tightly to the place they are needed. Also, if we are only going to perform a behavior once, inventing a function name for it is rather tedious.

Question: Can an anonymous function accept parameters and return a result?

Answer: Yes, it can. It is just declared in a slightly different way from a "traditional" function.

Question: Are arrow functions always anonymous?

Answer: An `arrow` function is simply a quick way of creating a function definition. Arrow functions can have names.

Question: What happens if I forget to return a value from a function?

Answer: A function that returns a value should contain a `return` statement followed by the value to be returned. However, you might forget to add the return statement, which sends the value back to the caller. The program will still run, but the value returned by the function will be set to `undefined`.

Question: What happens if I don't use the value returned by a function?

Answer: A program does not need to use the value returned by a function.

Question: What does the `let` keyword do?

Answer: The `let` keyword creates a variable local to the block of code in which it is declared. The local variable will be automatically discarded when the block is exited.

Question: Do JavaScript programs crash?

Answer: This is an interesting question. In some languages, the program text is carefully checked for consistency before running to ensure that it contains valid statements. With JavaScript, not so much. JavaScript does not check for program mistakes like using the wrong type of value in an expression, giving the wrong number of arguments to a function call, or forgetting to return a value from a function. In each of the above situations, the program would not fail when it ran; instead, the errors would cause variables to set to values like `undefined` or NaN (Not a Number). This means that you must be careful to check the results of operations before using them in case a program error has made them invalid.

So, the answer is that your JavaScript program probably won't crash, but it might display the wrong results.

2
Get into the cloud

What you will learn

In the last chapter, we discovered the origins of the cloud and ran some JavaScript code in a web page using the browser Developer Tools. We also learned a lot about JavaScript functions and how to connect them to events.

In this chapter, we will take our JavaScript code and put it into the cloud for anyone to access. We will start by getting the tools we will use and then move on to look at the format of the documents underpinning those web pages. Then we will use JavaScript to add programmed behaviors to pages and discover how we can put our active pages into the cloud.

Don't forget that you can use the glossary to look up any unfamiliar terms. Words defined in the glossary are shown in *italic*. Note that both *this* and *in* are in the glossary. You can find the glossary online at *https://begintocodecloud.com/glossary.html*.

Working in the cloud

Before building your applications, you need to find a nice place to work. There is a physical aspect to this. You work best if you are comfortable, so a decent screen, a nice keyboard, and a responsive computer are all great things to have. However, there is a "logical" element, too. You need to find a place to store all the materials that you're going to generate. You could just store all the files on your computer, but you might lose them if your machine fails. What's more, if you make the wrong modifications to the only copy of a crucial file, you can lose a lot of work very quickly (I have done this many times). So, let's look at how we can manage our stuff—starting with Git.

Git

Git was created in 2005 by Linus Torvalds, who was writing the Linux operating system at the time. He needed a tool that could track his work and make it easy for him to share it with others. So, he created his own. Git organizes data into "repositories." A *repository* can be as simple as a folder containing a single file or a *hierarchy* of nested folders containing thousands of documents. Git doesn't care what the documents contain or even what type of data they are. A repository can contain pictures, songs, 3D designs, and software code.

You ask Git to "commit" changes you have made to the contents of a repository. When you do this, the Git program searches through all the files in the repository and takes copies of the ones that have changed. These files—along with records of changes— are then stored by Git in a special folder. The great thing about Git is that you can return to any of your committed changes at any time. You can also send people a copy of your repository (including the special folder). They can work on some of the files in the repository, commit their changes, and send the repository back to you.

Git can identify which have been changed and handle contentions. If two people have changed a particular file, Git can show each person's changes. These changes can be used to establish a definitive version of the file, which is then stored back in the repository. You are correct if you think Git was a hard program to write. It turned out to be tricky to manage file synchronization and change resolution. However, it makes it much easier for people to work together on shared projects.

Figure 2-1 shows the repository containing all the sample code for this book. I have selected the **Hidden Items** option on the **View** tab, so File Explorer shows hidden files. At the top of the folder, you can see a **.git** folder, a special folder created and managed by the Git program. You can look inside if you wish, but you shouldn't change anything in it. When you copy a repository, this folder must be copied, too.

Figure 2-1 Sample Repository

The sample repository is exposed by GitHub as a web page containing an `index.html` file, so you can view any of the sample code in your browser without downloading it to your machine. Not all GitHub repositories are web pages, but hosting a website from a GitHub repository is very useful. (See the end of this chapter for how to do this.)

To work with repositories, you need to install the Git software, which is a freely available for download for all operating systems.

MAKE SOMETHING HAPPEN 4

Scan the QR code or visit: *https://www.youtube.com/watch?v=q8O_TEEnNC8* for a video walkthrough of this Make Something Happen.

Install Git

First, you need to open your browser and visit this web page:

https://git-scm.com

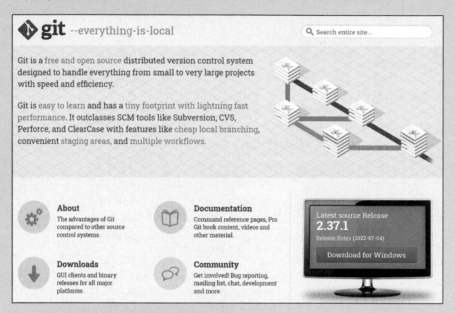

Now, follow the installation process selecting all the default options.

Storing Git repositories

You can use the Git program on a single computer to manage your work by putting each repository in a folder. If you want to store your files in a central location, you can also set up a computer as a Git server, which is a bit like a web server for software developers. You use the Git program to send copies of your repositories over the network to the server, where they are stored. You can also clone a repository from the Git server —a process called "checking out" a repository. You can work on the file and sync your changes with the original—known as "checking in." Git's user management allows users to have their own login names. Those users can work in teams with access to their particular repositories.

All the changes are tracked by Git so that they can be reverted or examined in detail. This makes it much easier for developers to collaborate (which is what Linus Torvalds wanted at the start) because Git can also detect multiple changes to the same file and require them to be resolved to create a single definitive version.

GitHub and open-source software

A Git server makes it easy for programmers in a company to work together. But what if you want anyone in the world to be able to work on your project? Lots of today's important software, including operating systems, network tools, and even games, are now developed as *open-source* projects. All the software code that comprises these applications is stored openly, frequently in a Git repository that is accessible to people who want to help with the project. Anyone can check out the repository, make some changes and then submit a "pull request" to the project owners, which means the project owners can "pull" in a copy of the changes. The changes could be a fix to a problem, a new feature, or even just improved error messages. If the owner approves the changes, they are incorporated into the application, making it that much better.

Figure 2-2 shows the book code sample repository as it appears on GitHub. GitHub also provides *organizations* for managing projects. A user can create an organization containing multiple repositories. For example, I've created one called "Building-Apps-and-Games-in-the-Cloud" for this book. The sample repository is one of several that are held in this organization. If you store group or project repositories that should not be directly associated with a particular GitHub user, you can create an organization to hold them.

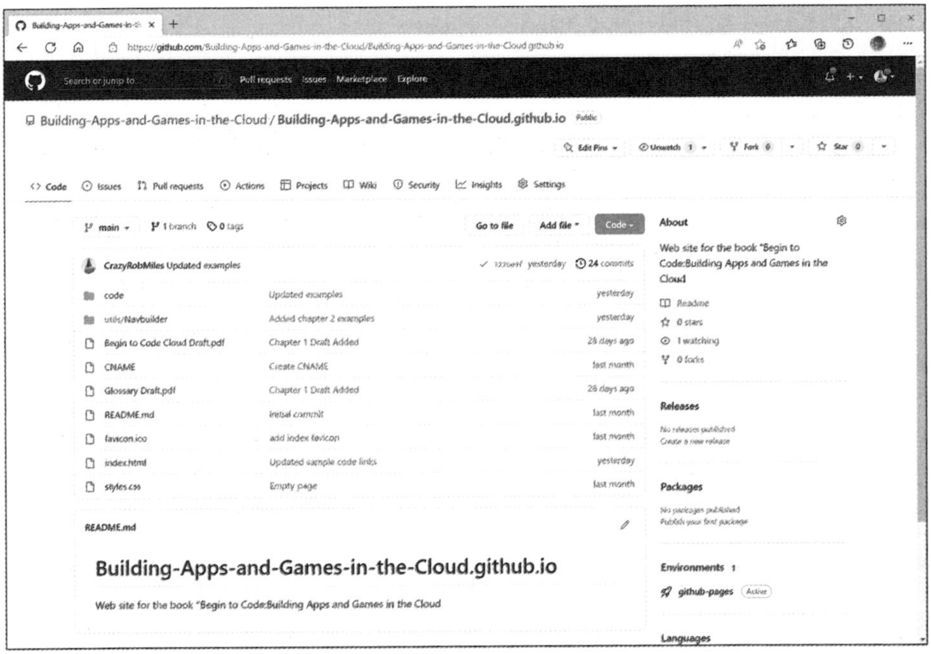

Figure 2-2 Sample repository on GitHub

The sample repository is public, so anyone can look inside the files. They can even clone the repository onto their computer, make some changes, and send me a pull request. You could regard the samples as a mini open-source project. Also, you can make private repositories that will not be visible to other GitHub users.

PROGRAMMER'S POINT

Open-source projects are a great place to start your career

You might think that you must become a great programmer before you can start to make a name for yourself in software development. This is not true. You can add value to an open-source project well before you're capable of creating complete programs. You can learn a huge amount just by looking at code written by other people. And working out how the internal pieces of a system fit together is very satisfying, even if you don't know how the whole thing works.

An important part of being a successful developer is working well with others, so being part of an open-source project prepares you well for this. Many developers also remember what it was like to start out and will be happy to help you improve as long as you keep your input constructive and focused.

In addition, a project needs lots of things that have nothing to do with programming. A large project will need people to test things, write documentation, make artwork, create different language versions, and so on. If you have any of those skills, you could find yourself in high demand just for those. And that alone could open a totally different career path for you.

GitHub hosts many open-source projects (and lots of commercial ones). Companies can rent space on GitHub rather than setting up their own Git servers, but GitHub also offers comprehensive free services for open-source developers. And you can host private repositories on GitHub for your projects.

I strongly advise you to set up an account on GitHub and use it for your projects. Doing so won't cost anything. When I start a new project, one of my first thoughts is, "what happens if I lose everything?" GitHub is a good answer to that question. If I put things into a GitHub repository, they will be as safe as they can be. And if I make good use of the ability to commit changes at regular intervals, I can save myself from losing work. Furthermore, once the repository is on GitHub, I can invite other people to my project to work on it with them or make it public so anyone can use it.

You don't need a GitHub account to make use of everything in this book, but if you want to get the most out of the contents, you should make one. It can completely change the way you work. If I want to do anything these days—from organizing a party to writing a book— I start by creating a GitHub repository for the project.

GitHub is a great place to store your data. However, it is also a great place to network with others. Each repository has a Wiki, which is a space for collaboratively creating documentation. A repository can host issue-tracking discussions that people can use to report bugs and request features, and you can create and manage projects within the repository.

GitHub also has a final ace up its sleeve—it can host websites. You can put your web pages in a GitHub repository and then make them available for anyone in the world to see. We will do that at the end of this chapter.

MAKE SOMETHING HAPPEN 5

Scan the QR code or visit *https://www.youtube.com/watch?v=JzaXvcX4WY8* for a video walk-through of this Make Something Happen.

Join GitHub

You can skip this section if you don't want to join GitHub. You can still grab the sample repositories and work on the code, but you won't be able to create your own repositories or use GitHub to host websites.

You will need an email address to create a GitHub account. Start by opening your browser and visiting the web page at *https://github.com/join*.

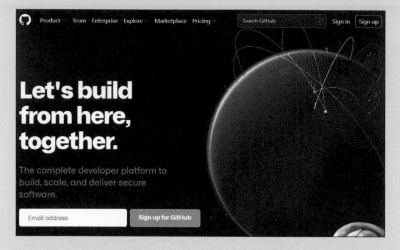

Enter your email address and click **Sign Up For GitHub**. It takes a few steps, and you have to wait for a message to validate your email address, but eventually, you will end up at the dashboard for your GitHub account.

You are now logged in to the GitHub website and can work with your repositories and clone the repositories created by other GitHub users. If you want to use GitHub from a browser on another machine, you will have to log in to the service on that machine.

You can work with your repositories using the web page interface. You can also enter Git commands into your Windows terminal or MacOS console. However, in this chapter, we will use the Visual Studio Code program to edit and debug our programs; it can also talk to Git and manage our repositories.

PROGRAMMER'S POINT

GitHub is also a social network

You can regard GitHub as a social network. If you make something that you think would be useful to other people, you can share it by creating a public GitHub repository. Other GitHub members can download your repository and use it. They can also make changes and send you "pull requests" to signal that they have made a new version you might like.

Members can award repositories "stars" and comment on their content. Many discussions happen on GitHub, which means GitHub is another place you can start making a name for yourself. However, just as you should be cautious when posting personal details on other social network sites, you should also be aware of the potential for misuse found on any social networking framework.

Make sure not to give out too much personal information and ensure that anything you put into a public repository does not contain personal data. Don't put personal details, usernames, or passwords into the program code you put on GitHub. In the section "Tiny Survey deployment" in Chapter 10, I explain how to separate sensitive information from the code in projects.

Get Visual Studio code

Now that we have Git installed and working, we will install Visual Studio Code, which we will use to create all our programs. It is free to download, and versions are available for Windows, Macintosh, and Linux-based computers, including the Raspberry Pi. It also supports lots of extensions that can be used to extend its capabilities.

MAKE SOMETHING HAPPEN 6

Scan the QR code or visit *https://www.youtube.com/watch?v=0uXD77feBoY* for a video walk-through of this Make Something Happen.

Install Visual Studio Code and clone a repository

The instructions here are for Windows, but the instructions for macOS are very similar. First, open your browser and visit this web page:

https://code.visualstudio.com/Download

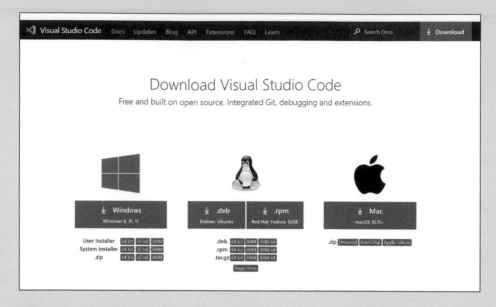

Click the version of Visual Studio Code you want and follow the instructions to install it. Once it is installed, you will see the start page.

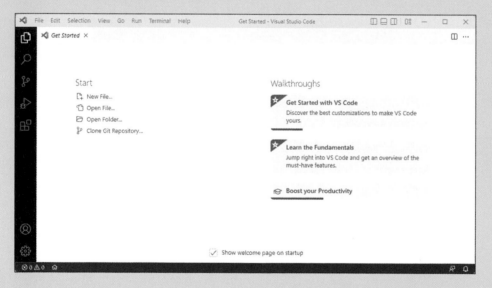

Now that you have Visual Studio installed, you next need to fetch the sample files to work on. To do this, click the **Clone Git Repository** link about halfway up the left-hand side of the page.

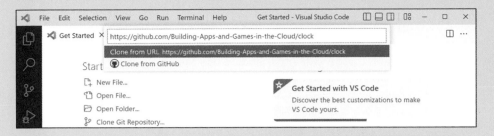

Enter the address of the repository into the dialog box, as shown above. Click the **Clone From URL** button beneath the address. If you click the **Clone From GitHub** button beneath **Clone From URL**, you will be prompted to log in to GitHub. This can be useful if you want to send local repositories from your machine to GitHub, but you don't need to do this just to fetch files.

The repository will be copied into a folder on your machine. The next thing that Visual Studio needs to know is the location of that folder. I have a special GitHub folder where I store my repositories. Because I'm using GitHub to keep my files safe, I don't need to use OneDrive to synchronize things.

> (i) Would you like to open the cloned repository?   ⚙ ✕
>
> Source: Git (Extension)   **Open**   **Open in New Window**

Once the files have been cloned, Visual Studio Code allows you to open the new repository. Click **Open**. You will be asked to confirm that you trust the author. It is best to choose **Yes** here. Then Visual Studio will open the repository and show you the contents. On the far left are the tools you can use to work on the repository. Click the top one to select **Explorer**. The examples are in the code folder, organized by chapter. Click **Ch02-Get_into_the_cloud** to open the folder, open the **Ch02-01_Simple HTML** folder, and then click the `index.html` file to open it in the editor.

```html
<!DOCTYPE html>
<html lang="en">

<head>
    <title>Ch02-01 Simple HTML</title>
</head>

<body>
    <p>
        This is <strong>strong</strong><br>
        This is <b>bold</b><br>
    </p>
</body>

</html>
```

Leave Visual Studio Code running; you will use it again in a moment. Next, you need to install your first Visual Studio Code extension.

Install the Live Server extension

Before we can work with our web pages, there is something we can do to make our job much easier. We will edit a web page with Visual Studio Code, view it in a web browser, edit it again, and so on. We could do this by repeatedly saving the web page to a file and opening it by hand each time. However, this would be a lot of work, and programmers hate doing a lot of unnecessary work. When faced with a problem like this, programmers create a tool that will do the work for them.

Ritwick Dey is a programmer who solved this problem by creating the Live Server extension for Visual Studio Code. You can add a new feature to Visual Studio Code by installing an extension. There are thousands of extensions available for download, but we will use the Live Server extension. Then, when we want to view HTML in our browser, we can simply press a button.

MAKE SOMETHING HAPPEN 7

Scan the QR code or visit *https://www.youtube.com/watch?v=juCQflxf9ss* for a video walk-through of this Make Something Happen.

Install the Live Server extension

Open Visual Studio Code and click the **Extensions** button on the left-hand toolbar. (It is the fifth one down, as highlighted below.) The Extensions Marketplace opens. Type **Live Server** into the search box.

The marketplace will show all the extensions with this name. Click the **Install** button on the one written by Ritwick Dey. The screenshot below is displayed when the extension has been installed.

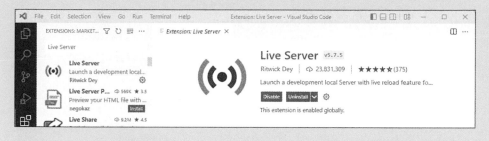

Once an extension has been installed, it will be loaded each time Visual Studio Code is started. You can test it by using the index page you opened earlier. If Visual Studio Code isn't already open, open the **Ch02-01_Simple HTML** folder repository and click the `index.html` file to open it in the editor.

Once an extension has been installed, it will be loaded each time Visual Studio Code is started. The first time you open the file, your firewall might ask if you want to allow this file to be opened. You should allow Visual Studio Code access to the ports it needs. In Windows, click **Don't Show Again**.

You will also see a message from Live Studio telling you the server has started; also, the networking port it is using will be specified. Then, the browser opens and displays this page:

Above, you can see the page as displayed by the browser. Note that the page address starts with `127.0.0.1`, which indicates that your computer is hosting the page. If you use Visual Studio Code to make changes to `index.html` and then save them, the browser will automatically reload the updated page. This is a very useful extension and has been downloaded more than 23 million times. It turns out that writing extensions for Visual Studio Code is also a great way to make a name for yourself. Next, you need to understand the web page's contents.

How a web page works

We have been using web pages in our browsers for years. In Chapter 1, we saw that a web page could contain JavaScript code. Now it is time to dig deeper and consider what makes a web page. We will not go into too much detail because there are books specifically about these topics that are much thicker than this one.

You might think you already know what a web page is, but I'd be most grateful if you would read this section anyway. You might find a few things you didn't know.

A web page is a "logical document." What do I mean by that? Well, a book is a *physical* document that exists in the real world. We can read it, add annotations, leave it on the bus, and do everything we can do with a physical book in the real world. An electronic book (or e-book) is a *virtual* document. It is created to play the part of a physical book in a virtual environment created by a computer. We can read it, annotate it, and if we delete the file containing the book, we could even manage to lose it. A web page is a *logical* document. It is a thing created by software and is hosted on a computer. A web page has no physical counterpart. No physical version of a book contains a ticking clock. As you can see in **Figure 2-3**, the best we can do is create a static image.

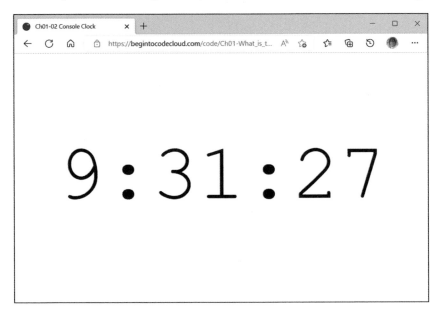

Figure 2-3 A static image of a clock

Loading a page and displaying it

The starting point for a web page is a text file hosted on a server. When you visit a website such as *www.robmiles.com*, the browser looks for a file called `index.html` at that location containing the site's start page. The text in this file describes the logical document that makes up the web page. The browser reads the text file from the server and uses it to build the logical document that is the web page. At this point, you might say, "Aha! The text file on the server describes the web page, so a web page is just a text file."

Well, no. A web page could contain JavaScript code that runs when the document is loaded into the browser. That code can change the contents of the logical document and even add new things. The logical document the HTML describes is held by the browser in a structure called the *Document Object Model (DOM)*. The DOM is a very important part of web programming. Our JavaScript programs will interact with the DOM to display output.

Once the browser has built the DOM, it is drawn on the display. The browser program then repeatedly checks the DOM for changes and redraws it if any changes are found. This is how the ticking clock we created in Chapter 1 works. In our ticking clock, a JavaScript function runs, changing the document and prompting the browser to redraw the page to reflect the changes. We don't have to do anything to trigger a redraw; our code can change the logical document's contents, and the updated page version is displayed automatically.

A logical document can contain images, sounds, and videos that are updated automatically. The initial contents of the document objects are expressed using a language called Hypertext Markup Language (HTML). Let's look at that next.

Hypertext Markup Language (HTML)

We can discover what Hypertext Markup Language really is by examining its name. Let's start with hypertext. Remember that we can call things *logical* to indicate they have no counterpart in real life. *Hypertext* is a logical version of text. Normal text, whether it is printed or displayed on a screen, is something you read from beginning to end. A computer can only display hypertext because hypertext can contain *hyperlinks*, which refer to other documents. You can start reading one document, open a hyperlink, and be moved to a completely different one, perhaps served by a completely different computer in a different country. When hypertext and hyperlinks were invented, it was thought cool to put the word *hyper* in front of them to make them sound impressive. So, that is where the name came from. At least, that's what I think.

So, the word *hyperlink* in HTML means that the language aims to express a page that can contain hyperlinks. HTML was invented to make it easier to navigate reports.

Before hyperlinks, if a report contained a reference to another report, you would have to find and open it to read it. After hyperlinks, you could just follow a link in the original report. Hypertext was designed to be extensible, meaning adding new features would be easy. The features provided by modern web pages are way beyond any foreseen by Tim Berners-Lee, the inventor of HTML, but a page's fundamental content remains the same.

The word *markup* refers to how an HTML document separates the author's intent from the page's content. Let's look at a tiny web page to discover how this works.

Figure 2-4 shows a tiny web page containing just six words. Let's look at the HTML file behind it and discover the role of markup in creating the page contents.

Figure 2-4 Simple HTML

Following is the HTML file that describes the page shown in **Figure 2-4**.

```
<!DOCTYPE html>
<html lang="en">
<head>
<title>Ch02-01 Simple HTML</title>
</head>
<body>
    <p>
        This is <strong>strong</strong><br>
        This is <b>bold</b><br>
    </p>
</body>
</html>
```

The most important characters in the file are the < and >, marking the start and end of HTML element names. The < and > are called *delimiters* and define the limits of something.

An *element* is a thing in the document that the browser knows how to work with. Elements can have attribute values. Name-value pairs are included in the element's definition. The `<html lang="en">` element in the preceding code has an attribute called `lang,` which specifies the language in the document. The value `en` means English.

Elements can be containers. A container starts with the element's name and ends with the name preceded by a forward slash (/). You can see that the `<title>` element contains the text to be used as the web page's title. You can see this title at the top of the web page in **Figure 2-4**. The title information is part of the page header, which is why it is enclosed in the `<head>` element.

The `<body>` element contains all the elements to be drawn by the browser. The `<p>` element (short for paragraph) groups text into a paragraph. The `<bold>` and `<strong>` elements give formatting information to the browser. However, an element can exist as the starting element name without another to mark the element's end. The `<br>` element tells the browser to add a line break in the text. You don't need to add a `</br>` element to a page to mark the end of a line break if the break doesn't contain anything.

The *L* in HTML stands for *language*. We use HTML to express things. HTML is very specific (it is used to tell a browser how to build a logical document), but it is a language.

🚀 **MAKE SOMETHING HAPPEN 8**

Scan the QR code or visit *https://www.youtube.com/watch?v=OvMsgb1QW54* for a video walkthrough of this Make Something Happen.

Web page editing

If you have been following this exercise, you will already have the first sample file open in your browser. If not, use Visual Studio Code to open the **Ch02-01_Simple HTML** file in the book examples and click the `index.html` file to open it in the editor. Then click **Go Live** to open the page in the browser.

Your desktop should now have both Visual Studio Code and your browser open, as shown below.

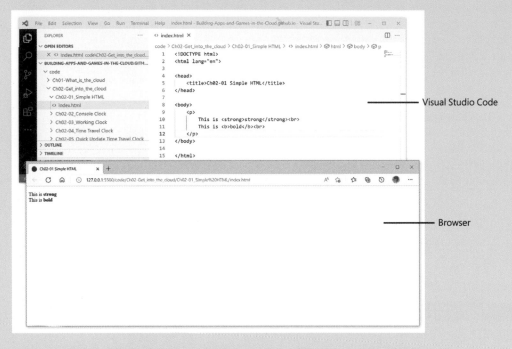

Now go back to Visual Studio Code and add the following element to the page:

```
This is <em>emphasized</em>
```

Visual Studio Code should now look like this:

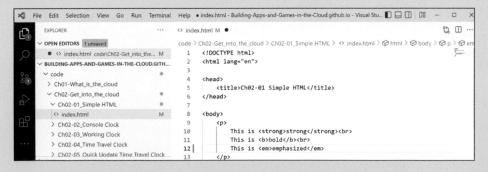

Now select **File > Save** from the Visual Studio Code menu bar to save the updated file:

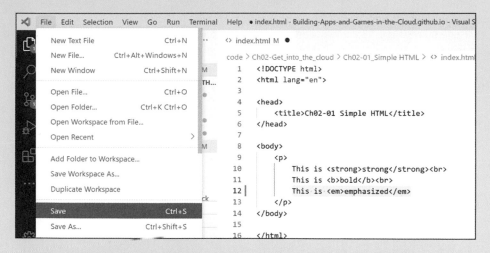

Because you are using Go Live, you should see the page in the browser updated automatically and displaying the new text on the page:

The page has been updated in the browser

This is a very nice way to work on web pages. Each time you save your file, the web page updates automatically.

Investigating HTML

If this is your first brush with HTML, you might have some questions.

Question: What is the difference between bold (`<b>`) and strong (`<strong>`)?

Answer: The HTML file marks one piece of text as bold (`<b>`) and another as strong (`<strong>`). But in **Figure 2-2**, they both look the same. You might think this means that `<b>` and `<strong>` are the same thing. However, they are intended to be used for different kinds of text. Text that needs to stand out should be formatted as bold (`<b>`). Text that is more important than the text around it should be formatted as strong (`<strong>`). I would format my name as `<b>` because I would like it to stand out. However, I would print "Do not put your head out of the window when the train is moving" in `<strong>` because that is probably more important than the text around it.

Remember, HTML contains instructions for the browser to display things in certain ways. The browser's default behavior is to display both `<b>` and `<strong>` as bold text, but you can change this for your web pages by adding styles, which we will discover in the Code Analysis section "Documents objects and JavaScript" later in this chapter.

Question: How do I enter a < or a > into the text?

Answer: Good question. HTML uses another character—&—to mark the start of a *symbol* entity. Symbols can be identified by their names. Some useful ones are

```
&lt; &gt; &amp;
```

Visit *https://html.spec.whatwg.org/multipage/named-characters.html* for a list of all the symbols. You can also use symbols to add emoticons to your pages. You can find the codes for emoticons at *https://emojiguide.org/*.

Question: What happens if I misspell the name of an element?

Answer: If the browser sees an element it doesn't know, it will just ignore it.

Question: What happens if I get the nesting of the elements wrong?

Answer: If you look at the sample HTML, you will see that some elements are inside others. For example, the `<p>` element is inside the `<body>` element. Putting items inside others is called *nesting*. It is important that nesting is performed correctly. If you get the nesting wrong (for example, you put the `</body>` element inside the `<p>`) the browser will not complain, and the page will display. However, it might not look how you were expecting.

Question: What does the `<!DOCTYPE html>` element mean?

Answer: The very first line of a resource loaded from a web server should describe what it contains. The resource could contain an image, a sound file, or any number of other kinds of data. The `!DOCTYPE` element is used to deliver this information. The browser doesn't always use this. A browser will try to display any text file it is given, but it is very useful to add information.

Question: How do I put JavaScript into a web page?

Answer: You use the `<script>` element to embed JavaScript into a page.

Question: Are there other kinds of markup language?

Answer: Yes, there are. The XML (eXtensible Markup Language) is used for expressing data structures. Lots of others have been developed for particular applications.

Question: How do I stop the Go Live server?

Answer: You might want to stop the Go Live server and open a web page from a different index file. You can do this by restarting Visual Studio Code, but you can also press the close button next to the port number on the bottom right of the Visual Studio Code window.

Make an active web page

We have reached a pretty powerful position. We have tools we can use to create and store web resources, and we are building an understanding of how web pages are structured. Now, we are going to take another big step forward and discover how a JavaScript program can modify the document object's contents and change the web page's appearance. This is how JavaScript programs running in the browser communicate with the user.

Interact with the document object

MAKE SOMETHING HAPPEN 9

Scan the QR code or visit *https://www.youtube.com/watch?v=IMTFkUQH3H0* for a video walkthrough of this Make Something Happen.

Interact with a web page

If you have files open in Visual Studio Code, you should close them now. If Go Live is displaying a page, stop it from running by pressing the close button next to the port number at the bottom of the Visual Studio Code window. Now use Visual Studio Code to open the **Ch02-02_Console Clock** folder in this book's examples and click the `index.html` file to open it in the editor. Click **Go Live** to open the page in the browser. Now open the Developer Tools and then select the **Elements** tab to see the document elements:

Page displayed in browser   Web page contents

In the figure above, I've resized the Developer Tools part of the screen to give me more space. On the left side of the window, you can see the page as the browser displays it. On the right, you can see the web page's contents. The selected paragraph contains an `id` attribute set to the `timePar` value. While this page looks a lot like the page's source code, it's actually a view of the elements in the Document Object Model (DOM) created from the HTML file.

Below, you can see the highlighted element. The clock program changes the content of this element to display the time:

```
<p id="timePar" class="clock">0:0:0</p>
```

The program looks for the element with an `id` attribute of `timepar` and then displays the time in this element. In the last chapter, we used the `showMessage` function to display a message on the page. Let's look at how it works.

```
showMessage("console hello");
```

We call `showMessage` by giving it an argument that is the message we want to be shown on screen. Type in the call of `showMessage` above and press **Enter**.

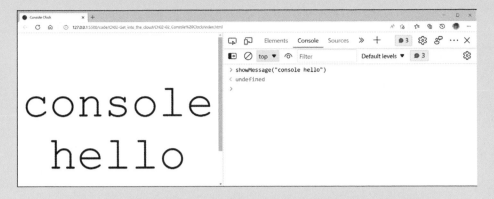

Above, you can see the effect of the `showMessage` call. The message is displayed because the browser redrew the document and the data in the document object has changed. Now, let's take a look at the `showMessage` function itself. The function below contains just two statements:

```
function showMessage(message) {
  let outputElement = document.getElementById("timePar");
  outputElement.textContent = message;
}
```

The first statement finds an HTML element in the document, and the second statement sets the `textContent` property of this element to the message supplied as a parameter. That sounds simple enough, especially if we say it very quickly. Or not. Let's break it down into a series of steps and enter them into the console. Select the **Console** tab in the **Developer Tools** window and enter the following statement:

```
let outputElement = document.getElementById("timePar");
```

This statement finds the element in the document displaying the output. (That's what `getElementById` does.) The DOM provides the `getElementById` method to search for elements by name. The element we have asked it to look for is a paragraph that has an `id` property set to `timePar`. The value returned by `getElementByID` is assigned to a variable called `outputElement`. Press **Enter** to perform the statement.

We know `let` does not return a value, so the console displays `undefined`. The display has not changed because all we have done is obtain a reference to a paragraph in the document. We need to change the text in that paragraph. Enter the following statement:

```
outputElement.textContent = "element hello";
```

This statement uses the `outputElement` reference we have just created. It puts the string `element hello` into the `textContent` property of the element that `outputElement` refers to. Press **Enter** to see what that does.

The page now shows the message `element hello` message because the `textContent` property of the `outputElement` is now `element hello`. The `showMessage` function performs these two steps and sets the `textContent` property to a parameter it has been supplied with, so we can use `showMessage` to show any message we like.

Documents objects and JavaScript

The way that JavaScript programs can interact with document is very powerful, but it can also be very confusing. You might have some questions.

Question: Why is the text that we are displaying so large?

> **Answer:** All the other text on the web pages we have made has been tiny. But the time message in our clock is huge, and in a different font. This works because we are using a feature called a *stylesheet*. Let's take a look at the HTML that defines the paragraph containing the clock output:

```
<p id="timePar" class="clock">0:0:0</p>
```

Initially, this is a paragraph contained 0:0:0. The id is timePar. (This is how our Java-Script finds the paragraph.) It also contains a class attribute, which is set to the value of clock. The class attribute tells the browser how to display an item when it is drawn. Alongside the HTML file containing the clock web page is a file that defines this page's styles. The link element in the head element for the clock web page tells the browser which stylesheet file to use.

```
<link rel="stylesheet" href="styles.css">
```

This document is using the styles.css file. Inside this file, you can find the following style definition:

```
.clock {
  font-size: 10em;
  font-family: 'Courier New', Courier, monospace;
  text-align: center;
}
```

This style information defines the clock *class*, which can then be assigned to elements in the web page. It sets the size, font, and alignment. When a web page is loaded, the browser also fetches the stylesheet file that goes with it. You can use stylesheet files to separate the page formatting from the code that creates it. If the designer and programmer agree on the names of the classes, the designer can create the styles, and the programmer can create the software. A running program can change an element's style class. We could create a style class called error that sets the color of the text in an element to red. If the program detects that the user has entered an invalid value into that element, it could change the style class of that element to error, which would turn the text in the element red.

Question: What if we try to find a document element that is not there?

```
let outputElement = document.getElementById("timeParx");
```

Answer: The statement above is valid JavaScript and is intended to get a reference to the element with an `id` of `timePar`. However, it will not do what we want because we have mistyped the `id`, and there is no element in the web page with an `id` of `timeParx`. When the statement runs, the `getElementById` function returns the value of `null`. This means that `outputElement` is set to `null`. The value `null` is another special JavaScript value. We've seen the `NaN` (not a number) and `undefined` (no value). The `null` value is how `getElementById` can say, "I looked for it, but I couldn't find it, so I'm returning a reference that explicitly means it was not found." If a program tries to set a property on a `null` reference, an error stops the program:

```
> let outputElement = document.getElementById("timeParx");
< undefined
> outputElement
< null
> outputElement.textContent = "hello";
⊗ ▶ Uncaught TypeError: Cannot set properties of null   VM542:1
  (setting 'textContent')
      at <anonymous>:1:27
>
```

Above, you can see the effect of trying to use a `null` reference. The message in red means that the program would stop at this point. In other words, any statements after the one that tries to set the `textContent` property on a `null` reference would not be performed. Later, we will discover how to detect `null` references and deal with statements that fail like this.

Question: What if we try to use an element property that is not there?

```
outputElement.textContentx = "hello";
```

Answer: The statement above is also legal JavaScript, but it won't display the `hello` message. This is because it sets the `textContextx` property rather than the correct `textContext` property. What happens next is really very interesting. You don't get the `hello` message because you've written to the wrong property. Instead, JavaScript creates a new property on the `outputElement` object called `textContextx`. It then sets the content of this property to `hello`. This is a powerful feature of the JavaScript language. It means that code running in the web page can attach its own data to elements on the page. We will explore this feature when we build the display for the Cheese Finder game in Chapter 3.

Question: What does the favicon do?

```
<link rel="shortcut icon" type="image/x-icon" href="favicon.ico">
```

Answer: You can find the above statement in the head section of the clock html. It specifies a tiny image to be displayed in the top left-hand corner of each web page, called the "favorite icon" or "favicon." The image is in a file called favicon.ico, which is held in a file on the server and fetched by the browser when the page is loaded. I use a little red ball as the favicon for my sample pages. You can see it on the page images in this chapter. You can create your own favicon image to personalize your pages. Look at *https://favicon.io/* if you want to do this.

Web pages and events

We will make a web page containing active content that runs when the page is loaded. The previous pages contained JavaScript functions, but we had to run them from the **Developer Tools** console. Now, we will give them control to make truly interactive websites. To do this, we will bind a function to the event fired when the browser loads a web page. In Chapter 1 (in the "JavaScript Heroes: Functions" section), we saw how we could pass a function reference to the event generator so the function is called when the event occurs. We used it to make a ticking clock. The clock used a tick function that could get the time and display it. You can see the tick function below. I've expanded it slightly from the version in Chapter 1 to clarify how it works.

```
function tick(){
    let timeString = getTimeString();          Get the time
    showMessage(timeString);                    Display the time
}
```

The first statement in the function puts the time into a string called timeString, and the second statement shows it on the screen. Each time tick is called, it will show the latest time value. To update the clock display continuously, we need to call the tick function at regular intervals. We can use the setInterval function to do this:

```
setInterval(tick,1000);
```

The setInterval function is called with two arguments. The first argument is a reference to tick, and the second argument is the interval between calls—in this case, 1,000 milliseconds. This will make our clock tick every second. The setInterval function causes an event to be created every second, so the clock will update every second. Next, we need a way of calling this function to start the clock each time the web page is loaded.

Below, you can see a function called `startClock`. If we can find a way of calling this function when the clock web page is loaded, we can make a clock that starts when the page is loaded.

```
function startClock(){
    setInterval(tick,1000);
}
```

When we began learning JavaScript in Chapter 1, we saw the importance of learning the Application Programming Interface (API) that provides functions. Now, we are starting to see the importance of another kind of interface—the one provided by properties of elements in the web page itself. We've seen how we can add properties to elements in an HTML document. Each element supports a set of properties. Some of the properties can be bound to snippets of JavaScript.

The `body` element shown below now has an attribute called `onload`, which is the string `"startClock();"`:

```
<body onload="startClock();">
```

Properties with names that start with the word `on` are event properties that will be triggered when the event occurs. The `onload` event is triggered when the body of a page is loaded. When the page is loaded, the string of JavaScript is performed by the browser in the same way the browser performs commands typed into the console.

MAKE SOMETHING HAPPEN 10

Scan the QR code or visit *https://www.youtube.com/watch?v=_-JXWgS-zw8* for a video walk-through of this Make Something Happen.

Make a ticking clock

If you have been following this exercise, you will already have the console clock open in your browser. Now use Visual Studio Code to open the **Ch02-02_Console Clock** folder in this book's examples and click the `index.html` file to open it in the editor. You will add some functions to the JavaScript code to the web page, so scroll to that part of the document:

```javascript
function tick(){
    let timeString = getTimeString();
    showMessage(timeString);
}

function startClock(){
    setInterval(tick,1000);
}
```

These are the two functions that make the clock work. Type them into the `index.html` page inside the `<script></script>` part of the page, near the two existing functions.

Now we need to modify the `body` element to add the `onload` attribute that will call the `startClock` function. Navigate to line 10 in the file and modify the statement as follows:

```html
<body onload="startClock();">
```

Now the body element has an `onload` attribute, which will call the `startClock()` function when the page is loaded. Now press the **Go Live** button to open the page in the browser. You should see the clock start ticking.

CODE ANALYSIS

Events and web pages

Events are great fun, but you might have some questions about them:

Question: My clock is not ticking. Why is this?

> **Answer:** There are a number of reasons why your clock might not tick. If you misspell the name of any function, it might not be called correctly. For example, if you call the starting function `StartClock` (with an uppercase S at the beginning), this will not work because the `onload` event expects to call a function called `startClock`. If you get completely stuck, head over to the **Eg 03 Working clock** folder, where there is a working version of the clock.

Question: What is the difference between an attribute and a property?

Answer: A property is associated with a software object. We have seen how objects can have properties that we can access when our programs run. For example, we looked at the name property of a function object in Chapter 1 in Make Something Happen 2, "Fun with function objects." An attribute is associated with an element in a web page. The body element can have an onload attribute.

Question: Can you run more than one function when a page loads?

Answer: You can do this but wouldn't do it by adding multiple onload attributes. Instead, you would write a single function that runs all the functions in turn and connect that to the onload event.

Making a time travel clock

Now that we know how to make a clock, we will make a clock that lets us travel through time. Sort of. In Chapter 1, in Make Something Happen 3, "Console clock," the Date object provides methods that could be used to set values in a date and read them back. If we use this to add 1,000 minutes to the minute value, the Date object will work out the date and time to be 1,000 minutes into the future. This code shows how this would work:

```
let d = new Date();            Make d refer to a new Date object
let mins = d.getMinutes();     Extract the minutes from the date
let mins = mins + 1000;        Add 1000 to the minutes value
d.setMinutes(mins);            Set the minutes in the future
```

- The first statement creates a variable called d that refers to an object containing the current date.

- The second statement creates a variable called mins that holds the number of minutes in the date stored in d.

- The third statement adds 1,000 to the value of mins.

- The fourth statement sets the minutes value of d to the value in mins. This moves the date in d 1,000 minutes into the future. The Date object sorts out the date value, updating the hours and even the day, month, and year if required.

We can use this to make a time travel clock that is fast or slow by an amount we can nominate. At some times of the day, perhaps in the morning, we can make the clock go fast, so we are not late for anything. At other times, perhaps when it is time to go to bed, we can make the clock go slow, so we can go to bed a little later.

Figure 2-5 shows how it would be used. The user clicks the buttons to select a fast, slow, or normal clock.

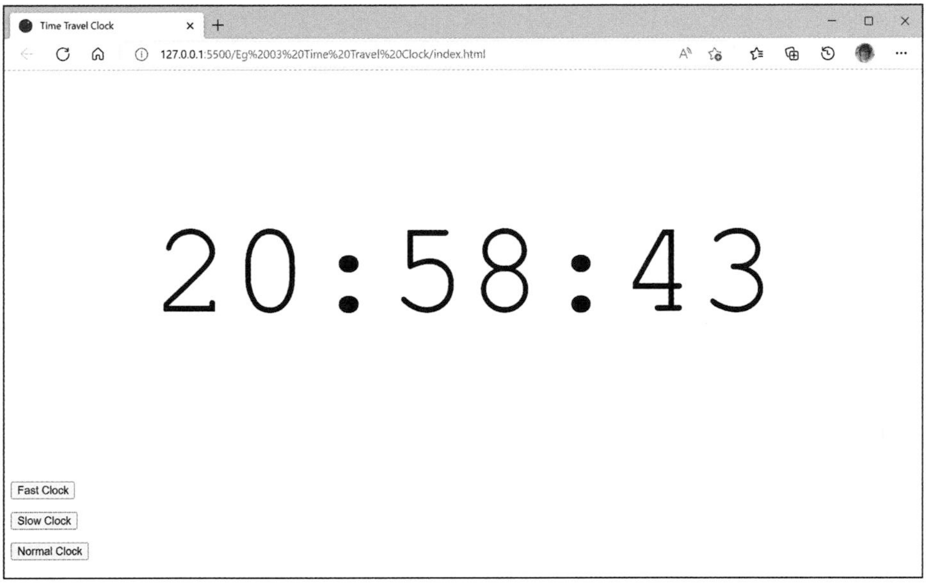

Figure 2-5 Time travel clock

Add buttons to a page

We first need to add some buttons to the page for the user to press. We do this with the `button` element. Here, you can see a paragraph that contains a `button`:

```
<p>
    <button onclick="selectFastClock();">Fast Clock</button>
</p>
```

The button encloses the text that will appear on the button. The button element can have an `onclick` attribute containing a string of JavaScript to be performed when the button is clicked. When this button is clicked, a function called `selectFastClock` is called. Now we need to create some code to put inside this function that will make the clock five minutes fast when it runs. We can do this by creating a *global* variable.

Share values with global variables

Until now, every variable we have created has been used inside a function body. We have used `let` to create variables that cease to exist when the program execution exits the block in which the variables were declared. So, when the function is completed, the variable is discarded. Usually, this is just what you want. It is best if variables don't "hang around" after you have finished with them. I'm very partial to using a variable with the identifier `i` for counting. This is because I am a very old programmer. However, I don't want an `i` used in one part of the program to be confused with an `i` used elsewhere. I like the idea of a variable disappearing as soon as the program leaves the block where it was declared.

However, in the case of the `minutesOffset` value, we want to share the value between functions. The `minutesOffset` mustn't disappear when the program exits a function where it is used. We can't declare `minutesOffset` in just one function. Instead, we must declare it so that it can be shared between all functions. We must make it global.

The variable `minutesOffset` below is not declared inside any code block. Instead, it is declared outside all the functions. It is also declared using `var` rather than `let`. This means that the variable can be used in any of the functions that follow it. The value in the variable will be shared by all the functions, which is exactly what we want.

```
var minutesOffset = 0;
```

If we change the value in `minutesOffset`, the next time the `tick` function updates the clock, it will draw the new time.

PROGRAMMER'S POINT

Global variables are a necessary evil

When you make a variable global by declaring it outside any function, you lose control of it. What do I mean by this? Suppose I'm working with a bunch of programmers, each writing some of the functions in my JavaScript application. If I declare all the variables in my functions by using `let`, I can be sure that those variables can only be changed by me. I can also be sure that I won't change any values in other functions.

However, if a variable is made global, it is possible for code in any of the functions to view and change it, which might lead to mistakes, making the program less secure.

Some things must be global. Making the clock work would be hard without creating a global variable called `minutesOffset`. But when you write code, you should start by making the variables as local as possible (by declaring them using `let`) and then make things global if necessary.

JavaScript gives you control of variable visibility. We will discover how to do this in Chapter 3, in the "JavaScript Heroes: `let`, `var`, and `const`" section.

Below is the code for the `selectFastClock` function. When the function runs, it sets the `minutesOffset` variable to 5. The contents of the `minutesOffset` variable are added to the `minutes` value when the time is displayed.

```
function selectFastClock() {
  minutesOffset = 5;                    ──────── Set the minutes offset to 5
}
```

Below is a modified version of the `getTimeString` function. This adds the value of `minutesOffset` onto the minutes in the time string. This means that when the fast button is clicked, the clock will display the time five minutes into the future. The page also has button handlers for `selectSlowClock` and `selectNormalClock`, which set the value of `minutesOffset` to the appropriate values.

```
function getTimeString() {
  let currentDate = new Date();                    ──────── Get the date
  let displayMins = currentDate.getMinutes()
                  + minutesOffset;                 ──────── Calculate the new minutes
  currentDate.setMinutes(displayMins);             ──────── Set the new minutes value
  let hours = currentDate.getHours();
  let mins = currentDate.getMinutes();
  let secs = currentDate.getSeconds();
  let timeString = hours + ":" + mins + ":" + secs; ──────── Build the time string
  return timeString;                               ──────── Return the time string
}
```

The complete HTML file for the Time Travel Clock is shown below. (You can view the code running in the **Eg 04 Time Travel Clock** example.)

```
<!DOCTYPE html>
<html lang="en">
<html>

<head>
  <title>Time Travel Clock</title>
  <link rel="shortcut icon" type="image/x-icon" href="favicon.ico">
  <link rel="stylesheet" href="styles.css">
</head>

<body onload="startClock();">
```

```
<p id="timePar" class="clock">0:0:0</p>

<p>
  <button onclick="selectFastClock();">Fast Clock</button>
</p>
<p>
  <button onclick="selectSlowClock();">Slow Clock</button>
</p>
<p>
  <button onclick="selectNormalClock();">Normal Clock</button>
</p>

<script type="text/javascript">

  var minutesOffset = 0;

  function selectFastClock() {
    minutesOffset = 5;
  }

  function selectSlowClock() {
    minutesOffset = -5;
  }

  function selectNormalClock() {
    minutesOffset = 0;
  }

  function tick() {
    let timeString = getTimeString();
    showMessage(timeString);
  }

  function startClock() {
    setInterval(tick, 1000);
  }

  function getTimeString() {
    let currentDate = new Date();
    let displayMins = currentDate.getMinutes() + minutesOffset;
    currentDate.setMinutes(displayMins);
    let hours = currentDate.getHours();
    let mins = currentDate.getMinutes();
```

```
        let secs = currentDate.getSeconds();
        let timeString = hours + ":" + mins + ":" + secs;
        return timeString;
    }

    function showMessage(message) {
        let outputElement = document.getElementById("timePar");
        outputElement.textContent = message;
    }
  </script>
</body>

</html>
```

CODE ANALYSIS

Time travel clock

You might have some questions about the time travel clock:

Question: Can we update the display immediately after a button is pressed?

Answer: There is a problem with the time travel clock. It takes a while to "catch up" when you click a button. You must wait up to a second before seeing the time change to reflect a new offset value. You can fix this by making the selectFastClock, selectSlowClock, and selectNormalClock functions call the Tick function once they have updated the offset.

```
function selectFastClock() {
  minutesOffset = 5;
  tick();
}
```

Now, when the user clicks the button, the clock updates instantly. This version is found in the **Eg 05 Quick Update Time Travel Clock** example.

Question: Can we make the clock display change color to indicate whether the clock is fast or slow?

Answer: Yes, we can. We could have a different style class of the display paragraph for each clock option.

```
.normalClock,.fastClock,.slowClock {
  font-size: 10em;
  font-family: 'Courier New', Courier, monospace;
  text-align: center;
}

.normalClock{
  color: black;
}

.fastClock {
  color: red;
}

.slowClock {
  color: green;
}
```

Above, you can see a stylesheet that creates three styles, normalClock, fastClock, and slowClock. You can see which settings are shared by all the styles and which just set the specific colors. The fast clock is displayed in red, and the slow one is displayed in green. When the selection button is pressed, you can set the style class to the appropriate style. The selectFastClock function below is bound to the Fast Clock button on the page and will run when the button is pressed.

```
function selectFastClock() {
  let outputElement = document.getElementById("timePar");
  outputElement.className = "fastClock";
  minutesOffset = 5;
  tick();
}
```

An HTML element has a className property that is set to the class's name. You can change the style class by changing this name. The selectFastClock function sets the className for the outputElement to fastClock so that the fastClock style class is used to display it. So, the text now turns red when the clock is fast. You can find this version in the **Eg 06 Color Coded Clock** example.

Question: Can this program be written without using a global variable?

Answer: The time travel clock currently uses a global variable called minutesOffset to determine whether the clock is fast or slow. Global variables should be avoided if possible, but how can you do this?

The web page contains a paragraph that displays the time. The clock program sets the TextContent property of this paragraph to display the time and the className property of the paragraph to select a different display style (fastClock, slowClock, or normalClock). You can also use the className property's value on the time paragraph to set the time offset.

```
function getMinutesOffset(){
  let minutesOffset = 0;
  let outputElement = document.getElementById("timePar");
  switch(outputElement.className) {
    case "normalClock": minutesOffset = 0;
    break;
    case "fastClock": minutesOffset = 5;
    break;
    case "slowClock": minutesOffset = -5;
    break;
  }
  return minutesOffset;
}
```

The function getMinutesOffset above uses the JavaScript switch construction to return an offset value, which is 0 if the className property of the timePar element is normalClock, 5 if the className is fastClock, and -5 if the className is slowClock. This can be used in getTimeString to calculate the time to be displayed.

```
function getTimeString() {
  let currentDate = new Date();
  let minutesOffset = getMinutesOffset();
  let displayMins = currentDate.getMinutes() + minutesOffset;
  currentDate.setMinutes(displayMins);
  let hours = currentDate.getHours();
  let mins = currentDate.getMinutes();
  let secs = currentDate.getSeconds();
  let timeString = hours + ":" + mins + ":" + secs;
  return timeString;
}
```

This version gets the value of the minutesOffset and then uses it to create a time string with the required offset. There is now no need for a global minutesOffset variable.

This is a very good way of solving the problem. The setting is an attribute of the element it will affect. There is also no chance that the display's color can get out of step with the minutesOffset value. This version is in the **Eg 07 No Globals Clock** example folder.

Host a website on GitHub

You now have something you might like to show off to the world. What better way to do this than putting it on a website for everyone to see? Then, anyone who wants a time-traveling clock can just go to your site and start it. One way to do this is to create a website repository on GitHub. To do this, you must have a GitHub account. You can only host one website on your account, but the site can contain multiple pages with links between them. We are going to start with a really simple website that just contains the time machine clock. If you want to experiment with styles, you can change the clock text color, size, and font. In the next chapter, I cover how to add images to pages.

🚀 **MAKE SOMETHING HAPPEN 11**

Scan the QR code or visit *https://www.youtube.com/watch?v=0sJyxBzAOwM* for a video walkthrough of this Make Something Happen.

Host a web page on GitHub

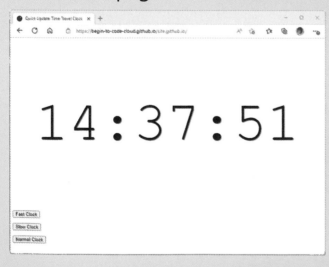

Above, you can see the endpoint of this exercise, which shows the clock program running on a website hosted by GitHub. I don't have the space to cover the process in detail here. In short, you need to do the following:

1. Create an empty repository.

2. Use Visual Studio Code to clone the repository onto your PC.

3. Add the clock files to the repository.

4. Configure Git on your computer with your GitHub username and email.

5. Check in the changes to your local Git installation.

6. Synchronize the changes from the PC up to the repository.

7. Configure GitHub to tell it which part of the repository to share on the web.

The good news is that you won't be doing this very often. The better news is that I've made a step-by-step video that takes you through the process.

What you have learned

This has been a very busy chapter. We've covered a lot of ground. Following is a recap plus some points to ponder.

- Git is a tool that makes working on large projects easier. It organizes units of work into repositories. A repository is a folder containing files; it also contains a special folder managed by the Git tool to track changes by making copies of changed files. You "commit" changes to the repository and take a snapshot of their contents. You can return to the snapshot at any time. You can also compare the snapshot with the current files.

- Git can be used on one machine by one person, or a Git server can be set up for network access to repositories by several people. Git also provides a means of resolving changes to the same file by multiple people.

- GitHub is a cloud-based service that hosts Git repositories. Users can take copies of (clone) repositories, work on them, and then check them back in over the network. A repository can be private to a particular user or public. Public repositories are the basis of open-source projects with managers accepting contributions and then committing them after testing. A GitHub repository can be exposed as a web page, making GitHub a good way to host a simple website.

- Git (and by extension GitHub) support can be added to software tools, which can then make use of repository storage and management. The Visual Studio Code integrated development environment (IDE) works in this way. We can check repositories in and out as we work on them.

- Visual Studio Code also provides an extension mechanism that can be used to add extra features. The Live Server extension allows you to deploy websites on your PC to test them.

- A web page is expressed by a file of text containing Hypertext Markup Language (HTML). The page contains elements that will be drawn by the browser when the page is displayed. The names of the elements are distinguished from text to be displayed by using < and > characters to delimit the element names. For example, <head> is how the start of the header element would be expressed. The end of the header is expressed by an element containing the name preceded by a forward slash: </head>. The <br> element (line break) does not need a corresponding </br> element.

- HTML elements can be nested. The <body> element contains all the elements to be displayed in the web page's body.

- HTML elements can have attributes that give information about the element. Attributes are added as named values in the element's definition. The HTML <p id="timePar"> marks the start of a paragraph. This paragraph has an id attribute that is set to the timePar value.

- Elements in an HTML document can be given a class attribute that maps back to a style definition in a stylesheet file loaded by the browser. The source HTML file specifies the stylesheet file location using a link element to the head of the document.

- The browser uses the HTML file to create a Document Object Model (DOM). The DOM is a software object that describes the web page structure. The DOM contains references to objects representing the elements described in the HTML page.

- Element objects in the DOM contain property values that are mapped onto the attributes assigned in the HTML. For example, an element's class attribute in an HTML document is mapped onto the className property in the element object in the DOM. This makes it possible for JavaScript programs to change the values of properties and their appearance on the page. We used this ability to change the color of the text in the time travel clock.

- You can use the **Elements** tab in the **Developer Tools** for the browser to look at the elements in the DOM.

- An element in an HTML document can be given an `id` attribute that allows a JavaScript program to find it in the DOM. The DOM provides a `getElementByID` method that will find an element by its `id`. If the method can't find an element with the requested `id`, it will return a `null` reference.

- You can change the `textContent` property of a paragraph element by assigning a string to it. The element will then display this new text on the web page.

- Some HTML elements can generate events. An event is identified by a name (usually starting with the word "on") and contains a string of JavaScript code to be performed when the event occurs. The `body` element can have an `onload` attribute that specifies JavaScript to run when the browser loads a web page.

- A web page can contain button elements that generate events when the user clicks them. When the web page user clicks the button, a JavaScript function can be called to respond to this event.

- GitHub can be made to host web pages and store repositories.

To reinforce your understanding of this chapter, you might want to consider the following "profound questions".

Question: What is the difference between Git and GitHub?

Answer: Git is the program that you run to manage your repositories. GitHub is a cloud based service that hosts repositories and is accessed using the Git program.

Question: Can I put any kind of file in a Git repository?

Answer: Yes, you can. However, you must be very careful not to put any credentials or confidential data into a file you add to a repository as it might get sent up to GitHub and end up being made public. In Chapter 8, I explain how to use the `gitignore` file to mark files that are not to be stored in a repository. In Chapter 12, we will use environment variables to pass credentials into a program when deploying it.

Question: Can I use Git on my machine?

Answer: Yes. You can use it to manage a repository stored on your machine, and you can also set up your own Git server and store private projects on your home network.

Question: Will I ever use the Git program directly?

Answer: I try to avoid doing this too much. Usually, Visual Studio Code will hide a lot of the complexities of Git, but every now and then (particularly if you work on group projects), you might have to type in a Git command to fix something.

Question: Are there different kinds of open-source projects?

Answer: Yes. This is controlled by the terms of the license agreement assigned to a particular project. It is worth reading through these to find out what permissions you can give people on the projects you make open source. You should also check when you use an open-source project that you are not breaking any of their conditions.

Question: Why is HTML called a markup language?

Answer: HTML is used to express the design of a view of a web page, such as which elements should be in paragraphs, which should be headings, and so on. In the days before computers, a printer would write instructions on the original copy of a document they were printing. The instructions would specify the fonts and type sizes for the text to be printed. This was called "marking up." HTML can be used to express how text is to be formatted, so it was given the name "markup."

Question: What would happen if I just gave a browser a file of text?

Answer: The browser tries very hard to display something, even if it doesn't look like a proper HTML document. It would display a file of text as a single line, but it ignores line feeds and reduces multiple spaces to 1. You must add appropriate formatting elements if you want to display separate lines and paragraphs.

Question: Where does the browser store the Document Object Model?

Answer: The browser stores the Document Object Model in the computer's memory when a web page is loaded. A software object provides data storage and methods used to interact with the data stored in the object. The HTML file sets the initial elements in the object and their initial values.

Question: What is the difference between HTML and HTTP?

Answer: HTML is a way of expressing the content of a web page. HTTP (Hypertext Transport Protocol) is all about getting that page from the server to the browser. The browser uses the HTTP protocol to get resources, and the server delivers them. The browser sends an HTTP `get` request (which actually includes the word GET). The server finds the resource and sends it back. A `get` request always returns a status value. A status of 200 means, "All is well. Here is the data." A 404 is the infamous "file not found" error that has become so notorious it now appears on T-shirts.

Question: Is HTML a programming language?

Answer: No. A programming language expresses a solution to a problem. Solving a problem might involve making decisions and repeating behaviors. HTML does not have constructions for doing either of these things. HTML is used to express the contents of a logical document, not to solve problems.

Question: What happens if a JavaScript program changes a visible property on an element very quickly?

Answer: We have seen that a JavaScript program can display messages in the browser by updating a property of an element in the document object. We set the `textContent` property on a paragraph to update the clock. If we do this very quickly, the browser will be unable to keep up. The browser updates at a particular rate, usually 60 times a second.

Question: Does every element on a web page need to have an `id` attribute?

Answer: We can add an `id` attribute to an element on a web page so that a program can get use the `getElementById` method to locate it. We used this in the clock program so that it could find the paragraph used to display the time and change the text in the paragraph when the clock ticks. However, we don't need to add an `id` attribute to every element on a page. We only need to add an `id` to the elements that the JavaScript code needs to find.

Question: What happens if an event function gets stuck?

Answer: Events can be assigned to JavaScript functions by attributes in web pages. We have seen how the `onload` attribute of the `body` element lets us call a JavaScript function when a page loads. But what happens if the function never returns? We've all had that experience where you visit a website, and your browser stops. This can be caused by a stuck JavaScript function that is triggered by an event on the web page. If you write a function that never returns (perhaps because it gets stuck in a loop) and then call this from an `onload` attribute, you will find that the web page will never complete loading. If a function called from `setInterval` doesn't return, the web page will not stop immediately. However, it will progressively slow down as the computer memory fills up with more and more unterminated processes. If a JavaScript function assigned to a button gets stuck, the user will not be able to press any other buttons until that function returns.

3
Make an active site

What you will learn

We now know how to create JavaScript applications and deploy them into the cloud as part of HTML-formatted web pages. We have seen how a JavaScript code can communicate with the user by changing the document element properties held in the Document Object Model (DOM) created by the browser from the original HTML. We made a ticking clock in which our JavaScript code changed the `textContent` property of a paragraph displaying the time. We can also deploy our web pages and their applications in the cloud so anyone with a web browser can use them.

In Chapter 2, we also discovered how a program could receive input from the user through button presses. In this chapter, we will discover how a JavaScript program can accept numbers and text from the user and store their values between browsing sessions. Then, we will start writing code that can generate web page content dynamically. And on the way, we will learn about a bunch of JavaScript heroes.

Don't forget that you can use the online glossary at *https://begintocodecloud.com/glossary.html* to look up unfamiliar things.

Get input from a user

You might find it strange, but people seem to quite like the idea of our time travel clock. However, like most people who like something you've done, they also have suggestions to improve it. In this case, they think it would be a good idea to be able to set how fast or slow the clock is. We know web pages can read input from the user. We have been entering numbers, text, and passwords into web pages since we started using them. Let's see how we can do this to make an "adjustable" clock.

Figure 3-1 shows that the time offset is entered as an input in the bottom-left part of the page. The entered value is set when the **Minutes offset** button is pressed. In this example, the user has entered **10** and pressed the **Minutes offset** button. Now, the clock is 10 minutes fast.

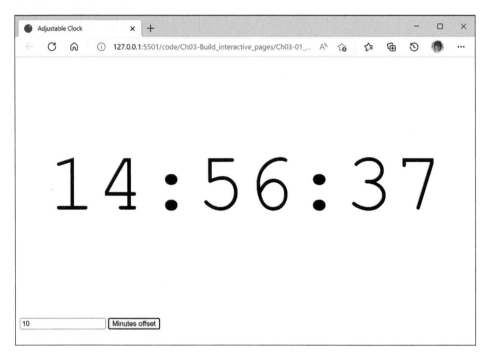

Figure 3-1 Adjustable clock

The HTML input element

First, we will need a place on the web page where the user can enter text. HTML provides the `input` element, which is used in two ways. It can send input back to the web server (we will do this in Chapter 8 when post a web form back to the server), and it can receive input from the user, which can be read by a JavaScript program and is what is happening here:

```
<input type="number" id="minutesOffsetInput" value="">
```

The HTML statement above creates an input element. The element has been given three attributes. The first attribute, input type, specifies the input type and has been set to number, which tells the browser to accept only numeric values in this input.

The second attribute, id, allows the JavaScript program to find this element and read the number out of it. This attribute has been set to "minutesOffsetInput".

The third element, value, is the initial value of the input and is set as an empty string—"".

Next, we need a button to press to set the new offset value. This will call a function to set the value when the button is pressed:

```
<button onclick="doReadMinutesOffsetFromPage();">Minutes offset</button>
```

We've seen buttons before for setting the clock modes in Chapter 2. A button can have an onclick attribute that specifies JavaScript to be run when the button is pressed. This button will call the function doReadMinutesOffsetFromPage when it is pressed:

```
function doReadMinutesOffsetFromPage (){
  let minutesOffsetElement =
      document.getElementById("minutesOffsetInput");    Get the input element
  let minutesOffsetValue = minutesOffsetElement.value;  Get the value out of the
                                                        input element
  minutesOffset = Number(minutesOffsetValue);
}                                                       Convert the string into a
                                                        number
```

You can see the doReadMinutesOffsetFromPage function above. It does what you might expect:

- Finds the input element into which the user has typed the number

- Gets the value property of that element containing the text of the number entered

- Converts the number text to a number

- Sets a global variable called minutesOffset to hold the new value

Scan the QR code or visit *https://www.youtube.com/watch?v=2jDfs2T01fM* for a video walk-through of this Make Something Happen.

Adjustable time travel clock

The code for this exercise is in the **Ch03-01_Adjustable_Clock** in **the Ch03-Build_interactive_pages** examples folder. Use Visual Studio to open the `index.html` file for this example, start Go Live to open the page in a browser, and open the **Developer Tools** for the page. Select the application's console view by clicking **Console**.

On the left, you will see the ticking clock. On the right is the console. You can check on the current value of `minutesOffset` by using the console. Type `minutesOffset` and press **Enter** to ask the console to show you the contents of the variable.

The following listing shows what happens. The variable is initially set as 0, so the clock will show the current time:

```
> minutesOffset
0
```

Now enter an offset value into the text box and click the **Minutes Offset** button:

```
10                                    ⬍    Minutes offset
```

You should see the clock time change to 10 minutes in the future. Now try setting the offset value to an empty string. Clear the contents of the input box and click the **Minutes Offset** button:

```
                                           Minutes offset
```

Watch what happens to the time displayed by the clock; it goes back to the correct time. The offset has been set to 0. This is strange because you didn't set it to 0; you set it to an empty string—"". Some programming languages would give you an error if you tried to convert an empty string into a number. JavaScript doesn't seem to mind. Let's have a look at what is going on.

The interesting thing here is the Number function, which takes something in and converts it into a number. We can give it a string containing a number, and Number will return a value. Let's try a few different inputs, starting with a string that holds a value. Type the following statement into the **Developer Tools** console in the browser. It will show you the result provided by the Number function when it is fed the string "99":

```
> Number("99")
```

Now press **Enter**. Remember that the console always shows you the value returned by the executed JavaScript. In this case, it will show you the value returned by Number function. Press **Enter**.

```
> Number("99")
99
```

The result of calling Number with the string "99" is the numeric value 99. Now, try a different string:

```
> Number("Fred")
NaN
```

For brevity, I'm showing the call of Number and the result it displays from now on. You can check these results yourself in the console if you like. Converting the text "Fred" to a number is not possible. Number returns NaN (not a number), which makes sense because "Fred" does not represent a number. Now, try one last thing:

```
> Number("")
0
```

Now, the Number function is working on an empty string from which it returns the value 0. You might expect to see NaN again here, but you don't. This is partly why you get a minutes-Offset of 0 when you enter an empty field. The other part involves using a type of number for an input element. When you try to set the minutesOffset value, a number input tries to prevent you from entering text. A device with a touchscreen might display a numeric keyboard rather than a text keyboard. If you do manage to type in an invalid number (or leave the text out), the input element value property is an empty string. This empty string is then fed into the Number function, producing a result of 0.

This might not be what you want. You might take the view that if the user doesn't enter a number, you want the minutesOffset to stay the same rather than go back to 0. We can fix this by adding some extra code to the doReadMinutesOffsetFromPage function. You can modify the function using Visual Studio Code or find this clock version in the **Ch03-02_Improved_Adjustable_Clock** sample folder.

```
function doReadMinutesOffsetFromPage() {
  let minutesOffsetElement =
              document.getElementById("minutesOffsetInput")    Get the value from the input
  let inputString = minutesOffsetElement.value;                                       element
  if (inputString.length == 0) {                                Check for an empty string
    alert("Please enter an offset value");
  }
  else {
    minutesOffset = Number(inputString);
  }
}
```

This version of the doReadMinutesOffsetFromPage function checks the length of the value received from the input element. The function displays an alert if the length is zero (meaning a number wasn't entered or an empty string was entered). Otherwise, it sets the minutesOffset value.

Below, you can see what happens if you click the **Minutes Offset** button with an empty string in the input element.

Input types

Figure 3-2 shows some of the input types available and what they look like on a web page when you enter data into them. Each input item in **Figure 3-2** has a paragraph containing an input field with the appropriate type and a button that is used to call a function that will display the input that the browser will receive. You can enter input data into an input and then click the button next to it to display the value produced. The `passwordIinput` element has just been used to enter `topsecret`, and the `password` button has been clicked to display the value in the input element. Note that the browser doesn't display the characters in the password as it is entered.

JavaScript input types

passwordInput : topsecret

hello	text
1234	number
••••••••	**password**
mail@someaddress.com	email
(12345) 567890	tel
19 / 08 / 2022 📅	date
19 : 26 🕐	time
www.robmiles.com	url
■	color

Figure 3-2 Input types

Below, you can see the HTML that accepts the password input. The outer paragraph encloses input and button elements. The `onclick` event for the button element calls a function called `showItem` with the `passwordInput` argument.

```
<p>
  <input type="password" id="passwordInput">
  <button onclick='showItem("passwordInput");'>password</button>
</p>
```

Note that the program uses two kinds of quotes to delimit items in the string containing the JavaScript to be performed when the button is pressed. The outer single quotes delimit the entire JavaScript text, and the inner double quotes delimit the `"passwordInput"` string, which is the argument to the function call. There are similar paragraphs for each of the different input types. The `showItem` function must find the entered value and display it on the output element.

```
function showItem(itemName){                                    Get the source element
  let inputElement = document.getElementById(itemName);
  let outputElement = document.getElementById("outputPar");     Get the destination element
```

```
    let message = itemName + " : " + inputElement.value          Build the message
    outputElement.textContent = message;                          Display the message
  }
```

The `showItem` function uses the `document.getElementByID` method to get the `inputElement` and `outputElement` values. It then builds the message to be displayed by adding the value in the `inputElement` to the end of the `itemName`. This message is then set as the content of the `outputElement`, causing it to be displayed.

The input types work differently in different browsers. Some browsers offer to auto-fill email addresses or pop up a calendar when a date is being entered. However, it is important to remember that all these inputs generate a string of text that your program will need to validate before use. The email input doesn't stop a user from entering an email address that doesn't exist. You can investigate their behavior by opening the HTML page in the **Ch03-03_Input_Types** sample folder.

Storing data on the local machine

When you show everyone your adjustable clock, they are very impressed—for a while. Then, they complain that the clock doesn't remember the entered offset. Each time the clock web page is opened, the `minutesOffset` is zero, and the clock shows the correct time. They want a clock that retains the `minutesOffset` value so that each time it is started, it has the same offset that they set last time it was used. They assumed you would know that was what they wanted, and now you must provide it.

PROGRAMMER'S POINTS

Engaged users are a great source of inspiration

Learning what users want a system to do can be very difficult. Even when you think you have agreed on what needs to be provided, you might still encounter problems like these. The solution is to provide a feedback workflow, which makes it very easy for the users to let you know what is wrong with your system and provide constructive suggestions in situations like these.

If you store your solution in a GitHub repository, an issue tracker allows users to post issues, and you can respond to them. If you do this correctly, you can build a team of engaged (rather than enraged) users who will help you improve your solution and even serve as evangelists for it.

JavaScript allows web pages to store data on a local machine. It works because the browser has access to the file storage on the host PC, and the browser can write small amounts of data into this storage and recover it when requested.

Below, the storeMinutesOffset function shows how we can use this feature from a JavaScript program. The storeMinutesOffset function accepts a parameter called offset, which holds the offset value to be stored in the browser's local storage. The value is stored by the setItem method provided by the localStorage object. This method accepts two arguments—the name of the storage location and the string to be stored there.

```
function storeMinutesOffset(offset){
  localStorage.setItem("minutesOffset", String(offset));
}
```

The loadMinutesOffset function below fetches a stored offset value using the getItem method, which is provided by the localStorage object. The getItem method is supplied with a string that identifies the local storage item to return. If there is no item in the local storage with the given name, getItem returns null. We've seen null before. It is a value that means "I can't find it." The code below tests for a return value of null from the getItem function and sets the offset to 0 if this happens. This behavior is required because the first time the clock is loaded into the browser, there will be nothing in local storage.

```
function loadMinutesOffset(){
  let offsetString = localStorage.getItem("minutesOffset");   ── Get the stored value
  if (offsetString == null){                                  ── Check for a missing value
    offsetString = "0";                                       ── Set the offset to 0 if nothing
  }                                                                is stored
  return Number(offsetString);                                ── Return a number
}
```

You can find this code in the example **Ch03-04_Storing_Adjustable_Clock**.

Scan the QR code or visit *https://www.youtube.com/watch?v=J-HvWOc1m6Q* for a video walkthrough of this Make Something Happen.

Setting sleuthing

The clock works fine. But there is no way that the user can see the value of the minutes offset when they use the clock. It is not displayed on the page, but does it mean anyone cannot discover this value? Let's see if we can use the debugger to get that setting value out of the browser. You can start by loading the clock page from the web. You can find it here:

https://begintocodecloud.com/code/Ch03-Build_interactive_pages/Ch03-04_Storing_Adjustable_Clock/index.html

Once you have loaded the page, open the **Developer Tools** window, select the **Sources** view, and open the `index.html` file. Then scroll down in the listing until you find the `get-TimeString` function. This function is called every second to display the time.

![Screenshot of the browser showing the clock displaying 10:12:6 and the Developer Tools Sources view with the index.html code listing]

Set a breakpoint at line 56 by clicking the margin to the left of the line number. This function is called every second, so the breakpoint will be hit almost instantly.

You should see a display like the one shown below in the code window. If you hold the mouse pointer over the `minutesOffset` variable, you can see the value `20` has been loaded from local storage. This shows how easy it is to view the values in a program as it runs.

Click here

Value loaded from local storage

```
53      func1 20 getTimeString() {
54          let currentDate = new Date(),
55          let minutesOffset = loadMinutesOffset
56  ▶       let displayMins = currentDate.getMinu
57          currentDate.setMinutes(displayMins);
58          let hours = currentDate.getHours();
59          let mins = currentDate.getMinutes();
60          let secs = currentDate.getSeconds();
```

However, if you want to see the values stored in local storage, there is an even easier way to do this. If you open the **Application** tab in the **Developer Tools**, you can view the contents of **Local Storage**. As you can see from the image below, the `minutesOffset` value is stored as `10`.

Contents of local storage   minutesOffset value

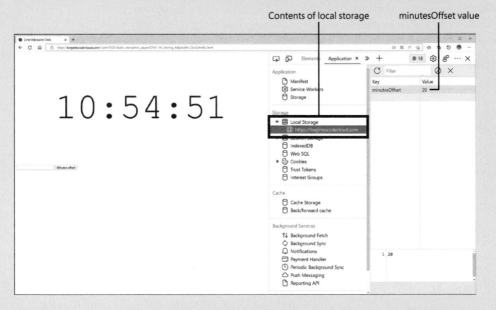

Note that this local storage is shared for all the pages underneath the **begintocode.com** domain. In other words, any of our example JavaScript applications can view and change that value. You can use this view to investigate the things web pages store on your computer.

Think hard about security when writing JavaScript

It's not really a problem if someone reads and changes the minutes offset for our clock, but I hope you now appreciate just how open JavaScript is. A badly written application that stores password strings in local storage would be very vulnerable to attack, although the attacker would need to get physical access to the machine. When you write an application, you need to consider how exposed the application is to attacks like these. Tucking something into a local store might seem to be a good idea, but you need to consider how useful it would be to a malicious person. And you should ensure that variables are visible only where they are used.

JavaScript heroes: `let`, `var`, and `const`

Some programming language features are there so you can use the language to make a working program. For example, a program needs to be able to calculate answers and make decisions, so JavaScript provides assignments and if constructions. However, `let`, `var`, and `const` are not provided to make programs work; they are provided to help us create code that is more secure. They help us control the *visibility* of variables we use in our programs. Let's look at why variable visibility is important and how we can use `let`, `var`, and `const` to manage visibility in JavaScript.

Making a variable in a program *global* is rather like writing your name and phone number on the notice board in the office. It makes it easy for your colleagues to contact you, but it also means that anyone seeing the notice board can call you. And someone else could erase the number you wrote and put up a different one if they wanted to redirect your phone calls to another person. In real life, we need to be careful about how much data we make public, and it's no different in JavaScript programs. Let's look at how we manage the scope of variables using JavaScript heroes `let`, `var`, and `const`.

Scan the QR code or visit *https://www.youtube.com/watch?v=DPnRL7k02wY* for a video walk-through of this Make Something Happen.

Investigate let, var, and const

You can start by loading the clock page from the web. You can find it here:

https://begintocodecloud.com/code/Ch03-Build_interactive_pages/Ch03-06_Variable_Scope/index.html

Load this page into your browser and open the **Developer Tools**. Now open the **Console** tab. You will see a page containing a list of sample functions you can call from the **Developer Tools Console** tab to learn more about variables and scope.

The variable's scope is the part of a program where the variable can be accessed. JavaScript has three kinds of scope: global, function, and block:

- **Global scope**   A variable with global scope can be accessed anywhere in the program.

- **Function scope**   A variable with function scope can be accessed anywhere in a function body.

- **Block scope**   A variable with block scope can be accessed anywhere in a block except where it is "scoped out."

Let's discover what all this means with some code examples. The function below creates two variables, both with the name i. The first version of i is assigned the value 99. This variable is declared in the body of the function. The second version of i is declared in the inner block and set the value to 100.

```
function letScopeDemo() {
    let i = 99;
    {
        let i = 100;
        console.log("let inner i:" + i);
    }
    console.log("let outer i:" + i);
}
```

Let's have a look at what happens when you run the function in the console

```
> letScopeDemo()
let inner i: 100
let outer i: 99
```

Above, you can see the letScopeDemo call and the results displayed when it ran. You can run the function on your machine. When you run this function, the value of each i is printed out. Note that within the inner block, the outer variable called i (the one containing 99) is not accessible. This is referred to as being "scoped out." When the program exits the inner block, the inner i (the one containing 100) is discarded, and the outer i becomes accessible again. You use let to create a variable that does not need to exist outside the block in which it was created. These are called global variables.

The function varScopeDemo below is similar to letScopeDemo, except that i is now declared using var.

```
function varScopeDemo() {
    var i = 99;
    {
        var i = 100;
        console.log("var inner i:" + i);
    }
    console.log("var outer i:" + i);
}
```

When we run it, we get a different result:

```
> varScopeDemo()
var inner i: 100
var outer i: 100
```

Variables declared using `var` have a function scope if declared in a function and a global scope if declared outside all functions. The second declaration of `i` replaces the original one with a new value, which persists until the end of the `varScopeDemo` function. So, variables declared using `var` within a block exist all the way to the end of the block and can be overwritten with new ones.

Let's build on your understanding of scope by trying some things that might not work. The `letDemo` function body contains a block of code nested inside it. Within this block, the `let` keyword is used to declare a variable called `I` and sets its value to `99`. Then the block ends, and the value of `i` is displayed in the console.

```
function letDemo() {
    {
        let i = 99;
    }
    console.log(i);
}
```

You can run the program by just typing `letDemo()` on the console:

```
> letDemo()
⊗ ▶ Uncaught ReferenceError: i is not defined                index.html:58
      at letDemo (index.html:58:21)
      at <anonymous>:1:1
>
```

The `letDemo` function fails because the variable `i` only exists within the inner block in the function. As soon as execution leaves that block, the variable is discarded, which means attempts to access that variable will fail because it no longer exists.

```
function varDemo() {
    {
        var i = 99;
    }
    console.log(i);
}
```

The function `varDemo` is very similar to `letDemo`, but this time, `i` is declared using `var`. Let's see what happens when you run this function.

```
> varDemo()
  99                                                                index.html:65
```

This time, the function works perfectly. Variables declared using `var` remain in existence from the point of declaration until the end of the enclosing scope, which, in this case, means the body of the `varDemo` function. So, if you try to use the variable `i` from the console, you will find that it no longer exists because the function `varDemo` has finished.

```
> varDemo()
  99                                                                index.html:63
< undefined
> i
⊗ ▶ Uncaught ReferenceError: i is not defined                           VM420:1
      at <anonymous>:1:1
>
```

So far, everything makes perfect sense. You use a `let` if you want the variable to disappear when the program leaves the block where the variable is declared. You use a `var` if you want the variable to exist in the entire enclosing scope.

So, let's try something weird.

```
function globalDemo() {
    {
        i = 99;
    }
    console.log(i);
}
```

The `globalDemo` function uses neither `let` or `var` to declare the variable `i`. You might think that this would cause an error, but it doesn't. Even stranger, the `i` variable still exists after the function has been completed.

```
> globalDemo()
  99                                                                index.html:70
< undefined
> i
< 99
>
```

In the introduction to the book, I said that I would flag up "JavaScript heroes," which are good things about the language, and "JavaScript zeroes," which are bad. This is a "JavaScript zero." It is one of the things about JavaScript that I really don't like. If you don't use `let` or `var` to declare a variable, you get a variable that has global scope, meaning it exists everywhere. This is perhaps the worst thing that could happen. I don't get an error if I forget the `var` or `let`. Instead, I get a global variable, which is visible throughout the program and is open to prying and misuse.

This behavior goes back to the very first version of JavaScript, which was intended to be easy to learn and use. At the time, it seemed a good idea to create variables automatically. Nowadays, JavaScript is used to create applications that need to be highly secure and resilient, so this behavior is a bad idea. To solve the problem, the latest versions of JavaScript have a `strict` mode, which you can turn on by adding this statement to your program:

```
function strictGlobalDemo() {
    'use strict';
    i = 99;
}
```

The `strictGlobalDemo` function sets `strict` mode and then tries to create a global variable. This function fails when it tries to automatically create the variable `i`.

```
> strictGlobalDemo()
⊗ ▶ Uncaught ReferenceError: i is not defined          index.html:107
      at strictGlobalDemo (index.html:107:11)
      at <anonymous>:1:1
>|
```

When I recorded the video for this Make Something Happen, I was surprised to discover that the `strictGlobalDemo` function did not fail for me. This is because I was running `strictGlobalDemo` just after I had run the `globalDemo` function, which creates a global variable called `i`. I had to reload the web page (which removes all variables) to get `strictGlobalDemo` to fail correctly.

Note that `strict` mode is only enforced in the body of the function `strictGlobalDemo` function. If you want to enforce `strict` mode on all the code in your application, you should put the statement at the top of your program, outside any functions.

Strict mode disallows lots of dangerous JavaScript behaviors, including the automatic declaration of variables. I add it to the start of all JavaScript programs I write.

The final hero you're going to meet is `const`. You use this when you don't want your program to change the value in a variable. In the `constDemo` function below, the variable `i` is declared as a `const`. This means the statement that tries to add 1 to the value of `i` will fail with an error.

```
function constDemo() {
    {
        const i = 99;
```

```
        i = i + 1;
    }
    console.log(i);
}
```

If you have a value in your program that shouldn't be changed, you can declare it as constant. Variables declared using const inside a block have the same scope as let. Variables declared using const outside any function have global scope.

It seems obvious when we need to use let or var. We use let when we want to create a variable that will disappear when a program exits the block where it was declared. We try to avoid using var at all unless we have something we really want to share over the whole program. But what about const? When I write code, I try to look out for situations where a bug can happen and then change the code to remove that situation. Look at these two statements from our adjustable clock, which store the minutesOffset value in the browser:

```
localStorage.setItem("minutesOffset", String(offset));
...
offsetString = localStorage.getItem("minutesOffset");
```

The first statement creates a local storage item called "minutesOffset", which contains a string of text specifying the offset value. The second statement gets this value back from local storage. Can you spot anything you might not like about this code? The thing I don't like about it is that I have to type the "minutesOffset" string twice. This string gives the name of the storage location that will be written to and then read back from later.

This is a situation where a bug could be introduced into the code. If I type one of the strings as "MinutesOffset" by mistake (I've made the first letter uppercase rather than lowercase), the program will either store the value in the wrong place or fail to find it when it looks for it. I can solve this problem completely by creating a constant variable that holds the name of the stored item:

```
const minutesOffsetStoreName = "minutesOffset";

localStorage.setItem(minutesOffsetStoreName, String(offset));
...
offsetString = localStorage.getItem(minutesOffsetStoreName);
```

The code above shows how I would do this. This makes it impossible to mistype the name of the store. The `minutesOffsetStoreName` is declared at a global scope outside every function, so it is available over the entire program. I don't mind constant values being global because they are not vulnerable to being changed. You can find this code in the **Ch03-06_Variable_Storage** example.

PROGRAMMER'S POINT

Use language features to make your code better

The `let`, `var`, `const`, and `strict` features of JavaScript are not there to allow you to do things; they are there to help you make programs safer. When I create a new variable, I consider how visible it needs to be. If I need to make the value widely available, I'll try to find ways to do it without creating a global variable. Also, I always use the `strict` mode. You should, too.

Making page elements from JavaScript

We have seen how the Document Object Model (DOM) is built in memory by the browser, which uses the contents of the HTML file that defines the website. The browser then renders the DOM to display the content of the pages for the user. We've also seen how a JavaScript program can interact with the elements in the DOM by changing their properties and how these changes are reflected in what the user sees on the page. We used this to change the time displayed by a paragraph in the clock.

Now we will discover how a JavaScript program can create elements when it runs. This is a very important part of JavaScript programming. Some web pages are built from HTML files that are entirely JavaScript code. When the page loads, the JavaScript runs and creates all the elements that are used in the display. We will show how this works by creating a game called Cheese Finder. It turns out to be quite compelling.

Figure 3-3 shows the Cheese Finder game, which is played on a 10x10 grid of buttons. One of the buttons contains a piece of cheese. Before you start, you agree whether you are play-ing to find the cheese or avoid it (if you don't like cheese). Then each player, in turn, presses a button. If the button does not contain the cheese, it turns pink and displays the distance that square is from the cheese. If the button is the cheese, a message is displayed, the cheese button turns yellow, and the game is over. Reloading the page creates a brand-new game and moves the cheese to a new location.

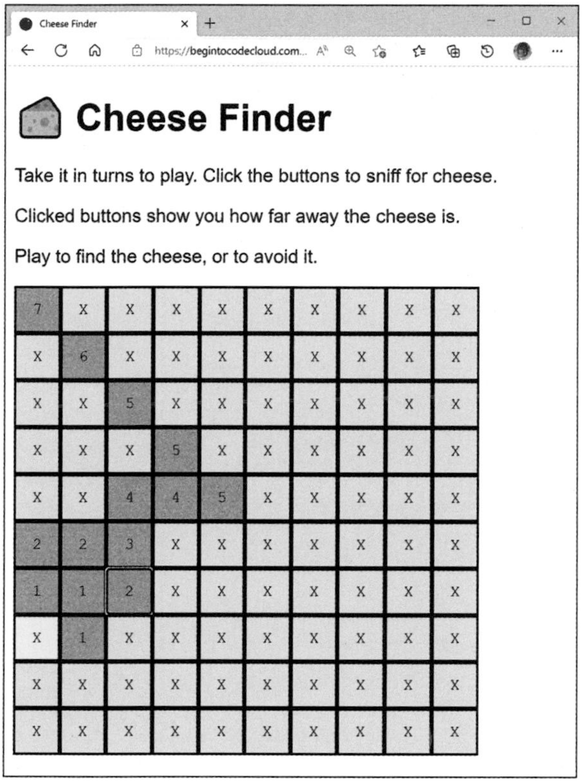

Figure 3-3 Cheese Finder game

Cheese Finder

You can have a go at the game by visiting the example page at

https://begintocodecloud.com/code/Ch03-Build_interactive_pages/Ch03-07_Cheese_Finder/index.html

Place the buttons

To make the game work, we need a web page that contains 100 buttons. It would be very hard to make all these buttons by hand. Fortunately, we can use loops in a JavaScript program to make the display for us. Below, you can see the paragraph that will contain the buttons:

```
<p id="buttonPar"> </p>
```

This paragraph is empty in the HTML file. The buttons will be added by a function called when the page is loaded. The paragraph has the `buttonPar` id so our code can locate it in the document.

```
function playGame(width, height) {

    let container = document.getElementById("buttonPar");         Find the destination paragraph

    for (let y = 0; y < height; y++) {                            Work through each row
        for (let x = 0; x < width; x++) {                         Work through each column in a row
            let newButton = document.createElement("button");     Make a button
            newButton.className = "upButton";                     Set the style to "upButton"
            newButton.setAttribute("x", x);                       Store the x position in the button
            newButton.setAttribute("y", y);                       Store the y position in the button
            newButton.textContent = "X";                          Draw an X in the button
            newButton.setAttribute("onClick", "doButtonClicked(this);");   Add an event handler
            container.appendChild(newButton);                     Append the button to the destination
        }
        let lineBreak = document.createElement("br");             Create a line break
        container.appendChild(lineBreak);                         Add the line break to the paragraph
    }

    cheeseX = getRandom(0, width);                                Set the X position for the cheese
    cheeseY = getRandom(0, height);                               Set the Y position for the cheese

}
```

This is the function that creates the buttons and sets the game up. Let's work through what it does.

The statement below creates a local variable called `container`, which refers to the paragraph that will contain all the buttons on the page. The paragraph has the id `buttonPar`:

```
let container = document.getElementById("buttonPar");
```

These two statements create a pair of `for` loops, one nested inside the other. The outer loop will be performed for each row of the button grid. The inner loop will be performed for each column in each row. The `y` variable keeps track of the row number, and the `x` variable keeps track of the column number.

```
for (let y = 0; y < height; y++) {
  for (let x = 0; x < width; x++) {
```

This next statement is something we've not seen before. The document object provides a method called createElement that creates a new HTML element. We specify the kind of element we want by using a string. In this case, we want a button. Note that creating an element does not add it to the DOM; we must do that separately.

```
let newButton = document.createElement("button");
```

The following statement sets the className for the button, determining the style used to display the button:

```
newButton.className = "upButton";
```

Following are the styles that are used for the buttons. There are some common style items (the font family, alignment, and minimum width and height) along with different colors for each button state.

```
.upButton,.downButton,.cheeseButton {
  font-family: 'Courier New', Courier, monospace;
  text-align: center;
  min-width: 3em;
  min-height: 3em;
}

.upButton{
  background: lightblue;
}
.downButton {
  background: lightpink;
}
.cheeseButton {
  background: yellow;
}
```

This statement sets the initial text content of the button, which will be replaced by the distance value when the button is clicked.

```
newButton.textContent = "X";
```

The following two statements set up a couple of attributes on the new button that give the button's location in the grid. We are going to bind a function to the button's onclick event. We don't want to create a different function for each button press because that would mean creating 100 functions. Instead, we want to store location values in each button so that a single button function can work the position of a particular button. We have already written code that sets existing attributes on an element (to change the class or the textContent of a paragraph). The two statements below create attributes called x and y that contain the x and y positions of the button. This is a very powerful technique. It makes elements in the DOM an extension of your variable storage.

```
newButton.setAttribute("x", x);
newButton.setAttribute("y", y);
```

The last statement that sets up the button is below. It binds the doButtonClicked method to the button's onClick event. If the button is clicked, this function will run. All buttons will call the same function when they are clicked. You might wonder how the doButtonClicked function will know which button has been clicked. Let's look at the JavaScript statement assigned to onClick to find out how this works.

```
newButton.setAttribute("onClick", "doButtonClicked(this);");
```

When executed in the context of a JavaScript statement running from HTML, the value of this is set to a reference to the element generating the event. Each time doButton-Clicked is called, it will be given an argument that refers to the button clicked. This is terribly useful. It makes it very easy for an event handler to know which element caused the event.

```
doButtonClicked(this);
```

If you are having trouble understanding what is happening here, remember the problem that we are trying to solve. We have 100 buttons. Each button can generate an onClick event. We don't want to make 100 functions to deal with all these onClick events. It's preferable to write just one function. But if we only have one function, it needs to know which button it has been called from. The this reference is an argument to the doButtonClicked call that is fed into the function when the button is clicked. In this context, the value of this refers to the button that has been pressed.

So, doButtonClicked is always told the button that has been clicked. This will make more sense when we look at what the doButtonClicked function does. Way back at the start of this description, we set up a container variable, which was a reference to the paragraph that will hold all our buttons. The container provides a method called appendChild, which is given a reference to the new element and adds it. This means that the paragraph now contains the newly created button. New elements are appended in order. So, the first element will be button (0,0), the second element will be button (0,1), and so on.

```
container.appendChild(newButton);
```

The following two statements are performed after we have added all the buttons in a row. They create a break element (br) and append it to the paragraph container. This is how we separate successive rows in the grid:

```
let lineBreak = document.createElement("br");
container.appendChild(lineBreak);
```

Figure 3-4 shows how we can use the **Elements** tab from the **Developer Tools** to look at all the buttons that our code has created. Remember that the original HTML for the page did not contain any buttons. These have all been created by our code. You can see that all the buttons have the properties that you would expect.

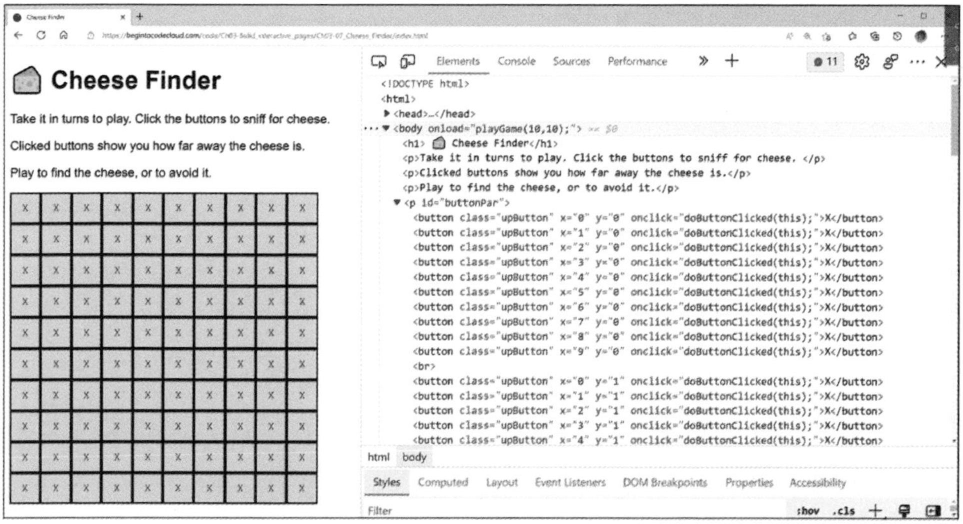

Figure 3-4 Cheese Finder buttons

Place the cheese

The next thing the game needs to do is place the cheese somewhere on the grid. For this, we need random numbers. JavaScript has a random number generator that can produce a random value between 0 and 1. It lives in the `Math` library and is called `random`. We can use this in a helper function to generate random integers in a particular range:

```
function getRandom(min, max) {
    let range = max - min;
    let result = Math.floor(Math.random() * (range)) + min;
    return result;
}
```

The `getRandom` function is given the minimum and maximum values of the random number to be produced. It then creates a value between the two values. The maximum value is an exclusive upper limit and is never produced. The function uses `Math.random` to create a random number between 0 and 1 and `Math.floor` to truncate the fractional part of a number and generate the integer value we need.

```
cheeseX = getRandom(0, width);
cheeseY = getRandom(0, height);
```

These two statements set the `cheeseX` and `cheeseY` variables to the cheese's position. These variables have been made global, so they are shared between all game functions.

```
var cheeseX;
var cheeseY;
```

Making these values global makes the game a bit less secure, but it also keeps the code simple.

Respond to button presses

The final necessary behavior is the function that responds to a button press. If you look at the buttons' definitions in **Figure 3-4** earlier in this chapter, you will see that the `onClick` attribute of each button makes a call to the `doButtonClicked` function. Let's have a look at this function:

```
function doButtonClicked(button) {
    let x = button.getAttribute("x");                          Get the x position of the button
    let y = button.getAttribute("y");                          Get the y position of the button
    if (x == cheeseX && y == cheeseY) {                     Check to see if this is the cheese button
        button.className = "cheeseButton";                      Set the button style to "cheese"
        alert("Well done! Reload the page to play again");     Tell the player they have
    }                                                                found the cheese
    else {                                                Do this part if the cheese was not found
        let dx = x - cheeseX;                                  Get the x distance to the cheese
        let dy = y - cheeseY;                                  Get the y distance to the cheese
        let distance = Math.round(Math.sqrt((dx * dx) + (dy * dy)));   Work out the distance
        button.textContent = distance;                     Put the distance value into the button
        button.className = "downButton";                      Set the button to the "down" style
    }
}
```

The doButtonClicked function has a single parameter, which refers to the button that has been clicked. This is obtained from the this reference, which is added when the event is bound in the element definition.

The first two statements in the function read the values in the button's x and y attributes. These give the button's grid location:

```
let x = button.getAttribute("x");
let y = button.getAttribute("y");
```

The next set of statements checks to see if this button is at the location of the cheese. If both the x and the y values match, the statements set the button's className style to "cheeseButton". This causes the button to turn yellow, and an alert is displayed, telling players the game is over.

```
if (x == cheeseX && y == cheeseY) {
    button.className = "cheeseButton";
    alert("Well done! Reload the page to play again");
}
```

The final part of this function is the behavior that is performed if the button is not the cheese. The first three statements use the laws of Pythagoras (the square of the hypotenuse is equal to the sum of the squares on the other two sides of a right-angled triangle) to work out the distance from this button to the cheese. It then sets the text content of the button to this value and changes the style to `downButton`, which turns the button red.

```
else {
    let dx = x - cheeseX;
    let dy = y - cheeseY;
    let distance = Math.round(Math.sqrt((dx * dx) + (dy * dy)));
    button.textContent = distance;
    button.className = "downButton";
}
```

Playing the game

The game is quite fun to play, particularly with two or more opponents. If you want to make the game larger (or smaller), you just change the call of `playGame`, which is bound to the `onload` event in the HTML body. This is where the number of rows and columns is set:

```
<body onload="playGame(10,10);">
```

The grid is made up of rows of buttons separated by line breaks. If the user makes the browser window too small, the rows of buttons wrap around. We could fix this by displaying the buttons in an HTML table element. We could create the table programmatically (as we have done when creating the buttons) and then add elements to the table to make the required rows and columns.

MAKE SOMETHING HAPPEN 15

Scan the QR code or visit *https://www.youtube.com/watch?v=xQVSNv1775M* for a video walkthrough of this Make Something Happen.

Play cheese finder

You can start by loading the Cheese Finder page from the web. You can find it here:

https://begintocodecloud.com/code/Ch03-Build_interactive_pages/Ch03-07_Cheese_Finder/index.html

Load this page into your browser and have a go at the game. Click the buttons and use the distance values displayed to work out where the cheese is. When you find the cheese, you can reload the web page to start a new game.

Now, take a look at how the code works. Open the **Developer Tools**, select the **Source** tab, and open the **index.html** file. You will put a breakpoint in the program so you can watch the program work. Click to the left of line 42 to set a breakpoint. This statement adds a newly created button to the document object model. Then reload the page to start another game. The program will hit the breakpoint and stop.

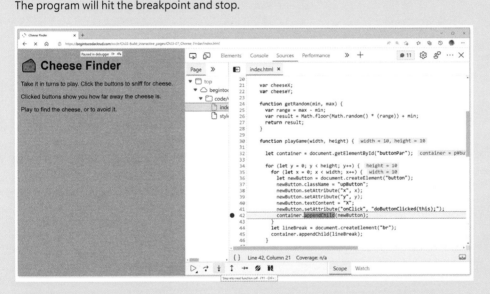

The statements above statement 42 create a new button, set its X and Y attributes and text content, and assign an event handler function that runs when the button is clicked. The program has paused at the statement that will add the button to the document. Click the **Step Into Next Function Call** button—the downward-pointing arrow in the program controls at the bottom of the screen—to perform the statement at line 42.

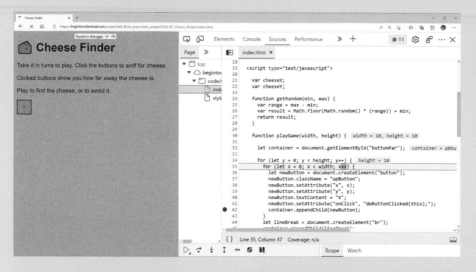

The `appendChild` method adds the new button to the document object model. The browser then displays the button on the page. You can repeatedly click the **Step Into Next Function Call** button and watch the game buttons being created. When you've seen enough buttons being created and displayed, you can clear the breakpoint at line 42 by clicking the red dot next to the statement and setting a breakpoint at statement 54, as shown below. This is the first statement of the `doButtonClicked` function, which will run when a button is clicked. Now click the **Resume Script Execution** button (the blue triangle in the program controls) to resume the program running. Next, click a game button, and the program will stop at the breakpoint.

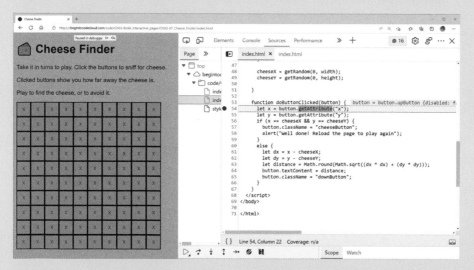

You can repeatedly click the **Step Into Next Function Call** button and watch the game button click being processed by `doButtonClicked`. First, the function gets the x and y positions of the button and then checks to see if they match the cheese position. If you hold the mouse over the cheeseX and cheeseY variables in the code, you can view their contents. Then, click that position in the grid of buttons (x gives the position on the left, starting counting at 0, and y gives the position down from the top, starting counting at 0). Watch what happens when the player finds the cheese.

Using events

The present version of Cheese Finder works perfectly, but there is a neater way of connecting events to JavaScript functions. Currently, we are using this statement to connect an event to an object:

```
newButton.setAttribute("onClick", "doButtonClicked(this);");
```

This works by creating an onClick attribute on a new button and then setting it to a string of JavaScript that calls the desired method (and uses this to provide a pointer to the button being clicked). This works because it is exactly what we would do if we set the event handler for an element in the HTML file. However, this is not the best way to do it when we are creating an HTML element from JavaScript code.

The major limitation of this technique is that we can only connect one event handler. We might have a situation where we want several events to fire when the button is clicked, but this is not possible because an HTML element can only have one of each attribute. However, we can use a different mechanism to connect the button click handler.

The statement below uses the addEventListener method provided by the newButton object to add an event listener function to a new button. The string specifies the event's name; in this case, the event we want is "click." The second parameter is the method's name to be called when the button is clicked—buttonClickedHandler. After the event listener has been added to the function, buttonClickedHandler will be called when the button is clicked.

```
newButton.addEventListener("click", buttonClickedHandler);
```

In the event handler code shown earlier, we used this to deliver a reference to the button that has been clicked. How does the buttonClickedHandler function know which button it is responding to? Let's look at the function code:

```
function buttonClickedHandler(event){
    let button = event.target;  ──────── Get the button reference from the event description
    . . .
}
```

The `buttonClickedHandler` function is declared with a single parameter called `event`, which describes the event that has occurred. One of the event object properties is called `target`. This is a reference to the element that generated the event. The `buttonClickedHandler` function extracts this value from the event and sets the value of `button` to it. The function then works in the same way as the earlier version. You can find this code in the **Ch03-08_Cheese_Finder_Events** example.

Improve Cheese Finder

The game is quite fun, but you might like to make some improvements. Here are some ideas for things that you might like to do:

- You could add a counter that counts the number of squares visited. Then you could have a version where the aim is to find the cheese in the smallest number of tries.

- You could add a countdown timer, so a player must find the cheese in the shortest time (clicking as many squares as they like).

- You could change the way the distance to the cheese is displayed. Rather than putting a number in the square, you could use a different color. You would need to create 10 or so new styles (one for each color), and then you could use an array of style names that you index with the distance value to get the style for the square. This might make for some nice-looking displays as the game is played.

What you have learned

This has been another busy chapter. We've covered a lot of ground. Here is a recap, along with some points to ponder:

- A web page can contain input elements that are used to read values from the user. An `input` tag can have different types, such as text, number, password, date, and time. The value of an `input` tag is always delivered as a string and needs to be checked for validity before it is used. The `input` tag behaves differently in different browsers.

- The `Number` function converts a string of text into a number. If the text does not contain a valid number, the function will return `NaN`. If the text is empty, the function returns `0`.

- A browser provides local storage where a JavaScript application can store values that persist when the web page is not open. Local storage is provided on a per-site basis (meaning each top domain has its own local storage). Local storage is implemented as named strings of text. The **Application** tab of the browser's **Developer Tools** can be used to view the local storage contents. Local storage is specific to one browser on one machine.

- JavaScript variables can be declared local to a code block using the keyword `let`. These variables are discarded when program execution leaves the block where they are declared. Using `let` to declare a variable in an inner block "scopes out" a variable with the same name declared in an enclosing block. An attempt to use a variable outside its declared scope will generate an error and stop the program.

- JavaScript variables can be declared global using the `var` keyword. Variables declared using `var` in a function body are global to that function but not visible outside it. Variables declared using `var` outside all functions are global and visible to all program functions.

- Global variables represent risk. Any code can view a global variable in the program (which represents a security risk), and any code can change it in the program, which represents a risk of unintentional change or attack vulnerability.

- Variables not explicitly declared (not declared using `let` or `var`) are global to the entire program. This dangerous default behavior can be disabled by adding a `"use strict'` statement to the function or at the start of the entire program.

- You can declare a variable using `const`, which prevents the value assigned to the variable from being changed.

- A JavaScript program can add elements to the DOM, making it possible for the contents of a web page to be created programmatically rather than being defined in the HTML file describing the page. You can view the elements in a web page (including those created by code) by using the **Elements** view in the **Developer Tools**.

- An element created in a JavaScript program can have additional attributes added to it. We used this to allow a button in the Cheese Finder game to hold its `x` and `y` grid position.

- Creating a new HTML element in a JavaScript program does not automatically add it to the page. The `appendChild` function can be used on the `container` element (such as a paragraph) to add the new element. When the element is added, the page will be redrawn, and the new element will appear on the display.

- The JavaScript `this` keyword can be used in the string of JavaScript bound to an event handler. In this context, the `this` keyword provides a reference to the object generating the event. In the case of the Cheese Finder program, we use `this` to allow 100 buttons to be connected to the same event handler. By passing the value of `this` into the event handler, we can tell the handler which button has been pressed.

- It is also possible to use the `addEventListener` method provided by an element instance (in our case, a button in the Cheese Finder game) to specify a function to be called when the event occurs. The event handler function is provided with a reference to the event details when it is called. These details include a reference to the object that caused the event.

- JavaScript provides a `Math.random` function that produces a random number in the range of `0` to `1`. We can multiply this value by a range to get a number in that range.

To reinforce your understanding of this chapter, you might want to consider the following "profound questions":

Question: Does the user always have to press a button to trigger the reading of an input?

Answer: You can use the `onInput` event to specify a function to be called each time the content of an input box changes. This means if the user was entering a number, the `onInput` function would be called each time a digit was entered.

Question: Is `Number` the only way to convert a string to a number?

Answer: No. JavaScript provides called `parseInt` and `parseFloat` functions, which can be used to parse a string and return a value of the requested type. These behave slightly differently from `Number`. A string that starts with a number would be regarded as that number. For example, parsing `123hello` would return the value `123`, whereas `Number` would regard this as NaN. The parse functions also regard an empty string as NaN. It doesn't matter whether you use `Number` or the parse functions; just be mindful of the slight differences in behavior.

Question: How much local storage can I have on a website?

Answer: The limit is about 5MB for a browser on a PC.

Question: How long are variables stored in local storage?

Answer: There is no limit to the time a value will be stored.

Question: Can I delete something from local storage?

Answer: Yes, you can. The `removeItem` method will do this. However, once deleted, it is impossible to get the data back.

Question: How do I store more complex items in local storage?

Answer: Local storage stores a string of data. You can convert JavaScript objects into strings of text encoded using the JavaScript Object Notation (JSON). This allows you to store complex items in a single local storage location. You can find out more about JSON in the section "Transfer data with JSON" in Chapter 5.

Question: How do I protect items stored in local storage?

Answer: You can't protect values in local storage. They are public. The only thing you could do is try to encrypt the values so that they can be read but not understood. Never store important data in local storage. You should store such data on the server that users cannot access. We will do this in Chapter 10.

Question: Can I stop someone from looking through my web page's JavaScript code?

Answer: No. There are tools you can use that will take your easy-to-understand code and make it much more difficult to read. These are called *obfuscators*. However, there are also some tools that can decode obfuscated code. The only way to make a properly secure application is to run all the code on the server, not on the client. We will do this in Part 2, "Make a Cloud-based application."

Question: What is the difference between `let` and `var`?

Answer: A variable declared using `let` will cease to exist if a program leaves the block in which the variable was declared. This makes `let` very useful for variables you want to use for a short time and discard. A variable declared using `var` has a longer lifetime. If it is declared in a function body, the variable will exist until the function exits. A variable declared as `var` at the global level (outside all functions) is global and will be visible to code in all the application functions. Global variables should be used with caution. They provide convenience (all functions can easily access their content) at the expense of security (all functions can easily access their contents).

Question: What does `strict` do?

Answer: `Strict` mode changes the behavior of the JavaScript engine so that dangerous program constructions are rejected. One of the things that `strict` does is stop the automatic creation of global variables when a programmer doesn't specify `let` or `var` at the variable creation.

Question: When do I use a constant?

Answer: You use a constant when you have a particular value that means something in your code. Using a constant makes it easy to change the value for the entire program. It also reduces the chance of you entering the value incorrectly. Finally, it lets you make a program clearer. Having a constant called `maxAge` in a program, rather than the value 70, makes it very clear what a statement is doing.

Question: Can document elements created by JavaScript have event handlers?

Answer: Yes, they can. We have actually done this. The best way is to use the `addEvent-Listener` to specify the function to be called when the event occurs.

Question: How does an event handler know which element has triggered an event?

Answer: We have done this in two different ways. In the first version of Cheese Finder, we added a `this` reference to the function call that handled the event. This function was specified in the text of a function call bound to the `onClick` attribute added to each button element. The function then received the `this` reference (which, in this context, is set to a reference to the element generating the event) and used it to locate the pressed button.

The second (and more flexible) way we did this used the `addEventListener` method on the new button to add the event handler. When the browser calls the event handler in response to the event, it is passed a reference to an `Event` object containing information about the event, including the `target` property containing a reference to the element generating the event.

4

Host a website

What you will learn

We now understand how a JavaScript program runs inside a web browser and can interact with a web page's Document Object Model (DOM) to create interactive websites. We know that the HTML page that defines a document might be only the starting point of the definition of a website. A JavaScript program can run in the browser when a page loads and dynamically create content and connect events to make an active web page. Next, we will discover how we can write JavaScript programs to create content sent to the browser. We will use a framework called Node.js to run JavaScript programs directly on our computer without needing a browser to run inside. We will also take a detailed look at how JavaScript programs can be broken down into modules.

As ever, you can find the glossary online at *https://begintocodecloud.com/glossary.html* to help you with terms you've not seen before.

Node.js

Figure 4-1 shows where we are now learning how to write applications for the cloud. We can write JavaScript programs running in the browser and communicate with the user via the DOM elements. Now we will learn how to write JavaScript programs that run on the server and respond to requests from the browser. The JavaScript programs we will write will run inside a framework called Node.js. Node.js was created by taking the JavaScript component out of a browser and turning it into a freestanding program. I often refer to it simply as node throughout this book. First, we need to get node running.

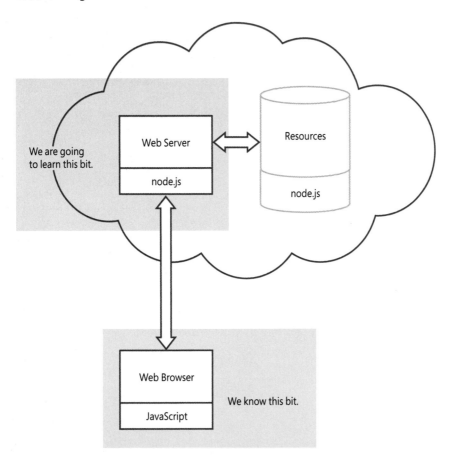

Figure 4-1 The role of node.js

Scan the QR code or visit *https://www.youtube.com/watch?v=_qrBYHa8xxA* for a video walk-through of this Make Something Happen.

Install node

Before you can use node, you need to install it. The application is free, and there are Windows, macOS, and Linux versions. Open your browser and go to *https://nodejs.org/en/download/*.

	node
HOME	ABOUT	DOWNLOADS	DOCS	GET INVOLVED	SECURITY	CERTIFICATION	NEWS

Downloads

Latest LTS Version: **16.17.0** (includes npm 8.15.0)

Download the Node.js source code or a pre-built installer for your platform, and start developing today.

LTS	Current
Recommended For Most Users	Latest Features

	Windows Installer	macOS Installer	Source Code
	node-v16.17.0-x64.msi	node-v16.17.0.pkg	node-v16.17.0.tar.gz

	LTS	Current
Windows Installer (.msi)	32-bit	64-bit
Windows Binary (.zip)	32-bit	64-bit
macOS Installer (.pkg)	64-bit / ARM64	
macOS Binary (.tar.gz)	64-bit	ARM64
Linux Binaries (x64)	64-bit	
Linux Binaries (ARM)	ARMv7	ARMv8
Source Code	node-v16.17.0.tar.gz	

Click the link for the installer for your machine and go through the installation process. Select all the suggested default options. Now, let's have a chat with node using the Visual Studio

Code Terminal. Now you start Visual Studio Code and open the GitHub folder containing the sample code. Start a terminal in the folder that contains a JavaScript program you will use to test your node installation. Open the explorer view in Visual Studio by clicking the icon at the top of the column on the left. Now look at the code samples and find the **Ch04-01_Tiny_Json_app** folder. Right-click this folder to open the context menu, as shown below.

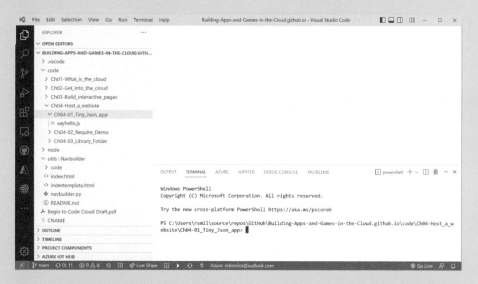

Select **Open In Integrated Terminal** from this menu to start a terminal session in this directory. A new terminal window will open at the bottom right of the page.

You use this window to send commands to your computer's operating system. I'm using a Windows PC, so my commands will be performed by a Windows PowerShell terminal program. If you are using a Mac or Linux machine, you will use the command processor on that machine. You will only use commands to control the node program, so the commands are the same on all platforms.

You tell the terminal what to do by entering text commands. For now, you will use the terminal to start node. Click in the terminal window to make it active, and then type **node** at the terminal command prompt as shown below.

Type node at the command prompt

```
Windows PowerShell
Copyright (C) Microsoft Corporation. All rights reserved.

Try the new cross-platform PowerShell https://aka.ms/pscore6

PS C:\Users\rsmil\source\repos\GitHub\Building-Apps-and-Games-in-the-Cloud.github.io\code\Ch04-Host_a_website\Ch04-01_Tiny_Json_app> node
```

Next, press **Enter** to start the node program inside the terminal. Any commands you enter will be processed by node, not the terminal.

```
PS C:\Users\rsmil\source\repos\GitHub\Building-Apps-and-Games-in-the-Cloud.github.io\code\Ch04-Host_a_website\Ch04-01_Tiny_Json_app> node
Welcome to Node.js v16.17.0.
Type ".help" for more information.
>
```

When node starts, it displays a console prompt. If you don't see the output above, make sure the install process completed correctly. Enter the sum below and watch what happens.

```
> 2+2+2
6
```

You should see how eager node is to help as you type in the calculation. It will execute the partial statement and show results before you've typed the whole line. You can use this console in the same way as you use the console in the browser developer tools. When you type in a JavaScript statement, it will be obeyed, and the result it generates will be printed.

You won't be using the node console very much. I suggested you run it to ensure that node works on your machine. You will be using node to run the JavaScript programs you have written. To exit node, type **.exit** (don't forget the period at the beginning) and press **Enter**. This will stop node and return you to the terminal.

The terminal has been opened in a directory containing a simple JavaScript source file. You can now use node to run this program. To do this, you issue the node command and follow it with the name of the JavaScript source file. You want to run a program in the sayhello.js file:

```
console.log("We can run this program using node");
```

Above, you can see the contents of the program file, which prints a message on the console. You can run this program by starting the node program and giving it the filename as an argument. Type **node sayhello**, as shown below, and press **Enter**:

```
Try the new cross-platform PowerShell https://aka.ms/pscore6

PS C:\Users\rsmil\source\repos\GitHub\Building-Apps-and-Games-in-the-Cloud.github.io\code\Ch04-Host_a_website\Ch04-01_Tiny_Json_app> node
Welcome to Node.js v16.17.0.
Type ".help" for more information.
> 2+2+2
6
> .exit
PS C:\Users\rsmil\source\repos\GitHub\Building-Apps-and-Games-in-the-Cloud.github.io\code\Ch04-Host_a_website\Ch04-01_Tiny_Json_app> node sayhello
```

The terminal will run the node program and pass the sayhello string as an argument to the program. The node program will open the sayhello.js file and run the JavaScript code in that file.

```
PS C:\Users\rsmil\source\repos\GitHub\Building-Apps-and-Games-in-the-Cloud.github.io\code\Ch04-Host_a_website\Ch04-01_Tiny_Json_app> node
Welcome to Node.js v16.17.0.
Type ".help" for more information.
> 2+2+2
6
> .exit
PS C:\Users\rsmil\source\repos\GitHub\Building-Apps-and-Games-in-the-Cloud.github.io\code\Ch04-Host_a_website\Ch04-01_Tiny_Json_app> node sayhello
We can run this program using node
PS C:\Users\rsmil\source\repos\GitHub\Building-Apps-and-Games-in-the-Cloud.github.io\code\Ch04-Host_a_website\Ch04-01_Tiny_Json_app>
```

Above is the result of running the sayhello program. The message has been displayed in the terminal, and both the sayhello and node programs have ended. You can now close the terminal session by typing the **exit** command.

CODE ANALYSIS

Running node

You might have some questions about the terminal and node.

Question: Why does mine not work?

> **Answer:** There are a few reasons why your program might not run. The most obvious is that you might have typed the wrong filename. If you enter the filename as **syHello**, the node program will be unable to find such a file, producing an error. The error is not a simple "Hey, you got the filename wrong" message. Instead, you get a whole bunch of error reports followed by the "MODULE_NOT_FOUND" message. You can also get this error if your filename doesn't have the .js language extension, which identifies a file as holding JavaScript code. And, most confusingly, you can get this error on some systems if you provide a sayhello filename.
>
> On a Windows PC, filenames are not case sensitive, so you could enter them in upper- or lowercase. If you enter the name as **sayhello**, the Windows file system will quite happily match this with **sayHello**. However, operating systems based on Unix—including those used in Linux and Apple systems—are case sensitive, so they don't do this matching. That

means we can issue commands that work on a Windows device but don't work on macOS or Linux devices.

Also, a command might not work because you are running the terminal program in the wrong directory. The terminal keeps track of its current directory, so it will look there for the file. We started the terminal by using the **Open In Integrated Terminal** command on the directory containing our example code. If we had opened the wrong directory, the node program would be unable to find the **sayHello** program.

Question: What happens if the `sayhello` program contains an infinite loop?

Answer: The node program will run a JavaScript program until the JavaScript program ends. If the JavaScript program never ends, node will keep running. This is frequently what we want. If node is hosting a web server program written in JavaScript, we want the server program to run forever, so the server program will run forever. We can stop a running JavaScript program in node by using keycode CTRL+C (hold down the Control key and press C) in the terminal window.

Question: How does a node program communicate with the user?

Answer: The node system will run a JavaScript program, but it doesn't provide a document object, so we can't create HTML elements and then change their properties to create a display for the user. A node program can use the `console.log` function to send messages to the console. There is also a module called `readline`, which can be used to read input from the terminal. You can find out more about `readline` at *https://nodejs.org/api/readline.html.* We will be learning about modules in the next section.

Question: How does the terminal program find the node program?

Answer: This is an interesting question. We've just discovered that the terminal program looks in the current directory to find files. However, the node program isn't in the current directory, but the Terminal program can find the node program and run it. How does this work?

The operating system manages a set of environment variables, which, as the name implies, describe the environment for programs on that computer. One of these variables is called the *path*, which is a list of "places to look" for things. If I can't find my keys, I'll check the front door, the kitchen door, the key hooks, my pocket, and finally, my right hand. This list of locations is my "path" for finding keys. In the case of my computer, the path is the place to look for a program to run.

When you enter the node command, the terminal program searches through all the directories specified in the `path` variable to see if any of them contain a program called node. When the terminal finds the node program, it runs it. The node application installation added the node program's directory location to the computer path. On a Windows PC, you can use the `$Env:path` command in the terminal to view the path. On Mac or Linux machines, the command is `echo $PATH`. You might be surprised by the number of different directories:

```
C:\WINDOWS\system32;C:\WINDOWS;C:\WINDOWS\System32\Wbem;C:\WINDOWS\System32\
WindowsPowerShell\v1.0\;C:\WINDOWS\System32\OpenSSH\;C:\Program Files\Microsoft SQL
Server\130\Tools\Binn\;C:\Program Files\Microsoft SQL Server\Client SDK\ODBC\170\
Tools\Binn\;C:\Program Files\Git\cmd;C:\ProgramData\chocolatey\bin;C:\Program
Files\dotnet\; C:\Program Files\CMake\bin;C:\Program Files\nodejs\; C:\Users\
rsmil\AppData\Local\Mu\bin;C:\Users\rsmil\AppData\Local\Microsoft\WindowsApps;C:\
Users\rsmil\AppData\Local\Programs\Microsoft VS Code\bin;C:\Users\rsmil\AppData\
Local\GitHubDesktop\bin;C:\Users\rsmil\.dotnet\tools;C:\Users\rsmil\AppData\Local\
Microsoft\WindowsApps;C:\Program Files\heroku\bin;C:\Users\rsmil\.dotnet\tools;C:\
Users\rsmil\AppData\Roaming\npm
```

Above, you can see some of the directories in the $Env:path variable on my machine. The directory containing node is in bold.

JavaScript heroes: modules

Node is much more than just a place you can run JavaScript programs. It also allows you to create programs that are made up of *modules*. Modules are another JavaScript hero you should know about. A module is a package of JavaScript code that you want to reuse. A module can contain functions, variables, and classes. Some elements in a module source file can be "exported" from the module for use in other programs. The first implementation of modules was created as part of the node framework. It uses a function called require to import items from a module that has exported them. Let's look at how it works.

Create a module and require it

Let's consider something we might like to turn into a module. In Chapter 3, we created a function called getRandom to generate random numbers. We used it to pick the position of the cheese in the Cheese Finder game we built.

Here, you can see the code for getRandom:

```
function getRandom(min, max) {
    var range = max - min;
    var result = Math.floor(Math.random() * range) + min;
    return result;
}
```

When a program needs a random number in a particular range, it can use the function to get one. The following statement creates a variable called spots that is set to the result of a getRandom call. The spots variable will contain a value in the 1 to 6 range. We could use the value of spots to replace dice in a board game. Note that the upper limit of our random number generator is *exclusive*. The number of spots returned will never be 7.

```
let spots = getRandom(1,7);
```

We might want to use getRandom in another application that also needs random numbers. We could just copy the text of the function into the new application, but if we ever find a bug in getRandom, we would then have to find all the applications where getRandom has been used and fix the code in each one. If our programs all used a single shared version, we'd just have to fix the fault in one file to fix it in all the programs. Modules have other advantages, too. A module can be developed independently of the rest of the application, perhaps by a different programmer.

We can make a JavaScript file into a module by adding an exports statement specifying what is being exported. The following code exports just one function, getRandom. The name of the function as it is exported is also getRandom:

```
function getRandom(min, max) {                        Create the function to be
    var range = max - min;                                          exported
    var result = Math.floor(Math.random() * range) + min;
    return result;
}
exports.getRandom = getRandom;                        Export the function with the
                                                          name getRandom
```

This code could be placed in a source file called randomModule.js. A program that wants to use the getRandom function can use the require function to load the module containing it. The two statements below show how a node.js application uses getRandom:

```
const randomModule = require("./randomModule");
let spots = randomModule.getRandom(1,7);
```
Import the function
Use the function in our program.

The variable randomModule is declared as a constant and then set to refer to the result from the require function. The require function is supplied with a string containing the file path to the randomModule.js source file. The character sequence "./" in front of the string tells the require function to look in the directory containing the program.

MAKE SOMETHING HAPPEN 17

Scan the QR code or visit *https://www.youtube.com/watch?v=Vi7xh9FvGD4* for a video walk-through of this Make Something Happen.

Use debug to explore the require statement

In Chapter 2, in the "Code Analysis: Calling functions" section, you used the debugger in the browser to discover how JavaScript functions are called. Now you will use the node.js debugger in Visual Studio Code to investigate how require is used to load modules into a program. Start Visual Studio Code and open the GitHub repository for this book's sample code. Now find the **Ch04-02_Require_Demo** directory and open the **useRandom.js** file:

This program uses `require` to load the `randomModule.js` file. Then it calls `getRandom` from the module. You can use the Visual Studio Code debugger to step through the code in this program. You do this by starting the debugger. Click the debug icon in the left-hand column. It looks like a run key button with a little bug sitting on it:

The first time you start the debugger, it will ask you which debugger to use:

Select **Node.js**, as suggested. The **Run And Debug** window is now displayed to the left of the Visual Studio Code window. Click the **Run And Debug** button.

Below, you can see that the program has run and displayed a throw result of 3 in the Debug Console. You can click the links next to the console log displayed to visit the lines of Java-Script that produced the outputs. This output shows that the program ran correctly, but you really want to use the debugger to discover how the `require` process works. You can do this by setting a breakpoint in this program and then stepping through the code.

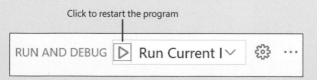

Throw result

We've already used breakpoints in the debugger in the browser, and they are set in the same way here. Click to the left of the line number to add a breakpoint. Add a breakpoint at the first statement in the program, as shown below:

```
Help                useRandom.js - Building-Apps-and-Games-in-the-Cloud.github.io - Visual Studio Code

JS useRandom.js  ✕

code > Ch04-Host_a_website > Ch04-02_Require_Demo > JS useRandom.js > ...
●    1    const randomModule = require("./randomModule");
     2
     3    let spots = randomModule.getRandom(1,7);
     4    console.log("Throw result:" + spots);
```

Breakpoint

The program will stop at the statement set with a breakpoint, so you can see what it is doing. Click the green triangle next to the Run Current dropdown at the top of the debugger pane to restart the program:

Click to restart the program

RUN AND DEBUG ▷ Run Current | ∨   ⚙   · · ·

The node environment will now run the JavaScript program until it hits the breakpoint. Below, you can see how the program stopped at the first statement in useRandom. At the top of the window, you can see a set of debug controls that look rather like those you saw in the browser's **Developer Tools**.

Breakpoint   Debugging tools

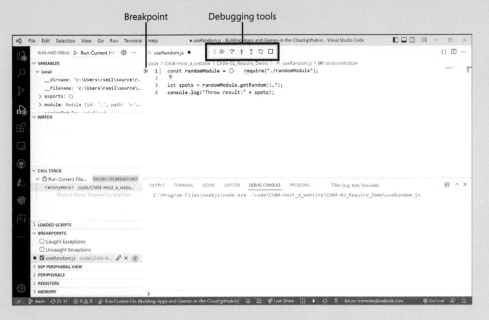

Press the **Step Into Function** control (the downward pointing arrow) to run the next statement. This will perform the `require` statement.

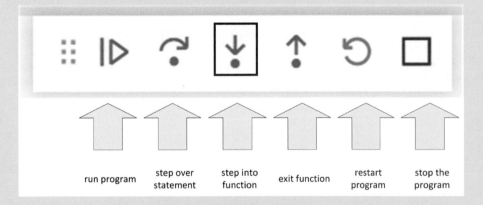

run program

step over statement

step into function

exit function

restart program

stop the program

When a JavaScript program performs a `require`, it executes the JavaScript in the module file, which is being loaded. Below, you can see that the module contains a statement that logs a message to the console before exporting the `getRandom` function. You can click the **Step Into Function** button to step through the program as it runs. When the execution reaches the end of the `randomModule` source file, it returns to `useRandom` and calls the `getRandom` function.

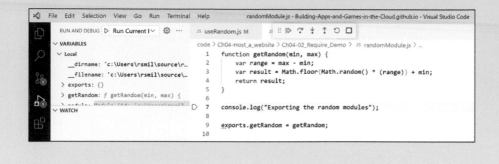

It makes sense to store modules separately from the application code. The `node` environment is designed to allow this. We can create a directory named `node_modules`, and `node` will search this directory to find required module files. The **Ch04-03_Library_Folder** example contains a `node_modules` directory containing the module files.

The following code shows how a module in the **node_modules** folder is accessed. We don't need to put the prefix in the module file path if we store the module file in the `node_modules` folder. You can open the programs in the debugger and step through them to see how they work.

```
const randomModule = require("randomModule");                    Load the module

let spots = randomModule.getRandom(1,7);              Use getRandom from the module
console.log("Throw result:" + spots);                  Print the result to the console
```

require and import

The `require` mechanism works, but it does have some disadvantages. A program can use `require` to load a module at any point in its execution. You might think this flexibility is a good thing. However, it might lead to delayed responses from an application if it has to fetch components using `require` as it is being used. It is always best if an application loads all external resources when it starts running.

Another issue is that the `require` mechanism runs *synchronously*. We saw that when a program uses `require` to load a module, it runs the entire contents of the JavaScript file containing the module code. This takes place when the `require` is performed, pausing the program while modules are loaded. If an application contains multiple `require` mechanisms, each must be completed before the next can be performed. It is also not possible to use `require` only to load particular elements from a module. The whole module must be scanned each time it is used.

To address these issues, later versions of JavaScript include `import` and `export` declarations that provide the same functionality as `require` but in a slightly different way. Below, you can see the JavaScript code for a module that exports the `getRandom` function. Another module can import this by using the `import` declaration:

```
function getRandom(min, max) {
    var range = max - min;
    var result = Math.floor(Math.random() * range) + min;
    return result;
}

export {getRandom} ;                                    Export the getRandom function
```

The following code imports the `getRandom` function from a local module file called `randomModule.mjs`. It then calls the function to generate a `spots` value:

```
import { getRandom } from "./randomModule.mjs";         Import the getRandom function

let spots = getRandom(1,7);
console.log("Throw result:" + spots);
```

There are some important things to remember when you are using import:

- The module file and any files that import modules must have the language extension `.mjs` rather than the usual `.js` which means JavaScript program.

- All the imports for a module must be performed at the start of the module.

You can find these example files in the **Ch04-04_Import_Demo** source code folder. If you are creating modules for your own projects, I think you should use the `import` mechanism. You might see modules created with either `require` or `import`, and older projects, in particular, might use `require`. In this book's examples, all the libraries used in `node` to create web servers use `import`.

Using import in the browser

Until now, we have created our JavaScript applications by embedding code directly in a web page. However, this is not a good solution if you're building large projects. We might also like to use code from modules in JavaScript applications running in the browser. Let's see how we can create a web page that uses a module.

Figure 4-2 shows when the Throw Dice button is clicked, a new random value between 1 and 6 is displayed. This page uses the same random number module we used earlier. You can find the files behind the site in the **Ch04-05_Browser_Import** examples folder. You can view the web page at

https://begintocodecloud.com/code/Ch04-Host_a_website/Ch04-05_Browser_Import/index.html

Figure 4-2 Throw dice

Following is the HTML file for the dice web page. It contains a definition for a Throw dice button. The application needs to know when this button is clicked so it can generate and display the new dice throw value:

```html
<!DOCTYPE html>
<html>

<head>
  <title>Dice using getRandom</title>
  <link rel="shortcut icon" type="image/x-icon" href="favicon.ico">
  <link rel="stylesheet" href="styles.css">
</head>

<body>
  <p>
    <button id="diceButton">Throw dice</button>
  </p>
  <p id="dicePar" class="dice">*</p>
```

```
  <script type="module">                          Specify that the script is a module
    import { doStartPage } from "./pageCode.mjs";   Import the doStartPage function
    doStartPage();                                  Call the doStartPage function
  </script>
</body>
</html>
```

Until now, the button's definition in the page's HTML contained an `onclick` attribute
that calls a handler function when the button is clicked:

```
<button onclick="selectFastClock();">Fast Clock</button>
```

This is a button definition from the web page for the **Ch02-04_Time Travel Clock**
example we worked on in Chapter 2, which defines the button to be clicked when we
want the clock to be five minutes fast. The `onclick` attribute contains the JavaScript
code `"selectFastClock();"` that is performed when the button is clicked. It means the
`selectFastClock` function runs when the button is clicked. This works, but it means
that the creator of the web page (which contains the button element) must agree with
the creator of the JavaScript (which contains the event handler) on the name of the
event handler function and how it is called.

A better way to do this is to put the developer in charge of connecting the event
handler to the button, so they can give the handler function whatever name they like.
All the developer needs to know is the button element's `id`. In the HTML for the dice
page, the button is given an `id` of `"diceButton"`.

```
<button id="diceButton">Throw dice</button>
```

Following is the HTML from the dice page, which defines a dice button that is clicked
when the user wants a new dice value displayed. The element has an `id` of `"diceBut-
ton"`. The binding of a function to the click event is performed in the `doStart` function,
which is held in a JavaScript module called `pageCode.mjs`. The HTML file imports the
`doStartPage` function from this module and then calls the function to run the page.
This is the `pageCode.mjs` source file:

```
import { getRandom } from '/modules/randomModule.mjs';          Import the getRandom
                                                                          function

function doThrowDice() {                                        Function that throws the dice
  let outputElement = document.getElementById("dicePar");
  let spots = getRandom(1,7);
```

```
    outputElement.textContent = spots;
}

function doStartPage(){                                    ──── Starts the page running
  let diceButton = document.getElementById("diceButton");  ──── Find the dice button
  diceButton.addEventListener("click", doThrowDice);       ──── Bind an event handler to it
}

export{ doStartPage };                                     ──── Export the doStartPage function
```

This file contains two functions:

- doThrowDice   Called to display a new dice value.

- doStartPage   Called to start the page running. This function connects the doThrowDice function to the button's click event.

The addEventListener function is used by doStartPage to add event listeners to the buttons in the Cheese Finder game we created in Chapter 3. The doStartPage function is exported from the module so it can be imported and used in the web page.

CODE ANALYSIS

Modules in the browser

You might have some questions about this code.

Question: Why must the JavaScript files have the language extension **.mjs**?

> **Answer:** JavaScript handles module files differently from "ordinary" files. The import declaration only works in a module file. Module files also have strict mode enabled by default. We first saw the JavaScript strict mode in the Make Something Happen 14, "Investigate let, var, and const," in Chapter 3. The strict mode asks JavaScript to perform extra checks to make sure your program is correct. This means JavaScript needs to know when it is processing a module file. This difference is indicated by language extensions, which are added to the end of a filename, preceded by a period (.):

- .js   JavaScript program
- .mjs   JavaScript module

If you want to indicate that JavaScript code in an HTML file is a module, use the type attribute of the JavaScript element in the HTML file. For a standard JavaScript program, the type is text/javascript, but for a module, the type is module, so the browser's JavaScript engine knows it is module code and can use import.

Question: Where is the `randomModule.mjs` file stored?

> **Answer:** Below is a statement that imports `getRandom` into a program. The word `from` is followed by the path to the file that contains the JavaScript code to be imported. The path starts with the `./` sequence, which tells JavaScript to look for the `randomModule.mjs` file in the same folder as the program source. This works, but it means every application has its own copy of the module file.

```
import { getRandom } from './randomModule.mjs';
```

> Following is the statement that imports the `getRandom` module for the dice website. Now the path doesn't start with a period (.). Leaving off the leading period tells JavaScript to look in the website's top directory rather than the directory containing the JavaScript program. I've created a directory called `modules` at the top of my website that stores all my module files. A copy of the `randomModule.mjs` file is in that directory, meaning all the pages in my website can import from this module.

```
import { getRandom } from '/modules/randomModule.mjs';
```

> Below, you can see how this all fits together. The **Sources** view in the browser's **Developer Tools** shows where all the files are located, and you can browse each one.

Question: Can a `node` application and a browser share the same module files?

> **Answer:** Yes, as long as you are careful where you put the shared module files. If you leave the leading period off a file path given in a `node` application, this means "look at the root of the storage device holding the `node` program," which is slightly different from the website root.

Question: Can a module export more than one item?

> **Answer:** Yes. You just add the items to the list of exported things. You can export variables and functions.

Question: Can you declare variables in a module file?

> **Answer:** Yes, you can. Variables declared *global* to the module file (declared outside any function in the file) will only be visible to the code in that module file. To understand how this works (and why we are doing it), suppose you wanted to make the doThrowDice function count the number of times it has been used. We would need a variable to hold this number and then increment it each time the function is called.
>
> Below, you can see how we could do this. This code is in the pageCode.mjs source file and uses a modified version of the doThrowDice function. The throwCount variable is used by the doThrowDice function, which is called each time the **Throw Dice** button is pressed. The function increments the throwCount variable and displays it after the number of spots. You can find this version of the dice in the **Ch04-06_Throw_Counter** example.

```
var throwCount = 0;

function doThrowDice() {
  let outputElement = document.getElementById("dicePar");
  let spots = getRandom(1,7);
  throwCount = throwCount + 1;
  outputElement.textContent = spots + " " + throwCount;
}
```

> This is a neat way of "hiding" variables you don't want people to have access to. If the variable is declared inside a module, it is only useable by code outside the module if it is explicitly imported.

The dark side of imported code

In the next section, we will build a working web server using just a few lines of JavaScript and a lot of code imported from modules. However, before we do that, we should look at the "dark side" of modules and what you should consider when you use them. Let's start with a look at a special new version of the getRandom function that is supposed to return a random number.

We've used the getRandom function to generate values for the Cheese Finder program and the dice. However, the following version of getRandom has an special feature. For the first ten minutes of every hour, the function subtracts 1 from the result. You might be wondering why you might write code like this. For ten minutes in every hour, I can say, "I'll give you a million pounds if this dice rolls a six," and be sure I won't lose any money because it is impossible to roll a six in that time. If this version of getRandom ended up in a program used by a casino, I could use this knowledge to my advantage.

You can find this tampered version of the program in the **Ch04-07_Tampered_Random** example:

```
function getRandom(minimum, maximum) {
    let range = maximum - minimum;
    let result = Math.floor(Math.random() * range) + minimum;

    let currentDate = new Date();                          Get the current date
    if (currentDate.getMinutes() < 10) {           Are we in the first 10 minutes of the hour?
        if (result > minimum) {                      If we are, subtract 1 from the result
            result = result - 1;
        }
    }
    return result;
}
```

When you are using code that might come from an untrusted source, you need to be careful that the code inside them doesn't have any nasty extra features like the function above. A module may contain faulty code, but it is also possible for a module to contain malicious code. There have even been reports of people copying GitHub repositories and making tampered versions of libraries for unwary developers to use in their applications. Make sure you are using the "proper" version of a library by checking the activity level on the GitHub site.

Make a web server

In Chapter 2, we installed the Live Server Extension in Visual Studio Code and used this extension to view the web pages we created in Visual Studio. Live Server provides a tiny web server that runs on our machine. When the browser asks for a web page, the Live Server program finds the file containing the page and sends it back to the browser. Now, we will create a web server powered by JavaScript code running inside node. This can send files back to a browser, but it can also generate HTML directly from code.

You might think hosting our own site would mean we must put something in the cloud, but that is not the case. We can use node to run a web server on our local machine and then connect to it with our browser. Our server will listen on a network *port* for incoming requests. When a message comes in, the server will generate an HTML-formatted response and send it back. We will give the browser a *localhost* network address for the server address so that it connects to our local computer. The server will use the Hyper Text Transfer Protocol (HTTP) to interact with the browser. We will connect event handler functions that will respond when requests arrive.

Once the server code is complete, it can be moved to the cloud so that anyone around the world can use the service we have created. Cloud-hosting services can take our JavaScript code and run it for us. There is even an extension for Visual Studio code that can take our site and place it in the cloud.

Serving from software

The program below hosts a web page that returns a web page containing the text "Hello from Simple Server" when accessed from the web. The web page is hosted on the local machine at port 8080:

```
import http from 'http';                                    Load the http library

function handlePageRequest(request,response){               Function to deal with a request
    response.statusCode = 200;                              Set the status code for the response
    response.setHeader('Content-Type', 'text/plain');       Set the content type to text
    response.write('Hello from Simple Server');             Add the content
    response.end();                                         Send the response
}

let server = http.createServer(handlePageRequest);          Create a server

console.log("Server running");

server.listen(8080);                                        Start the server listening on port 8080
```

Let's use the debugger to step through the code and watch the server build a web response and return it.

MAKE SOMETHING HAPPEN 18

Scan the QR code or visit *https://www.youtube.com/watch?v=F2ixu-RQiaw* for a video walk-through of this Make Something Happen.

Use debug to investigate the server

You can use the Visual Studio Code debugger to watch your tiny web server in action. Start Visual Studio Code and open the GitHub repository for the sample code for this book. Now use the **Explorer** to find the **Ch04-08_Simple_Web_Server** directory and open the server. mjs file.

This is the most complicated exercise you have performed so far. You will use two programs, Visual Studio Code and your browser. Visual Studio Code will use node to run a web server written in JavaScript, and the browser will visit the server. Make sure you follow all the steps in the sequence given.

You used breakpoints and the debugger in Make Something Happen 17, "Use debug to investigate the require statement," earlier in this chapter. Before performing this exercise, refresh your knowledge of breakpoints, how to start a program in the debugger, and the debug controls. Now add two breakpoints to server.mjs at statements 4 and 11, as shown below.

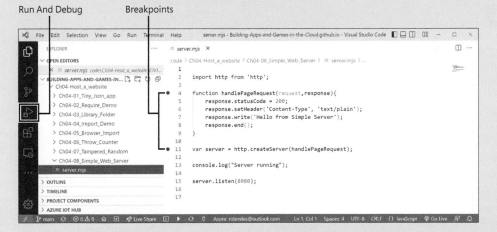

Now start the program running in the debugger. It will hit the breakpoint at line 11. This is the statement that starts the server. The breakpoint at line 5 wasn't hit because that statement is inside the handlePageRequest function, which has not been called yet. The handle-PageRequest function is passed into the createServer function so the server knows which function to call when a page request is received. Click the **Step Into Function** button in the debug controls (or press F11) to execute that statement in the program.

Breakpoint not hit

Breakpoint hit

Step Into Function

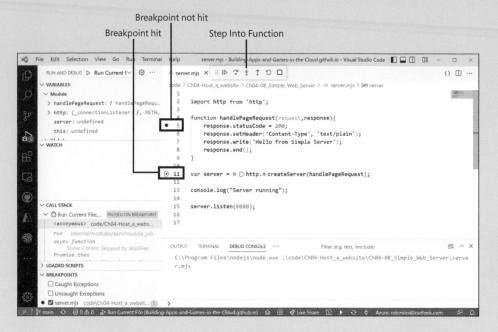

The program will now move onto a statement that logs `"Server running"` on the console.

```
● 11    var server = ● http.● createServer(handlePageRequest);
  12
▷ 13    console.log("Server running");
  14
  15    server.listen(8080);
```

Click the **Step Into Function** button again to perform this statement. You should see the message appear on the console, and the execution moves on to the next statement, which starts the server listening by calling the `listen` function.

```
● 11    var server = ● http.● createServer(handlePageRequest);
  12
  13    console.log("Server running");
  14
▷ 15    server. ▷ listen(8080);
  16
  17
```

Above, you can see the output from the program and the program positioned at line 15, ready to start the server listening for web requests. The call to `listen` is provided with the number of the port to listen to (in this case, 8080). **Click Step Into Function** to perform the `listen` function. The `listen` function is now running and waiting for a web request on port 8080.

You can use your browser to make a web request of the site that your server is hosting. The address you will use is `http://localhost:8080`. The first part of the address is the address of the machine (in this case, it is `localhost`), and the second part of the address is the port number (in this case, it is `8080` because that is where your server program is listening). Open your browser, type the address into the address bar, as shown below, and press **Enter** to open the site.

You will see that the browser will pause, waiting for the site to arrive from the server. Now, go back to the Visual Studio. The program has hit the breakpoint in the `handlePageReq-uest` function. This function is called by the server when a page is requested. The function's job is to assemble a response and then send it back to the server. If you wait too long before allowing `handlePageRequest` to run, the browser will time out the web request. Let's take a look the function now.

Return to Visual Studio Code and click the **Continue** button in the debug controls (the right-pointing blue triangle) to continue the `handlePageRequest` function. You might expect the web page to appear in the browser, but it doesn't. Instead, you will find that the breakpoint in the `handlePageRequest` is hit a second time. Click the **Continue** button again.

Now, you can go back to the browser and see what has happened:

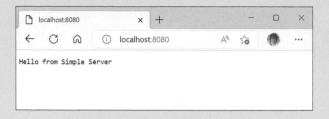

Above, you can see the page produced by the server. This works because the browser has been told that the content returned by the server is plain text, so it just displays it. (I'll explain how this works in the next section.)

Now stop the server (press the red square in the debug controls), edit the text in the call of `response.write` on line 7, and run the program again to confirm the served text has changed. When you have finished with the server, you can stop it again.

This is a big moment. You now know how both ends of the World Wide Web work. You've seen how browsers download web pages and display them, and now you know how a program can serve a web page.

Running a server

You might have some questions about what we have just done:

Question: What would happen if the server never sent back a response?

> **Answer:** The browser sends a request to a website and then waits for the response. If the response takes too long to arrive, the request will time out, and the browser will tell you the page is inaccessible.

Question: How does the server build the response to the browser?

```
function handlePageRequest(request,response){
    response.statusCode = 200;
    response.setHeader('Content-Type', 'text/plain');
    response.write('Hello from Simple Server');
    response.end();
}
```

When the `handlePageRequest` function is called, it is given two parameters:

- `request`   The first parameter, `request`, is a reference to an object that describes the request from the browser.

- `response`   The second parameter, `response`, is a reference that refers to an object that describes the response to be sent to the browser. At the moment, we are not using the `request` parameter.

The `handlePageRequest` function builds the same response to any request. The first thing the function does is set the `statusCode` property of the `response` to 200. This value is sent back to the browser at the beginning of the response. The value 200 means, "All is well; here is the page." We could use other values to signal error conditions. The value 404 means "page not found."

Next, the function uses the `setHeader` method in the response to set a value in the header to be sent to the browser. It sets the "Content-Type" value to the "text/plain" string. The browser uses the Content-Type value to decide what to do with the incoming data. If the content type were "text/html", the browser would build a document object and display it. However, our server just serves out plain text.

The third statement in the `handlePageRequest` function uses the `write` method in the response to write the page's actual content. In this case, it is just a simple message, but this content could be much longer.

The final statement calls the `end` function on the response. This is the point at which the response is assembled and sent back to the browser.

Question: How does the server know which page is being requested by the browser?

Answer: The `request` parameter (which we have not used yet) contains a property called `url` that contains the URL (uniform resource locator) for the requested page. If the browser requests the index page, the `url` property is the "/" string. We will use the path in our next server to serve files.

Question: Why did the browser make two requests of the server?

Answer: In Make Something Happen 17, "Use debug to investigate the server," earlier in this chapter, we set a breakpoint in the `handlePageRequest` function. The breakpoint is hit when a server requests a page. The breakpoint was hit twice when we tried to load the page into the browser, which means that the browser has asked the server for two responses. Why?

This has to do with the way the web works. Many web pages, including the ones for the sample code for this site, have "favicons" on them. A favicon is a little image displayed in the top left-hand corner of the page.

Favicon

Above, you can see the favicon for the *begintocodecloud.com* site—a shiny red ball that I think is quite artistic. When a browser loads a website, it makes two requests. One request is for the favicon image file; the other is for the site's actual content. Our server returns the same response to both requests: "Hello from Simple Server." The browser can't change a text message into a favicon, so it ignores the favicon. If we want our site to have a working favicon, we have to create a bitmap file of the correct type and then serve it out when the file is requested.

```
import http from 'http';
import fs from 'fs';

function handlePageRequest(request, response) {
    let url = request.url;

    console.log ("Page request for:" + url);

    if (url == "/favicon.ico") {
        console.log("  Responding with a favicon");
        response.statusCode = 200;
        response.setHeader('Content-Type', 'image/x-icon');
        fs.createReadStream('./favicon.ico').pipe(response);
    }
    else {
        console.log("  Responding with a message");
        response.statusCode = 200;
        response.setHeader('Content-Type', 'text/plain');
        response.write('Hello from Simple Server');
        response.end();
    }
}
```

This version of `handlePageRequest` checks the incoming request's URL. If the request is for a favicon, it will open the icon file and send it back to the server. Otherwise, it sends the "Hello from Simple Server" message. You can find this version of the simple server in the **Ch04-09_Simple_Web_Server_with_favicon** sample code folder for this chapter. If you use this server, you should see that the browser displays a shiny red favicon for the page.

In the next section, we will take a close look at how pages are sent back to server.

Serving out files

The server we have just created always delivers the same text back to the browser—the string "Hello from Simple Server." We can turn it into a more useful server by allowing the browser to specify the file that the server is to return. When we ask a browser to show us a particular page, the page's address is expressed as a "universal resource locator" or **url**. This tells the browser where to go to look for a page.

Figure 4-3 shows an overview of a URL. The protocol and the host elements tell the browser the computer's address and how to talk to it. The path specifies the file on the server that is to be read. The port value (if present) specifies the network port on the computer to connect to. If the port elements are missing, the browser will try to connect to port 80

https	://	begintocodecloud.com				/index.html
protocol		host				path

https	://	begintocodecloud.com	:	8080	/index.html
protocol		host		port	path

Figure 4-3 URL structure

The web server uses the path's value to find the requested file. The path in **Figure 4-3** is for the `index.html` file for the *begintocodecloud.com* website. If you leave the path off the address, the server will send the index file automatically. Our server can use the `url` property of a web request to determine what is to be sent back to the browser.

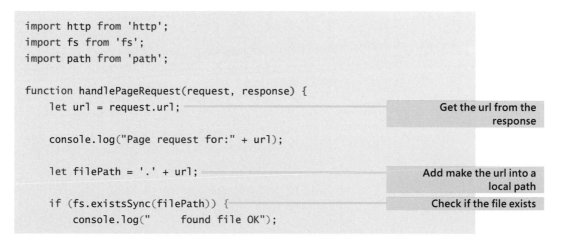

```
import http from 'http';
import fs from 'fs';
import path from 'path';

function handlePageRequest(request, response) {
    let url = request.url;                              Get the url from the
                                                                response

    console.log("Page request for:" + url);

    let filePath = '.' + url;                           Add make the url into a
                                                                local path

    if (fs.existsSync(filePath)) {                      Check if the file exists
        console.log("    found file OK");
```

```
            response.statusCode = 200;
            let extension = path.extname(url);                        Get the file extension of the url
            switch (extension) {                                          Select the content type
                case '.html':
                    response.setHeader('Content-Type', 'text/html');
                    break;
                case '.css':
                    response.setHeader('Content-Type', 'text/css');
                    break;
                case '.ico':
                    response.setHeader('Content-Type', 'image/x-icon');
                    break;
                case '.mjs':
                    response.setHeader('Content-Type', 'text/javascript');
                    break;
            }
            let readStream = fs.createReadStream(filePath);       Create a read stream for the file
            readStream.pipe(response);                                Pipe the stream into the
        }                                                                       response
        else {                                                        If the file doesn't exist, send
            console.log("    file not found")                               file not found
            response.statusCode = 404;
            response.setHeader('Content-Type', 'text/plain');
            response.write("Cant find file at: " + filePath);
            response.end();
        }
    }
}

let server = http.createServer(handlePageRequest);

console.log("Server running");

server.listen(8080);
```

Scan the QR code or visit *https://www.youtube.com/watch?v=BXeNydBTQhA* for a video walkthrough of this Make Something Happen.

Using the file server

You can use the program from the earlier "Serving out files" section to serve the entire website for this book. Start Visual Studio Code and open the GitHub repository for the sample code. Now use the **Explorer** to find the **Ch04-10_File_Web_Server** directory and open the `server.mjs` file.

```
File  Edit  Selection  View  Go  Run  Terminal  Help         server.mjs - Building-Apps-and-Games-in-the-Cloud.github.io - Visual Studio C...

EXPLORER                                    JS server.mjs  ×
                                            code > Ch04-Host_a_website > Ch04-10_File_Web_Server > JS server.mjs > handlePageRequest
OPEN EDITORS                          1     import http from 'http';
  × JS server.mjs  code\Ch04-Host_a_website\Ch04-10_File... 2     import fs from 'fs';
BUILDING-APPS-AND-GAMES-IN-THE-CL...  3     import path from 'path';
  > Ch04-01_Tiny_Json_app             4
  > Ch04-02_Require_Demo              5     function handlePageRequest(request, response) {
  > Ch04-03_Library_Folder           6         let url = request.url;
  > Ch04-04_Import_Demo               7
  > Ch04-05_Browser_Import            8         console.log("Page request for:" + url);
  > Ch04-06_Throw_Counter             9
  > Ch04-07_Tampered_Random          10         let filePath = '.' + url;
  > Ch04-08_Simple_Web_Server        11
  > Ch04-09_Simple_Web_Server_with_favicon  12         if (fs.existsSync(filePath)) {
  ∨ Ch04-10_File_Web_Server          13             console.log("     found file OK");
    <> index.html                    14             response.statusCode = 200;
    JS server.mjs                     15             let extension = path.extname(url);
  ∨ Ch04-11_Picture_File_Web_Server  16             switch (extension) {
    <> index.html                    17                 case '.html':
    🖼 seaside.JPG                    18                     response.setHeader('Content-Type', 'text/html');
    JS server.mjs                     19                     break;
  > Ch05-Build_applications          20                 case '.css':
  > Ch06-Shared_Experiences          21                     response.setHeader('Content-Type', 'text/css');
  > Ch07-Application_Design          22                     break;
  > Ch08-Application_Build           23                 case '.ico':
  > Ch09-Turn_professional           24                     response.setHeader('Content-Type', 'image/x-icon');
  > Ch10-Store_data                  25                     break;
                                     26                 case '.mjs':
> OUTLINE                            27                     response.setHeader('Content-Type', 'text/javascript');
> TIMELINE                           28                     break;
> PROJECT COMPONENTS                 29             }
> AZURE IOT HUB                      30
                                     31         let readStream = fs.createReadStream(filePath);
                                     32         readStream.pipe(response);
main   0 0    Live Share    Azure: robmiles@outlook.com         Spaces: 4  UTF-8  CRLF  {} JavaScript    Go Live
```

Now select the debugger and start the program. Below, you can see a debugging session running. I used the browser to open the *http://localhost:8080/index.html* file, which is served by this program. The server outputs the name of each file as the browser requests it. The server has sent two files, `index.html` and `styles.css`. If you move to other pages on the site, you will also see them displayed. I find it rather impressive that such a tiny program can act as quite a capable web server.

CODE ANALYSIS

Simple file server

You might have some questions about the server:

Question: How does the server send a file back to the browser?

Answer: A `node` installation includes a few built-in modules. One of these is the HTTP module we are using to host our website. Another library is the file system module, `fs`, which `node` programs use to interact with the local file store.

```
let readStream = fs.createReadStream(filePath);
readStream.pipe(response);
```

These statements send a file back to the browser. The first statement uses the `create-ReadStream` function from the `fs` module to create a `ReadStream` connected to the file. The second statement uses the `pipe` function on the `ReadStream` to send the file to the web page response. You might need to think about this a bit. A stream is a bunch of data you want to send somewhere like you might use a tank of water to fill a washbasin. You would use a physical pipe to link the two in real life. Our server has a `response` object that needs to be given some data to send (the wash basin), and a `file` object that supplies that data (the water tank). We use the `pipe` method on the `ReadStream` object to tell it to send the `file` to the `response` object. We don't need to worry about precisely how this works. The response will automatically end when the file has been received from the stream. If this seems hard to understand, consider what we want to do. We have data and a thing that wants to receive some data. The pipe method will perform that transfer using a stream.

Question: What happens if the browser asks for a page that doesn't exist?

Answer: The server uses a function from the `fs` module called `existsSync` to check whether a requested file exists. This function is part of the file system library. The server responds with a 404 "resource not found" error code if the file is not found.

Question: How does the server know what type of file to send back to the server?

Answer: When a server sends a response to a request, it must always include `Content-Type` information, so the browser knows what to do with the incoming data. The server works out the type of data to send back by looking at the file extension of the incoming URL.

```
let extension = path.extname(url);
```

The statement above uses the `path` module's `extname` method to get the URL extension. The extension is the character sequence preceded by a period (.) at the end of a file path or URL. As an example, the path `index.html` path has the `.html` extension. The extension specifies the type of data contained in the file. So `index.html` should contain HTML text that describes a web page. The server uses the extension string to decide what `Content-Type` to add to the response:

```
switch (extension) {
    case '.html':
        response.setHeader('Content-Type', 'text/html');
        break;
}
```

The case construction selects the response type matching the extension string.

Question: What happens if the browser asks for a file type that doesn't exist?

Answer: As far as the server is concerned, a content type is a mapping of a file extension (which specifies the type of data in a file) to a Content-Type value to be sent back to the browser. The server we have just created uses a switch construction to perform this mapping and can handle html, css, mjs, and ico file types. If the supplied file extension doesn't match any of these file types (for example, the browser requests an image file with .jpg language extension), the switch construction has no matching case element for .jpg and so doesn't add a Content-Type to the response.

If we want to add more content types (including .jpg images), we could add extra case elements to the switch, but a neater way would be to create a lookup table for the content types:

```
let fileTypeDecode = {
    html: "text/html",
    css: "text/css",
    ico: "image/x-icon",
    mjs: "text/javascript",
    js: "text/javascript",
    jpg: "image/jpeg",
    jpeg: "image/jpeg",
    png: "image/png",
    tiff: "image/tiff"
}
```

The code above creates a variable called fileTypeDecode that can be used as a lookup table that maps language extensions onto Content-Type strings. For each file extension, there is a matching Content-Type string. It allows our browser to handle a range of different image file types. To use the lookup table, you must first get a variable that contains the language extension (for example, html) from the path received by the browser. The code below does this.

```
let extension = path.extname(url);
extension = extension.slice(1);
extension = extension.toLowerCase();
let contentType = fileTypeDecode[extension];
```

These four statements get the content type from the URL. The first statement creates a variable called extension from the URL containing the extension string for the file that the browser has requested. This would create ".html" from a request for "index.html." The second statement removes the leading "." from the extension. It would convert ".html" to "html." The third statement converts the extension to lowercase. It would convert "HTML" to "html." The fourth statement gets the file type that matches the extension from the fileTypeDecode object.

The lookup process works because JavaScript allows you to specify the property of an object by using a string. In other words, both of the two statements below would set the value of contentType to "text/html."

```
let contentType = fileTypeDecode.html;
```

```
let contentType = fileTypeDecode["html"];
```

If you try to look up an extension that is not present in the fileTypeDecode object, the value undefined is returned. Code in the server can test for this and respond with an error 415 when it happens. Otherwise, the file is piped out to the response as before. You can find this server version in the **Ch04-11_Picture_File_Web_Server** sample code folder for this chapter. You can use it to view the picture on the home page for that example. You can expand the server to deliver audio and video files if you wish. You just have to identify the content types for each file type and then add them to the FileTypeDecode object.

```
let contentType = fileTypeDecode[extension];
if (contentType == undefined) {
    console.log("     invalid content type")
    response.statusCode = 415;
    response.setHeader('Content-Type', 'text/plain');
    response.write("Unspported media type: " + filePath);
    response.end();
}
else {
    response.setHeader('Content-Type', contentType);
    let readStream = fs.createReadStream(filePath);
    readStream.pipe(response);
}
```

Active sites

You now know how a JavaScript program running under node can serve out both active content (messages from a running program) and file content (the contents of files on the server). Most web applications use a mix of these. Fixed elements of pages will use files, and then the program-generated content will be inserted as required. It would be useful to have a framework where you could create "templates" containing the fixed parts of a site and then allow you to inject the program-generated content when required. The good news is that you will be learning how to do this in the next chapter. The better news is that you are now well on the way to understanding how the web works in both browsers and servers.

What you have learned

This has been another busy chapter. We've covered a lot of ground. Following is a recap plus some points to ponder:

- Node.js is a framework that allows JavaScript programs to run outside of the browser. It is a free download for all machines. It doesn't provide a document object model to communicate with the user. Instead, it is controlled via a terminal interface. It provides a console on which you can enter commands to run Java-Script statements. It can also be given a JavaScript program to load and execute.

- The node framework provides support for modules. A file of JavaScript code can contain statements that export data or code elements that can then be introduced into other programs using the require statement.

- A module file can contain elements that are not exported, which can be used internally by that module.

- When elements are fetched by a require call, the node framework will execute all the code in the module source file before exporting the elements. This execution takes place synchronously, meaning the program performing the require will be paused until the require call completes.

- A module source file can contain elements that are not exported. These are local to the module and are not visible outside it.

- Node applications can be debugged in Visual Studio Code like JavaScript code running in the browser. You can add breakpoints to the code and view the contents of variables.

- The JavaScript language offers an alternative to the require mechanism using the import keyword. Modules containing import statements must have the file .mjs extension rather than the .js extension.

- It is not possible to use require in JavaScript code that is held in a web page and executed by the browser. However, JavaScript code running in a browser can use the import statement. JavaScript code in an HTML file containing import statements must have the module type. It is not possible for JavaScript code embedded in HTML element attributes to access elements in a `module`. Instead, code in a `module` must obtain a reference to a named element in the HTML file and then act on that directly.

- When you use code you didn't write (for example, when importing a downloaded module), you should make sure that the code doesn't contain any unwanted behaviors.

- A `node.js` installation contains several built-in modules. One is the `http` module, which can create a JavaScript program that acts as a web server.

- The `http` module contains a `createServer` function that is called to create a web server. The `createServer` function is supplied with a reference to a function that will service incoming page requests from the browser. This function is supplied with two parameters that refer to `request` and `response` objects. The `response` object must be populated with page information by the function servicing incoming page requests. The contents of the `response` object are sent back to the browser making the request.

- A response to a web request contains a `statusCode` property that gives the response's status. A `statusCode` of 200 means the page was found correctly.

- A response to a web request contains a `Content-Type` property that the browser will use to decide what to do with the page when it arrives. A `text/plain` type specifies that the file contains plain text.

- You can add plain text to a web request response by using the `write` method exposed by the request.

- A function servicing incoming requests to an HTTP server also receives a `request` parameter describing the request made by the browser. The `request` parameter contains a `url` property that provides the path to the file on the server that is requested. The server can map this URL onto the local filestore to locate the file to be sent back to the server.

- The `node` framework provides modules called `fs` and `path` that are used to interact with the file system on a machine. The `fs` module can make stream objects that are connected to local files. A stream contains a `pipe` method that can direct a stream's content into another object. The response object sent to the server in a web request can receive file streams and send them back to the browser.

- When a browser accesses a website, it will also request a favicon.ico file containing a bitmap displayed by the browser.

- A server must ensure that the reply's Content-Type element reflects the file's content.

To reinforce your understanding of this chapter, you might want to consider the following "profound questions."

Question: What does node.js do?

> **Answer:** The node.js framework lets you run JavaScript programs on a computer without using a browser.

Question: When would you use a module?

> **Answer:** You should use a module if you write code you want to use in several applications. You can also use a module to share work with others. Once you have decided what each module needs to do, they can be developed separately. Another reason to use a module is that it gives your code more privacy. Code and variables in a module that are not exported are not visible outside the module. Modules are also useful when testing. For example, we could test a program that uses our random number generator module by creating a random number generator module to produce a fixed sequence of values. Waiting for the random number generator to produce a dice throw of 6 during testing would be tiresome. It's much better to have a "testing dice" module that produces the values that you need.

Question: Why do we have two mechanisms for using modules in JavaScript, require and import?

> **Answer:** It turns out that programming languages are continually evolving as people think of new things that they want them to do. Also, the first attempt to solve a problem might not be the best one. require was developed specifically for use in node.js applications. import was developed as a language element that built on what require does.

Question: Can the same module be both required and imported?

> **Answer:** Yes, it can. We have been importing modules into our node.js applications. We can also use require in node.js applications to bring in the same modules.

Question: Where would you run a web server program?

> **Answer:** A web server program accepts page requests from browsers and responds with content for the browser to display. You can run a web server on any computer. In this chapter, we have written programs that act as web servers. Web servers for public use are run on machines that have permanent network connections or as processes in the cloud.

Question: Can two applications on one computer share the same port number?

> **Answer:** A port is a numbered connection to a program running on a machine. We have used 8080 as the port number that our server is running behind. Once a program has claimed a port number on a machine, it is not possible for any other program running on the machine to use that port for connections. Port numbers below 1024 are reserved for "well-known" applications, so we should make sure that our applications don't use these numbers.

Question: What is the difference between a port and a path?

Answer: A program running on a computer can open a network port that can be used by other programs to connect to it. Ports are specified by numbers. Port number 80 is traditionally used by web servers. A path is a string of text specifying how to traverse a storage system to get to a particular file or location. For example, the path `code/Ch04-Host_a_website/Ch04-10_File_Web_Server/index.html` tells a program to find the code directory and then look in that for the `index.html` file in the `Ch04-Host_a_website` folder.

Question: What happens if a server gets the `Content-Type` wrong?

Answer: A server adds `Content-Type` to each response it sends back to the browser. The browser can then work out what to do with that content. If the server makes a mistake— perhaps sending back a jpeg image with the content type `text/plain`—the browser will render the content incorrectly. If an image is marked as text, the browser will show a collection of random-looking characters rather than a picture. Remember, a computer has no real understanding of data. We must tell it what is in the file so that it can do the right thing with it.

Question: Is hosting a server on your machine a dangerous thing to do?

Answer: It might be. The server we have made can only serve the contents of the file types that we have specified. In other words, it will serve a JPEG image but not a spreadsheet or a word document. This means if someone managed to browse to any of the other directories on my hard disk, they would not be able to look at passwords or system files. However, they could probably learn a lot about me from the other types of files. You should never host a public-facing (visible to the outside world) website on your own computer. Instead, you should move just the files you want to share onto a separate machine or cloud service and host them there.

Part 2

Make a cloud-based application

First, we investigate the HTML Document Object Model in the browser and use it to create a playable game. Then we deploy the game into the cloud for anyone in the world to access. Next, we move on to make our game a shared user experience powered by connected code running in both the browser and server. We finish with an application design and build exercise, starting with an idea and ending with a cloud-ready application.

5

Build a shared application

What you will learn

In the previous chapter, we created a JavaScript application running in **node** that could act as a web server. We used the server application in two ways: to serve out the contents of files and to run JavaScript code in response to web requests. We found that we could access our site using a standard browser. In this chapter, we'll discover how we can create a server that can host components of an application. Part of our application will run inside the browser, and the rest will run on the server. We'll create services on the server and access them from code running in the browser to spread our application across the two platforms. We'll also find out how JavaScript Object Notation (JSON) can transfer the contents of JavaScript variables between the server and browser. But first, we will revisit the game we made in Chapter 3 and add some compelling gameplay elements as we learn more about JavaScript development and debugging.

And don't forget that the glossary is always out there at

https://begintocodecloud.com/glossary.html

Upgrade Cheese Finder

In Chapter 3, we made a simple game called Cheese Finder. Players click squares in a grid, trying to find the square containing the cheese. When a square is clicked, it shows a number giving the distance from that square to the cheese. **Figure 5-1** shows how the game is played. People seem to like it, but they would like to see a few improvements.

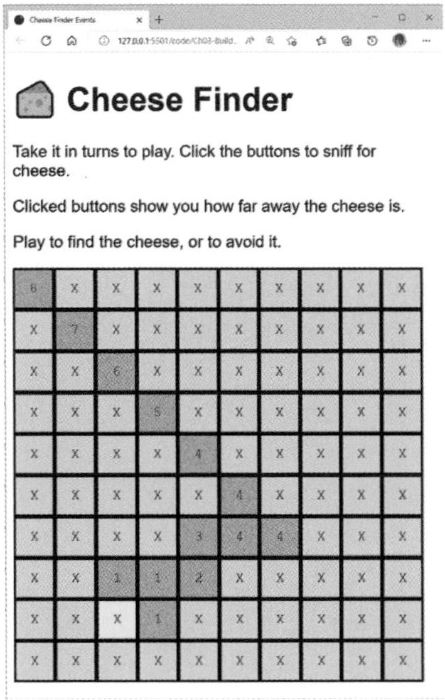

Figure 5-1 Cheese Finder game

Adding some color

Cheese finder works well, but players don't seem to like looking at numbers in the squares. Someone suggests that it might be a good idea to use colors rather than numbers to indicate the distance a square is from the cheese. This turns out to be quite simple to do. First, we need to make some styles that contain colors for the squares:

```
.cheese,
.dist1,
.dist2,
.distFar {
```

```css
    font-family: 'Courier New', Courier, monospace;
    text-align: center;
    min-width: 3em;
    min-height: 3em;
}
.cheese {
  background: lightgoldenrodyellow;
}
.dist1 {
  background: red;
}
.dist2 {
  background: orange;
}


....


.distFar {
  background: darkgray;
}
```

I've removed some of the styles to make the above listing shorter. There are actually 10 distance styles called `dist1` to `dist10` in the game's stylesheet. All the styles are based on a starting style, and the background color for each is set individually. Next, we need a way to convert distance values into style names. We can use an *array* for this.

 **MAKE SOMETHING HAPPEN 20**

Scan the QR code or visit *https://www.youtube.com/watch?v=NvkVpcq1H7E* for a video walk-through of this Make Something Happen.

Arrays as lookup tables

A JavaScript program can use arrays as lookup tables. The `colorStyles` array is a lookup table. Let's investigate how this works. Start your browser and open the `index.html` file in this chapter's **Ch05-01_Colored_Cheese_Finder** example folder. This is a color version of the Cheese Finder game. If you feel like a little fun first, play the game a few times, and then open the Developer Tools window in your browser when you're ready to get to work. Then open the **Console** tab:

You can now investigate how the array works. In the console, you can view the contents of an item just by entering its name. Type the following text and press **Enter**:

```
colorStyles
```

The console shows you the contents of the `colorStyles` array, which is used to convert distance values into style names. Items in an array are called *elements*.

```
> colorStyles
< ▶ (12) ['cheese', 'dist1', 'dist2', 'dist3', 'dist4', 'dist5', 'dist6', 'dist7', 'dist8', 'dist9', 'dist10', 'distFar']
>
```

Let's look at the elements in the array, starting by looking at the element at the beginning of the array. You specify the element you want to look at by providing an index value that tells JavaScript how far down the array to go to get the desired element. The index is given enclosed in brackets. Type the following and press **Enter**:

```
colorStyles[0]
```

```
> colorStyles[0]
< 'cheese'
> |
```

Arrays in JavaScript are indexed from 0, so cheese is the first element in the array.

Let's see what happens when you try to step outside the array's bounds. Type the following and press **Enter**:

```
colorStyles[1000]
```

```
> colorStyles[1000]
< undefined
>
```

There is no element with an index of 1000. Some programming languages would get upset at this point, but JavaScript returns an undefined value.

You can also assign values to the elements in an array. In some languages, an array is declared as having elements of a particular type. Let's see what happens in JavaScript. Type the following and press **Enter**:

```
colorStyles[0] = 99
```

This statement will attempt to put the number 99 into the element at the start of the array. The statement seems to have worked. The element at the start of the array (with index 0) is now the number 99.

```
> colorStyles[0]=99
< 99
```

Type the following and press **Enter** to view the contents of the array:

```
colorStyles
```

```
> colorStyles
< ▶ (12) [99, 'dist1', 'dist2', 'dist3', 'dist4', 'dist5', 'dist6', 'dist7',
      'dist8', 'dist9', 'dist10', 'distFar']
```

This demonstrates that a single array can hold different types of data. The `colorStyles` array now contains numbers and strings. Changing the array like this has broken the game program. The cheese will not be detected or displayed correctly. You can fix this by just reloading the page, but not before you've tried something really interesting. Let's try putting a value into an array element we know is not there. Type the following and press **Enter**:

```
colorStyles[100]='hello world'
```

```
> colorStyles[100]='hello world'
< 'hello world'
```

This seems to work. No error has appeared. Type the following and press **Enter** to view the contents of the array and see what has happened:

```
colorStyles
```

```
> colorStyles
< ▶ (101) [99, 'dist1', 'dist2', 'dist3', 'dist4', 'dist5', 'dist6', 'dist7',
      'dist8', 'dist9', 'dist10', 'distFar', empty × 88, 'hello world']
```

The console shows us that the array is now 101 elements long, contains a block of 88 `empty` elements, and has `hello world` at the end.

CODE ANALYSIS

JavaScript arrays

You might have started off thinking that there is nothing special about how arrays work in JavaScript, but you might have some questions now.

Question: How do I create an empty array?

```
let arr = [];
```

Answer: This will create an empty array called `arr` for use by pirates.

Question: Can I create an array of a particular size?

Answer: Some programming languages require you to create an array before you use it. In JavaScript, you can't do this. Instead, you can use the push function to add an item to the end of an existing array. The statement below would put the value 8 into the arr array:

```
arr.push(8);
```

Question: How do I find an array's length?

Answer: An array has a length property that gives the array length.

Question: Can I create two-dimensional arrays?

Answer: Some languages allow you to create multidimensional arrays that can hold grids and layers. In JavaScript, an array can only hold a single row of items. If you want a two-dimensional array (for a grid), you will need to create an array of arrays.

Question: What happens when I use an array as a parameter into a function call?

Answer: When an array is given as an argument to a function call, a reference to the array is passed to the function parameter.

The colorStyles decode array

The colorStyles array is shown below and contains a list of style names. We can feed an index value into the array to get a style name representing a particular distance. A distance of 0 will select the "cheese" style, whereas a distance of 11 gets the "distFar" style.

```
const colorStyles = ["cheese", "dist1", "dist2", "dist3", "dist4", "dist5",
                     "dist6", "dist7", "dist8", "dist9", "dist10", "distFar"];
```

We can create a function that is fed a distance value and returns the style that should be used for that square:

```
function getStyleForDistance(styles, distance){
  if(distance>=styles.length){          Check if the distance fits in the array
    distance = styles.length-1;                    Pick the far style if it does
  }
  let result = styles[distance];            Look up the name of the style to use
  return result;
}
```

The `getStyleForDistance` function is given a list of styles and a distance value and returns the style matching the distance. It ensures a very large value won't cause an invalid style to be selected. I can use this to set the style for a square:

```javascript
function setButtonStyle(button) {
    let x = button.getAttribute("x");                                    Get the x position of the button
    let y = button.getAttribute("y");                                    Get the y position of the button
    let distance = getCheeseDistance(x, y);                              Get the distance to the cheese
    button.className = getStyleForDistance(colorStyles, distance);       Set the button style
}
```

The `setButtonStyle` function is given a button reference and sets the button's style to match the button's distance from the cheese. It uses the `getCheeseDistance` function to calculate the distance to the cheese. The `setButtonStyle` function is called in the button's event handler:

```javascript
function buttonClickedHandler(event) {
    let button = event.target;                                           Get the button that was clicked

    if (button.className != "empty") {                                   If the button is not empty return
        return;
    }

    setButtonStyle(button);                                              Set the style for the button

    if(button.className == "cheese"){                         If the cheese has been found, end the game
        alert("Well done! Reload the page to play again");
    }
    else {
        counter++;                                                       Update the turn counter
        showCounter();                                                   Display the turn counter
    }
}
```

The `buttonClickedHandler` function is called when the player clicks a button in the grid and is supplied with a parameter describing the `buttonClicked` event. The `target` property of the event refers to the button that was clicked. The `buttonClicked-Handler` function can determine if the button has already been clicked because an unclicked button has a `className` of "empty". If the button has not been clicked, the function sets the button's style. It then checks to see if the style is "cheese". If it is, the game is over, and the function displays an alert. If the game is not over (the player has not clicked the "cheese" button), the function increments, displays a turn counter, and then continues.

Figure 5-2 shows how a game is played in the color version. You can see the path I followed to get to the cheese. The cheese square is pale yellow. This version of the game is available in **Ch05-01_Colored_Cheese_Finder** example folder.

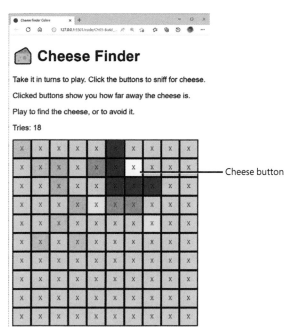

Figure 5-2 Color Cheese Finder

Add a game ending

Players like the new colors, but then someone says it would be nice to display all the colored squares when the game ends. This would add nothing to the gameplay, but it sounds like fun, so we agree to do it. All our program needs to do is work through all the buttons and set their styles. Of course, this means the program will need an array of buttons to work through:

```
var allButtons = [];
```

The variable `allButtons` is an array that will hold an entry for each button. It is declared outside all the functions as a var, so any function in the application can use it. We add buttons to the array as we create them:

```
for (let y = 0; y < height; y++) {
  for (let x = 0; x < width; x++) {
    let newButton = document.createElement("button");
    newButton.className = "empty";
    newButton.setAttribute("x", x);
    newButton.setAttribute("y", y);
    newButton.addEventListener("click", buttonClickedHandler);
    newButton.textContent = "X";
    container.appendChild(newButton);
    allButtons.push(newButton);                                Add the button to the list of
  }                                                                          all buttons
  let lineBreak = document.createElement("br");
  container.appendChild(lineBreak);
}
```

Above is the nested for loop that creates all the game buttons. Each button is now added to the `allButtons` array using the `push` function. Now that we have the array, all we need to do is create a function that uses it to set the style for all the buttons:

```
function fillGrid(buttonList){
  for(let button of allButtons){
    if(button.className == "empty"){                           Does this button need filling?
      setButtonStyle(button);
    }
  }
}
```

The `fillGrid` function is supplied with a list of buttons as a parameter. It works through all the buttons in the list using the `for-of` construction. Any buttons with the `className` of "empty" have their styles set. The `fillGrid` function is called when the player finds the cheese.

Figure 5-3 shows what the end of a game looks like now. You can find this version of the game in the **Ch05-02_Color_Fill_Cheese_Finder** example files folder.

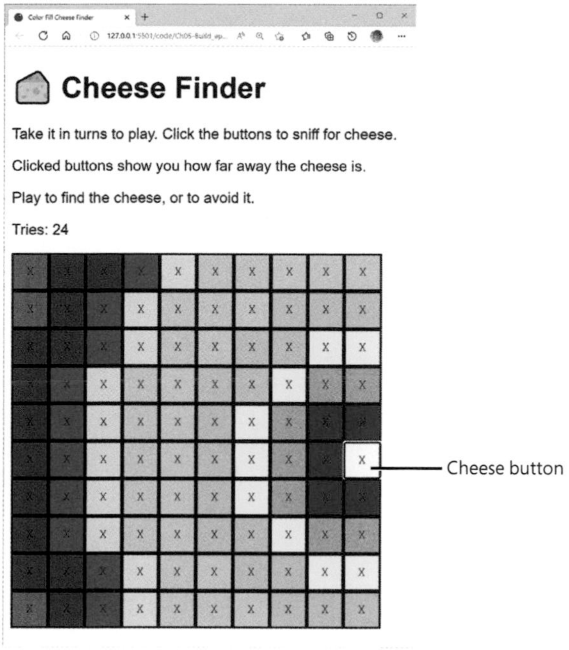

Figure 5-3 Completed color Cheese Finder game

Add randomness

People like playing the game and really like the colored display at the end. But fairly soon, they discover that the game is actually quite easy to win. Once you have learned the colors, you can quickly find the cheese. Someone suggests that it might be more fun if the distance colors are mixed up at the start of the game. Players must now deduce the distance each color represents.

Figure 5-4 shows how the game will work. In this game, green means a distance of 1, and gray means a distance of 2. The mapping between colors and distance is different each time the game is played. We use a lookup table to map the distance values onto the style names, and we need to shuffle the style names before each game.

Figure 5-4 Cheese Finder shuffled

```
const colorStyles = ["white", "red", "orange", "yellow", "yellowGreen",
                     "lightGreen", "cyan", "lightBlue", "blue", "purple",
                     "magenta", "darkGray"];
```

Above, you can see the colorStyles array used to convert a distance into a style name. The game must shuffle this list into a random order. We can create a function to shuffle arrays:

```
function shuffle(items){
  for(let i=0;i<items.length;i++){
    let swapPos = getRandom(0,items.length);
    [items[i], items[swapPos]] = [items[swapPos], items[i]];
  }
}
```

The shuffle function works through an array, picking a random position for each item in it. I've used a rather neat way of swapping two items you might not have seen before. It performs the swap by assigning one array to another, avoiding using a temporary variable. This function is used to shuffle the colorStyles array:

```
shuffle(colorStyles);
```

Now, each distance's style will be different each time the game runs. Note that we can use the shuffle function to shuffle any collection, not just names of styles. We will be using shuffle later to shuffle something else.

Finding the cheese

In the previous version of the game, the "cheese" style was in the colorStyles array at element 0. When a button style became "cheese", the cheese had been found. In this random version of the game, we can't put cheese in the colorStyles array because it could get shuffled to any of the distance values. We must modify the setButtonStyle function to check whether the player has found the cheese and set the style to "cheese" if they have.

The version below checks to see if the button is at the cheese position and sets the style to "cheese" if it is. If the button is not at the cheese position, the function uses the distance to index the colorStyles array. Now, when the game ends, it calls fillGrid to fill in all the colors:

```
function setButtonStyle(button) {
  let x = button.getAttribute("x");
  let y = button.getAttribute("y");

  let distance = getCheeseDistance(x, y);

  if (distance == 0) {                    ── Have we found the cheese
    button.className = "cheese";          ── Set the style if we have
  }
  else {                                  ── Otherwise, set the style for the distance
    button.className = getStyleForDistance(colorStyles, distance);
  }
}
```

```
if (button.className == "cheese") {
  fillGrid(allButtons);
}
```

You can find this version of the game in the **Ch05-03_Cheese_Finder_Color_Shuffle** folder. This is quite an interesting game to play.

> **PROGRAMMER'S POINT**
> ## Always consider accessibility
>
> Showing the cheese distance as colors makes the game display look nice, but it does lead to problems for players who may not be able to resolve the different colors. This issue could be addressed by providing a game option to use letters or symbols to represent the distance values. Whenever you make something for general use, you should consider accessibility. The Web Content Accessibility Guidelines at *https://www.w3.org/TR/WCAG21/* provide a wealth of information, including the use of distinguishable colors.

Add more cheese

I strongly believe that you can improve anything, even cheese, by adding cheese. Some game players feel the same way. They think the game would be even more challenging if more than one square contained cheese. Each time the game starts, it will need to set the position of both cheeses and then display the distance of a square to the nearest cheese.

This is how the single cheese version of the game works. The two variables give the x and y coordinates of the cheese. A random number generator sets the cheese's x position (the distance across the grid) and the cheese's y position (the distance down the grid).

```
var cheeseX = getRandom(0, width);
var cheeseY = getRandom(0, height);
```

If we want to handle two cheeses, we can add some extra variables:

```
var cheese1X = getRandom(0, width);
var cheese1Y = getRandom(0, height);
var cheese2X = getRandom(0, width);
var cheese2Y = getRandom(0, height);
```

We have made two new variables to store the position of a second cheese. We could then test for the two cheese locations when calculating the distance to the nearest cheese:

```
function getCheeseDistance(x, y) {
  let d1x = x - cheese1X;
  let d1y = y - cheese1Y;
  let distance1 = Math.round(Math.sqrt((d1x * d1x) + (d1y * d1y)));

  let d2x = x - cheese2X;
  let d2y = y - cheese2Y;
  let distance2 = Math.round(Math.sqrt((d2x * d2x) + (d2y * d2y)));

  let distance;

  if(distance1 < distance2){
    distance = distance1;
  }
  else {
    distance = distance2;
  }

  return distance;
}
```

This version of the `getCheeseDistance` gets the distance to each of the two cheeses and then returns the smallest value. The only other thing that is required is a cheese counter value to keep track of how many cheeses have been found:

```
let gameCheeseCounter = 0;
```

This counter is increased when a cheese is found (see **Figure 5-5**). The game ends when it reaches two:

```
if (button.className == "cheese") {
  gameCheeseCounter = gameCheeseCounter + 1;
  if (gameCheeseCounter == 2) {
    showCounter();
    fillGrid(allButtons);
  }
}
else {
  gameMoveCounter++;
  showCounter();
}
```

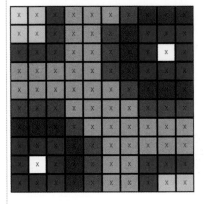

Figure 5-5 Two cheeses

This version of the game seems to work fine. You can find it in the **Ch05-04_Broken_ Cheese_Finder_2_Cheeses** example folders. However, the name might not inspire confidence. Every now and then, something bad will happen. Let's investigate.

MAKE SOMETHING HAPPEN 21

Scan the QR code or visit *https://www.youtube.com/watch?v=rfmyGJReBxk* for a video walk-through of this Make Something Happen.

Find the bug

There is definitely a bug in the two-cheese version of the game, and perhaps you've already spotted it. For the rest of us, I've made a version that always goes wrong. Let's take a look at it. Start your browser and open the `index.html` file in the **Ch05-05_Really_Broken_Cheese_Finder_2_Cheeses** example folder. If you play this game to completion, you'll notice the problem.

You can see below that every square has been clicked, but only one cheese is on the board.

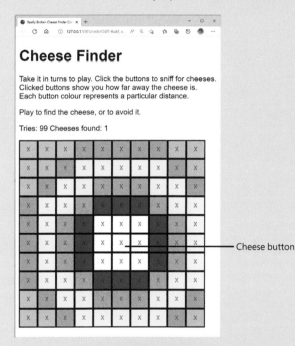

— Cheese button

You can investigate what is going on by using the debugger in the Developer Tools. Perform the following steps:

1. Open the browser's **Developer Tools**.

2. Select the **Sources** tab.

3. Open the `index.html` file.

4. Find the `getCheeseDistance` function and put a breakpoint on the function's first statement.

5. Reload the page to start a new game.

6. Click any button in the grid.

As shown below, the program has reached the first statement of the `getCheeseDistance` function. If you look closely, you will see that I clicked the button located at x=7 and y=4.

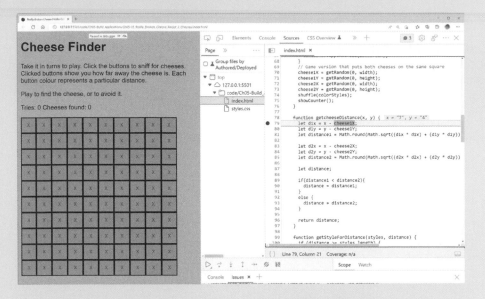

Let's take a look at some of the other values in this code by hovering the mouse pointer over the code variables. Below, you can see the value of cheese1X is 5. In fact, if you look at all the cheese locations— cheese1X, cheese1Y, cheese2X, and cheese2Y—you will find they are all 5.

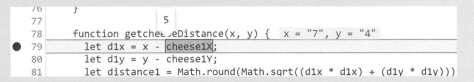

This makes the random number-generating process look very suspect. You can find that code in the source in line 38:

```
38      function getRandom(min, max) {
39          var range = max - min;
40          var result = Math.floor(Math.random() * (range)) + min;
41          return 5;
42      }
```

— Random number generator

The getRandom function calculates a random result and returns a fixed value of 5. This means all the position values for the cheese are 5. In other words, both cheeses are at the same location. This will cause the program to break because there is no second cheese; there is only one. In real life, the game will put both pieces of cheese on the same square every now and then. When this happens, finishing the game will be impossible.

This code simulates the situation where both cheeses are placed in the same place on the grid, something that will happen sometimes. We've found out what is wrong—now we need to fix it.

Testing for duplicated locations

We have seen that our two-cheese version of the Cheese Finder game has the worst kind of bug—one that only appears sometimes. There is a 1-in-100 chance the second cheese will be placed in the same square as the first cheese. If this happens the game becomes impossible to finish. The fix is to ensure the second cheese is not on the same square as the first. The code below shows how we do this:

```
cheese1X = getRandom(0, width);
cheese1Y = getRandom(0, height);
do {
   cheese2X = getRandom(0, width);
   cheese2Y = getRandom(0, height);
} while (cheese1X == cheese2X && cheese1Y == cheese2Y);
```

The position of the second cheese is repeatedly chosen until both values are different from the first cheese. You can find this version of the game in the **Ch05-06_Working_Cheese_Finder_2_Cheeses** folder.

Even more cheese

The problem with giving people extra cheese is that they come back asking for even more. The two-cheese version of the game has become so popular that people now want even more cheese—at least three cheeses, and probably even more. This is the point that the cheese placement code starts to betray its simple origins. To make three cheeses work, we must add quite a few more statements to select cheese positions, check for clashes, and test for distance. Code to support 10 cheeses doesn't bear thinking about. At this point, we need to stop and think about how the program works.

> **PROGRAMMER'S POINT**
>
> ## Avoid kludges
>
> Our two-cheese solution works but doesn't scale very well when adding more cheese. Worse still, the solution performance decreases dramatically as the number of cheeses increases. The code repeatedly generates possible cheese locations until it finds an unused one. More cheeses mean more chances for the program to pick a location that has been used. It is also impossible to predict exactly how long the program will take to place the cheese. If the program was spectacularly unlucky, it could be stuck trying locations for a very long time. One of the aims of JavaScript and node is to make a system that can handle requests as quickly as possible. The last thing we want is a process that might take a while to complete and could even get stuck.

If you think about it, the original upgrade to add the second cheese is a bit of "kludge." A kludge is a solution that works despite how it is put together. It will be hard to understand, maintain, and expand. Handling additional cheeses by duplicating the code for one cheese turns out to be a kludge. We made it work for one extra cheese, but using same approach for even more cheeses would make the code extremely complex.

It is important to recognize that a change in application requirements might mean completely changing how your solution works. This is one of those situations. We should have recognized two things as soon as we were asked to make a two-cheese version:

- Our one-cheese solution was a bad place to start if we needed to handle more than one cheese.

- The demand for extra cheese would not stop at two cheeses. We have to make a solution that can handle a very large number.

Make maximum cheese

Fortunately, it's not too complicated to create a version of the game that can support a very large number of cheeses—up to the size of the grid. We can use the same technique we used to create a list of randomized style names to be mapped to the distances for the random-colors version of the game. We make a list of all the buttons, shuffle the list, and then work through the elements in the list. Each time the list is shuffled, the element at index 0 will be different, as will the index 1 and so on.

The game already has an array containing all the buttons in the grid. When the game starts, it creates an array called allButtons containing references to all the buttons in the grid. The fillGrid function works through this array to set the color style for all the buttons in the grid. See "Add a game ending," earlier in this chapter if you have questions.

The statement below shuffles the allButtons array to get a list of buttons in random order. We could say that allButtons[0] holds the first cheese in the game, allButtons[2] the second, and so on. The function that checks for the nearest cheese can work through this array for the number of cheeses the game contains.

```
shuffle(allButtons);
```

The getDistToNearestCheese function is given an x and y value and returns the distance to the cheese nearest to that location. It works through the allButtons array to get cheese locations, gets the distance of each cheese, and returns the smallest one.

```
function getDistToNearestCheese(x, y) {
  let result;
  for (let cheeseNo = 0; cheeseNo < gameNoOfCheeses; cheeseNo = cheeseNo + 1) {
    let cheeseButton = allButtons[cheeseNo];                    Get this cheese button
    let distance = getDistance(cheeseButton, x, y);            Get the distance to this cheese
    if (result == undefined) {                                 Has result been set yet?
      result = distance;                                       Set it to the first value
    }
    if (distance < result) {                                   Is the distance less than result?
      result = distance;                                       Set result to distance
    }
  }
  return result;                                               Return the result
}
```

The variable `gameNoOfCheeses` is set with the number of cheeses being used in the game. See **Figure 5-6**.

Four Cheese buttons

Figure 5-6 Four cheeses

You can find this version of the game in the **Ch05-07_Infinite_Cheese_Finder** folder in this chapter's example code. The number of cheeses in the game is set in the range 2,5 by the following statement, which runs when the game starts. (Remember that the upper limit supplied to the `getRandom` function is *exclusive*, which means that the call of `getRandom` below will never return the value 6.)

```
gameNoOfCheeses = getRandom(2,6);
```

This version of Cheese Finder creates a good single-player experience, running entirely inside the browser. But now, we are going to create a shared version.

Create a shared game

We have spent quite a lot of time creating a fun little cheese-finding game. Then someone suggests that it might be fun to make a version that lots of people could play at the same time. Perhaps a room full of cheese finders could compete to discover who could find a hidden cheese the fastest. Rather than each game placing the cheese randomly at the start, everyone would start with the same cheese positions, and it would be a race against time to find them all first.

This would be easy enough to do, but there is a snag. As we have seen when using the browser's debugger in the Developer Tools, someone can look at the code behind a web page and extract information from it. A cunning player could win the big prize simply by pressing F12 to get the cheese position variable values from the code in the debugger.

This is a problem faced by any browser-based application that wants to keep secrets. We could try to hide how our browser code works using *obfuscation*, which renames all the variables in a program and generally makes the text hard to understand. However, no matter how clever the obfuscation is, the cheese position is still held in the browser, making it vulnerable to attack.

We can keep the cheese position completely secret by storing it on the server hosting the web page containing the page. In our game, the user clicks a button, the game looks up the style for that button (based on the button's distance from the nearest cheese), and then sets that style on the page. It then checks to see if the style indicates that a cheese has been found and updates the game state accordingly. With the current game version, this lookup process takes place in the browser.

For a shared game, we will make the browser ask the server for a particular square's style. In Chapter 4, in the "Make a web server" section, we saw how a JavaScript program running under `node` could respond to web queries and serve messages and files. Now, we will discover how a program running in a browser can ask questions of a server and update its display accordingly.

Design a protocol for a conversation

When our server-based Cheese Finder game runs, the browser and server exchange messages. We first need to decide the form and meaning of the messages to be exchanged. Then we can work on how the programs will send and receive them. This is an important part of application design. In a way, we are creating our own language for a conversation. This is sometimes called a *protocol*. Let's describe the protocol in general terms and then look at how we would implement this:

1. The player navigates to the website to play "Cheese Finder."

2. The browser loads the web page from the server and starts running a JavaScript program on the web page.

3. The program running in the browser asks the server for some details about the game. It needs to know the grid's width and height and the number of cheeses being searched for.

4. The browser builds the web page containing the grid and displays the count of how many cheeses are left to be found and the number of turns taken.

5. The player clicks a button on the grid. The browser sends the location of the clicked button to the server. The server responds with that location's style. The browser updates the game's state on the display and then waits for the next button click.

6. This continues until the game detects that the player has found the last cheese.

It is important to check this protocol carefully. A good way to test it is for one person to be the browser and another the server. Then work through playing a game and look at the information that is sent back and forth.

Now we create the code that implements the protocol between the browser and the server. **Figure 5-7** shows what we are going to make. It shows the game being played in the browser and the server providing the cheese management. The code running in the browser asks the server for the game details when it starts. It uses the details to draw the grid for the game. Then, each time the user clicks one of the buttons in the grid, the browser will send a message asking for that button's style. The server responds with a string containing this style. The browser then updates the game.

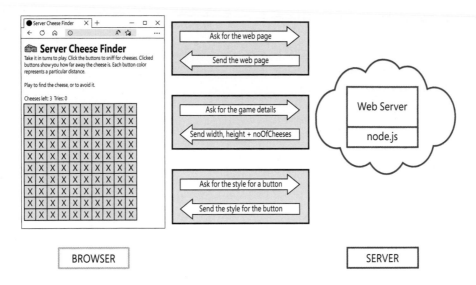

Figure 5.7 Browser and server messages

The game will be implemented by two JavaScript programs. One runs on the browser and provides the game user interface; the other runs on the server and manages the cheese position. We will be running both the server and the browser on our computer. Later, we can put the server program on the cloud so anyone can try it.

> **IMPORTANT** When looking at code samples in this text, it is useful to remember where the code will run. In the remainder of this chapter, samples of code running in the browser will have a light-yellow border, whereas code samples running on the server will have a light-blue border.

Create endpoints

An endpoint is a web address a browser uses to get something. We need to create three endpoints for the Cheese Finder server. The first endpoint will return the pages and files that make up the Cheese Finder website content. The second endpoint will return the game details when the browser asks for them. The third will return the style of a particular button on the grid when the player clicks that button.

The code that responds to these requests will run on the server. During development, we will host the server on our local machine. Once the game works, we can host the server in the cloud and make the game available to anyone on the Internet. I've obtained the domain name `cheesefinder.xyz` for the finished implementation of the game. If you want to play the final version, you can visit that site and have a go.

The JavaScript below runs in the browser and sets the values `hostAddress`, `start-Url`, and `getStyleUrl`, which the browser code will use as the endpoints. We will run a `node.js` server behind port 8080 on our machine, which will respond to these requests. The browser will use these endpoints to connect to the server. It is important that the server and browser agree on the names of these endpoints. Otherwise, the application will not work. When I move the server to the cloud, I will change the string `http://localhost:8080` string to `https://cheesefinder.xyz`.

```javascript
let hostAddress = "http://localhost:8080/";
let startUrl = hostAddress + "getstart.json";
let getStyleUrl = hostAddress + "getstyle.json";
```

Start the game

If a user wants to play Cheese Finder, they will start by opening the website. The server will send back a page of HTML for the browser to display. Then the browser will build the Document Object Model (DOM) and run the JavaScript program in the HTML file.

Following is the HTML file for the web page sent from the server to the browser. The page contains two paragraph elements, one with the id `counterPar` that is used to display the counters and another with the id `buttonPar` that will hold all the grid's buttons.

```html
<!DOCTYPE html>
<html>

<head>
  <title>Server Cheese Finder</title>
  <link rel="shortcut icon" type="image/x-icon" href="favicon.ico">
  <link rel="stylesheet" href="styles.css">
</head>
<h1>&#129472; Server Cheese Finder</h1>

<body>

  <p>Take it in turns to play. Click the buttons to sniff for cheeses.
    Clicked buttons show you how far away the cheese is.
    Each button colour represents a particular distance.</p>
  <p>Play to find the cheese, or to avoid it.</p>
  <p id="counterPar"></p>    ────────────────────────  Counter paragraph
  <p id="buttonPar"> </p>    ────────────────────────  Button grid paragraph
```

```
<script type="module">
  import { doPlayGame } from "./client.mjs";          ──────── Import the game start function
  doPlayGame();                                       ──────── Call the game start function

</script>
</body>

</html>
```

There are only two JavaScript statements in the HTML file. The first statement imports the function doPlayGame from the client.mjs library, and the second statement calls it. The doPlayGame function is shown below. It doesn't do much. It sets the moveCounter and the cheesesFound variables to 0 and then calls another function, getFromServer. This function will get the game details from the server and use them to set up the game grid. The first argument sent into the getFromServer function is startUrl, the endpoint address of the server's getstart service. The second argument references the setupGame function, which will set up the game.

```
function doPlayGame() {
  moveCounter = 0;
  cheesesFound = 0;                                   ──────── Clear the game counters
  getFromServer(startUrl, setupGame);                 ──────── Start the game
}
```

If we were organizing a party, I might ask, "Could you go to the store to pick up the balloons and then put them up in the hall?" My request gives you a location to fetch something from (the store) and something to do with what was fetched (put the balloons up in the hall). If you look at the call of getFromServer in doPlayGame above, you will see a location to get something from (startUrl) and a function to work on what was fetched (setupGame). Let's have a look at how the getFromServer function works.

```
function getFromServer(url, handler) {
  fetch(url).then(response => {                       ──────── Start the fetch
    response.text().then(result => {                  ──── The then part runs when the fetch completes
      handler(result);                                ──── Call the handler to deal with the message that was fetched
    }).catch(error => alert("Bad text: " + error));   ──────── Catch errors in the handler
  }).catch(error => alert("Bad fetch: " + error));    ──────── Catch errors in the fetch
}
```

The getFromServer function uses a JavaScript function called fetch that fetches a response from a server. The fetch function is given the URL specifying the server address. Fetching something can take a while, and we don't want our game to be held up waiting for the response to come back from the server. To address this, the `fetch` function returns a JavaScript `promise` object representing the fetch operation being performed. (We will learn about promises and asynchronous code in Chapter 6.) A `promise` object contains a method called `then`, which can be used to specify a function to be called when the promise is fulfilled (when the information has been fetched from the server). In the case of the preceding code, an anonymous arrow function passes the call onto the handler function supplied as a parameter to `getFromServer`.

If you are having difficultly understanding what this code does, recall the problem it is solving. The `getFromServer` function lets a program ask for some data from the web (in an address specified by the `url` parameter) and specify the function that will deal with the data when it arrives (in a function specified by the `handler` parameter). It is a very useful little function; the game uses it to fetch the settings at the start of a game and get the style settings for particular game squares. At this point in the application, we are using the `getFromServer` function to call `setupGame` when the server receives a response. Let's take a look at that next.

```
function setupGame(gameDetailsJSON) {

  let gameDetails = JSON.parse(gameDetailsJSON);          Get the game details from
                                                                     the response

  noOfCheeses = gameDetails.noOfCheeses;                 Save the number of cheeses
                                                                    from the details

  let container = document.getElementById("buttonPar");

  for (let y = 0; y < gameDetails.height; y++) {           Create the button grid
    for (let x = 0; x < gameDetails.width; x++) {
      let newButton = document.createElement("button");
      newButton.className = "empty";
      newButton.setAttribute("x", x);
      newButton.setAttribute("y",y);
      newButton.addEventListener(«click», buttonClickedHandler);
      newButton.textContent ="X";
      container.appendChild(newButton);
      allButtons.push( newButton);
    }
    let lineBreak = document.createElement("br");
    container.appendChild(lineBreak);
  }
  showCounters();
}
```

You've seen most of this code before in Chapter 4, in the "Place the buttons" section, where we created the first Cheese Finder game. The interesting part of this code is right at the very top, where the response from the server is decoded to get the width, height, and number of cheeses values. This is all done with a single line of JavaScript, using the magic of JavaScript Object Notation or JSON. Let's briefly digress to see how that works.

Transfer data with JSON

The program in the browser uses the `startUrl` endpoint to ask the server, "Can I have the screen width and height and number of cheeses, please?" It would be useful if we could encode and decode these values without doing much work. Well, it turns out that there is—JavaScript Object Notation (JSON). JSON lets us convert an object into a string of text. Let's explore it.

🚀 **MAKE SOMETHING HAPPEN 22**

Scan the QR code or visit *https://www.youtube.com/watch?v=697mRY3DjM0* for a video walkthrough of this Make Something Happen.

Investigate JSON

JSON is a tremendously powerful part of JavaScript. Start your browser and open the `index.html` file in the **Ch05-08_JSON_Investigation** example folder. Open the **Developer Tools** and click **Console**.

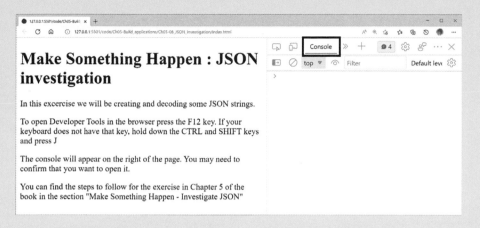

JSON works with JavaScript objects. We know we can create a JavaScript object anywhere in the code. (It is one of the things we love about the language). Let's make a tiny object that answers the browser's first question—the width and height of the grid and the number of cheeses. Type in the following statement and press **Enter**:

```
let answer = { width:10,height:10,cheeses:3};
```

This statement creates an answer variable, which refers to an object containing the width, height, and cheeses properties. You can ask the console to show you this value. Type in the following statement and press **Enter**:

```
answer
```

The console will now show the object that answer refers to:

```
> let answer = { width:10,height:10,cheeses:3}
< undefined
> answer
<  ▶ {width: 10, height: 10, cheeses: 3}
>
```

You can see that the properties are inside the object. This display of the object is very similar to the JSON code representing the object contents. You can use the wonderfully named stringify function to turn an object into a JSON string. Type the following statement and press **Enter**:

```
let jsonString = JSON.stringify(answer)
```

The `stringify` method accepts an object reference and then returns the JSON string describing the object contents. The preceding statement creates a variable called `json-String`, referring to a string containing the JSON representation of your object. Now, take a look at this string. Type the following statement and press **Enter**:

```
jsonString
```

The console will now show the JSON string describing the object:

```
> let jsonString = JSON.stringify(answer)
< undefined
> jsonString
< '{"width":10,"height":10,"cheeses":3}'
> |
```

You can see that the JSON-encoded string looks almost identical to how you would declare an object in JavaScript program code. The only difference is that the property names are enclosed in double-quotation characters (""). You can convert this string back into an object by using the JSON `parse` function. Type the following statement and press **Enter**:

```
JSON.parse(jsonString)
```

The console will perform the parse and show the object created by the `parse` function.

```
> JSON.parse(jsonString)
<  ▶ {width: 10, height: 10, cheeses: 3}
```

The result is an object holding the exact values you need. The JavaScript code in the browser can read the width, height, and cheeses properties from the object and use them to set up the page.

CODE ANALYSIS

JSON

JSON is wonderful, but you still might have questions about it.

Question: What kinds of values can I save in a JSON string?

   Answer: You can write numbers, strings, Boolean values (true or false), and objects.

Question: Can I save an array of items in JSON?

Answer: Yes, you can. An array of the required size is created when the JSON is parsed.

Question: Is there a limit to the length of a string that can be produced when you encode an object with JSON?

Answer: A JavaScript string can be very long, certainly longer than the size of the hard disk in your computer. This means you could create JSON strings representing large amounts of data. However, these might take a while to be transferred between devices via a network. If you find yourself trying to store very large amounts of data in JavaScript objects, you should look at databases, which are covered in Chapter 10.

Question: What happens if a program tries to parse a string that does not contain valid JSON?

Answer: The `parse` function will stop the program and throw an exception if it is given invalid JSON to decode. We will discuss exceptions in Chapter 10.

Question: Is JSON only used by JavaScript?

Answer: No. JSON has become ubiquitous. Every modern development platform supports JSON. It is used throughout modern computing to send structured data from one place to another.

The game server

We've spent a lot of time on how the browser works. Now let's look at what the server is doing. The server serves the files making up the website, including index.html, code libraries, and stylesheets. We created a very basic server in Chapter 4 in the section "Make a Web Server," and we'll use that server here to serve the game website. Then, we will add the code to handle the `getstart` and `getstyle` endpoints. We'll do this in the server's `handlePageRequest` function.

```
function handlePageRequest(request, response) {

    let filePath = basePath + request.url;

    if (fs.existsSync(filePath)) {            Is there a file with this path?
        // If it is a file - return it           Open the file and send it
    }                                                            back
    else {
        // If it is not a file it might be a command
        console.log("Might have a request");
```

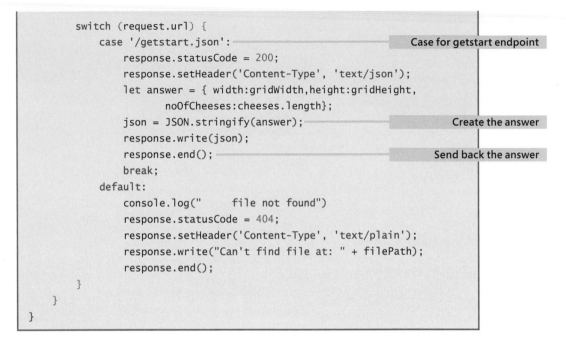

```
switch (request.url) {
    case '/getstart.json':                           Case for getstart endpoint
        response.statusCode = 200;
        response.setHeader('Content-Type', 'text/json');
        let answer = { width:gridWidth,height:gridHeight,
            noOfCheeses:cheeses.length};
        json = JSON.stringify(answer);                Create the answer
        response.write(json);
        response.end();                               Send back the answer
        break;
    default:
        console.log("    file not found")
        response.statusCode = 404;
        response.setHeader('Content-Type', 'text/plain');
        response.write("Can't find file at: " + filePath);
        response.end();
    }
  }
}
```

The first part of the handlePageRequest function serves out files on the server. You can find an explanation of this code at the end of Chapter 4 in the section "Serving out files." If the function can't find a file matching the request, it uses a switch construction to check whether the request is for the endpoint getstart.json. The code handling this endpoint assembles the required JSON and sends it back.

MAKE SOMETHING HAPPEN 23

Scan the QR code or visit *https://www.youtube.com/watch?v=Brm0jRnr7Uk* for a video walk-through of this Make Something Happen.

Browser and server

This might be a good time to use your debugging skills to discover how the browser and server work together. You've done this kind of thing before in Make Something Happen 18, "Use the debugging tools to investigate the server," in Chapter 4. It's a bit complicated but totally worth it.

Start Visual Studio Code, open the examples for this chapter and find the **Ch05-09_Browser_and_Server** example folder. You'll run both the server and the browser simultaneously. You'll put breakpoints in the code to watch the two programs interact.

Open the file `server.mjs` file, which contains the code implementing the game server. Now click the left of line 60 to insert a breakpoint. This breakpoint will be hit when the browser uses the `getstart.json` endpoint.

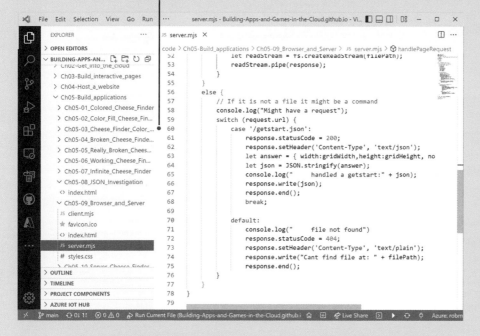

Now press the **Run And Debug** button (the triangle with the little bug on it in the left column of buttons) to open the debug window and start the program.

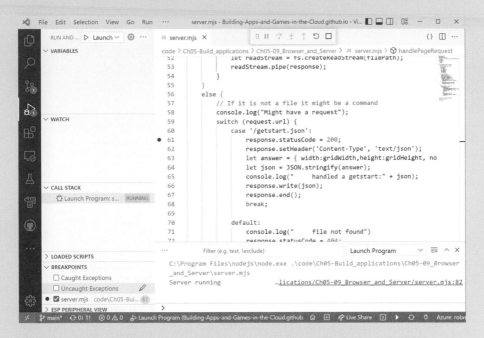

The program is now hosting a web server at *http://localhost: 8080/.* Open the browser and load the game website into it. Start the browser and enter the *http://localhost:8080/index.html* address to open the game's index page. Don't forget to include *index.html* at the end of the address.

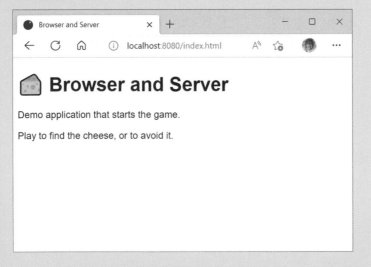

You will notice that the game board has not appeared in the browser. This is because the game made a request to the `getstart` endpoint, but the server hit the breakpoint before it could send anything back. Let's take a look at Visual Studio Code window.

Run

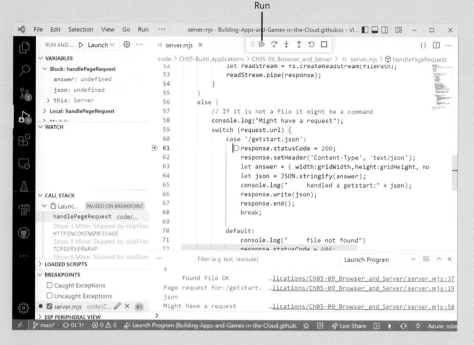

You can step through the code after the breakpoint, but you had better be quick before the fetch request from the browser times out. If you click the blue **Run** button (the right-pointing arrow) in the debug controls (or press F5), the server will continue, and you should see the game board appear in the browser. You can use the browser's debugger (in **Developer Tools**) to watch the code in the browser pick up the messages from the server and use them to build the pages. This version of the game doesn't respond to button presses in the grid. We will be doing that in the next section.

Play the game

We've seen the `getstart` endpoint deliver game information to the browser. Now, we need to create the `getstyle` endpoint as well. The browser code will use this to get the style for a button clicked in the grid. In the original game, this task was performed by code running in the browser. Now, the distance calculation and style selection take place on the server. The good news is that because both the browser and server are running JavaScript, we can take these parts of the solution out of the browser code and drop them into the server code. The bad news is that the browser needs to send the button's location to the server so the server can work out which style string to return.

The browser program can use the HTTP query mechanism to pass the x and y values to the server. Let's look at the code that does this.

```
function setButtonStyle(button) {
  let x = button.getAttribute("x");
  let y = button.getAttribute("y");                    Get the x and y position of the button
  let checkUrl = getStyleUrl + "?x=" + x + "&y=" + y;              Assemble the query
  getFromServer(checkUrl, result => {              Get the result from the endpoint
    button.className = result
    if (button.className == "cheese") {              If we got cheese – check for game end
      cheesesFound++;
      if (cheesesFound == noOfCheeses) {
        fillGrid(allButtons);              Fill the grid if the game has ended
      }
    }
  });
}
```

The setButtonStyle runs in the browser when the player clicks a button in the grid. In the browser-based versions of the game, this function calculated the distance of the button from the cheese and used that distance to set the button's style. In the server-based version, the browser creates a query and sends the query to the checkUrl endpoint in the server. The query part of the endpoint starts with a ? (query) character and is followed by name-value pairs separated by & characters. Below, you can see the endpoint address with query information added at the end. This query requests the style name for the button at location (2,0):

```
http://localhost:8080/getstyle.json?x=2&y=0
```

The address string above is used by the browser in a request to the server. When the server receives this address, it must extract the values of x and y and work out the style for that location. We could write our own code to extract the values of x and y, but JavaScript provides a url library that will do all the work for us. The code below uses the parse function from the url library to create a parse object referred to by parsedUrl. The parse call has two arguments. The first is the url string being parsed. The second argument specifies whether query elements in the url should be parsed. We want them to be parsed (that's why we are doing this), so we set this to true. Now code running on the server can extract the local path and the queries.

```
let parsedUrl = url.parse(request.url, true);              Make a url object from the
                                                                       request
```

Always use the helper libraries

Some programmers like making their own solutions to problems. They quite enjoy solving things as a form of mental challenge. Splitting a URL into its various components is an example of a simple-looking task that might be more complicated than you think. This is particularly true if you consider that nasty people might try to make an endpoint URL that will confuse your application and make it misbehave, so you should always look for a helper library (preferably one that is part of JavaScript) rather than making your own solutions.

The code below is part of the `switch` construction on the server, which handles requests to the different endpoints. This code runs when the browser makes a request to the `getstyle.json` endpoint. It uses the `parsedUrl` value that has just been created to extract the x and y coordinates of the location for which the style string is to be returned. It then gets the style for that location, builds an object containing the style, and returns it as a JSON-encoded string.

```
case '/getstyle.json':
    let x = Number(parsedUrl.query.x);
    let y = Number(parsedUrl.query.y);          ← Get the button x and y
    response.statusCode = 200;
    response.setHeader('Content-Type', 'text/json');
    console.log("Got: (" + x + "," + y + ")");
    let styleText = getStyle(x,y);              ← Get the style of this button
    let styleObject = {style:styleText};        ← Make an object that contains the style value
    let styleJSON = JSON.stringify(styleObject);  ← Convert the object to a JSON string
    response.write(styleJSON);                  ← Send the string to the browser
    response.end();
    break;
```

CODE ANALYSIS

The getstyle.json handler

The following code runs on the server to handle the `getstyle.json` endpoint. You might have some questions about it.

Question: When does this code run?

> **Answer:** When a player clicks one of the buttons in the grid, the browser needs to know the button's style. It gets the button's x and y location, assembles a web request, and sends it to the server. The web request is sent to the address `getstyle.json`. The server recognizes this address, gets the button's style, and sends it back to the browser as a JSON-encoded string.

Question: How does this code get the x and y values for the button location?

Answer: Earlier, we created a `parsedUrl` object containing the web request with the `query` property sent to the server. The `query` property refers to an object containing properties for all the elements in the query. Below, you can see the statement that extracts the x value from this property. There is a similar statement for the y property.

```
let x = Number(parsedUrl.query.x);
```

Question: How does the server determine the style for a grid location?

Answer: The style for a grid location is determined by its distance from the cheese. The `getStyle` function is given the button's x and y location and calls the `getDistanceToNearestCheese` function to get the distance to the cheese. It then looks up the required style in the `colorStyles` array. This is the same code we used in the browser version of the game.

```
function getStyle(x, y) {

    let distance = getDistToNearestCheese(x, y);

    if (distance == 0) {
        return "cheese";
    }

    if (distance >= colorStyles.length) {
        distance = colorStyles.length - 1;
    }
    return colorStyles[distance];
}
```

In browser versions of the game, the cheese locations were determined randomly. For a shared version of the game, all the players must get the same cheese locations. Currently, the game contains an array of cheese location objects we can use for testing. A future version of the game will create random cheese locations at regular intervals, perhaps hourly.

```
const cheeses = [
    { x: 0, y: 0 },
    { x: 1, y: 1 },
    { x: 2, y: 2 }
];
```

Question: What happens if a request doesn't contain query x and y values?

Answer: The endpoint below doesn't contain query values for x and y. It just has a value for `wally`. The game server would try to decode it, but if a JavaScript program tries to access an object property of an object that is not present, the result is the `undefined` value. If the x and y values were left off the query, the handler would feed the undefined values into the `getStyle` call. This would end up sending an empty JSON object back to the browser, resulting in the button style being set to `undefined`. There is no `undefined` style in the stylesheet, so the button will not have the correct style.

```
http://localhost:8080/getstyle.json?wally=99
```

In this case, it looks like nothing bad has happened to the game, but this has been more by luck than judgment. A battle-hardened version of the server would need to check for the query values and then send back an "error" style to indicate that the grid location could not be determined. The same thing should happen if the browser asks for the style for a grid location that is not present, such as x=99 and y=100.

MAKE SOMETHING HAPPEN 24

Scan the QR code or visit *https://www.youtube.com/watch?v=YD128hPjAxQ* for a video walk-through of this Make Something Happen.

Play Server Cheese Finder

You can find the code for the browser and server in the **Ch05-10_Server_Cheese_Finder** example folder. The process of starting and debugging the code is exactly the same as it was in the previous Make Something Happen sidebar. Start the game running and play it through. Below, you can see the completed game. Note that the cheeses are always in the same places. You can move them to other squares by editing the code in `server.mjs`. In the next chapter, you will add the code to hide the cheese in different locations each time it is run.

What you have learned

This has been another busy chapter. We've covered a lot of ground. Here is a recap, plus some points to ponder:

- Until now, we have used arrays to store data in indexed locations. We can also use an array as a lookup table. The index can specify a matching value stored at that position in the array.

- Arrays in JavaScript are indexed from zero. An array is never created with a particular size. Instead, an array is created from constant data, or values are automatically added to the array when values are placed in elements.

- Writing to an indexed value in an array will cause an array to expand to that size automatically. In other words, if you store a value with an index value of 10 in an array that only contains 4 values, JavaScript will automatically add the extra values (set to the value undefined) to fill in the gap.

- You can use the function push on an array instance to add an element to the end of an array.

- An array exposes a length property providing the number of elements in the array.

- It is not possible to create multidimensional arrays in JavaScript, but an array can contain elements that are themselves arrays.

- Arrays are passed into JavaScript functions as references to the array object.

- A program running entirely in the browser is not secure because a user can look at the code and variables in the program. The Developer Tools debugger can even be used to step through the code and view the contents of variables.

- We create secure applications by running part of the application on a server. Code running in the browser sends web requests to the server, which responds to the requests. The browser has no access to the code on the server. It just asks questions and gets responses.

- When designing an application that runs on the browser and the server, it is important to work through the application behaviors and identify the requests to be made by the browser and the content of the replies.

- An endpoint is a URL (uniform resource locator) that can be used by a program to request that the server behind the URL perform an action.

- JavaScript provides a fetch function that sends a request to a web server and returns the response to the program.

- The JavaScript fetch function uses the JavaScript promise mechanism to ensure that a slow fetch operation will not pause a program. A fetch operation can be made to run a callback function when the fetch has been completed.

- JavaScript Object Notation (JSON) can be used to transfer the data in a JavaScript object. A JSON-encoded object is a string of text. The JSON.stringify function will act on an object to encode the object contents into a string. When an object is encoded, numbers and text values are stored directly. If the object being encoded contains a reference to another object (for example, a customer object contains a reference to an address object for that customer), the contained object is added to the encoded string. The JSON-encoded string can contain arrays.

- The JSON.parse function will decode an object description string and build an object containing the values described in the string. The parse function will throw an exception if the string does not contain valid JSON.

- We can watch a browser/server-based application run by using the debug tools in the server and browser. The server will serve the application on the localhost address. When the server code is transferred into the cloud, the HTTP address of the server will be changed to the cloud address.

- A URL can contain query information consisting of name-value pairs that can be picked up by the server and used to control the behavior of code running on the server.

- If the server receives invalid query information (perhaps a value in the query is missing or out of range), this may lead to the server returning an invalid response (or perhaps no response at all). The implantation of a command endpoint needs to deal with invalid queries correctly.

To reinforce your understanding of this chapter, you might want to consider the following "profound questions."

Question: How can you determine the type of elements in an array?

Answer: Each element in an array will have a type, but an array itself does not have a type. It is just a collection of items.

Question: How do you clear an array?

Answer: There is no way to clear an array. However, in JavaScript, you can delete an object by assigning its reference to another object. The first statement below creates a variable called x, which refers to an array containing four elements. Then x is made to refer to a three-element array. At this point, the initial array is inaccessible (there are no references to it), so it can be considered to have been deleted. A process called the "garbage collector" runs alongside an application and recovers the memory space used by such inaccessible objects.

```
let x = [1, 2, 3, 4];     // create an array
x = [0, 1, 2];            // set x to refer to a different array
```

Question: How can I make the server tell the browser that something has happened?

Answer: An HTTP interaction starts when the browser sends a request to the server. But what if we want the server to send a message to the browser? One way to do this is by using web sockets. We use them in Chapter 12 to create a web page that reponds to a message from the server. Take a look at the "Use WebSockets to send values from a server" section in Chapter 12.

Question: What is the difference between an endpoint and a web page URL?

Answer: From a functional point of view, there is nothing different about the two, although an endpoint request might have the language extension `json` rather than the `html` extension of a URL. It is up to the server to examine the incoming address and decide what to send back in response.

Question: Can you use a JSON message to send binary information?

Answer: If you want to send binary information (perhaps a graphic or sound), you must encode the binary information as text before sending it.

Question: Can you use a JSON message to send a reference?

Answer: No. When stringifying an object, JSON will always follow each reference and insert the JSON text that describes that object. Note that this means that if an object being stringified contains three references to the same object, the JSON string will contain three copies of the object's contents.

Question: Can you use a JSON message to send a method contained in an object?

Answer: No. If the object being stringified contains methods, they will be ignored.

6

Create a shared experience

What you will learn

Humans enjoy sharing things. The feeling of being part of a crowd at a football match or watching the same TV show together is a great thing. The Internet can host shared experiences, from streamed video gameplay to puzzles we can all work on at the same time. In this chapter, we will create a version of the Cheese Finder game that is a shared experience. All game players will solve the same grid at any given time. To do this, we will discover how to synchronize the server and browser, use pseudo-random numbers to generate "repeatable" random behavior, and spend some time optimizing our code for the cloud. And finally, we will place our shared Cheese Finder in the cloud where anyone can play it.

Sharing gameplay

The first versions of Cheese Finder ran inside the browser on the player's computer. Every player's experience differed because the distance colors and cheese positions differed each time the game ran. These games used JavaScript's `Math.random()` function to get the random numbers used to position the cheese and select the distance colors. This made for good gameplay for individuals, but running the game engine on a server allows us to create shared experiences where everybody gets to play the same game simultaneously. Let's see how we would go about doing this.

Figure 6-1 shows a completed game of Cheese Finder. You can play this game by running the code in this chapter's **Ch06-01_Fixed_Cheese_Finder** sample code folder. This version provides a shared experience (everybody plays the game with the cheese in the same fixed positions and distance colors), but it is not a very good one because the experience is the same every time the game is played.

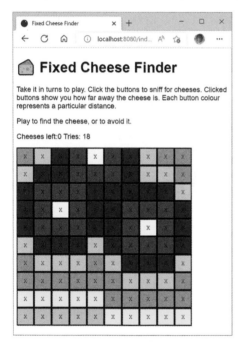

Figure 6-1   Fixed cheese positions

The following code shows why you always get the same experience when you play this version of the game. The `gameSetup` variable is an object literal that contains properties that define the game setup. We've been using object literals for a while; you first saw them in Chapter 1 in the "Returning an object from a function call" section.

There, we learned how to make an object that contained a set of values that could be returned as one object from a function call. In this code, we will create a literal object containing the initial setting values for the random number generator.

```
const gameSetup = {

    colorStyles: ["white", "magenta", "red", "lightGreen", "orange",
                  "yellow", "yellowGreen", "cyan", "lightBlue", "blue",
                  "purple", "darkGray"],
    cheeses: [
        { x: 4, y: 0 },
        { x: 2, y: 3 },
        { x: 7, y: 4 }
    ]
}
```

If you look at **Figure 6-1**, you will see that the locations in the code correspond to what the player gets when they play the game. Remember that the grid's origin (0,0) is the top left-hand corner of the grid. The gameSetup variable refers to an object containing two properties. The colorStyles property is an array that contains a particular sequence of style names, and the cheeses property is an array holding three specific cheese locations. When the game runs, these are used to place the cheeses and pick the distance colors. This means that the game is always the same. The first time you play it with your friends, you might find it fun to see who can find the cheeses the fastest. But the second time around is much less challenging because the cheeses are in the same locations.

We want to change the shared experience at regular intervals like a popular word puzzle provides a different word to find every day. Everyone would play with the same cheese positions and distance colors, but these would change regularly.

Create shared gameplay

Currently, the only way to change colors and cheese positions is to edit the contents of the gameSetup.mjs file and change the values in the gameSetup variable. Doing this would rapidly become very tiresome, particularly as we might like to provide a different grid design every hour. We could create an array of objects with a setup for each hour of the day.

```
const gameSetups = [

    { // hour 0
        colorStyles: ['darkGray', 'purple', 'white', 'blue', 'lightGreen',
        'red', 'lightBlue', 'yellowGreen', 'yellow', 'cyan', 'magenta', 'orange'],
        cheeses: [{ x: 4, y: 0 }, { x: 2, y: 3 }, { x: 7, y: 4 }]
    },
    ...
    { // hour 11
        colorStyles: ['orange', 'cyan', 'darkGray', 'lightBlue', 'blue',
        'red', 'magenta', 'yellow', 'purple', 'yellowGreen', 'white', 'lightGreen'],
        cheeses: [{ x: 9, y: 5 }]
    }
];
```

The array `gameSetups` in `server.mjs` contains 12 elements (though the listing above only shows 2), each containing a list of colors and a set of cheese positions. When the game starts, it uses the current time to decide which map to use.

```
let date = new Date();                    ──────── Get the current date
let hour = date.getHours() % 12;          ──────── Extract the hour value mod 12
gameSetup = gameSetups[hour];             ──────── Get the game setup for that hour
```

This code runs in the server at the start of the code that processes commands from the browser. It gets the setup for the current time. It uses the `Date` object we first saw when we made a clock in Chapter 1. It extracts the hour from the data and then uses the modulus operator (%) to restrict the hour to the 0 to 11 range. (I did this because I didn't want to make another 12 game setups.) It then looks up the appropriate game setup for the hour in the `gameSetups` array and sets it. This means game players will get a different game setup for each hour of the day.

There is an implementation of this game in the folder **Ch06-02_Hourly_Cheese_ Finder**. You can start it and play it if you like. Remember that because this game is hosted on a server, you must start the server running using the `node` runtime debugger in Visual Studio Code and then open the `index.html` file on localhost. Use the *http://localhost:8080/index.html* URL in your browser. You did this in Chapter 5 in Make Something Happen 23, "Browser and server." Just follow the same process to start the server and visit the page. You will find that you are presented with a different game depending on which hour of the day you play the game. Unfortunately, you might also find that there is a serious bug with this implementation of the game.

Debug shared gameplay

As a programmer, you will have to get good at debugging. That's just as well because we now have a bug in our game. Players report that sometimes the cheese moves about while they are playing the game. They don't think this is fair, and I'm inclined to agree. Let's investigate to see if we can find out what is happening.

MAKE SOMETHING HAPPEN 25

Scan the QR code or visit *https://www.youtube.com/watch?v=Z5DkHyr5d4M* for a video walkthrough of this Make Something Happen.

Debug timed gameplay

We can investigate how this code works by debugging it. Use the steps from the Make Something Happen 25, "Browser and server," in Chapter 5 to open the `server.mjs` file in the **Ch06-02_Hourly_Cheese_Finder** folder and start the server. Now, open your browser and navigate to *http://localhost:8080/index.html*. The browser will open the page, and the game will start. Play a game and watch how it runs. It will probably run correctly with no fault. It seems that the user reports are wrong.

At this point, we could just tell the players that we can't find the fault and that the game is perfectly okay. But we don't. Instead, we ask them for more detail. Were there any special circumstances when they were playing the game? When did they start playing? When did the game go wrong? It turns out that the game seemed to go wrong when the hour changed. A-ha! Perhaps when the hour changes, the game server switches to a different grid in the middle of the game, causing the cheeses to change position. We can use the debugger to test our theory.

First, play a complete Cheese Finder game and note where the cheeses are. The cheeses will be in the same place the next time you play the game during the same hour. Reload the game and click a few locations to validate that the grid is the same. Now, you will interrupt the program and move to the next hour by changing the contents of one of the variables.

Click next to line 155 to add a breakpoint

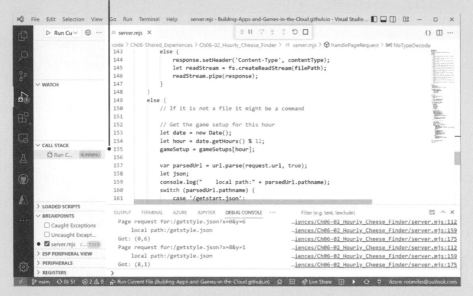

One of the great things about the Visual Studio Code debugger is that you can add breakpoints to the program as it is running. Find line **155** and click next to it, as shown above, to set a breakpoint. Now go back to the browser and click a square in the grid for which you know the color.

The server program will hit the breakpoint you just set because the browser program has asked the server for the style to use for a square, and the server is selecting the `gameSetup` for this hour. Find the `hour` value in the **Variables** section in the top-left part of the window (in the **Block:handlepagerequest** section, as shown below). The hour value is 1, meaning I created this figure in the hour between 1 and 2. As explained earlier, the hour values range from 0 to 11. When the hour reaches 12, it is wrapped around to 0. I created this example at 1:30 PM. The hour value you see represents the hour in which you debug the program.

Continue

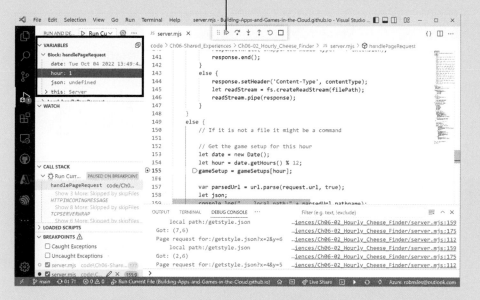

You could wait until the next hour to test the theory about the fault, but you can also change the values inside variables using Visual Studio Code. Double-click the hour value and increase it by 1. Below, I am in the process of changing the hour to 2.

Do not click this to continue the program

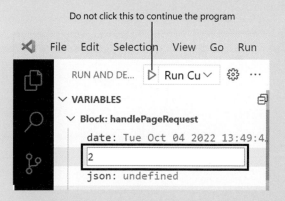

Press **Enter** once you have updated the value. Click the right-pointing Continue button in the debug controls to continue the program. (Don't click the tempting Run button in the above screenshot to continue the program; doing so will start another instance of the server, which you don't want to do).

Now, go back to the browser and look at the grid. The grid location you clicked will now have a color, but you should find that it is the wrong color because the server is using a different gameSetup. The cheese has moved because the hour has changed, and the server is now sending out style settings for its new location.

We could have tested our theory by starting a game in one hour, waiting a while, and continuing it in another hour. However, being able to change the values in a variable inside the code made testing the code much easier.

There are many other ways you can use debugging to make your life easier. You can create a breakpoint that fires when a certain condition is true or after it has been hit a particular number of times. It is well worth finding out more about these features. Leave Visual Studio Code running and the browser open. We will use it to test our bug fix.

CODE ANALYSIS

Fault analysis

The story so far: Players play the Cheese Finder game by clicking squares on a grid displayed by their browser. The squares change to a color representing the distance that location is from the nearest cheese. By working out which color represents which distance, a clever player can work out which squares contain the cheese in the smallest number of clicks. The first version of the game ran entirely in the browser. The code running in the browser calculated the color of the squares. We then created a server version of Cheese Finder. When this version is played, the locations of grid clicks are sent from the browser to the server, which then responds with that square's color. We've modified the server version to deliver a different player experience every hour by changing to a different grid each hour. Players have complained the cheese sometimes moves to a different location during play. We have discovered that if the hour changes during a game, the cheese location will change as the server moves onto a different game setup. Now, we must fix this error.

One of the hardest aspects of debugging is that faults often end up being a two-for-one deal. Fixing one fault can sometimes create two more. Chapter 5 discussed the dangers of using "kludges" when designing a program. We also need to be careful not to fix our bug with a kludge that might cause other problems. So, let's consider some questions.

Question: Whose fault is the bug?

> **Answer:** When things go wrong, we naturally tend to look for someone to blame. You should never do this when debugging. I've worked on many projects and discovered that everybody writes faulty code. If you make a big fuss about someone else's faults, you can expect them to make a similar fuss about yours. That's not to say you shouldn't discuss how a fault occurred and what you can do to ensure similar ones happen again. However, you should do this while recognizing bugs are a consequence of writing code in the same way that we get smoke with fire.
>
> In this case, the fault lies with the person who designed how the game works because they didn't think about the hour changing in the middle of the game. We need to fix that

fault and remember that if we make any time-based behaviors in new games, we must consider what happens when the time changes during gameplay.

Question: How do we fix the fault by adding code to the server?

Answer: We can't. This is not a fault that can be fixed at the server end. The server is completely unaware of the history of browsers requesting style values for particular squares. As we have seen before, one of the fundamental principles of the world wide web is that each transaction (a browser asks for a web page, and the server sends it back) is independent of any other. Our server program cannot know if a game on a particular browser started in the previous hour. In the next chapter, we will discover how we can add extra code and behaviors into the browser and server code so the server can know who is using it, but for now, we don't have this, so we can't fix the fault in the server.

Question: How do we fix the fault in the code in the browser?

Answer: Before we fix the fault, we must consider what we want to happen in this situation. Perhaps it might be nice if a game started in one hour continued into the next. The browser sends the x and y positions of a grid location to the server when it wants to know that location's color. We could add an hour value to the request so the server can send back the correct color response for the specified hour. A problem with this solution is that it breaks the "shared experience." People will be playing versions of the game from different hours at any given time.

A better solution would be for the browser to abandon a game when the hour changes. This adds some interesting jeopardy to the gameplay. You might find people who deliberately wait until the last minute in the hour before starting to play to complete the game in the nick of time. We will need to change the responses from the server, so they include the hour value for each response. The browser will store the hour value received when the game started and check it against an hour value sent by the server in each response. The browser will display an alert and reload the latest game if a different hour value is received.

Question: If the browser and server have access to the time, why must the server send the hour value to the browser?

Answer: This is a good question. You might think the browser program could use the Date function to get the hour value and use it to decide when a game should be abandoned. However, I don't think this is a very good idea. Usually, the browser and server clocks correspond, changing the hour on both simultaneously. However, we can't be completely sure the server and browser hour values will change simultaneously. If the dates are obtained independently, there is always a chance that an error could arise occasionally. An error that happens every hour is hard to debug. An error that happens every week is *really* hard to debug. Sending the hour value from the server removes the possibility of this error altogether.

If the server sends an hour value to the browser, the application is much easier to test. A different hour value from the server should trigger the browser to abandon a game. We can set a Visual Studio Code breakpoint in the server code, which stops the program when the browser requests the style for a particular location. We can then change the hour value the server sends to the browser and ensure the browser reacts correctly by displaying that the game has timed out.

Synchronize the browser and the server

The code we will add will keep the browser and the server "in sync." If the hour changes, the server will move into the new hour. The browser must detect this and abandon the game it was playing in the old hour. Each message the server sends to the browser must include an hour value so the browser can use it to work out whether it is still in sync.

The server sends two messages to the browser when the game is played. One is sent at the start of the game. It tells the browser the size of the grid and the number of cheeses in the grid. The browser uses this information to draw the grid that is used to play the game. It turns out to be very easy to add an hour value to the answer object that is sent back to the browser in response to a request from the browser to get the contents of the `getstart.json` URL.

Below, you can see the answer object created in the server when the browser sends a request to the `getstart.json` URL. This will be encoded and sent in a JSON string to the browser. If you are unclear about how this works, see "Create endpoints" in Chapter 5.

```
let answer = { width: gridWidth,
               height: gridHeight,
               noOfCheeses: gameSetup.cheeses.length,
               hour: hour };
```

Send back the hour value when the game was started

Below, you can see the function in the browser that receives the answer object sent from the server. It stores the noOfCheeses and hour properties from the object in the browser. The noOfCheeses value is used by the browser, so the game can detect when the player has found the last cheese. The gameHour value is used to detect when the server becomes out of sync with the browser.

```
function setupGame(gameDetailsJSON) {

  let gameDetails = JSON.parse(gameDetailsJSON);

  noOfCheeses = gameDetails.noOfCheeses;
  gameHour = gameDetails.hour;

  // rest of setupGame here
}
```

Save the hour value sent by the server

When the server sends a style value back to the browser, it also includes the hour value:

```
let styleObject = { style: styleText, hour: hour };
```

The statement above shows how the style information is added to the `styleObject` being sent back to the browser. In the previous version of the program, the style object only contained the style text. Now it contains the current hour value as well. Now let's see how code in the browser can use this to decide when to restart the game:

```
let checkDetails = JSON.parse(result);
if(checkDetails.hour != gameHour){
  // we have reached the end of the hour
  // end the game
  alert("The game in this hour has ended.");
  location.reload();
}
```

The statements above are performed when the browser receives a response from the server. If the hour in the received object (called `checkDetails`) differs from the one saved when the game started, the browser displays an alert to the player and then reloads the page, restarting the game. The `location.reload()` JavaScript function is used to reload the page. You can find a version of the game that synchronizes the server and browser in the **Ch06-03_Synchronized_Cheese_Finder** example folder. We can use the debugger to test it.

MAKE SOMETHING HAPPEN 26

Scan the QR code or see *https://www.youtube.com/watch?v=qlU8RpaSZtQ* for a video walk-through of this Make Something Happen.

Test synchronized gameplay

We can test whether our fixed version of the game works correctly by going through the same sequence of tests we used earlier in this chapter in the Make Something Happen 25, "Debug timed gameplay." Open the `server.mjs` file in the **Ch06-03_Synchronized_Cheese_Finder** folder and start the server. Now open your browser and navigate to *http://localhost:8080/index.html*. The browser will open the page, and the game will start. Click a few squares and note that they update correctly. Now you are going to do some time travel. You can use the debugger to change the hour value sent from the server back to the browser. This should cause the browser to abandon the game. Set a breakpoint at line **177** in `server.mjs`, as shown below. This statement creates the response sent to the browser when it asks for a particular square's style.

Breakpoint

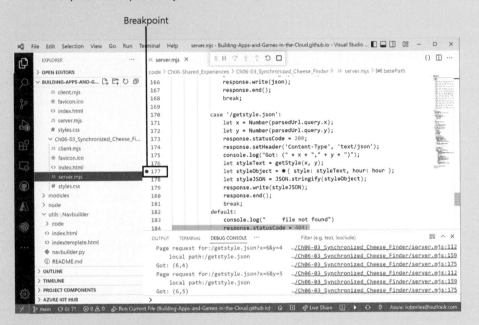

Now, click a grid location in the browser. The browser will ask the server for the style for that location, and the code in the server will hit the breakpoint.

Change the hour value to 2   Continue

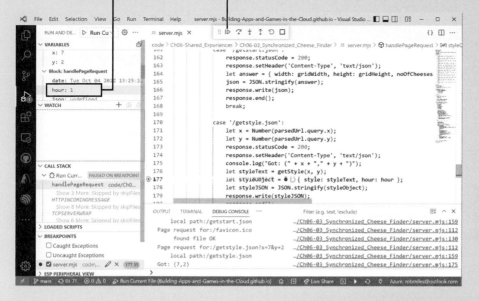

Above, you can see that the program has hit the breakpoint at the statement that creates the object to be sent back to the browser. You will change the hour value to make the browser decide it is out of sync. Open the **Block:handlePageRequest** item in **Variables** displayed in the top left. This is where the hour variable is described. Double-click the **hour** value and increase its value by 1. This exactly what you did earlier in this chapter when you were looking for the bug. Now you are making the change to determine if you have fixed the bug. Click the blue arrow in the debugging controls to make the program continue. The server will continue running. Now, look at the browser window. The browser displays a message indicating that the game has ended. If you click **OK**, the game will be reloaded with the new cheese positions. The fix seems to work.

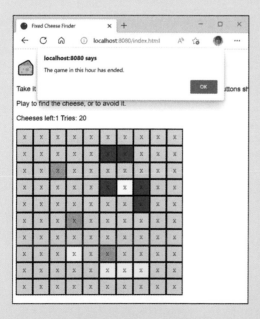

Make pseudo-random values

We now have a version of Cheese Finder that we can put on the Internet for anyone to use. However, I'm not keen on having to keep updating the grid with new cheese locations and style colors by hand. I would really like a way to have the server automatically create a unique game every hour. It turns out this is possible. We will use a technique called "pseudo-random" numbers, which is used throughout the Internet and is the basis of technology that secures network traffic. Let's look at it.

Computers have a real problem with randomness. A computer that behaves randomly is called "broken." However, programs frequently need random numbers, so we need a way to get randomness out of the machine. A computer can make random numbers in the same way I look like I can do lots of things—by faking it. It is hard for a program to make a random number from nothing, but we can make a function that takes in a number and uses it to make another number that seems to have no connection to the input value. It can do this by multiplying the incoming number by a large number, adding another large number, and then taking the modulus of the result. This technique for making random numbers is called the Linear Congruential Generator and was published by Thomson & Rotenberg in 1958.

To create a random number generator, we need to decide on values that will be used to make each successive value. These values are called the *seed* values for the random number generator. They are

- `randValue` (keeps track of our current random number)

- `randMult` (the number we multiply the current value by to get the next one)

- `randAdd` (the number we add)

- `randModulus` (the modulus)

Below is the `startRand` function, which sets the seed values for a pseudo-random number generator. The seed values are stored in variables used by the random number functions. They need to be visible to these functions, so they are declared outside the function:

```
let randValue;
let randMult;
let randAdd;
let randModulus;

function startRand() {
  randValue = 1234;           // set initial random number
```

```
    randMult = 8121;          // set the multiplier
    randAdd = 28413;          // set the amount to add
    randModulus = 134456789;  // set the modulus value
}
```

The pseudoRand() function below generates a value in the range 0 (inclusive) to 1 (not inclusive). This is the same range of values that JavaScript Math.random() produces, meaning it can be used in place of Math.random in our programs. The pseudoRand() function uses the current value of randVal to calculate a new one. The previous random number is multiplied by a large value (randMult) and has another value added (randValue). The statement then applies the modulus value (randModulus) to produce the next random value. If we divide this value by randModulus, we will get a value between 0 and 1 (but not including 1 because the modulus operator ensures that randValue will never reach randModulus).

```
function pseudoRand() {
    randValue = ((randMult * randValue) + randAdd) % randModulus;
    return randValue/randModulus;
}
```

CODE ANALYSIS

Making random numbers

You might have some questions about how this function works.

Question: What does the modulus operator (%) actually do?

Answer: This is an important part of the process. Each time we calculate a new random number, we multiply the previous value by randMult. We need to do something to stop the value of randValue from getting larger and larger. The modulus operator divides one number by another and returns the remainder of the division. The value 19 modulus 16 is 3. This is because 16 goes into 19 once, with a remainder 3. So, in our program, using the modulus value will ensure that the value of randValue never goes above 134456789.

Question: Are the randMult, randAdd, and randModulus seed values particularly special?

Answer: Some combinations of seed values can cause the successive random values to get "stuck" at particular values or to bounce between them. The ones we are using generate a usable stream of random values. You can find more discussion of this random number technique at *https://en.wikipedia.org/wiki/Linear_congruential_generator.*

Question: Will the sequence of random numbers ever repeat?

Answer: The earlier set of starting values returns to the original `randvalue` of 1234 after 33,614,190 random values have been generated. In other words, you would have to calculate more than 33 million random numbers before you saw the sequence repeat. You might like to ponder how I worked out that value of 33,614,190. I'll answer later in this section.

Question: Will the random sequence be different on different computers?

Answer: Great question. The JavaScript language specification describes how numeric values are stored and manipulated, so the random number sequence should be the same on every computer running standard JavaScript.

🚀 **MAKE SOMETHING HAPPEN 27**

Scan the QR code or see *https://www.youtube.com/watch?v=KDTNcxQV4oQ* for a video walkthrough of this Make Something Happen.

Random dice

The web page in the **Ch06-04_Pseudo_Random_Dice** can implement random dice. The present version implements a single dice using the `pseudoRand` function you have just seen. Let's have a look at it. Open your browser and navigate to the **index.html** file in the **Ch06-04_Pseudo_Random_Dice** folder.

Click the **Roll Dice**. The dice always rolls a 1 when it starts. In fact, the sequence of values it produces is always the same. If you reload the page in the browser, it will take you back to the start of the sequence.

This page has hidden features in the form of functions we can use to test the randomness of the die. Open the **Developer Tools** and switch to the **Console** tab. Now, type the statement **testDice(pseudoRand,1000000)** and press **Enter**:

Above, you can see the output from this function. It displays an array containing the fraction of the rolls for each dice score, from 1 to 6. For a perfect roll, each score should have a probability of one-sixth (0.166666). The `testDice` function is supplied with two arguments:

- `pseudoRand` identifies the random number function to be used.

- `1000000` is the number of tests to be performed (in this case, 1,000,000).

The call above throws the die one million times using the `pseudoRand` random number function. We can test the performance of the `Math.random` function by using that instead. Type the **testDice(Math.random,1000000)** statement and press **Enter**:

This time, the `testDice` function does one million tests using `Math.random` to generate the random numbers. As you can see, the values are very close to the ones produced by our pseudo-random function.

Test random numbers

You might have some questions about how `testDice` works.

Question: Why do I get different results from the ones you get?

Answer: When you test the `pseudoRand` function, the program is positioned in the random number stream, affecting each roll's scores. If you perform the test directly after the dice page has loaded, you will see the same numbers as above before you click to roll any dice yourself.

The `Math.random` function has been designed to provide a totally random value each time it is called, so the results using that function will be different each time it is tested.

Question: How does the `testDice` function work?

Answer: Good question. Here's the code:

```
function testDice(testFunction,noOfTests) {
  randFunction = testFunction;                    Set the random number function
  let totals = [0, 0, 0, 0, 0, 0];                Create the totals array
  for (let i = 0; i < noOfTests; i++) {           Test loop
    let roll = getRandom(1, 7);                    Get a dice roll
    totals[roll - 1]++;                            Update the count
  }
```

```
    let fractions = totals.map((v) => v / noOfTests);
    console.log(fractions);
}
```

Get the fractions
Log the values

The dice roll page contains a `randFunction` variable that refers to the random number generator being used by the page. Initially, this variable is set to `pseudoRand`:

```
let randFunction = pseudoRand;
```

The `testDice` function is supplied with a reference to the function that will generate the random numbers. The first thing the function does is set the value of `randFunction` to this reference.

```
randFunction = testFunction;
```

Then it creates an array to hold the totals for each dice score, from 1 to 6. The initial values for each total are `0`.

```
let totals = [0, 0, 0, 0, 0, 0];
```

Then the test function performs a loop 1,000,000 times. Each time around the loop, the function gets a random value into a variable called `roll`. The `roll` value is then used as an index to specify the element in the totals array, which will be increased by 1. The function deducts 1 from the roll value because a dice value goes from 1 to 6, and the array is indexed from 0 to 5. For example, if the roll value returned 4, the element at index 3 in the totals array would be increased by 1 (that is what the `++` operator does).

```
for (let i = 0; i < noOfTests; i++) {
  let roll = getRandom(1, 7);
  totals[roll - 1]++;
}
```

When the loop has finished, the program uses the `map` function provided by the `totals` array to make a new array (called `fractions`), which contains each element of the `totals` array divided by the number of tests. This provides a fraction of the total results for that particular dice throw. This value should be one-sixth (0.16666) because there are six possible outcomes, and each is equally likely.

```
let fractions = totals.map((v) => v / noOfTests);
```

We can feed any function to `testDice` to generate random values.

```
testDice(()=>0.9,10000);
```

This provides `testDice` with a function literal that returns the value `0.9` every time it is called. This would result in a die that always rolls a six. The `testDice` function leaves the `randFunction` variable referring to the function it was supplied with, so performing the above test would result in a die that always returns the value 6. You can reset the behavior by reloading the page.

Question: How did you determine how long the random sequence takes to repeat?

```
function getRepeatLoopSize() {
    startRand();                              Reset the random number generator
    let firstValue = randValue;               Remember the first random value
    let counter = 1;                          Start a counter
    while (true) {                            Start a loop
        pseudoRand();                         Get the next random number
        if (randValue == firstValue) {        Have we got the first value again?
            break;                            Break if we have reached the first value
        }
        counter = counter + 1;                Increment the value counter
    }
    console.log("Loop size: " + String(counter));   Display the value counter
}
```

Answer: The `getRepeatLoopSize` function starts the random number generator and records the first value in the sequence. It then repeatedly gets random numbers until it sees the first value again. It counts each time around the loop in a `counter` variable and displays the result at the end.

```
> getRepeatLoopSize()
  Loop size: 33614190
< undefined
> |
```

Above, you can see the result of calling the function. This took a couple of seconds to return as the program worked through all the random values.

Create a pseudo-random library

The following code is stored in a file called `pseudo-random.mjs`, which can be imported into any application that wants to use a pseudo-random number sequence. It is the same code we have already seen but repacked as a library. The `setupRand` function accepts a `settings` object used to set the initial values of the variables controlling the random number generation.

```
let randValue;
let randMult;
let randAdd;
let randModulus;

function setupRand(settings) {                           Copies the settings into the library
    randValue = settings.startValue;
    randMult = settings.randMult;
    randAdd = settings.randAdd;
    randModulus = settings.randModulus
}

function pseudoRand() {                                   Gets the next number
    randValue = ((randMult * randValue) + randAdd) % randModulus;
    return randValue / randModulus;
}

function getRandom(min, max) {                            Gets an integer in a range
    var range = max - min;
    var result = Math.floor(pseudoRand() * range) + min;
    return result;
}
export {setupRand, pseudoRand, getRandom};                Exports the functions
```

The following codes below shows how we use the library. First, we import the two functions from the library that we need to use. The dice program only needs two functions. It uses `setupRand` to set the initial values and `getRandom` to get random numbers. The configuration values are provided as an object literal. The properties in the object are the values used by the random number generator in the original dice application. You can find a version of the dice application that uses the random library in the **Ch06-05_Dice_using_library** folder.

```
import {setupRand,getRandom} from "./pseudorandom.mjs";

let randSettings = {
    startValue:1234,
    randMult:8121,
    randAdd:28413,
    randModulus:134456789
}

setupRand(randSettings);
```

Generate timed randomness

We now understand how computers generate random numbers, but we don't seem to have solved our original problem, which was to find a way that our game can create different cheese positions and style colors every hour. However, now that you know the effect of the seed values of the random numbers produced, you might be able to think of how we could do this. Look at the following function:

```
function getAbsoluteHour(date){
    let result = (date.getFullYear() * 372 * 24) +
        (date.getMonth() * 31 * 24) +
        (date.getDate() * 24) +
        date.getHours();
    return result;
}
```

It works out the approximate number of hours until the supplied date. We could call this an "absolute hour" value. It is a value that will be unique for every hour. However, it is not completely accurate; all months are assumed to be 31 days long, and a year is 12 × 31 (372) days long. It works by multiplying the year value by the length of a year in hours, adding the month number multiplied by the length of a month in hours, and so on. We don't mind that this is not an accurate number. We want to ensure that each hour has a different number because this will lead to a different (but repeatable) sequence of random numbers for each hour the game is played.

The following code starts a game, gets the date, and uses it to calculate the absolute-Hour. The absoluteHour value is then used as the startValue for the random number generator. We will now get a sequence of random numbers specific to the hour the program runs.

```
// get the date
let date = new Date();

// get the absolute hour for this date
let absoluteHour = getAbsoluteHour(date);

// Use the absolute hour to setup the random number generator
let randSettings = {
    startValue: absoluteHour,
    randMult:8121,
    randAdd:28413,
    randModulus:134456789
}

setupRand(randSettings);
```

The setupGame function shown below runs in the server and builds the colorStyle and cheeseList lists for the game. It then shuffles the colorStyles and cheeseList and sets the number of cheeses to be used in the game. It is based on the original setup code for the browser-based version of Cheese Finder.

```
let colorStyles;
let cheeseList;
let noOfCheeses;

function setupGame() {
    // set up the initial positions for the game elements
    colorStyles = ["white", "red", "orange", "yellow", "yellowGreen", "lightGreen",
                   "cyan", "lightBlue", "blue", "purple", "magenta", "darkGray"];
    shuffle(colorStyles);
    cheeseList = [];
    // build the grid
    for (let y = 0; y < gridHeight; y++) {
        for (let x = 0; x < gridWidth; x++) {
            let square = { x: x, y: y };
            cheeseList.push(square);
        }
    }
    shuffle(cheeseList);
    noOfCheeses = getRandom(2,6);
}
```

Before the server processes an incoming request from a server, it gets the date and time and uses it to set up the random number generator before processing the request. This means the game updates with a new map every hour. You can find this version in the **Ch06-06_Time_Synchronized_Cheese_Finder** sample code folder. If you repeatedly play the game, you will notice that the grid changes every hour.

> **PROGRAMMER'S POINT**
> ## Pseudo-random technology is very powerful
>
> We can use the magic of pseudo-random sequences in all kinds of ways. Rather than spending time designing a game world by hand, we could create a landscape using pseudo-random values to decide where the trees, rivers, and mountains go. Lots of games do this. We could send people secret files that can only be decoded by the right pseudo-random sequence. We would just need to give them the keys (the seed values) to decode them. This technology is the basis of secure communications on the Internet. When you visit a secure website, your browser and server exchange "keys," which are reused in a pseudo-random-based encryption process to keep transmitted data secure from eavesdroppers.
>
> One word of warning, however: It took my computer just a few seconds to create 33 million values and discover how regularly our random number sequence repeats. This would be an important first step in "cracking" the sequence and working out the seed values. If you want to use random numbers in your encryption, make sure you use the versions provided by JavaScript, which are cryptographically secure. These are slower, but the sequences they produce are much harder to "crack."

Use worldwide time

We can now create a shared experience of the Cheese Finder game that updates the cheese position every hour. The browser will "time out" games that are not completed within the hour that the games were started, and the server uses pseudo-random numbers based on the time's hour value to set the cheese position and distance colors for each game. However, we do have one more problem to deal with—the issue of worldwide time.

The current game version uses the local time to generate the starting value of the pseudo-random sequence of values that describe the board. This means if there are multiple server versions worldwide, they will give the players an experience based on their local date and time. This means I might not have the same shared experience as someone using a different server. I can't talk to a friend in a distant land about how hard the current grid is because if their local server time is different from mine, they won't be using the same game layout.

This happens because the JavaScript `Date` object provides your program with correct date information in your present location. Normally, this is what you want. But sometimes, you write code that needs to use a time independent of any location adjustments. UTC (or Coordinated Universal Time) is the time from which all other times in JavaScript are derived. The `Date` object in your machine applies an offset to the UTC time, which is determined by the location of the computer running the program.

```
function getAbsoluteHour(date){
    let result = (date.getUTCFullYear() * 372 * 24) +
        (date.getUTCMonth() * 31 * 24) +
        (date.getUTCDate() * 24) +
        date.getUTCHours();
    return result;
}
```

This version of `getAbsoluteHour` uses UTC versions of all the functions that get time values from a `Date` object. It is used in the version of Mine finder in the **Ch06-07_World_Synchronized_Cheese_Finder** folder.

Prepare for the cloud

We are nearly ready to install our Cheese Finder game in the cloud for anyone to use. But before we do this, we might want to take a look at what we have done to see if there are any more steps we can take to make the application cloud ready.

Optimize performance

Before we place our solution on a server, we might want to look for ways to optimize its performance. Most programs can be written without much need to consider their performance. Modern computers are so powerful that we don't have to hunt for the fastest solution when we write software. Instead, we build applications that are easy to understand and maintain. There are only two situations when I worry much about performance:

- When I (or a user) notice something seems to be running a bit slowly

- When I'm paying for the computer time being used

Cloud providers will give you an amount of free hosting, but at some point, you might have to part with some cash for the computer time you use. Any free provision we can get will have a limit on use, so it might be a good idea to look at our code to see if we can improve its efficiency.

In Chapter 5, we talked about "kludges" and how it can be a bad idea to modify an existing solution to a problem if the problem changes. We saw this in the context of adding more cheeses to the Cheese Finder game, but it looks like we have created something rather similar here. The first version of Cheese Finder was written to work in a browser. The player selects a square by clicking a button. This triggers code that uses the x and y position of the square to calculate the distance to the nearest cheese. Then it selects the style color for that distance and sets that style on the button.

This is a good way to structure the code for a single user where a given square has only been clicked once by the player. But the server is used differently. It will receive lots of requests about the same square. It is wasteful of computer resources to calculate the distance values every time we get a request for that square. The program should create something that can quickly look up a distance and return it to the browser without having to do any calculations.

Create a cache

A cache is a copy of data made to speed up the execution of a program. Hardware caches are used in your computer to speed up access to memory and mass storage devices. They are small pieces of very fast memory that hold values the computer is working on. A software cache does something similar. It holds a value to save it from being recalculated each time it is needed. When the server sets up a new game, it could set the position of the cheeses and then fill a grid with the style values for each x and y coordinate pair. The grid would serve as a cache of the style values. We would feed x and y values into the grid and get back the style for that grid.

Build a two-dimensional array in JavaScript

We have seen how we can use arrays as lookup tables. We already use a lookup table to convert distances into style names. The style lookup is "one-dimensional." We want to convert a single value into the name of the style to be used for that distance. The lookup table for the grid will have to be two-dimensional, converting an x and y coordinate pair into the style value for that square. Some programming languages support arrays with multiple dimensions, but JavaScript does not. We can, however, create multidimensional arrays by creating "arrays of arrays."

The following code creates the grid by using a nested pair of for loops. The outer loop takes us through all the x values in the grid and creates a column array for each x value. The column is filled with all the squares in that column by a loop that goes through all the y values. The column is then added to the grid array. Each square contains three properties, the x position of the square, the y position of the square, and the style string for that square.

```
// build the grid and cheese list
let grid = [];
let cheeseList = [];
for (let x = 0; x < req.width; x++) {
    let column = [];
    for (let y = 0; y < req.height; y++) {
        let square = { x: x, y: y, style: "empty" };
        // put the square into the cheese list
        cheeseList.push(square);
        // put the square into the column
        column.push(square);
    }
    // put the column into the grid
    grid.push(column);
}
```

Each square is also added to a one-dimensional array called cheeseList, which is a linear array of squares. We need a one-dimensional array of square locations that we can shuffle to create a list of cheese positions. When this code has been completed, we can access individual squares in the grid by using to index values:

```
grid [9][0].style = "cheese";
```

The preceding statement would set the style property of the square at the top right-hand square to "cheese." The square at the "origin" (such as the one with coordinates 0,0) is at the top left of the grid. Once we have created our grid, the next thing to do is populate it with style values.

```
shuffle(cheeseList);
noOfCheeses = getRandom(req.minCheeses, req.maxCheeses);
// set the styles for these cheese positions
for (let x = 0; x < req.width; x++) {
    for (let y = 0; y < req.height; y++) {
        grid[x][y].style = getStyle(x, y);
    }
}
```

This is the code that creates the "cache" of style strings. The cheese list is shuffled, and then the number of cheeses is determined. Then, a second pair of nested `for` loops goes through all the grid locations and sets the style string for each. Now, rather than calling `getStyle` to get the square's style, the program can just look up the style in the grid.

```
let styleText = game.grid[x][y].style;
```

CODE ANALYSIS

Creating caches

You might have some questions about how the caches are created.

Question: How can the same square object be in two different lists simultaneously?

```
let square = { x: x, y: y, style: "empty" };
// put the square into the column
cheeseList.push(square);
// put the square into the cheese list
column.push(square);
```

Answer: The code above creates a square object and then adds that object to two lists. This works perfectly because the lists hold references to the object. The square object is not "in" either list. The lists just contain references to objects, not the objects themselves.

You could use the same technique if you wanted to have a list of objects ordered in more than one way, such as a list of books. You might want to work through these in order or by author name or book title. You could create two lists of references, one ordered by author and the other by title. Each book object would exist once but appear in both lists.

Question: What happens to the old grid when we create a new one?

Answer: The code above creates square and grid objects as it builds the cache. This code will run every hour, meaning a new grid is created every hour. What happens to the old grid? Does it remain in memory somewhere, taking up space forever? It turns out that we don't have to worry about this. When the new grid is created, the old one is no longer accessible by the program because the `grid` variable now refers to the new grid, not the old one. JavaScript contains a process called the "garbage collector," which automatically searches for objects not referred to by the program code and removes them from memory.

Question: Can an array have more than two dimensions?

Answer: Yes. You can write code that creates arrays of arrays of arrays, but I've rarely had to do this when creating an application. If you think, "What I need here is a 4D array," you should take a long hard look at how you are structuring your data.

Avoid recalculations

The original version of the server set up the game for every request. However, it only needs to do this once every hour. Once the game has been set up, there is no need to set it up again. The code from the last section will reduce the load on our server significantly. Now the game is only set up once an hour, not every time a request is received. It works the same way as the code in the browser, which checks to see if the hour has changed and reloads the page if it has.

```javascript
// get the date
let date = new Date();

// get the absolute hour for this date
let newabsoluteHour = getAbsoluteHour(date);

if (newabsoluteHour != absoluteHour) {

    // Set up the new game

    // update the absoluteHour value
    absoluteHour = newabsoluteHour;
}
```

CODE ANALYSIS

Avoiding recalculations

You might have some questions about avoiding recalculations.

Question: What happens the very first time that the server program runs?

> **Answer:** We need to force the server to set up the game the very first time that a request is received. We can do this by setting the initial value of absoluteHour to something which will force an update.

```javascript
let absoluteHour = 0;
```

> The value of absoluteHour will never be 0, so the first time a request is received, a game setup will be triggered.

Question: What happens if a web request comes in while the server updates the game setup?

> **Answer:** This can never happen. The Node.js system is single-threaded, meaning web requests are queued up and processed one at a time.

Question: Why don't we care about performance on the browser?

Answer: As long as the application gives the user a good experience, there is no need to spend time trying to make it go faster. However, we should test the application on low-performance machines to ensure it works on them. I use a cheap laptop and a Raspberry Pi computer to test the performance of my applications. It will be okay for most people if it runs well on those.

Question: Could we improve efficiency even more?

Answer: Yes, we could. The present version creates a new grid every hour. We could make the `getGame` function reuse the existing grid rather than make a new one each time. There are other tricks we could use to make `getGame` even faster. However, this function is only used once an hour, so doing this doesn't seem worthwhile. When considering the efficiency of code, you must remember that computer time is usually much cheaper than programmer time. If an ultra-efficient solution is extremely hard to understand and maintain, this might not represent good value.

Improve structure

Improving structure will not really improve performance, but it will make the program easier to manage and maintain. When you write a program, you must be mindful that others might have to work with it. That means you should make the code easy to understand and try to reduce the number of ways the code could be inadvertently damaged. We can do this by changing the structure of our code slightly.

Put the game engine in a library file

Currently, the functions and variables that manage the gameplay are in the `server.mjs` file. We can extract these from the game and put them in their own library. We could create a library called `game.mjs` that exports the behaviors and variables the game needs. This is a good idea because someone looking at the code now knows exactly where to look for code that manages gameplay. It also makes the application more flexible.

```
export {setupGame, grid, noOfCheeses};
```

The statement above shows the items that are exported from the engine. The `setupGame` function is called to set up the game, and the `grid` and `noOfCheeses` variables give the styles for the squares and the number of cheeses in the game.

One big advantage of putting the game engine in a separate library is that it can be incorporated into other applications. We can use `game.mjs` to create a browser-based version of the Cheese Finder game. The sample folder **Ch06-08_Optimized_Cheese_Finder** contains a browser-based version of the game alongside the server-based one. You can play this version on your computer by opening the `local.html` file in your browser. The JavaScript code that uses the `game.mjs` file to implement a local version of the game can be found in the file `local.mjs`.

Use object literals in function calls

In Chapter 1, when we discussed functions, we discovered that arguments to Java-Script function calls (the things you provide when the function is called) are matched by position with the parameters in the function (the things that the function works on when it runs). If you get the order of your arguments wrong when you call a function, you can expect it to do strange and wonderful things you won't want. We noted that one way to resolve any ambiguity about arguments to functions is to use object literals.

```
let gameRequest = {
    width: gridWidth,
    height: gridHeight,
    colorStyles: ["white", "red", "orange", "yellow",
        "yellowGreen", "lightGreen", "cyan",
        "lightBlue", "blue", "purple", "magenta", "darkGray"],
    minCheeses: 1,
    maxCheeses: 6,
    startValue: newAbsoluteHour,
    randMult: 8121,
    randAdd: 28413,
    randModulus: 134456789
}
```

Above, you can see the definition of an object literal that contains all the information needed to create a new game. This is passed as an argument to the `getGame` function, which builds and returns a new game description.

```
setupGame (gameRequest);
```

This statement calls the `setupGame` function to set up a game. The `gameRequest` object contains everything the `setupGame` function needs to know as named items.

Buy a domain name

The domain name is the first part of the address you enter to access a site on the web. You will be familiar with popular domains such as `microsoft.com`, `apple.com`, and `robmiles.com`. When you create a web application hosted in the cloud, the domain name will contain your hosting provider's name. If hosted on Azure, the Cheese Finder game could have the `cheesefinder.azurewebsites.net` URL. This will work fine, but it would be better if the address on the web had a bit more personality. It would be nice if the game could have the `cheesefinder.com` URL. However, that web address turns out to be rather expensive. Fortunately, other domain names are available at very low prices. A service such as **namecheap.com** allows you to search for and register your own domain name. You will have to pay an annual fee for the registration and hosting of the name, but this need not be too expensive. I have managed to obtain the *cheesefinder.xyz* domain and will be setting this as the game's address.

Put your name on it

```
// Cheese Finder server by Rob Miles October 2022
// Version 1.0
// If you move the server to a different location you will
// have to update the base path string to reflect the new location

// Rob Miles www.robmiles.com
```

If you have made something you are proud of, you should put your name on it. Great artists always sign their paintings, so there is nothing wrong with you putting your name in your code. At the very least, you should provide a way for users to find you. A good way to do this is to create an email account (and maybe even a web page) specifically for your creation.

Deploy an application

Until now, we have been using a computer to simulate the server. Both the server and the browser programs have been running on one machine. But now we want to put the server part of the game, plus all the other files it needs, into a cloud-based host. To do this, we will have to modify the files so that they will run correctly in their new home. We will also need to create a file that describes the application.

package.json

You might think that programming is just about writing code and solving problems. While you do get to do a lot of this, you also have to do a fair bit of organization and management. This is because any nontrivial solution will have components that must be managed. A very large part of the wonderfulness of JavaScript comes from the node package manager (NPM) system, which we will explore in detail in the next chapter. This makes it easy to make applications out of existing elements. The package manager can also ensure that your system uses the latest (or particular) versions of components and can manage different application configurations you might like to use for development, testing, and deployment.

A key component of the package management process is a file that contains the package settings for any given application. This file has the name package.json and should be placed in the folder along with the files comprising your application. In the next chapter, we'll discover tools to create this file automatically. However, we can create one by hand for the Cheese Finder application. The package.json file does not contain a list of all the files in the project. It is assumed that all the files in the project folder are part of it. In other words, we don't have to include any mention of files such as pseudo-random.mjs and index.html.

Below, you can see a package.json that describes the Cheese Finder application. The most important elements are the ones specifying the name of the file that starts the application. We want to run the server application in the file server.mjs. If we were using features of a specific version of JavaScript or wanted to ensure that an "upgraded" version does not break our application, we could specify the versions to use in the "engines" property. If we put this file in the folder containing our application, Node.js (and other programs) will pick it up automatically when required.

```
{
    "name": "cheesefinder",                                          Name of the application
    "version": "1.0.0",                                                  Version number
    "description": "A cheese finding game",                                Description
    "main": "server.mjs",                       File that contains the body of our application
    "scripts": {
      "test": "echo \"Error: no test specified\" && exit 1",                    No tests
      "start": "node server.mjs"                             Command to start the server
    },
    "engines": {                                      Versions of node and npm to use
      "node": ">=7.6.0",
      "npm": ">=4.1.2"
    },
    "author": "RobMiles",
```

```
    "license": "ISC",
    "dependencies": {                                                    No dependencies
    },
    "devDependencies": {},                                          No dev dependencies
    "repository": {                                          Tell people where to find the source
      "type": "git",
      "url": "https://github.com/Building-Apps-and-Games-in-the-Cloud.github.io"
    },
    "homepage": "https://begintocodecloud.com/"                Provide a homepage link
  }
```

Set the port for the server

The Internet uses port numbers to identify program connections to external clients. A program can listen behind a particular port on a machine. We can use whatever port numbers we like when running servers on our local machine. The Live Server Extension we installed in Visual Studio Code in Chapter 2 (see the "Install the Live Server Extension" section) creates a web server that listens on port 5050. When we created a web server in Chapter 4 (see the "Make a web server" section), we created one that listens on port 8080. When we use the browser to access one of the locally hosted files, we add the port number to the URL (unified resource locator).

Figure 6-2 shows that we have used our browser to open a website hosted on our local machine by a process running a server program that is listening on port 8080.

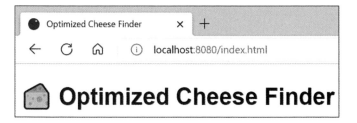

Figure 6-2   Local address and port

The Azure hosting I use for Cheese Finder is *cheesefinder.azurewebsites.net*, which was set up when I created the application. **Figure 6-3** shows this site being accessed. The browser uses port 80 to access this server because that is the default port for HTML requests. The server we deploy into the cloud must listen on port 80.

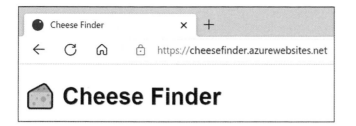

Figure 6-3 Web address and port

Ideally, we'd like our server to listen on port 80 when it runs in the cloud and on port 8080 when it runs on the local host. The following two statements make this work.

```
const port = process.env.PORT || 8080;

server.listen(port);
```

The first statement creates a constant called `port`, which is set to the value of the PORT property of the process environment variables (which will be set by the cloud service) or the value 8080 if this PORT property has not been set. In this context, the || operator means "here is a default value to use if the given value is undefined, NaN, or null." So, if there is no PORT property (or process object), the port value is set to 8080. The Azure infrastructure sets an appropriate environment variable before it runs the server program. We need to add this code where the server starts to listen. The environment variables are very useful. We will be doing more with them later.

Set the server path

The client program (the one that runs in the browser to display the Cheese Finder game to the player) sends requests to the server for game setup information:

- Grid size and number of cheeses

- Square style (color style string for a square at a given x and y location)

The `hostAddress` variable below is declared in the `client.mjs` file and gives the first part of the address for any request. Currently, this is set to `localhost` because while we have been testing, we have been running both the client and the server on our machine, so the server's address is the local host running the client program.

```
let hostAddress = "http://localhost:8080/";
```

When we move our application to the cloud, we will need to change this address so that it refers to the location in the cloud where the application is hosted. When a browser connects to that site, it will trigger the Node.js application that implements the server. The following statement is the updated host address I must put in the client.mjs file so that web requests are sent to the server in the cloud. When you move your application to the cloud, you must update the address to point to the location where your application is hosted.

```
let hostAddress = "https://cheesefinder.azurewebsites.net";
```

Set the local file path

We have been running different versions of the Cheese Finder server from the sample program folders we copied from GitHub in Chapter 1. Each folder holds a set of files for use by that example. Each server version contains a file path set to refer to the files it uses. This path is held in server.mjs in a variable called basePath. This path is needed because of how files are located when Visual Studio Code runs a program in the local debugger.

```
const basePath = "./code/Ch06-Shared_Experiences/Ch06-08_Optimized_Cheese_Finder/";
```

Above, you can see basePath value for one of the example applications. The string in basePath is added to the file path that has been requested, so the correct files are loaded. When the program runs in the cloud, we must change this path to direct the server to the local folder.

```
const basePath = "./";
```

This will cause the server to look in the local folder for the files, which is what we want. When we make larger applications with lots of resources, we will put them in separate folders to make them easier to manage.

Scan the QR code or visit *https://www.youtube.com/watch?v=jDMJd5Eqlkc* for a video walk-through of this Make Something Happen.

Create an Azure app service

This is a very exciting Make Something Happen. Here is where you put something into the cloud for others to find and use. The code you want to deploy to the cloud should be held in a GitHub repository on your machine. You can test the application by using the local settings as we have been doing and then make the modifications described above to make it ready for deployment.

If you don't have an application to deploy and just want to practice the deployment process, you can find a deployable version of Cheese Finder in the **Ch06-09_Azure_Deployment** folder.

Sign up for Azure at *https://azure.microsoft.com/*. You will need a Microsoft Account to do this.

Open Visual Studio Code and install the Azure App Service extension. Follow the process we used to install Live Server in Chapter 2, but search for **Azure App Service**. You will be asked to sign in to your Azure Account when the extension starts. Do this.

Your application should be in a GitHub repository; open this repository before you begin deployment. If you want to use the sample project, just create an empty repository and copy all the source files from the example folder into that repository.

Open the Azure extension, click the arrow next to the **Resources** item, and then open the dropdown for your account. Right-click the **App Service** item and select **Create New Web App** from the menu that appears.

You will now be asked for the name of the app you are creating. This name will be used in the URL identifying the app on the Internet. I called mine **cheesefinder**:

Next, you need to select the runtime stack for the app. You are using Node.js, so select the latest version (Node 16 LTS).

Now Azure wants to know the pricing option for your service. Select Free (F1). You will get limited service, but it will be enough to get started. The Azure extension will work while building your application.

Once you have set your pricing tier, you will get the option to deploy to the application.

Note that the dialog shows the URL for the application that will be created. Press the **Deploy** button to deploy your site to the cloud. Once the deployment has been completed, you should be able to view your application in the browser.

Once the application has been deployed, you should be able to connect to it using your browser. If you go to *portal.azure.com*, you can open the dashboard for your new application and watch as requests come through.

What you have learned

This chapter has been super busy. We have learned lots of things. We've done some programming, debugging, optimization, and deployment. And we've learned a lot about how random numbers run the net. Here's the recap, plus some points to ponder.

- We can create applications that give a shared experience to all those who access them. The site can give a different experience to visitors by using the date and time to determine what is served by the site.

- If the content served by a site can change over time, an application must determine when the content being viewed in the browser is out of date. This can be achieved using timestamps that are sent along with content. The browser can check these against the current time and act when content is outdated.

- When debugging a program, it is possible to set a breakpoint while the program is running. This can be done within the Visual Studio Code debugger and the debugger built into the browser's **Developer Tools**.

- When debugging code, it is useful to be able to change the contents of variables in a program to test theories about the location of faults in the program.

- Faults in a program can arise when an existing design is modified to work in a different context. A new context might give rise to fault conditions or considerations that the original program was not designed to handle.

- A computer cannot generate a truly random value, but it can perform a combination of multiplication, addition, and modulus to create a "new" random number from an existing one. Repeating this process on the "new" number generates a "pseudo-random" stream of values. Different initial values (or seed values) will result in different sequences of values, but each sequence is repeatable with the same seeds.

- Pseudo-random number sequences can be used in games to generate realistic-looking artifacts and behaviors. Their repeatability means that they can also be used for encryption and decryption. The JavaScript libraries include functions that can be used to create "encryption-quality" random number streams with successive values that cannot be easily analyzed and predicted.

- Pseudo-random numbers can be combined with time inputs to create random sequences that are unique to a particular time.

- Under normal circumstances, it is not necessary to optimize the performance of your programs. However, you should consider some optimization if code is going to be called repeatedly (as it would be in a web server responding to requests from clients) and you are paying for the computer time to run the program (as you do in a web server running on a cloud service provider).

- One way to optimize a server is to create a precalculated cache of values that can be sent back in response to requests.

- JavaScript does not provide support for two-dimensional arrays. However, these can be created as an "array of arrays."

- Placing components of an application into library files makes the code clearer and raises the possibility of code reuse.

- Applications built to run in `Node.js` can be given a `package.json` file that describes the application, how to run different application configurations, and any dependencies the application might have on both runtime systems and software libraries used by the application.

- Visual Studio Code provides an Azure App Service plugin that can be used to deploy into the cloud the contents of a `Node.js` application described by a `package.json` file.

To reinforce your understanding of this chapter, you might want to consider the following "profound questions."

Question: What do we mean by a "shared experience"?

> **Answer:** Before computers and the Internet, a shared experience would be provided by a football game or a "must-watch" TV show. Today, people can get the same experience at the same time by visiting a website that provides changing content they all interact with.

Question: How can we make a client that automatically determines when the content it displays is out of date?

> **Answer:** In the current version of Cheese Finder, the browser checks to see if the game is out of date (the server has moved into the next hour) when the player clicks a square. The response from the server includes an hour value that the browser can check.

A browser could detect that the content is out of date is by repeatedly asking the server, "is the content still in date?" When we wrote the clock program, we saw that it can cause trigger events at regular intervals in a JavaScript program running inside the browser. We used the events to update a clock display, but they could be used to trigger a request to the server to check the hour value. We could use this to add a feature to Cheese Finder where the browser automatically detects when a game has timed out, rather than waiting for the player to click a square and trigger an action on the server.

Chapter 12 covers WebSockets, which can be used by a server to send a message to a JavaScript program running in a browser. A browser could make a WebSocket connection to the Cheese Finder game server. The server could then inform browser clients that a game had expired. However, this would require the server application to maintain a list of active WebSocket clients and send a message to each client when the hour changes. This would make the server more complex and more expensive to operate.

Question: Could a computer work out how people play Cheese Finder by watching game players?

Answer: This is a very interesting question. To answer it, we must consider what information goes into the server. The server receives requests when users click buttons on the game grid. The browser sends the x and y values of a particular square, and the server sends back the color style for that square. The server doesn't know which player each request is from, so it can't work out what any given player is doing. However, it can determine the most "popular" squares on the grid. The server might be able to combine the knowledge of square popularity and the actual cheese positions to get some broad ideas of strategy, but it would not be possible to learn more than that. However, changing the game so that the browser sent the server a user ID with each request would make a huge difference. The server could then observe individual players and watch what they do.

Question: How do we use pseudo-random numbers to encode data?

Answer: The key to this is the `exclusive-or` logical operator. You have probably heard of the `and` logical operator (output a `true` if both inputs are true) and the `or` operator (output a `true` if either or both inputs are true). The `exclusive-or` operator outputs a `true` if either input is **true** but `false` if both inputs are `true`). You could say that `exclusive-or` outputs a `true` if the inputs are different.

The interesting thing about `exclusive-or` is that if you apply the operation twice, you will get back to the value you started with. What do I mean by this? Let's look at some JavaScript. The JavaScript operator to perform `exclusive-or` is ^. If we apply this between two values, we will get a result that is the `exclusive-or` of all the bits in the values.

```
99^45
78
```

If we `exclusive-or` the value 99 with the value 45, we get the value 78. The `exclusive-or` operation combines the bits used to store the values 99 and 45 using the `exclusive-or` operation and generates a result of 78.

```
78^45
99
```

The interesting thing about `exclusive-or` is that if I now `exclusive-or` the value 78 with 45, I get back to the value 99 again. Now, consider that 99 is the number I want to keep secret, and 45 is my encryption key. I can send the value 78 as a public message because only someone with the key can convert it back into the actual value. I would like a repeatable stream of numbers to encrypt successive values in a block of data, and that is what pseudo-random numbers give me. I can send you a block of data over a public channel, and I only need to use a super-secure connection to send you the seed values for the pseudo-random stream that will be used to decrypt it.

Question: How do we make pseudo-random numbers harder to "crack"?

Answer: We have seen that we can use multiplication, addition, and modulus to create a new pseudo-random value based on the previous one. However, someone with a lot of computer power could look at the sequence of values and work out the seed values by trying lots of combinations.

To counter this, we could generate two streams and then combine a successive value in some way to produce the output. This would require more computing effort to create the random sequence and more complex seed values, but it would make it much harder to crack. JavaScript provides the random function that generates "general purpose" random numbers, and it provides a crypto version that provides sequences that are harder to "crack."

Question: Do pseudo-random numbers have anything to do with cryptocurrencies?

Answer: Cryptocurrencies assign value to the process of solving mathematical puzzles based on pseudo-random sequences. For example, I could give you a sequence of 10,000 numbers and ask you to work out the random number seed values that were used to create it. When you find the seeds, we could give that solution some value in our economy and move on to the next problem to calculate some more money. The "puzzles" set are much more complex than simple pseudo-random sequences, but the underlying principle is the same.

Question: How do you get "proper" random numbers?

Answer: We now know that most computer-generated random numbers are made from a stream of pseudo-random values. But the `Math.random` function provided by JavaScript seems to be random each time we use it. How does this work? The `Math.random` function uses something that is "random enough" as a starting value. This might be the time in microseconds (a value that will differ each time the program runs). For "professional" quality randomness, you have to use additional hardware, perhaps a component that produces a "noisy" electrical signal that can be measured to get a truly random value.

Question: When should you use a cache?

Answer: The aim of a cache is to reduce the amount of time a program spends calculating values that it uses a lot as it runs. When deciding when to add a cache, you must consider how often the value is recalculated, how much memory it would take to store the cache, and how long it would take to get values from the cache. You should also consider the value of your time to write the extra code that will perform the caching.

Question: What does the default operator do?

Answer: The default operator (||) allows us to specify a value to be used if a given value is invalid. We used it to select a port value for our server.

```
const port = process.env.PORT || 8080
```

Node.js includes a `process` object that provides our application information about the currently running process. The `process` object contains an `env` property, a list of environment variables used to send settings information to our program. The external environment can set an environment variable to tell our program something. The external environment might want to tell our server the network port on which the server is to run. It can do this by adding a `PORT` environment variable. On the other hand, the external environment might not add a `PORT` value, so the server will need to have a default-to value to use.

The || operator makes it easy to create a default value. You could also use it in a function to assign default values to function parameters that have not been provided or are invalid. Default values can be useful, but you must ensure a default value is appropriate for every kind of invalid input.

7

Design an application

What you will learn

We can now create applications that use the browser and server to deliver a user experience. The browser downloads HTML pages from the server and runs JavaScript programs on those pages that interact with the server's services. Our first versions of the Cheese Finder game ran entirely in the browser. This made their operation vulnerable as it is possible to view the execution of a JavaScript program on the browser using the Developer Tools. We improved the security of Cheese Finder by moving some functions into the server and creating a protocol of requests and responses that allow code in the browser to display the game to the player. We've seen that a part of developing an application that works this way involves designing the interactions between server and browser and deciding where tasks should be performed.

In this chapter, we will design an application from the ground up. We will start with an idea, make sure the idea is ethically sound, and then create the workflow that will be followed when running the application. Then we will move on to create the underlying data structures the application will need as it runs. This will provide the perfect platform for building the application itself, which we will do in the next chapter. On the way, we will learn about another JavaScript hero—the *class*.

As we move deeper into this book, your need for the glossary might be dropping, but don't forget that it is always online at *https://begintocodecloud.com/glossary.html*.

The Tiny Survey application

We are going to create a voting application called "Tiny Survey." When a bunch of people decide to do *something*, the first problem is deciding what that *something* is. The decisions could range from pizza toppings, movies to see, or perhaps even the person to marry. We can help this process by creating an application to manage voting. We will use the application to pick the best of several possible options. Anyone can create a Tiny Survey for a particular topic on our web application, and then people can vote for the option they want. Once someone has voted, they get to see the state of the votes, and after the last person has had their vote, you can then use the result to decide what to do. Or perhaps you might decide to have another vote about something else.

Ethics, privacy, and security

Now that we have decided what Tiny Survey will do, we should consider whether we should do it and the implications of building it. This is not necessarily a programming consideration, but I think it is a necessary one. Just because something can be built does not necessarily mean that it is a good idea to build it. We need to consider

- The ethical aspects (can this application be used to make people unhappy?)

- The privacy aspects (can this application be used to violate the privacy of its users?)

- The security (can this application be provided securely?)

Let's take each of these in turn.

Ethics

Ethics is all about "right" or "wrong." You might think a programming book is a strange place to discuss right or wrong, but I think this is a worthwhile exercise. Companies take ethical stances on what they do and will examine their products and business process from this perspective.

The Tiny Survey application does not appear to raise any ethical issues. It is simply a way that a group of people can agree on a preferred option. It doesn't encourage bad behavior or steer the users in any particular direction. It could be used for a group of people to choose the most appalling insult for a rival football team, but they could also use a piece of paper or email for that.

However, we might consider adding an "Option Recommendation" feature that offers survey options based on the first three entered when a survey is being built. The feature would look through all the submitted surveys and find matches. This would mean that once I had entered the first three types of pizza for my `robspizza` survey, the program would suggest "vegetable supreme" as one of the options because other lists containing pizza names also contained this. I might find this useful if I had forgotten to add "vegetable supreme" to my list, but is it ethical?

This is an interesting question. It might be useful but also dangerous, particularly if the feature ranks options and recommends the most popular ones. Now the options take on a life of their own. Nasty people could "game" the application by creating lists containing options they want other people to see. At this point, I don't think we have an ethical application anymore.

I might be overthinking things a bit here—I am a programmer after all—but I think an "ethical check" of applications you are about to build is a good idea. And, like other risks to a project that should be monitored, you should regularly review a project during development to check if any new ethical issues have arisen.

Privacy

At this point, I'm not considering issues around the dangers of people stealing data from our application. That is for the security section coming next. Instead, I'm thinking about how someone providing the application could compromise the users' privacy. What do I mean by this? Well, after a few uses, the Tiny Survey system could end up knowing my five favorite pizzas and five favorite movies. The application could track its users so that it knows who created a survey and whether a given person has responded to it. This tracking would need to use the local storage of my browser, which means that the survey can only work out that my browser likes pepperoni pizza and the *Clueless* movie, not that Rob Miles has those preferences. And if I clear out my browser's local storage or use multiple browsers, I can't be tracked like this. However, gathering information in this way could be very useful. Next time I use Tiny Survey, it might pop up a recommendation for a movie or a pizza topping that other people with my preferences also like. Or it could find a movie and tell me about that. The fact that many people who like pepperoni pizza also like *Clueless* might also have value. Once some data has been collected, it can be used in many ways.

Someone using Tiny Survey has no way of knowing whether the information they enter is being used in these ways; they just have to trust that the application is respecting their privacy. Data protection codes of practice require an application to ask the user for informed consent if data is to be used for anything other than the purpose for which it was entered. In our case, Tiny Survey will not use responses anywhere else, so there is no need to ask for consent. However, you might want to consider these issues next time you fill in a survey on your favorite social media platform. They already have your consent to do anything they like with your surveys and the responses they receive. The European Union has created the General Data Protection Regulation, which sets out data protection and privacy laws. We need to make sure that our application works in accordance with these. You can find out more at *https://en.wikipedia.org/wiki/General_Data_Protection_Regulation*.

Security

The Tiny Survey application doesn't take any steps to keep the responses in a survey private. Once someone has the name of a survey, they can access it, pick favorites, and see the current scores. This might be a problem if a group of people uses the application to pick the best password, but anyone who does that probably deserves all the problems they get.

However, when considering security, you also have to consider the system's vulnerability to attack. The application will expose endpoints used to enter lists of responses, vote on options, and read back results. The application uses these endpoints in the browser as it runs. But what if someone creates a program that talks directly to these endpoints? The program could use the endpoints to create surveys, search for surveys by repeatedly asking for different survey names, and then randomly vote on them. It could create spurious surveys containing skewed data, trying to convince people that ham and pineapple is the best pizza topping by giving it thousands of votes.

These problems could be addressed by requiring users to log in before using the application. However, this would make it harder to use and raise a whole new set of problems regarding user management. In the next chapter, we will discover how to implement logins on an application.

Happy endings

I've always considered programming the "science of the happy ending." If you do everything right, you end up with a happy user running a program that does what they want and keeps them safe. Considering ethics, privacy, and security before you build any application is a very good idea to get you to that happy place. Now we can move on to consider how our application will work.

Don't reinvent the wheel

One final point worth mentioning is that you should check whether a product already exists before you start building it. We are using Tiny Survey as a learning exercise, but if I was asked to build such an application, my first action would be to search for any existing ones. Much as I love to write code, I try to avoid writing something already made.

Application workflow

The absolute worst thing we could do right now is to start writing JavaScript. Before we write any code, we must decide how the application is used. We have a text description of what Tiny Survey is going to do. But we need more detail. We need to create a *workflow* that sets out the steps to be performed when a survey is created. We use workflows all the time. We implement a workflow when we follow a recipe to bake a cake. Workflows have a particular sequence (we need to turn the oven on before we put the cake in) and conditional elements (we need to have all the ingredients for our cake before we start). A good way to design a workflow for the Tiny Survey application is to make a prototype version. This will have all the pages that will be present in the finished version, but the pages will not be functional. They will just set out what the user will see when using the application. We can work through each page in the same order they would be used, starting with the index page.

Figure 7-1 shows a prototype index page for the Tiny Survey application. The user can either enter the topic of an existing survey (to select their preferred option) or the name of a survey that doesn't exist (to create a new survey).

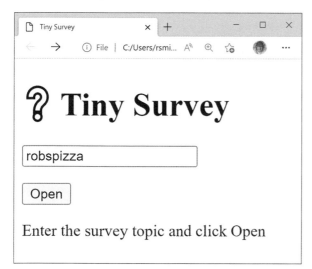

Figure 7-1   Tiny Survey start page

Index page

Let's follow the workflow to make a new survey. I'm buying everyone pizza, so I want to know what toppings people prefer. I'm going to create a survey topic of robspizza.

When I click **Open**, the page will change to one where I can enter the toppings I want people to choose from.

Below, you can see the HTML for the index page. The content is very simple, with a question mark emoji as the application logo.

```html
<!DOCTYPE html>
<html>

<head>
  <title>Tiny Survey</title>
</head>

<body>
  <h1>&#10068; Tiny Survey</h1>                          Question emoji in the title
  <p>
    <input type="text" spellcheck="false" value="robspizza">
  </p>
  <p>
    <button onclick="doEnterOptions();">Open</button>
  </p>
  <p>Enter the survey topic and click Open</p>

  <script>
    function doEnterOptions() {                          Open button event handler
      window.open("enteroptions.html", "_self");
    }
  </script>
</body>

</html>
```

At the bottom of the page, you can see the function doEnterOptions, which is called when the **Open** button is clicked. This uses the window.open function to open a page called enteroptions.html. Let's look at that page next.

Enter options

The enteroptions.html page displays five inputs that are used to set the options for the survey. The demonstration survey is all about pizza toppings. **Figure 7-2** shows that I've entered the name of the toppings I want everyone to choose from. When I click **Start**, the survey will go live and allow me to vote.

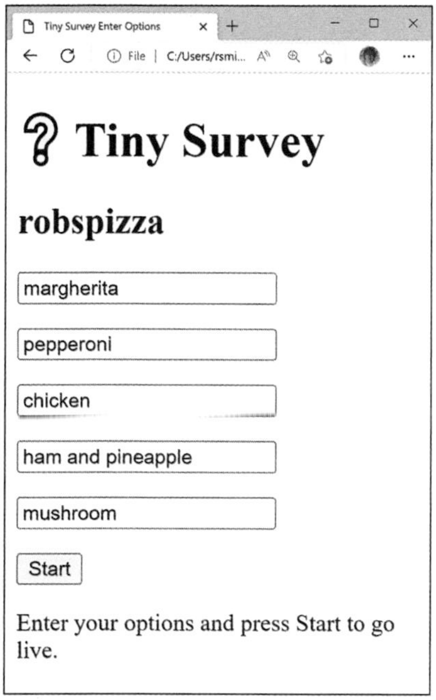

Figure 7-2 Tiny Survey entry options

The content of the `enteroptions.html` page is shown below. This contains five HTML input elements which have been pre-set with the demonstration pizza topping names. We will add the working HTML elements to read options from the user once we have decided we are okay with the workflow through the application.

```html
<!DOCTYPE html>
<html>

<head>
  <title>Tiny Survey Enter Options</title>
</head>

<body>

  <h1>&#10068; Tiny Survey</h1>
  <h2>robspizza</h2>
  <p><input value="margherita"></p>
  <p><input value="pepperoni"></p>
  <p><input value="chicken"></p>
  <p><input value="ham and pineapple"></p>
  <p><input value="mushroom"></p>
  <p>
    <button onclick="doStartSurvey();">Start</button>
```

Enter options title

Survey topic

Pre-set inputs

```
    </p>
    <p>
      Enter your options and press Start to go live.
    </p>

    <script>
      function doStartSurvey () {                         Start button event handler
        window.open("selectoption.html", "_self");
      }
    </script>
  </body>

</html>
```

When the **Start** button is clicked, a page called `selectoption.html` is displayed. Let's look at that.

Select option

Figure 7-3 shows the select option page. The `selectoption.html` page holds five radio button inputs.

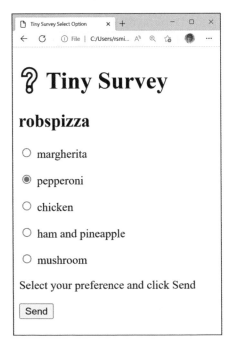

Figure 7-3   Selection page

The selection buttons are grouped so that only one can be selected anytime. Users can click the button to select the option they want. I'm a big fan of pepperoni. When I click the **Send** button, my selection will be saved, and the count for that option will be updated. The listing below shows the `selectoption.html` page. It uses HTML labels associated with the radio buttons used to get the option selection. Radio buttons that have the same name attribute are part of a group. Only one button can be pressed at any time.

```html
<!DOCTYPE html>
<html>

<head>
  <title>Tiny Survey Select Option</title>          Select option title
</head>

<body>
  <h1>&#10068; Tiny Survey</h1>
  <h2>robspizza</h2>
  <p>
    <input type="radio" name="selections" id="option1">   Radio button
    <label for="option1">margherita</label>   Label for the button containing the option
  </p>
  <p>
    <input type="radio" name="selections" id="option2">
    <label for="option2">pepperoni</label>
  </p>
  <p>
    <input type="radio" name="selections" id="option3">
    <label for="option3">chicken</label>
  </p>
  <p>
    <input type="radio" name="selections" id="option4">
    <label for="option4">ham and pineapple</label>
  </p>
  <p>
    <input type="radio" name="selections" id="option5">
    <label for="option5">mushroom</label>
  </p>
  <p>
    Select your preference and click Send
  </p>
  <p>
    <button onclick="doSendSelection()">Send</button>
  </p>
```

```
<script>
  function doSendSelection() {                                Event handler for Send button
    window.open("displayresults.html", "_self");
  }

</script>
</body>

</html>
```

The user of the survey will select an option and then click **Send**. This runs the `doSend-Selection` function, which loads the `displayresults.html` page.

Display results

Figure 7-4 shows the results page. Currently, my favorite seems to be getting the most votes, which is nice. The user can click **Reload** to see new count values. This version of the survey doesn't automatically update the display.

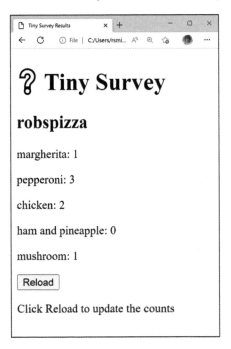

Figure 7-4   Results page

Following is the HTML that shows the results display. The results values are all fixed strings of text that show what the page will look like when the Tiny Survey is used. The **Reload** button does nothing when it is pressed.

```
<!DOCTYPE html>
<html>

<head>
  <title>Tiny Survey Results</title>
</head>

<body>
    <h1>&#10068; Tiny Survey</h1>
    <h2>robspizza</h2>
    <p>margherita: 1</p>
    <p>pepperoni: 3</p>
    <p>chicken: 2 </p>
    <p>ham and pineapple: 0</p>
    <p>mushroom: 1</p>
    <p>
      <button>Reload</button>
    </p>
    <p>
      Click Reload to update the counts
    </p>
  </div>
</body>

</html>
```

Extra workflows

We have just worked through the workflow for creating a survey, entering the options, selecting an option, and then displaying the results. The workflow will be slightly different if the user enters the name of an existing survey. In that case, they will be taken directly to the **Select Option** page, followed by the **Show Results** page.

Scan the QR code or click *https://www.youtube.com/watch?v=-2-i4ZJsqls* for a video walk-through of this Make Something Happen.

Play with the Tiny Survey pages

Now that you have your prototype, you can work through it to understand what you are trying to build and ensure there aren't any ambiguities or unknowns. Start your browser and open the `index.html` file in the **Ch07-01_Tiny_Survey_Prototype** folder. You can work through the screens above to examine how the application would be used.

🏭 **CODE ANALYSIS**

Tiny Survey

This is not really a code analysis because we don't have any code yet, but it does seem rather complicated, and you might have some questions about it.

Question: Does the prototype need to simulate opening an existing survey?

Answer: The current prototype shows the workflow for creating a new survey (called `robspizza`) which is all about pizza toppings. It doesn't show the situation where a user enters the name of a survey that someone else has created and selects an option. You could do this by creating two `index.html` files—one called `indexNew.html` and the other `indexSel.html`, which show the two different workflows. Software designers talk about "user stories," where they describe a scenario for a workflow in which a user comes to the system with a particular need.

Question: Is it possible for someone to vote more than once?

Answer: Yes, they can. This is to keep the workflow simple. In later chapters, we will discover how an application running on a server can use "cookies" (small amounts of data stored by the browser) to track the actions of users and prevent users from voting more than once.

Question: Can the count values be viewed without selecting an option?

Answer: If the user opens an existing survey, they are taken to the option selection page for the survey, not the results page, so they have to vote to see the count values. Tiny Survey is only designed for quick "which movie shall we watch" surveys in which everyone in the room picks their option, and the survey ends.

If we were making the Tiny Survey application for a customer, and they really wanted the application to allow users to view the counts without selecting an option, we could allow users to click **Send** on the **Select Option** page without clicking any radio button. Or, we could add a **No Selection** radio button to the **Select Option** page. If the application uses cookies (see above), it could record in the browser which surveys a user has voted for and take them straight to the results page if they select a survey in which they have already voted.

PROGRAMMER'S POINT

Make good use of sample pages

Temporary pages like these are a great way to design a workflow. If you work for a customer, you can show them exactly how the application will be used. Simple HTML files like the ones we have used are very quick to make, and once you have made a few, you can copy and reuse them for each new application you design. Try very hard not to put any actual working code in your sample pages; just populate them with sample data. However, I think it is worth spending a few minutes picking a logo on each page. Emojis are a great source for simple "place-holder" images that you can replace with better ones later.

If you don't want to use HTML for your workflow designs, you can draw out the different screens on sticky notes, put them on a whiteboard and then draw lines between them to show the workflow. If you do this, remember to photograph your finished design. There are also prototyping tools like Adobe XD, which can be used effectively when creating workflows.

Application data storage

So far, we've talked about the data elements in the Tiny Survey application in general terms. Now that we have an idea of the application's workflow, we can identify what data should be stored and how it should be structured. This is a great point to introduce a new JavaScript hero who can help with this.

JavaScript hero: classes

We know some data items, such as `option`, `survey`, and `count`, will be needed in the Tiny Survey application, but we haven't really considered how we will structure them. Now, we will look at a JavaScript hero, which makes this much easier. Many other programming languages use "classes" to structure their solutions. We've managed to create quite a few useful applications without using any classes at all. JavaScript provides classes and supports useful class-based features such as *inheritance*, but you are not forced to use them. However, the Tiny Survey application would benefit from some classes, so let's take a look at them and how they work.

Classes versus objects

The first thing we need to do is work out the difference between classes and objects. Until now, the data in our applications has been made up of individual values. There has not been much of a need to "lump" things together. And when we needed to lump things together, we used an object literal. An example of an object literal in action is what we did in Chapter 1 in the Programmer's Point, "Make good use of object literals."

A problem with object literals is they are created without any form of validation. Consider the two object literals below. The intention of the code is to create two objects which contain `name` and `address` properties. However, the variable `invalidPerson` does not contain the correct properties. The properties are called `Name` and `newname`.

```
Let validPerson = { name:"Rob", address:"House of Rob"};
let invalidPerson = { Name:"Jim", newname:"House of Jim"};
```

The variable `invalidPerson` would not be used correctly by a function that expects to receive an object containing a `name` and an `address` property. The following `displayPersonDetails` function displays the contents of a person. It would work correctly with `validPerson` but display an undefined name and address if used with `invalidPerson`.

```
Function displayPersonDetails(person){
    console.log("Name: "+ person.name);
    console.log("Address: "+ person.address);
}
```

We could add tests to the displayPersonDetails function to ensure an object's correct properties are present. The code below shows how we would do this. Values of missing properties are set to undefined, so the code will display the error message if the person object doesn't contain a name.

```
if(person.name == undefined){
    console.log("Name property missing from input");
}
else{
    console.log("Name: "+ person.name);
}
```

However, adding these tests to all the code that works with person details would be time-consuming. It would be useful if we could create something that defines the required properties for a PersonDetails object so that someone using it could be sure that it has all the required ones. We can do this with a class.

The class PersonDetails is defined below. The important thing to note about the definition is that it doesn't make a data store that can hold PersonDetails information. Instead, it tells JavaScript how to make an object that is an instance of the Person-Details class. Every class has a constructor method that runs when a new instance of that class is created. The constructor creates properties that are part of the class—in this case, name and address.

```
Class PersonDetails {
    constructor(name,address){
        this.name = name;
        this.address = address;
    }
}
```

The following statement creates a new PersonDetails object, which is referred to by the rob variable. This object is called an *instance* of the PersonDetails class. The object has name and address properties, which the constructor sets. The keyword new tells JavaScript to make a new instance of the class. The arguments to the call are passed into the constructor function for the class.

```
Let rob = new PersonDetails("Rob","Rob's house")
```

MAKE SOMETHING HAPPEN 30

Scan the QR code or click *https://www.youtube.com/watch?v=m4XRLdq3jjM* for a video walk-through of this Make Something Happen.

Investigate classes

Let's take a look at how you can create instances of classes and work with them. Start your browser and open the index.html file in the **Ch07-02_Classes_Investigation** example folder. Open the browser's **Developer Tools** and select the **Console** view.

The JavaScript code in this sample file contains a definition of a PersonDetails class. It is exactly the same as the definition you saw earlier, but an extra statement in the constructor method logs a message to the console each time a PersonDetails instance is created.

```
class PersonDetails {

    constructor(newname, newAddress) {
        this.name = newname;
        this.address = newAddress;
        console.log("I just made a PersonDetails object: " + this.name +
                " :  " + this.address);
    }
}
```

Type the statement below and press **Enter**:

```
let rob = new PersonDetails("Rob","Rob's house")
```

When a program makes a new class instance, the `constructor` method for the `Person-Details` class gets control and displays a message. Properties are assigned to values inside the new object using `this` keyword. Let's take some time to consider what `this` means.

A keyword is a word in JavaScript that has special meaning. We've seen a few. The words `if` and `function` are keywords. These words have special meanings in the language. The word `this` is another keyword. Humans use this all the time. It's a shorthand that means "the thing we are talking about." My wife occasionally picks up a T-shirt I have just gotten out of the wardrobe and says, "You're not going to wear this?" In this context, the word *this* means "this ugly shirt you insist on wearing." In JavaScript, the keyword `this` is a shorthand for "a reference to the object in whose context this code is running." In the `constructor` of a class, a `this` reference refers to the object being created.

```
> let rob = new PersonDetails("Rob","Rob's house")
  I just made a PersonDetails object:Rob :Rob's house
```

The statement below from the `constructor` method adds the `address` property to the object that `this` refers to (the object being set up by the `constructor`). The `newAddress` variable is a parameter to the constructor that contains the address value to be put into the `PersonDetails` object.

```
this.address = newAddress;
```

The confusing thing about `this` in JavaScript is that it refers to different things according to the context in which it is being used. We will discuss these contexts when we get to them, or you can read the whole story of `this` in the glossary.

When the `constructor` has finished, it creates a new instance of the class, which will contain `name` and `address` properties that the `constructor` set.

You might now wonder what happens if the constructor is not provided with `name` and `address` values. Type the statement below and press **Enter**:

```
let badPerson = new PersonDetails()
```

The `constructor` has not been provided with `name` or `address` values, so it will create a `badperson` object showing `undefined` for the `name` and `address` values, as shown next.

```
I just made a PersonDetails object:undefined :undefined
```

You might think that this means that classes don't represent an advance in object literals. It looks like it is still possible to create invalid PersonDetails objects. However, classes have a crucial advantage: We can write code that runs when a new PersonDetails value is created, and that code can ensure that a person is created with valid contents. Leave the **Console** window open; you will use it in the next section.

Class construction

You might have some questions about the class construction process.

Question: What does new do?

> **Answer:** The new keyword starts the creation of a new class instance. The new keyword is followed by the class name. When a running JavaScript program encounters new, it then looks for the class that has been specified and copies the arguments following the class name into a constructor call.
>
> In the case of the new keyword below, JavaScript will look for the PersonDetails class definition, create an empty object, and then call the PersonDetails constructor method, passing it "Rob" as the first argument and "Rob's house" as the second. The constructor will then fill in any properties of that object, and it will then be returned. In the case of the earlier statement, the variable rob would be made to refer to the new object. If a program tries to create a new instance of a class that has not been defined, the program will stop with an error.

```
let rob = new PersonDetails("Rob","Rob's house")
```

Question: Do we ever call the constructor method in a class?

> **Answer:** We never call the constructor ourselves. It is called when a new is performed.

Question: What does this mean again?

> **Answer:** Rather than think about what this means, start by thinking about the problem it is being used to solve. The PersonDetails constructor makes a new class instance, which is given name and address properties. For the PersonDetails constructor to work, it will need a reference to the new object being created. The reference is provided in the form of a keyword called this.

Question: What is the difference between a function and a method?

Answer: A function is a code block with a name that exists outside any object. We've created quite a few functions as we've been learning JavaScript. A method is a code block with a name declared inside an object; it allows the object to perform behaviors. Currently, the only method we've created has had the special name `constructor` and runs when an object instance is created. We can add other methods to a class and do so later in this chapter.

Question: What is the difference between a class and an object?

Answer: The class is the recipe. The object is the cake. In other words, the class provides the instructions that tell JavaScript how to make the object, which is made from the class.

Class advantages

At the moment, you might be wondering why you would use a class. You can put an object literal directly into your code any time you want one. You must make the class definition with a class and then write the `constructor` function. One answer is that using classes makes your programs more reliable. Code in a `constructor` can validate incoming properties and only create an instance if they are correct.

🚀 MAKE SOMETHING HAPPEN 31

Scan the QR code or click *https://www.youtube.com/watch?v=56VDk-YKa6U* for a video walk-through of this Make Something Happen.

Valid objects

You should already be in the `index.html` file in the **Ch07-02_Classes_Investigation** example folder. If not, browse to this file, open it with the browser, and then open the **Console** in the **Developer Tools** view. Now type in the following:

```
let x = new PersonDetails(1/"fred")
```

This is completely legal JavaScript, which will run successfully. It is also a very bad thing to do. The result of dividing a number by a string is the JavaScript value NaN. The result of leaving off an argument to a function call (the above construction of `PersonDetails` does not have an address value) is a parameter set to `undefined` when the function runs. So, we are asking the `PersonDetails` constructor to create an object that is a `PersonDetails` instance with a name of NaN and an address of `undefined`. Press **Enter** to run the statement:

```
> let x = new PersonDetails(1/"fred")
  I just made a PersonDetails object:NaN :undefined
```

The `constructor` has made a `PersonDetails` object with a name of NaN and an address of `undefined`. If the program subsequently uses this object, it will produce spurious results. If you've ever seen a web page display the NaN or `undefined` messages, you might understand why this happens now.

You want a way to ensure that a `PersonDetails` object always has valid content. I've made a class that has taken a course in self-defense. It won't let you create an invalid person. I call it `ValidPersonDetails`. Let's see if you can break that. Type in the following to test it:

```
let y = new ValidPersonDetails(1/"fred")
```

This is trying to make a new `ValidPersonDetails` instance using the same invalid arguments as before: The name is not a number, and the address is undefined. Press **Enter** to see what happens this time.

```
> let y = new ValidPersonDetails(1/"fred")
⊗ ▶ Uncaught  ▶ (2) ['Invalid name', 'Invalid address']
```

This time, the program displays an error. The `constructor` for the `ValidPersonDetails` class has thrown an *exception*. You will learn more about exceptions in Chapter 9. An exception is an object that describes something bad that has just happened. A program can throw an exception at any point in the code. When an exception is thrown, JavaScript transfers the program execution to a piece of code designed to catch and handle the exception. In this case, the exception information is an array containing the "Invalid name" and "Invalid address" messages describing what has gone wrong. The program stops if there is no code to catch and deal with the exception. Our program will stop if it tries to create an invalid PersonDetails instance.

You might like to try creating more ValidPersonDetails objects. You will discover that creating a ValidPersonDetails object with anything other than two strings for name and address is impossible.

```
> let z = new ValidPersonDetails("Rob", "Rob's House")
  I just made a ValidPersonDetails object:Rob :Rob's House
```

Above, you can see proof that it is possible to create an instance of ValidPersonDetails as long as you provide the correct kind of arguments. Let's look at how this works.

Create valid objects

We've seen that a crucial difference between creating a literal object (by just creating the object in the code) and creating a new instance of a class (by using the new keyword) is that our code gets control during construction. Code in the constructor for an object can enforce rules that will ensure that the object contains valid content. Let's see how this works.

```
class ValidPersonDetails {

  constructor(name, address) {
    let error = "";                                  Create an empty error string
    if (typeof (name) == 'string') {                 Make sure that the name is a string
      this.name = name;                              If it is, create the property
    }
    else {                                           If the name isn't a string...
      error = "Invalid name. ";                      ...add an error message
    }
    if (typeof (address) == 'string') {              Make sure the address is a string
      this.address = address;                        Set the address property if it is valid
    }
    else {                                           Add to the error string if the address is invalid
      error = error + "Invalid address. ";
    }

    if (error != "") {                               If the error string is not empty, something failed
      throw error;                                   Stop the function and throw an exception
    }
```

```
    }
    console.log("I just made a ValidPersonDetails object:" + name + ":" + address);
  }
}
```

CODE ANALYSIS

Constructor validation

We've just seen a `constructor` that ensures an object is only created with valid content. You might have some questions about how it does this.

Question: What does `typeof` do?

> **Answer:** The `typeof` operator acts on a JavaScript variable and returns a string containing the type of that variable. We've seen that all variables have a particular type, which is inferred when a variable is created.
>
> The following pair of statements would display the message "number" on the console because the variable type is number. If you assign the value 99 (or any expression that evaluates to a number) to a variable, JavaScript will set the variable type to number.

```
let age = 99;
console.log(typeof age);
```

> The following statements would output the message "string" because JavaScript has worked out that name contains a string. The `constructor` for `ValidPersonDetails` uses `typeof` to ensure that the `name` and `address` parameters are both strings.

```
let name = "Rob";
console.log(typeof name);
```

> The following code would output the `PersonDetails` message because the `rob` reference has been made to refer to an object of that type. This means we could make a function that only works on particular parameter types. It could check the type of an incoming object and only accept certain types.

```
let rob = new PersonDetails("Rob","Rob's house");
console.log(typeof name);
```

Question: What does the `throw` operation throw in our `constructor`?

Answer: As the `constructor` runs, it creates a tiny "error report" about the construction process in the `error` variable. The `error` variable starts as an empty array. If the `constructor` detects that the name is not a valid string, it adds "Invalid name" to the error array. It adds another message if the address is not valid. If everything works correctly, the constructor's `error` variable will contain an empty array at the end of the construction process. If the error contains anything else, the `constructor` decides that the construction process has failed and throws the error array as an exception description.

Question: Could the `constructor` enforce other rules?

Answer: Yes, it could. At the moment, the `ValidPersonDetails` is quite happy to create an object with an empty string for the name or address. You might want it to reject empty strings for those items. It could even test to make sure that the name was only made up of alphabetic characters or had a minimum length and that the address contained a valid zip code. All these tests would occur when the object was created, making it much more difficult to make an invalid person.

Question: Is there anything to stop a program from assigning an invalid value to a property of an existing `ValidPersonDetails` object?

Answer: No. The construction gets control when the object is created and can stop bad things from happening, but once the object has been created, there is nothing to stop changes to the properties of the object.

The following two statements would result in a `ValidPersonDetails` object with a `name` property with the value of `NaN`.

```
let rob = new ValidPersonDetails("Rob","Rob's house");
rob.name = 1/"fred";
```

If you want to create managed properties of objects that have `get` and `set` behaviors, you can use the object `defineProperty` method, which is described at
https://developer.mozilla.org/en-US/docs/web/javascript/reference/global_objects/object/defineproperty.

Question: Could we use an object literal to provide the values for a `constructor`?

Answer: This is a very good idea. We have already seen how we can use object literals to reduce the chance of mistakes when calling functions. It makes sense to do this with the `constructor` method, too. The following statement creates an instance of the `PerfectPersonDetails` class.

```
let rob = new PerfectPersonDetails({address:"House of Rob",
                                    name:"Rob Miles"});
```

The `constructor` for the class looks like this:

```
class PerfectPersonDetails {

  constructor(newValue) {
    let error = [];
    if (typeof (newValue.name) == 'string') {
      this.name = newValue.name;
    }
    else {
      error.push("Invalid name");
    }
    if (typeof (newValue.address) == 'string') {
      this.address = newValue.address;
    }
    else {
      error.push("Invalid address");
    }
    if (error.length != 0) {
      throw error;
    }
    console.log("I just made a PerfectPersonDetails object:" +
              newValue.name + " : " + newValue.address);
  }
}
```

The `constructor` has a single parameter called `newValue`, which is an object containing all the setup information required to create a new `PerfectPerson`. This class is provided in the **Ch07-02_Classes_Investigation** example, so you can create an instance yourself if you want.

PROGRAMMER'S POINT

Catch errors "before they happen" with TypeScript

You might find the heading for this programmer's point confusing. Surely, catching errors before they happen would involve using a time machine? It turns out that there are two types of error handling. The code we are adding to the `ValidPersonDetails` constructor is reacting to an error when it occurs during program execution. However, a better idea might be to have a programming language that allows you to specify the type of an element in a program and then reject code where the element is being used incorrectly before the program even runs. TypeScript is an extension to the JavaScript language that allows us to do this and is well worth investigating.

If you want to refresh your understanding of object literals, take a look at Chapter 1's Programmer's Point, "Make good use of object literals."

Classes for Tiny Survey

Now that we know how to use classes, we can create some to hold the data items in the Tiny Survey application. We need three classes, which we can call Survey, Option, and Surveys. We learn what properties they should hold by examining the workflow we have created.

The Option class

We can start by creating the class for the option object. The code below declares the Option class and shows the constructor method for the class.

```
class Option{
  constructor(newValue) {
    this.text = newValue.text;
    this.count = newValue.count;
  }
}
```

The constructor accepts an object containing the initial values for the Option, the Option's text (for example, "pepperoni"), and the Count, which will usually be 0.

The statement below creates a variable called option1, which refers to a new Option instance with "pepperoni" as the option text and a Count of 0.

```
let option1 = new Option({ text: "pepperoni", count:0 });
```

Option methods

Until now, all our classes have only contained the constructor method. However, we can add our own methods to a class, allowing the class to do things for us. Putting methods in a class allows us to make our code slightly safer. For example, consider the effect of the code below:

```
option1.Count = option1.count + 1
```

This code was intended to increment the Count value for an option. Unfortunately, it won't work. You might have to look hard to find the mistake. However, if you look carefully, you will see that the identifier Count has been misspelled. One version has Count, with an uppercase C. This is not going to cause the program to fail. JavaScript will just add a new property called Count to the object referred to by option1 and continue happily on its way. However, you will not be happy because the value of the count property is not going up when it should. A better solution is to create a method in the Option class, which increments the count property for us. We could also add a method that returns the count property value.

```
class Option{
  constructor(newValue) {
    this.text = newValue.text;
    this.count = newValue.count;
  }

  incrementCount(){
    this.count = this.count+1;
  }

  getCount(){
    return this.count;
  }

  getText(){
    return this.text;
  }
}
```

A program can now call the incrementCount method on an option to get the option to make the count value for that option larger by 1. It can also use the getCount function if it needs to know the value of the count. I've also added a method called getText, which returns the option's text.

You might think I have made a mistake by leaving the word function off the front of the method declarations above. However, this is not the case (as if!). When creating a method in a class, you start with the method name; there is nothing in front of it.

PROGRAMMER'S POINT

Use methods to improve resilience

Using methods like `incrementCount` and `getCount` in the `Option` class make the class operation more secure. If someone tries to call `incrementcount` to increment the counter, the program will fail at run time because the method name has been spelled incorrectly. But at least you won't have to spend ages trying to work out why a counter is not updating when it should.

Providing an `incrementCount` method rather than expecting people to increment the `count` property inside an `Option` object also improves security slightly. If the only thing the application is supposed to do with the `count` value is make it larger, it should not be possible to do anything else with it. Some programming languages can mark class members as *private*, which means they can only be used in methods running inside the class. It would be wonderful if we could make the `count` property private to the `Option` class and prevent external access to it. Unfortunately, JavaScript doesn't support this, so any code outside an `Option` object can access and change any class member, including `count`. This means that methods such as `incrementCount` don't bring as much extra security as they should, but they are still worth doing because they clarify the code. It is never a good idea to expect users of a class to directly access the properties in the class, which is why there is now a `getText` method to get the option's text.

The Survey class

Each survey will have a topic (what the survey is about) and a list of options. The survey's constructor is given the survey's topic and a list of options.

```
constructor(newValue) {
  this.topic = newValue.topic;                    Set the topic name
  this.options = [];                              Make an option array
  newValue.options.forEach(optionValues => {      Work through the supplied option texts
    let newOption = new Option(optionValues);     Make a new option
    this.options.push(newOption);                 Add the option to the list
  });
}
```

The constructor above makes a new `Survey` instance from the values supplied to it. The parameter `newValue` refers to an object containing the new `Survey` values.

```
let newSurveyValues = {
  topic: "robspizza",
  options: [
    { text: "margherita" },
    { text: "pepperoni" },
    { text: "chicken" },
    { text: "ham and pineapple" },
    { text: "mushroom" },
  ]
};

let pizzaSurvey = new Survey(newSurveyValues);
```

The code above creates a literal object referred to by `pizzaSurvey` containing all the initial settings for a `Survey` object. It then uses this object to initialize a new instance of the `Survey` class referred to by the variable `pizzaSurvey`. The `newSurveyValues` object has all the properties of a `Survey`; these will be copied into the new `Survey` instance by the `constructor`.

CODE ANALYSIS

Survey constructor

You might have some questions about what this `constructor` does.

Question: What does `forEach` do?

> **Answer:** A JavaScript array object provides a `forEach` method that can work through all the array elements. `forEach` is supplied with a function that is called for each element in the array with the Survey `constructor`; the program must work through all the supplied option values and create an option for each one.

```
newValue.options.forEach(optionDetails => {
  let newOption = new Option(optionDetails);
  this.options.push(newOption);
});
```

> The first parameter to the function called by `forEach` is the array element currently being processed. In the above code, this parameter has been called `optionDetails` and contains the details for creating the new option. The details are fed into the `Option`

constructor to make a new `Option` instance, which is then pushed onto the list of options the `constructor` is building.

Question: Why do we allow the `Option constructor` to set the `Count` value for a new `Option` instance?

> **Answer:** Since all options should have an initial `Count` of 0 (the option has been picked 0 times), you might wonder why the `Option`'s constructor accepts a `Count` value because we might want to create an `Option` from a string of JSON that has been sent to us. In that case, we wouldn't want to set the `Count` to 0; instead, we want to set the `Count` to whatever was in the object we received.

Survey methods

One of the fundamental principles of object-oriented programming (that sounded very posh, didn't it?) is that you shouldn't need to know how an object works internally to use it. When the Tiny Survey application is using the `Survey` object, it should not know (or care) how the `Survey` object works or what is inside it. The `Survey` object should provide methods that can be called to do exactly what the application needs and nothing more. Once a `Survey` has been created, an application only needs three things. It needs to increment the counter for a particular option, get the option texts and their names for display when an option is being picked, and get the option texts and their `Count` values to display the results. Let's look at each of these methods in turn.

```
incrementCount(text){
  let option = this.options.find(          Find the option
    item=>item.text == text);              Match the option name
  if(option != undefined){                 Is the option defined?
    option.incrementCount();               Increment the counter if it is
  }
}
```

The `incrementCount` method increments the `count` for an option. We give it the text of the option (perhaps "pepperoni"), and it finds the option with that text. If the option is defined, it then calls `incrementCount` on that option to make the `count` bigger by 1. If you are unsure how this process works, we will take a more detailed look at `find` in the next section.

The `getOptions` method returns an object that contains the topic of the survey and a list of objects that contain the option texts (for example `{topic:"robspizza",options:`

[{text:"pepperoni"}, {text:"chicken"]}] for a really Tiny Survey). This list is used to build the display of radio buttons that the user will use to select their preferred option.

```
getOptions(){
    let options = [];                                          Make an empty option array
    this.options.forEach(option=>{                             Work through all the options
        let optionInfo = { text: option.text };      Make an object that contains the option text
        options.push(optionInfo);                               Add the option to the list
    });
    let result = {topic:this.topic, options:options};              Make a result object
    return result;                                                  Return the result
}
```

The getCounts method returns an object containing the topic of the survey and a list of objects containing the option text and the Count for each option (for example {topic:"robspizza",options: [{text:"pepperoni",count:1}, {text:"chicken",count:0}]}).

It uses ForEach loop that works through all the options in the survey and builds an object containing the option text and the Count value for each. It then creates a result object containing the survey's topic name and option list. The list is used to build the page showing each item's counts.

```
getCounts(){
    let options = [];                                          Make an empty option array
    this.options.forEach(option=>{                          Work through the options in the survey
        let countInfo = { text: option.text,
            count: option.getCount() };      Build an object containing the count and the option text
        options.push(countInfo);                               Add the object to the options
    });
    let result = {topic:this.topic, options:options};              Make a result object
    return result;                                                  Return the result
}
```

Scan the QR code or click *https://www.youtube.com/watch?v=v0lIiQS-L4I* for a video walk-through of this Make Something Happen.

Tiny Survey classes

Open the `index.html` file in the **Ch07-03-Tiny_Survey_Classes** example folder using your browser. Open the **Console** in the **Developer Tools** view. The page contains the Tiny Survey classes and a function called makeSampleSurvey, which creates a sample survey.

```
function makeSampleSurvey() {

  let newSurveyValues = {
    topic: "robspizza",
    options: [
      { text: "margherita",count:0 },
      { text: "pepperoni", count:0 },
      { text: "chicken", count:0 },
      { text: "ham and pineapple", count:0 },
      { text: "mushroom", count:0 },
    ]
  };

  let result = new Survey(newSurveyValues);
  return result;
}
```

The function makes an array of options and a topic name value to create a Survey instance. Type in the following to use this function to make a sample survey.

```
let pizzaSurvey = makeSampleSurvey()
```

The variable pizzaSurvey now refers to an instance of the Survey class. You can use the **Console** to view the contents of the survey. Type **pizzaSurvey** into the command prompt and press **Enter**. The contents of the object will be displayed. Expand the items in the object to see the entire contents.

Below, you can see the contents of the class.

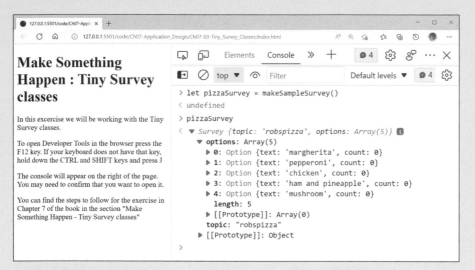

Now, get it to do some work for you by adding a vote for pepperoni. Type the following command and press **Enter**. This will increase the value of the Count for the option with the name item2.

```
pizzaSurvey.incrementCount('pepperoni')
```

You can check that this works by asking the survey object to give you an object that contains the results of the survey. Type the command below and press **Enter**.

```
let counts = pizzaSurvey.getCounts()
```

The Counts variable now refers to an object containing the survey results information. You can take a look at the content of the Counts object. Type **counts**, press **Enter**, and then expand the object's contents.

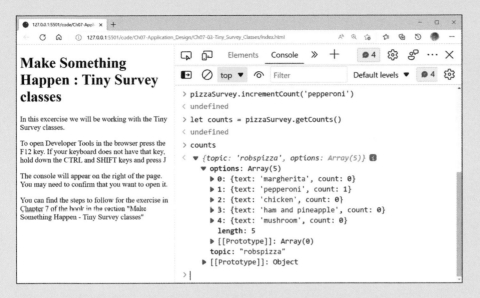

Make Something Happen : Tiny Survey classes

In this excercise we will be working with the Tiny Survey classes.

To open Developer Tools in the browser press the F12 key. If your keyboard does not have that key, hold down the CTRL and SHIFT keys and press J

The console will appear on the right of the page. You may need to confirm that you want to open it.

You can find the steps to follow for the exercise in Chapter 7 of the book in the section "Make Something Happen - Tiny Survey classes"

You can add more votes for other topics and take a look at what the `getOptions` method returns. Leave your browser open. You will use this sample page in the next Make Something Happen.

Tiny Survey classes

The Tiny Survey classes work well, but you might have some questions.

Question: What is the difference between an instance of the `Option` class and a JavaScript object that just happens to contain `text`, and `Count` properties?

> **Answer:** This is a brilliant question. From a data property perspective, there is no difference at all. JavaScript does not distinguish between an `Option` instance and any other object with matching properties. JavaScript uses what is called "duck typing," from the saying, "If it walks like a duck and talks like a duck, it's a duck." So, any part of an application that could work with the data in an `Option` instance would also work with an object containing `Count` and `text` properties. However, only an instance of the `Option` class would contain the `getCount` and `getText` methods.

Question: If you turn an instance of a class into JSON string, do the methods get encoded into the string as well?

> **Answer:** This is a good question. The answer is no. A JSON string contains only the data properties in an object, not the methods. However, we could feed the JSON string into the `Option constructor` to make a "proper" `Option` with all the methods. We could use this to send options from one place to another. Perhaps we want to send our `pizza-Survey` somewhere. We can do this:

```
let pizzaSurveyJSONString = JSON.stringify(pizzaSurvey);
```

> This creates a string called `pizzaSurveyJSONString` containing a JSON description of the survey contents. We can send that string to someone else, and they can create an object from it using `JSON.parse`:

```
let receivedObject = JSON.parse(pizzaSurveyJSONString);
```

> Now we can turn the `receivedObject` into a `Survey` just by feeding it into the `Survey` constructor.

```
let receivedSurvey = new Survey(receivedObject);
```

> This `receivedObject` will have all the data properties from the original `Survey` object, so the `receivedSurvey` will have those set by the `constructor`.

The Surveys class

The application needs to store active surveys. We can create a class called `Surveys` that will do this. There are many ways to store the survey values, but to start with, we will use a simple array. We save a survey by adding it to the array. We find a survey by searching the array for one with a matching topic.

```
class Surveys {
  constructor() {
    this.surveys = [];
  }

  saveSurvey(survey) {
    this.surveys.push(survey);
```

```
  }

  getSurveyByTopic(topic) {
    return this.surveys.find(element => element.topic == topic);
  }
}
```

The complete Surveys class is above. The constructor method for a survey creates the array that holds the surveys. The saveSurvey method pushes a received survey value onto the survey list. The getSurveyByTopic method returns the survey with the matching topic name.

🚀 MAKE SOMETHING HAPPEN 33

Scan the QR code or click *https://www.youtube.com/watch?v=cqqQ1Pj73fg* for a video walk-through of this Make Something Happen.

The Surveys class

The index.html file in the **Ch07-03-Tiny_Survey_Classes** example folder also contains the Surveys class for us to look at. You can start by making a new pizza survey:

```
let pizzaSurvey = makeSampleSurvey()
```

Type the statement above and press **Enter**. The variable pizzaSurvey now refers to an instance of the Survey class. You now need to create a survey store:

```
let store = new Surveys()
```

Type the statement above and press **Enter**. The variable `store` now refers to a `Surveys` instance. Now you can store the survey in the store:

```
store.saveSurvey(pizzaSurvey)
```

Type the statement above and press **Enter**. You now have a survey in the store. You can take a look at the store contents.

```
store
```

Type the statement above to get the **Console** to display the `store` object.

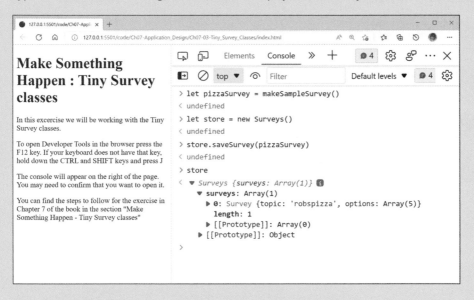

Now you can use the `getSurveyByTopic` function to get a survey out of the store. There is only one survey in there, and it has the topic `robspizza`. Type the following statement to make `loadedSurvey` refer to the survey with the topic `robspizza`.

```
let loadedSurvey = store.getSurveyByTopic("robspizza")
```

Now you can view the content of `loadedSurvey`. Type in the name of the variable and press **Enter** to see what it contains.

```
loadedSurvey
```

Here, you can see that `loadedSurvey` contains the same values as `saveSurvey`. The correct survey has been located.

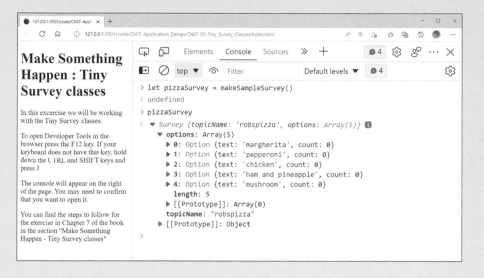

The Surveys class

The `Surveys` class is very small, but you still might have some questions about it.

Question: How does `findSurvey` work?

> **Answer:** The `findSurvey` method is given the topic of the survey (for example `robs-pizza`), and it then finds the survey with that topic.
>
> It uses the `find` method provided by the `surveys` array. All arrays provide a `find` method. You give the `find` method a function that accepts a parameter (which will be an element of the array) and returns `true` when the required element has been found. In the case of `findSurvey`, the element is found if it has a `topic` matching the one supplied as a parameter, so the provided function tests for this.

Question: What does `findSurveysByTopic` return?

> **Answer:** The method returns a reference to the survey with the matching topic. Changes to this survey will be reflected in the survey "in" the store because they are both actually the same survey object.

Question: What happens if the topic name is not matched?

> **Answer:** If we ask `findSurveyByTopic` to find a survey that doesn't exist, it will return the value `undefined`. Any program using `findSurveyByTopic` must check for undefined in case the survey was not found.

Question: Why have we made a `Surveys` class? The `Surveys` class is very small. Each function in the class contains a single statement. Would it not be easier just to put these statements in the Tiny Survey application code and use them directly?

> **Answer:** Creating a `Surveys` class separates the survey storage from the application. It makes it very easy for us to change from an array to a database. We would just have to change the find and save methods in the class and not change the application at all.

Question: How are old surveys removed?

> **Answer:** At the moment, they aren't. The `surveys` array just keeps getting larger as more surveys are pushed onto it. However, we could modify the `saveSurvey` method to set an upper limit on the size of the surveys array and remove the oldest one each time a new survey was added beyond that limit.

We now have a workflow and data storage for our Tiny Survey application. In the next chapter, we will create the working web pages and the code to make Tiny Survey work.

What you have learned

This has been another busy chapter. We've covered a lot of ground. Here is a recap, plus some points to ponder.

- Companies that create applications and regulating bodies have ethical standards against which new applications will be judged before release. It is important that issues of ethics, privacy, and security are considered during the design process of a new application.

- Before you start writing code or building web pages for a new application, you need to create the "workflow" for it. The workflow expresses the items the user will see, the order they are presented, and how the user will move from one item to the next. Workflow can be designed initially on paper. Creating a prototype application from web pages containing only fixed text is a good idea. These are very useful when documenting the steps through the workflow.

- Once the workflow of an application has been designed, you can move on to consider the data storage the application will require. Initial discussions can talk about the storage items in general terms (for example, survey), but these can be refined to consider what is held in each item.

- The JavaScript class defines an object that has a `constructor` method that can create specific object properties set at values determined by those supplied to the `constructor` as parameters. The parameters are best sent into the `constructor` as a literal object holding properties with values that are transferred into the new object being created.

- The JavaScript keyword `this`, when used in a `constructor` method, means "a reference to the object currently being created."

- A class `constructor` can validate initial values supplied as parameters, but the only way that the `constructor` can indicate invalid parameter values is by throwing an exception.

- An instance of a class is created using the keyword `new`. This will invoke the `constructor` method for the class. The `constructor` is given parameters that contain values to be used to initialize the instance.

- A JavaScript class can contain methods as well as properties. A method is equivalent to a function but exists within a class. In the code for a method, the keyword `this` means "a reference to the instance in which this method is running."

- Code external to a class instance should not have to manipulate the contents of the instance to change the data in it. Instead, the instance should provide methods that can be called to perform the specific action required. For example, the `Option` class in TinySurvey provides a method that can be used to increment the `count` value. External code should not access the internal `count` property directly.

- Arrays provide a `forEach` function that can be made to perform a given function on every array element.

- JavaScript doesn't regard objects in terms of their particular type. Any object with a particular set of properties is interchangeable with any other object with the same set of properties.

- Converting an instance of a class into a JSON string does not encode the particular type of the instance or any of the method properties into the resulting string.

To reinforce your understanding of this chapter, you might want to consider the following "profound questions."

Question: When starting an application, how much effort should you put into ethical, privacy, and security issues?

> **Answer:** Considering these things when you start development is always useful. It is often the case that simple changes to the behavior of an application can make it more ethical. The reverse is also true. Attempts to monetize an application can convert it from ethical to unethical. Ethical considerations need to be tracked during a project regarding the effects of changes to the application and observations of what people are doing with the application.

Question: Are there other issues to consider beyond ethics when building an application?

> **Answer:** Other issues worthy of consideration are

> - Does an existing application perform the same function as the proposed application?
>
> - What is the business model? How you will make money from the application, and who owns what?
>
> - Are you building something as a team?
>
> - How will profits be shared?
>
> - Who claims ownership of different parts of the application?

Question: Do you need a workflow diagram if you are only creating a single-page application?

> **Answer:** The Tiny Survey application is spread across several pages. However, you can also create single-page applications. In this case, rather than documenting the navigation between pages, you should document the workflow between the different states the page can occupy as the user works with the application.

Question: What is the difference between a class and an object?

> **Answer:** A class sets out what behaviors the object should have and provides a mechanism (the `constructor`) for setting initial values in the object. You can think of a class as the recipe (how to bake a cake) and an instance of a class as the result of following the recipe (a cake).

Question: Can a class have multiple `constructors`?

> **Answer:** The `constructor` method in a class is used to set up initial values held in the class. It might be useful to have multiple `constructors` to create an instance from a JSON-encoded string or some other means. JavaScript does not allow this. There can only be one `constructor` method in a class. However, you could make a `constructor` that examines the type of parameter coming into the `constructor` and acts appropriately.

Question: How can a program detect the class of a particular object?

> **Answer:** The `typeOf` function will return the type of an object, but this does not work with classes. An instance of a class always has the type of "Object." However, the `instanceOf` operator can determine whether a reference to an object refers to an object of a particular type.
>
> The following statement shows how `instanceof` is used. The message will be logged if the reference `pizzaSurvey` refers to a `Survey` object.

```
if (pizzaSurvey instanceof Survey) console.log("A Survey")
```

Question: Can classes be exported from a library?

> **Answer:** Yes, they can. When we create the Tiny Survey application in the next chapter, we will use a `SurveyStore.mjs` library file that exports the `Survey`, `Option`, and `Surveys` classes for use by the application.

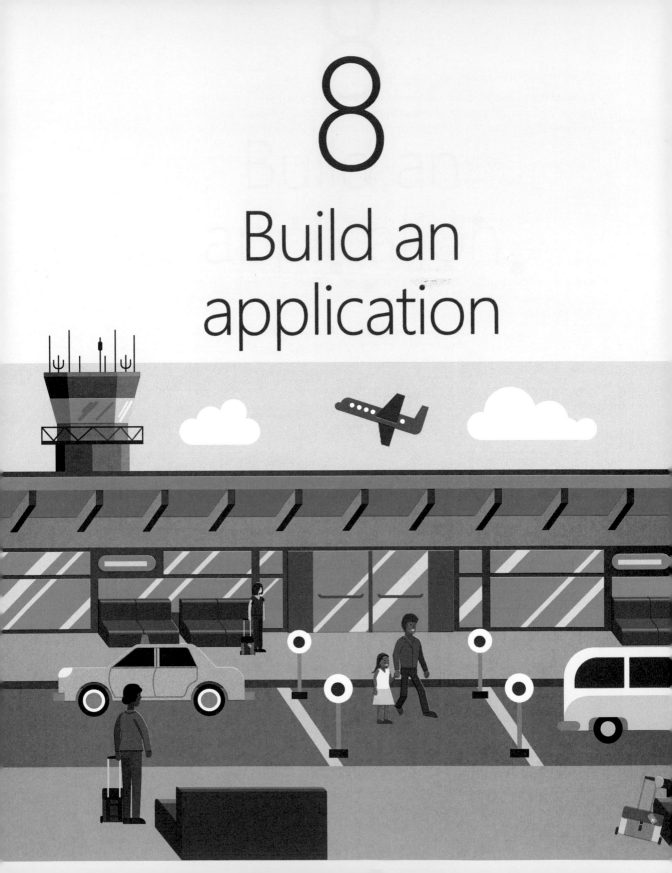

8

Build an application

What you will learn

In the last chapter, we designed the Tiny Survey application. We set out the pages the user will interact with and the workflow followed as the application is used. Then, we designed the data storage to underpin the application and implemented a set of classes that provide the storage behaviors the application needs.

In this chapter, we are going to build the application. We will learn how to add style to our pages and how the Express framework makes it easy to create web applications. We'll also create our first project that uses node package manager and discover how to create and configure applications that use multiple libraries. Along the way, we'll learn some new tricks with Git to help us manage changes to our code. And at the end, we will have our working survey ready for deployment into the cloud.

This is the point where I remind you about the glossary. I'd hate to disappoint you, so don't forget about the online glossary.

Put on the style with Bootstrap

Before we start creating the pages to be used in Tiny Survey, we should consider how they will be styled. So far, the prototype pages we have created have used the standard HTML styles for the elements. This will work, but it doesn't provide a very good user experience. In previous applications, we have added our own stylesheets to set the styles for the elements on the page. We first saw stylesheets in chapter 2 when we used them to set the text size displayed by our JavaScript clock. See the Code Analysis section "Document objects and JavaScript" to find out what we did. Since then, when we have created web pages, we have created a stylesheet file to go with them. The stylesheet file contains definitions of styles applied to the HTML files' elements. The header for the document contains a reference to a local file called `style.css`.

```
<link rel="stylesheet" href="styles.css">
```

The `style.css` file contains the definition of classes that give display settings for the elements on our page. Creating good stylesheets that work on multiple devices is hard work that has already been done by lots of people who are very good at it. Some of those people are at Bootstrap (*https://getbootstrap.com/*). They have made stylesheets that we can use in our applications. The stylesheets are powerful and include dynamic behaviors that adjust pages for different-sized displays. We will not use all these features in our Tiny Survey application, but they are well worth exploring.

Before we link to the Bootstrap stylesheet, we need to add a statement to the HTML to tell Bootstrap how to scale the page on different devices. The statement below creates an item of *metadata*, which says, "use the full width of the device and start with an initial scaling value of 1". This metadata, which has the `viewport` identifier, is read by Bootstrap when it starts.

```
<meta name="viewport" content="width=device-width, initial-scale=1.0">
```

We can use a Bootstrap stylesheet by setting it as the stylesheet for a document:

```
<link rel="stylesheet"
href=https://cdn.jsdelivr.net/npm/bootstrap@4.3.1/dist/css/bootstrap.min.css
integrity="sha384-ggOyR0iXCbMQv3Xipma34MD+dH/1fQ784/j6cY/iJTQUOhcWr7x9JvoRxT2MZw1T"
crossorigin="anonymous">
```

This does the same job as the previous link; it sets a stylesheet for a document. However, the stylesheet is now downloaded from the internet. The `integrity` property contains a *hash* of the content of the stylesheet, which is used to validate the contents. We can use this stylesheet to format the index page for the Tiny Survey application.

Figure 8-1 below shows the index page for Tiny Survey. The user will enter the name of the topic for the survey. We will select the best pizza topping, so the topic has been called "robspizza" This page is styled using the Bootstrap stylesheet.

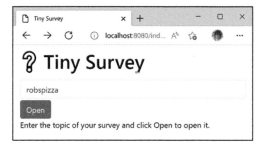

Figure 8-1   Tiny Survey Bootstrap

Let's take a look at the HTML behind the page:

```
<!DOCTYPE html>
<html>

<head>
  <title>Tiny Survey</title>
  <meta name="viewport" content="width=device-width, initial-scale=1.0">
  <link rel="stylesheet" href="https://cdn.jsdelivr.net/npm/bootstrap@4.3.1/dist/
css/bootstrap.min.css"
    integrity="sha384-ggOyR0iXCbMQv3Xipma34MD+dH/1fQ784/j6cY/
iJTQUOhcWr7x9JvoRxT2MZw1T"
  crossorigin="anonymous">
</head>

<body>
  <div class="container">
    <h1 class="mb-3 mt-2">&#10068; Tiny Survey</h1>
    <p>
      <input type="text" class="form-control" id="topic" spellcheck="false">
    </p>
    <p>
      <button class="btn btn-primary mt-1" onclick="doEnterOptions();">Open</button>
    </p>
```

```
    <p>
       Enter the topic of your survey and click Open to open it.
    </p>
  </div>
  <script>
    function doEnterOptions() {
       window.open("enteroptions.html", "_self");
    }
  </script>
</body>
</html>
```

CODE ANALYSIS

Styling Tiny Survey

You can find the Bootstrap version of Tiny Survey in the **Ch08_01_Bootstrap_Tiny_Survey** folder. All the application pages are now styled using Bootstrap. You might have some questions about the index file.

Question: What does the line starting `<meta` do?

   Answer: This describes Bootstrap's viewport to scale the page appropriately for different devices.

Question: What does `div` do?

   Answer: Sometimes, you want to lump some page content together to apply things to it. The `div` encloses all the content on the page, which we want to assign style with the class `container`. The `container` class is provided by Bootstrap and allows us to group related items on the page.

Question: What does `&#10068;` mean?

   Answer: You can find this in the heading for the page. It is the code for an emoji that displays a white question mark. This is a low-cost way of getting a simple logo for the application.

Question: What does `class="mb-3 mt-2"` mean?

   Answer: These are class names that contain layout instructions for Bootstrap. `mb-3` sets the bottom margin, and `mt-2` sets the top margin. You can use these to position items vertically on the page.

Question: What does `spellcheck="false"` mean?

```
<input id="topic" spellcheck="false">
```

Answer: Topic names chosen by the user might not match words in the dictionary. I've called my topic "robspizza" If the input is not meant to be correctly spelled, you can add this property to tell the browser not to complain if words in the input are not in the dictionary.

Question: What does `window.open` do?

Answer: When the user presses the **Open** button, we want the application to move to another window. For our demonstration application, it will move to the page where the survey options will be entered. The page that will do this is called **enteroptions.html**.

```
window.open("enteroptions.html", "_self");
```

The `window.open` function tells the browser to open the specified URL. The second parameter, `"_self"`, tells the browser to open the URL in the existing window.

Getting started with Express

We created the "Cheese Finder" game by writing two JavaScript programs. A client program runs in the browser and talks to a server program running in the cloud. The client JavaScript builds the HTML pages seen by players. The server JavaScript runs the game itself. The server also serves out the web pages used by the browser to build the page. We could use the same technique to build Tiny Survey. A JavaScript program running in the browser could build each of the four pages depending on what part of the application the user was interacting with. However, it turns out that there is a framework we can use that makes the construction of multi-page applications much easier. It is called Express, and you can find it at *http://expressjs.com/*. Before we can start using Express, we have to look into just how libraries are incorporated into `Node.js` applications.

Express and node package manager

In Chapter 6, we used a `package.json` file to describe the elements of the Cheese Finder application that we wanted to deploy into the cloud. The Cheese Finder program didn't depend on any other code to run. Everything it used was part of JavaScript, the `Node.js` framework or a library file we created for the application (for example, `pseudorandom.mjs`). The Tiny Survey application will depend on many external libraries. The code in these libraries will need to be added to our application, and something will have to make sure they are all kept up to date. The node package manager will do this for us.

The npm (node package manager) program is supplied as part of a Node.js installation and talks to servers managed by a company called npm (*https://www.npmjs.com/*). These servers host the library files, and the npm program reads the package.json file to discover which library files a project needs. The npm program manages the contents of package.json, starting with creating a new application. Let's see how we do this.

🚀 **MAKE SOMETHING HAPPEN 34**

Scan the QR code or visit *https://www.youtube.com/watch?v=Un7tL7v4rR4* for a video walk-through of this Make Something Happen.

Create the Tiny Survey project

This is a different Make Something Happen. Rather than use pre-built code as a starting point, we will start with a completely blank folder and then create an application in it. Later we will add some pre-built components. We will use the integrated terminal in Visual Studio Code to do this. In Chapter 1, we installed the git program on our computer. We have not used it from the terminal before, but in this exercise, we will use Git to make a new repository on our computer and then add the files we need to get started.

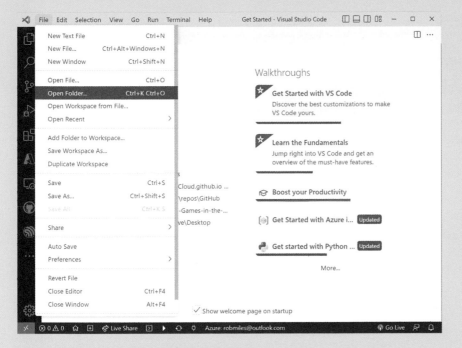

The first thing to do is to start Visual Studio Code. Then close any folders that might be open in Visual Studio and select the **Open Folder** option from the **File** menu. This will open the folder browser.

Click **New Folder** in the **Open Folder** window to make a new folder. You can put the folder anywhere on your machine. I have a folder called `projects` where I keep the projects I'm working on. Create a folder called **tinysurvey**, click **Select Folder**, and select it in Visual Studio.

Now that we have a folder, we can use the terminal interface in Visual Studio Code to set it up. Select **New Terminal** from the **Terminal** menu. The terminal window will open at the bottom of the Visual Studio Code window.

The first thing we will do is create a Git repository for this folder. This will track the changes in our files. We use the Git program to do this.

```
git init
```

Type the command as shown above and press **Enter**.

The command will confirm that it has been completed. Now that we have a Git repository, we can start adding files to our application. The node package manager (npm) program will do this for us. We will be asked a series of questions, and the answers will be used to build a package.json file for the project.

```
npm init
```

Type the command as shown above and press **Enter**.

```
PS C:\Users\rsmil\projects\tinysurvey> npm init
This utility will walk you through creating a package.json file.
It only covers the most common items, and tries to guess sensible defaults.

See 'npm help init' for definitive documentation on these fields
and exactly what they do.
```

```
Use 'npm install <pkg>' afterwards to install a package and
save it as a dependency in the package.json file.

Press ^C at any time to quit.
package name: (tinysurvey)
version: (1.0.0)
description: Tiny Survey application
entry point: (index.js) tinysurvey.mjs
test command:
git repository:
keywords:
author: Rob Miles
license: (ISC)
About to write to C:\Users\rsmil\projects\tinysurvey\package.json:

{
  "name": "tinysurvey",
  "version": "1.0.0",
  "description": "Tiny Survey application",
  "main": "tinysurvey.mjs",
  "scripts": {
    "test": "echo \"Error: no test specified\" && exit 1"
  },
  "author": "Rob Miles",
  "license": "ISC"
}


Is this OK? (yes)
PS C:\Users\rsmil\projects\tinysurvey>
```

For most of the questions, you can just press **Enter**. The answers you give are shown above in **bold**. You only have to supply the `entry point` (the name of the file that will be run to start the project) and the `author`. Now we have a `package.json` file for our application. We can look at it (shown above), but we usually let npm look after the file's contents. The next step is to add the Express library to our project. The `npm install` command followed by the name of the package to be installed does the trick.

```
npm install express
```

Type the command as shown above and press **Enter**. The npm program looks for Express on the server and discovers that it uses 57 other packages. These are all copied into a folder called `node_modules`, which is added to the application, along with two package files.

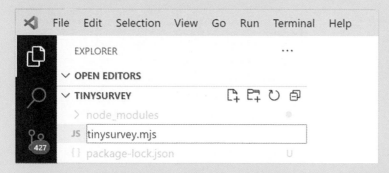

Open the `package.json` file in the Visual Studio Editor to see the changes. As you can see above, an entry in the dependencies section indicates that this application uses Express and needs a version newer than 4.18.2. The only thing we are missing is the `tinysurvey.mjs` file, which contains the JavaScript that will run the application.

Click the **New File** icon to the right of the **TINYSURVEY** item in the Explorer and name the file **tinysurvey.mjs**.

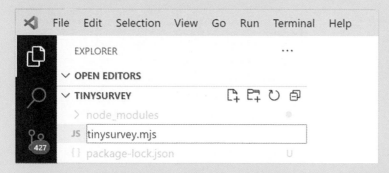

This will create an empty file. You can find the contents of the **tinysurvey.mjs** file we will use in the folder **Ch08-02_Express_Hello_World** in the sample programs for this chapter. Find the file on your machine and copy its contents to the **tinysurvey.mjs** file and then save the **tinysurvey.mjs** file. Now, we can use `node` to run it.

```
node tinysurvey.mjs
```

Open a terminal window, type the command above, and press **Enter** to start your program.

The Express framework is hosting a web server running on port 8080. Let's use the browser to see what it is serving (although the listing above might contain some strong hints). Open your browser and navigate to *localhost:8080/index.html*.

Above, you can see the response from the index page. You might like to find out what happens when you visit *localhost:8080/extra.html*.

You might wonder what happens if the browser tries to access a page that is not present. Try to access *localhost:8080/fred.html*.

The Express server will generate the correct response. There is no route for `fred.html`. We can add as many endpoints as we wish to the Express project. The code behind each endpoint sends out a simple response, but we can also run code to generate the page content. More on this later.

We can debug our application by using the debugger to start the `tinysurvey.mjs` program like we have been debugging the Cheese Finder code. However, we must first stop the `Node.js` application by pressing CTRL+C in the terminal window. Stop the application now, but leave Visual Studio Code running so you can use it in the next exercise.

Express routes

The following code deals with a `get` request for the `index.html` page. A browser generates a `get` request when it wants something from the server. The `get` method in Express defines a *route*.

```
app.get('/index.html', (request, response) => {
  response.send('Hello from Index');
})
```

A route is a mapping between an endpoint and a JavaScript function that will deal with it. The first argument to `get` is a string containing the endpoint that the route is handling. In this case, it is the page `index.html`. The second argument to `get` is a function that accepts two arguments: `request` and `response`. To deal with this route, we could have declared a function called `handlePageRequest` (as we did in Chapter 4 in the "Serving from software" section) to deal Instead, we have created an anonymous arrow function that calls the `send` method on the `response` parameter to send a reply to the browser. We can create as many routes as we like to deal with different endpoints. But before we do this, we will save this working demonstration.

Manage versions with Git

Racing drivers and programmers have one thing in common. They both hate going backward. When you work on code, one of the worries is that you might break your application and be unable to get it back to how it was before. The Git program provides a solution to this problem. We currently have a working application, so we should probably commit these changes to Git to prepare for the next part of the development. **Figure 8-2** shows the **Source Control** item on the left side.

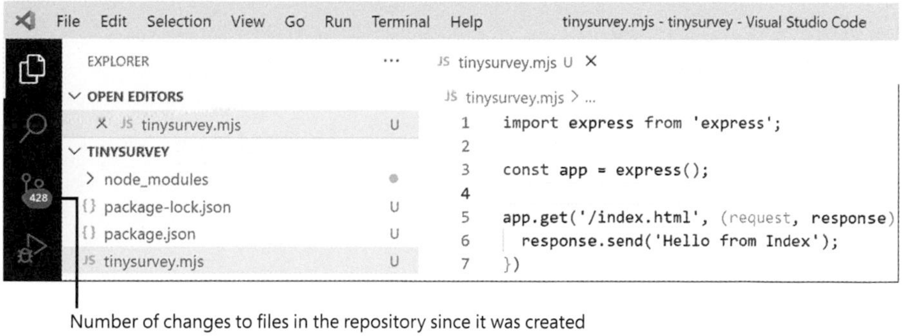

Number of changes to files in the repository since it was created

Figure 8-2   Git Changes

The number 428 on the control means there have been 428 changes to files in the repository since it was created. Visual Studio Code uses the Git repository we created to track changes to the files in the application folder, and installing Express and its dependencies creates a lot of new files.

Use gitignore

We could just commit all the changes to Git, as shown in **Figure 8-2**. This would add 428 files to the repository for our application. However, we didn't create most of the files. They were created when npm installed Express. The package.json file contains a list of dependencies that set out the libraries needed by this project. There is no need to keep all the Express files in our repository because anyone wanting to build our application could look in the package.json file, find the dependencies, and get all the required files. It would be useful if there was a way of saying to Git, "Don't bother putting these files like these in the repository because they are from a library."

It turns out that there is. It is called gitignore. You can add a file called gitignore to your repository. This file contains a list of patterns matching files and folders that should not be included in the repository. How you create a gitignore file is a bit beyond this book's scope, but you don't need to because GitHub has a list of gitignore files you can use for any project at *https://github.com/github/gitignore*. We are using the `gitignore` file for `node` projects. Let's see how all this works.

MAKE SOMETHING HAPPEN 35

Scan the QR code or visit *https://www.youtube.com/watch?v=pOdsCSJEhVM* for a video walkthrough of this Make Something Happen.

Check in your code

We saw that when we used `git init` to create the repository, Git replied with the "Initialized empty git repository" message. The repository is a folder managed by Git, which holds all your files' versions. A commit takes a snapshot of the files in your application that have changed and stores it in the repository. If you click the **Source Control** icon on the left, you can see all the files that have changed. Type a summary of this commit (I've entered **First Express test**). You use this comment to identify this version, so adding some useful detail is a good idea.

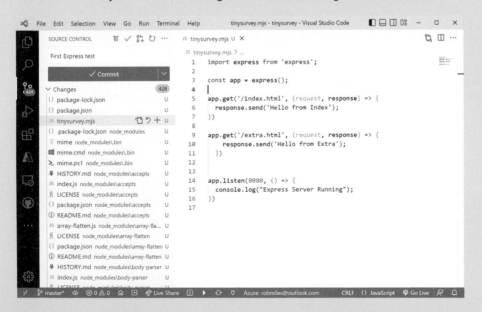

If you click the **Commit** button, the new files are copied to the repository. Don't press it just yet, though, because we want to reduce that value of 428 changes to something more manageable by adding a gitignore file. You can find the file in the **Ch08_03_Node_gitignore** folder. Copy it into your application folder. Now, go back and look at **Source Control** view.

The only files that will now be added to the repository are the ones we created, plus the gitignore file. Press the **Commit** button to check them in. You will see a screen like the one below when it is finished. The number of changes since the last commit is zero, so no number is shown.

After changes are committed, no number is shown

The **Publish Branch** button allows you to publish this repository on GitHub. If you click it, you will be asked to log in with your GitHub username to begin the publishing process. However, you don't need to use GitHub just to get the file tracking; you can keep your repositories local. We can see the tracking in action by changing one of our files. Return to the Explorer view and make a change to the **tinysurvey.mjs** file. (I've added an **extra1.html** endpoint.) Save the file.

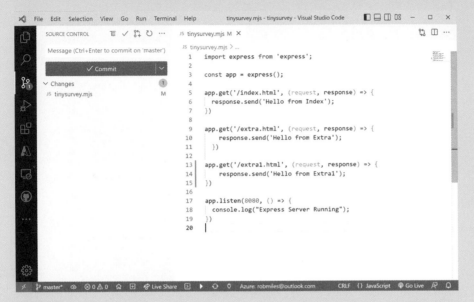

The **Changes** counter now shows 1 change to the committed repository. Click the **Source Control** button to open the **Source Control** view, and click `tinyserver.mjs` to view the changes made to this file.

Click Undo to revert a highlighted change

Visual Studio Code shows you a view of both files—the original and the changed version—so you can see what you have been doing. If you press the undo arrow next to the filename, you can revert the file to its original version.

Use page templates with EJS

At the beginning of Chapter 7, we created a set of web pages showing how the Tiny Survey application will be used. It would be great if we could use these pages to start making our application. Well, it turns out that we can. EJS (*https://ejs.co/*) is a piece of "application-level middleware" that can be used with the Express framework. Wow. That sounds seriously impressive. Tonight, you can tell your family (or the cat) that you spent the day installing "application-level middleware," and I'm sure they will be very impressed.

It really means that you've told the Express application to use the EJS engine to generate the pages to be set to the browser. Middleware is software that works with an application and does something useful. There are several different types of middleware. "Application level" middleware is used within an application to perform a particular task. In this case, the task is to render an HTML source page to provide the text to be sent to the browser. We will see some other forms of middleware later. We must install the `ejs` engine before we can use it, which we can do using the node package manager (npm) command in the terminal:

```
npm install ejs
```

This command is given at the terminal. Another 200 or so files are added to our project to support `ejs`. Now, we can tell the Express application to use this engine by adding the following statement to `tinyserver.mjs`:

```
app.set('view-engine', 'ejs');
```

The call of the `app.set` function is given two arguments. The first is a string specifying what the middleware is used for. (In this case, it is being used as the view engine.) The second argument is the library's name providing the function. In this case, it is the `ejs` library we just installed.

The application can now call the `render` function on the `response` object we received from route and tell it to render the required EJS file:

```
app.get('/index.html', (request, response) => {
  response.render('index.ejs');
})
```

The `render` action has been added to the route for `index.html`. This means that when a browser client requests the page at `index.htm`, it will now be sent the contents of `index.ejs`. By convention, the EJS files are stored in a folder called **Views**. We can have as many EJS page files as we need for a particular application in the **Views** folder.

MAKE SOMETHING HAPPEN 36

Scan the QR code or click *https://www.youtube.com/watch?v=2ep9Zoi5-e8* for a video walk-through of this Make Something Happen.

Use EJS template files

We will make an Express application that displays the prototype web pages we created earlier. The first thing we need to do is install the `ejs` library.

```
npm install ejs
```

Enter the command above into the Visual Studio Code terminal window and press **Enter**. Watch as `ejs` is installed in your project. Now you need to add some items to your project. You can find these extra items in the **Ch08-04_Express_EJS_Prototype** folder in the sample files for this chapter.

You'll need an updated **tinysurvey.mjs** file and the contents of the **views** folder. The EJS middleware looks in the **Views** folder for any templates used in your application. Once you have copied the files into place, use Visual Studio Code to open your application and open the **tinysurvey.mjs** file.

Your Visual Studio Code window should look like the above. You can see from the Explorer window at the top left that the views folder contains the four template files used by the application: `build.ejs`, `entry.ejs`, `index.ejs`, and `results.ejs`. If you look inside them, you'll see that they contain exactly the same text as the original HTML files. Click `index.ejs` to take a look.

Now we have our Express-powered version of the application, we can start it. Open a terminal and type the following command to start the application.

```
node tinysurvey.mjs
```

If you open your browser and view the page at *http://localhost:8080/index.html*, you will see the same example pages as before, but now they are hosted by Express. We can use these template EJS pages as the basis for the finished application.

Get the example application

We now have a set of page template files and an Express application that we can use to navigate between the pages. Now, we will discover how each page works by examining a complete implementation of TinySurvey. The application is stored on GitHub in the *https://github.com/Building-Apps-and-Games-in-the-Cloud/TinySurvey* repository. We can use the Git tool in the terminal to clone this to our machine.

Scan the QR code or click *https://www.youtube.com/watch?v=64ojgggvH5I* for a video walk-through of this Make Something Happen.

Get the example application using Git

We will use the `git` command line to clone the example application. You can use the terminal in Visual Studio code. Start the terminal and navigate to a folder where you want to put the clone of the survey application.

```
git clone https://github.com/Building-Apps-and-Games-in-the-Cloud/TinySurvey
```

Now, enter the above command to clone the sample application. This will create a new folder called `TinySurvey` which contains all the files for the application. Note that it will not copy all the library files. You will need to install those yourself. Navigate into the `TinySurvey` folder that was created by Git and enter the following command:

```
npm install
```

The `npm` program will open the `package.json` file and load all the dependencies for the application. Now you can run the program by using the `node` command:

```
node tinysurvey.mjs
```

Enter the command above and press **Enter**. Open your browser and navigate to *localhost:8080/index.html*, and you will find a working Tiny Survey application. To stop the server, press CTRL+C.

You can open the `TinySurvey` application using the **Open Folder** command in Visual Studio Code. Any changes you make to the application on your machine will not affect the version stored on GitHub.

The index page

We now have an application that contains working versions of each page plus the JavaScript program that navigates between them. Now we are going to investigate how each of the pages works. We will follow the same sequence we used when designing the application. We will start with the index file, which serves as the "home page." The page takes the survey topic from the user and either creates a new one with that topic (if the topic does not exist) or allows the user to select options for the survey (if the topic exists).

Figure 8-3 shows the home page for the application.

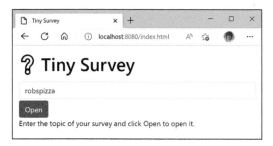

Figure 8-3   Tiny Survey home page

The HTML for this page is held in the `index.ejs` template file in the `views` folder.

```
<!DOCTYPE html>
<html>

<head>
  <title>Tiny Survey</title>
  <meta name="viewport" content="width=device-width, initial-scale=1.0">
  <link rel="stylesheet"
 href="https://cdn.jsdelivr.net/npm/bootstrap@4.3.1/dist/css/bootstrap.min.css"
    integrity="sha384-ggOyROiXCbMQv3Xipma34MD+dH/1fQ784/j6cY/
iJTQUOhcWr7x9JvoRxT2MZw1T"
crossorigin="anonymous">
</head>

<body>
  <div class="container">
    <h1 class="mb-3 mt-3">&#10068; Tiny Survey</h1>
    <form action="/gottopic" method="POST">                          Input form
```

```
        <input type="text" name="topic" required class="form-control"
               spellcheck="false">
        <button type="submit" class="btn btn-primary mt-1">Open</button>
    </form>
    <p>
        Enter the topic of your survey and click Open to open it.
    </p>
  </div>
</body>

</html>
```

Above, you can see the HTML for the index file. The Express server sends this file back to the browser when the browser asks for the endpoint `index.html` endpoint.

```
app.get('/index.html', (request, response) => {
  response.render('index.ejs');
})
```

Above is the Express route that deals with a request for the `index.html` page. The contents of `index.ejs` is rendered in response to the request. Now, let's look at what `index.ejs` does. The user enters the survey topic (`robspizza`), and when the Open button is clicked, it is sent to the server. We have already seen one way a page can send data to the web server. We used the HTTP query mechanism in the Cheese Finder game to send a grid square's X and Y coordinates to the game engine when the button in that square was clicked. Look for details in the "Play the game" section in Chapter 5. We could use the same query mechanism to send the topic information to the application, but when we are reading input from the user, the best way to do this is by using `HTTP post`.

Post data from a form

A browser can send content to the server using a `post` command. We specify a `post` action by creating a web page form. A form can contain multiple input elements, so you could post a user's name, address, and age in a single form. In the case of the index page for Tiny Survey, we just need one input—the survey topic.

```
<form action="/gottopic" method="POST">
  <input type="text" id="topic" name="topic" required
         spellcheck="false">
  <button type="submit">Open</button>
</form>
```

Above, you can see the HTML in `index.ejs` that defines a form containing a text input field and a button containing the "Open" text, which will submit the form. The form's `action` attribute specifies the server endpoint that will be used when the form is submitted. The form above sends the result to the `gottopic` endpoint. The `method` attribute is set to `POST` because that is what we will be using to transfer the data.

We first saw the `input` element in Chapter 3 in the "The HTML input element" section when we needed to read an offset value for our time travel clock. In that application, the input was read by JavaScript running inside the browser. In the code above, the input will be transmitted to the server using the `post` action. The input element has `id` and `name` attributes, both of which are set to the string `topic`. The `HTML document uses the id attribute` to refer to the element. The `name` property gives the name this input will have when it is sent to the server. It makes sense for both these attributes to be set to the same string.

We have used buttons in our HTML pages before. This button has a `type` attribute that is set to `submit`. When the button is pressed, the form is submitted by the browser. To do this, the browser assembles a message containing the contents of the input fields encoded as a JSON string and sends it to the server in a `post` command. Now, let's see how code in the server application can receive that input and do something with it.

Receive input from a post

We now know how to create an HTML page that can post a form of data to the server. Now we need to find out how to write code in the server that responds to the post and receives its input. To do this, we will use another piece of middleware that is part of the `Express` framework, so we don't need to install anything new. We just need to enable it. This piece of middleware takes incoming post requests, decodes the JSON in them, and converts this into an object that can be used by the code dealing with the post message.

```
app.use(express.urlencoded({ extended: false }));
```

We've seen `app.use` before; it is how we told Express to use the EJS framework to render the pages to be sent to the browser. The statement above enables and configures an Express component called `urlencoded`. This takes in post messages and converts them into objects. It is configured using an object literal that contains setting values. The only setting that we are using is "`extended:false`." The `urlencoded` middleware can do lots of clever things, such as decode compressed data in a post. We don't want any of that, so turn off the extended options. Once you have added this middleware to the `Express` application, something magical happens. The `request` object in our route now has a `body` property containing the items in the submitted form.

```
// Got the survey topic
app.post('/gottopic', (request, response) => {                      Route for a post to gottopic
  let surveyTopic = request.body.topic;                             Get the survey topic from the post

  let survey = surveys.getSurveyByTopic(surveyTopic)                Find the survey for this topic
  if (survey == undefined) {                                        If there is no survey – make one
    // need to make a new survey
    response.render('enteroptions.ejs',                             Select the page to get options
      { topicName: request.body.topic, numberOfOptions: 5 });
  }
  else {                                                            This survey exists – select option
    // enter scores on an existing survey
    let surveyOptions = survey.getOptions();            Get the options for display from this survey
    response.render('selectoption.ejs', surveyOptions);             Select the page to get
  }                                                                               a selection
});
```

If you look back at the HTML page that set up the Form element, you will see that the action for this form was specified as /gottopic. Above is the post route in our server code that responds to this action. This is the point in the workflow where the server decides whether the user is making a new survey or selecting an option in an existing one. The code above uses the survey storage classes that we created in Chapter 7. The Surveys class provides a method called getSurveyByTopic which is given a survey topic (in our case, "robspizza") and will return a reference to that survey if it exists in the survey store. If the survey is not found, the getSurveyByTopic method returns the value undefined. If the survey is found, the application should allow the user to enter their options by sending them to the selectoption.html page. If the survey is not found, the application will create a new survey with that name by sending the user to the enteroptions.html page.

🚀 MAKE SOMETHING HAPPEN 38

Scan the QR code or click *https://www.youtube.com/watch?v=7reMQoHYfS8* for a video walk-through of this Make Something Happen.

Handle a post

You might have found the above explanation a bit confusing. Seeing the system in action will make it a lot clearer. The next few Make Something Happen exercises will use the completed application, so open that in Visual Studio Code. Now open the **tinysurvey.mjs** file.

Add breakpoints at lines 20 and 25

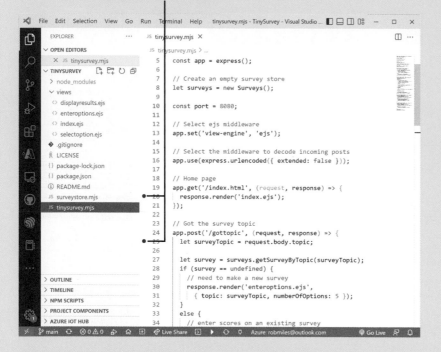

The **tinysurvey.mjs** file controls the application. Add a pair of breakpoints at lines 20 and 25, as shown above. One will be hit when `the browser requests index.html`. The other will be hit when the user posts the topic for the survey. Select the **Run And Debug** option from the **Debug** menu and start the application. Open your browser and navigate to *localhost:8080/index.html*. You will notice that no page appears. Look back at Visual Studio to find out why.

```
 18     // Home page
 19     app.get('/index.html', (request, response) => {
 20       response. render('index.ejs');
 21     });
```

The program has stopped at a breakpoint in `tinysurvey.mjs`. The browser has asked for the `index.html` file, and the server is running the Express route for that endpoint. The breakpoint is on the statement that will open the `index.ejs` file and send it back to the browser.

Click the Run Program button

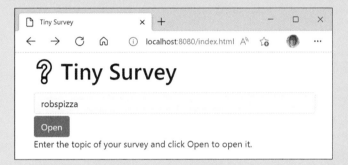

run program | step over statement | step into function | exit function | restart program | stop the program

Click the **Run Program** button in the **Debug** controls to continue the program, which will call the render function and serve out the page. Now, look back at the browser to see that the index page has appeared.

Tiny Survey   ×   +   —   □   ×

← → C ⌂   ⓘ localhost:8080/index.html A⁣ⁿ ☆   👤   ···

? Tiny Survey

robspizza

Open

Enter the topic of your survey and click Open to open it.

Enter the topic of the survey, and click **Open**. The browser will appear to get stuck again. Move back to Visual Studio Code to investigate.

```
23    // Got the survey topic
24    app.post('/gottopic', (request, response) => {
25      let surveyTopic = request.▷ body.topic;
26
27      let survey = surveys.getSurveyByTopic(surveyTopic);
28      if (survey == undefined) {
29        // need to make a new survey
30        response.render('enteroptions.ejs',
31          { topic: surveyTopic, numberOfOptions: 5 });
32      }
33      else {
34        // enter scores on an existing survey
35        let surveyOptions = survey.getOptions();
36        response.render('selectoption.ejs', surveyOptions);
37      }
38    });
```

The application has stopped at a breakpoint in the function that services the `gottopic` route. The first thing the function does is get the survey topic from the request's body. The browser puts this information into the post message. Click the **Step Into Function** button to perform the statement. If you hover the mouse pointer over the `surveyTopic` variable, you will see that it contains the topic you entered into the index page. This is how code in the application gets values from a form in a web page.

Click the **Step Into Function** button in the **Debug Controls** to step through the code. The `getSurveyByTopic` method in the survey storage is called to get a survey with the given topic. There is no survey with this topic (the program has just started), so the `getSurveyBy-Topic` function will return undefined. This will cause the application to make a new survey.

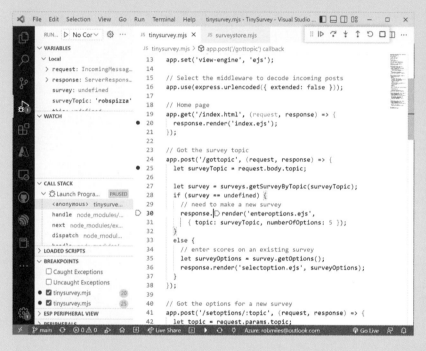

Above, you can see that the program has reached statement 30. If you look in the top-left corner in the **VARIABLES** area, you will see that the variable `surveyTopic` holds the "robspizza" value, which is what was entered into the form. The server is about to render the `enteroptions.ejs` page, which will build a form to read the five survey options from the user. Press the **Run Program** button in the **Debug Controls** to continue running the server. Leave everything as it is for the next Make Something Happen.

We are following this path through the program because there is no existing survey with the "robspizza" topic. If the survey exists, the `selectoption.ejs` page will be rendered.

If you are having problems with this exercise, two things are important:

- The first is that if you start the program using the command `node tinysurvey.mjs` command in the command line, the program does not run within the debugger, so no breakpoints will be hit.

- Secondly, you must have the `tinysurvey.mjs` file as the selected file in the Visual Studio Code editor before you use **Run And Debug** to run it. If you have another file selected, you will not get the correct run options.

This is a big step toward making the Tiny Survey application. In fact, this is a huge step in making any web-based application. You can now create a form to capture any information you want a user to enter and then process the data in a server-based application. If you want to capture more details from your user, you just have to add more input elements to the form and give them `name` attributes to identify them. They will appear as properties of the `body` object, which is a property of the request object passed to the function that handles the route. In the next section, we will discover how the `enteroptions.ejs` page works.

Enter the survey options

We are implementing the pages behind our Tiny Survey application. We've created an index page that receives the topic for the survey. The index page contains a form with one text input that was used to set the topic for the survey. When the user presses the Open button, the contents of that form are submitted to a post route called `settopic`. We've just seen how this works and that the topic entered by the user can be picked out of the post from the browser. Now we need to generate a page for the user to enter the five items we choose. We have seen this done by a page called `enteroptions.ejs`. Let's take a look at what this produces.

The enteroptions page

Figure 8-4 shows the enter options page generated from the `enteroptions.ejs` template. The user has entered the five options, and when the `Start` button is clicked, the survey will go live for users to select their preferences.

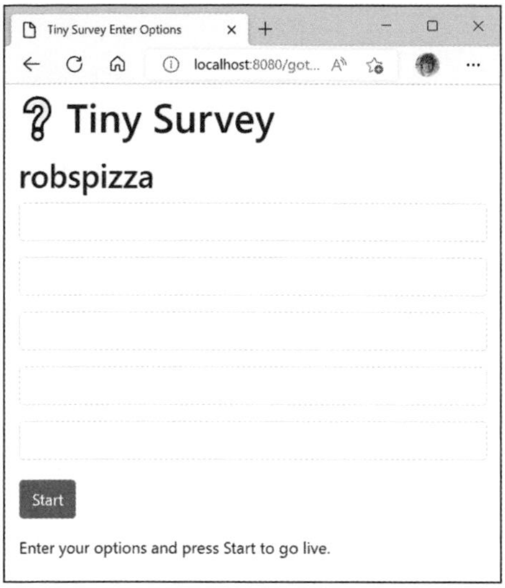

Figure 8-4 Enter Options page

The HTML below is a simplified version of the HTML behind **Figure 8-4**. The HTML specifies a heading of "robspizza" and contains a form that accepts the five survey options:

```
<h1>&#10068; Tiny Survey</h1>                               Page heading
<h2>robspizza</h2>                                          Name of topic
<form action="setoptions/robspizza" method="POST">         Form for items
  <input type="text" value="" name="option1">              Input for an item
  <input type="text" value="" name="option2">
  <input type="text" value="" name="option3">
  <input type="text" value="" name="option4">
  <input type="text" value="" name="option5">
  <button type="submit">Start</button>                     Start button
</form>
<p>Enter your five options and press Start to go live.</p>
```

We could create an HTML file that contained the above code, and it would work, but only for a survey called "robspizza" which contained five items. If I wanted a survey called "Robs Movies," I would need to generate a different page. In a perfect world, we could generate different pages automatically from the enteroptions.ejs page. The great news is that we are going to do exactly that.

Generate pages using an EJS template

This next part might hurt your head a little. It certainly did mine when I found out about it, but once you know how to do it, you will see just how awesome it really is. Before looking at the contents of the `enteroptions.ejs` file, I want to remind you of the problem we are trying to solve. We want to make a page for the application that looks like **Figure 8-4**. The page must contain the survey topic (`robspizza`) and input elements for five options. We have received the survey topic from the post to the `set-topic` route, and now we need to produce a page that contains input elements for the names of the options in the survey. Let's look at the JavaScript that does this.

```
response.render('enteroptions.ejs',                    Render enteroptions.ejs
  { topic: surveyTopic,                          Values to send to enteroptions.ejs
    numberOfOptions: 5 });
```

My favorite way of solving a problem is to get someone else to do it. That is what this code does. The function `render` how has two arguments. The first is the name of the template file (in this case, `enteroptions.ejs`). The second argument is an object literal that contains two properties:

- The `topic` of the survey (which is loaded from the post we received from the user)

- The number of options (in this case, `5`)

The `enteroptions.ejs` template uses these values to make an HTML page. Let's look at how it does this.

```html
<!DOCTYPE html>
<html>

<head>
  <title>Tiny Survey Enter Options</title>
  <meta name="viewport" content="width=device-width, initial-scale=1.0">
  <link rel="stylesheet"
 href="https://cdn.jsdelivr.net/npm/bootstrap@4.3.1/dist/css/bootstrap.min.css"
    integrity="sha384-ggOyR0iXCbMQv3Xipma34MD+dH/1fQ784/j6cY/
iJTQUOhcWr7x9JvoRxT2MZw1T"
crossorigin="anonymous">
</head>

<body>
  <div class="container">
```

```
<h1 class="mb-3 mt-2">&#10068; Tiny Survey</h1>
<h2>
  <%= topic %>————————————————————————————— Display the topic in the heading
</h2>
<form action="/setoptions/<%=topic%>" method="POST">
  <% for(let i=1;i<=numberOfOptions;i++) { %>———————— Loop to create options
    <p>
      <input type="text" required class="form-control"
      spellcheck="false" value="" name="option<%=i %>">——— Counter in option name
    </p>
  <% } %>————————————————————————————————————————————————— End of loop
    <p>
      <button type="submit" class="btn btn-primary mt-1">Start</button>
    </p>
</form>
<p>
  Enter your options and press Start to go live.
</p>
  </div>
</body>

</html>
```

This is the `enteroptions.ejs` page. At first glance, it looks like ordinary HTML, but if you look closer, you will find something interesting. There are pieces of JavaScript code in there too. This code runs as the HTML is generated. The first time we see this is when the topic is included on the page.

```
<h2 class="mb-2 mt-2">
  <%= topic %>
</h2>
```

The HTML above puts the value of `topic` into the page text. This value was passed into the page when the render method was called. The value displayed is enclosed in `<%=` and `%>` delimiters, which means "include the value of this expression in the content of the page at this point." This is how we get the `robspizza` text into the heading on the page.

```
<% for(let i=1;i<=numberOfOptions;i++) { %>———————— Loop to count through the options
  <p>
    <input type="text" required class="form-control" spellcheck="false"
```

```
        value="" name="option<%=i %>">                    Create the option name using i
    </p>
    <% } %>                                                End of the loop
```

This loop runs when the page is rendered. It creates as many input boxes as are required for the survey. Each input box will have a different name based on the word `option` followed by a count. The JavaScript statements are enclosed in `<%` and `%>` delimiters. The `numberOfOptions` value was passed to the page when `render` was called, just as the page received the `topic` value.

🚀 MAKE SOMETHING HAPPEN 39

Scan the QR code or visit *https://www.youtube.com/watch?v=svhrZpM2nTo* for a video walk-through of this Make Something Happen.

Rendering enteroptions

It is very useful to run JavaScript code inside a page as it is being generated, but it takes a little while to get used to seeing HTML and JavaScript quite so close. So, let's watch a page being rendered. We can continue working through the example application. Go back to Visual Studio Code, clear the breakpoints in **tinysurvey.mjs** and open the **enteroptions.ejs** file in the **Views** folder.

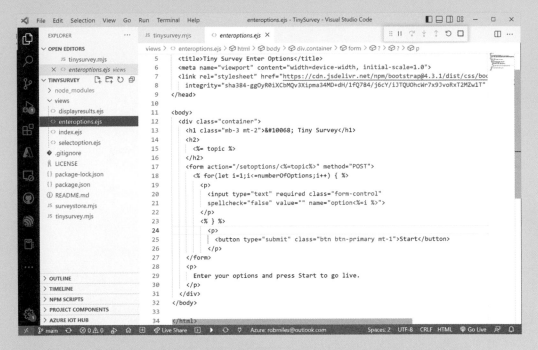

This page generates the input options. We can see how it works by changing the page and seeing the effect on the output. The page uses a JavaScript `for` loop to generate the input elements on the page. The `for` loop is on line 18 of the template.

```
<% for(let i=1;i<=numberOfOptions;i++) { %>
```

The loop is controlled by the `numberOfOptions` value. We could change the number of options by changing this value. Edit the code so that instead of using the `numbeOfOptions` value, the loop now uses the value 3:

```
<% for(let i=1;i<=3;i++) { %>
```

Save your updated version of `enterOptions.ejs` and run the application again. Enter a topic for the survey, and you will see the options page has only three options.

Our change to the loop limit has affected the amount of HTML. We don't want just three options, so we should put enterOptions.ejs back into the original file. We can use the **Source Control** in Visual Studio Code to do this. Click the **Source Control** button in the left-hand button strip.

Click to discard changes

Source Control will show you that one file has changed: enteroptions.ejs. Click the file-name to open the file to see the changes. Now, click the **Discard Changes** button next to the filename to select discard the changes. You will be asked if you want to discard the changes. If you do, the changes will be removed. Changes that have been discarded in this way cannot be recovered, but the command can be useful if you've made a terrible mess of editing a file and you want to get back to how things were before.

Rendering in Express

You might have some questions about what we have just seen.

Question: What happens if the JavaScript in `enteroptions.ejs` contains errors?

> **Answer:** If you make a mistake in a JavaScript program, you will get an error when it runs. The same is true with JavaScript in a template. The error will be displayed in the browser output and in Visual Studio Code. It will tell you the statement which caused the error.

Question: Can we use JavaScript code like this to validate input values entered into the web page?

> **Answer:** This is an interesting question. We've seen situations where we've put JavaScript into a web page to respond to inputs entered onto the web page. Can we do this here? It turns out the answer is no. Understanding why goes to the heart of understanding what these templates do. If you think about it, the JavaScript code in an EJS file only gets to run as the HTML text is generated. If you look at the HTML produced by the build page, you won't find any JavaScript code. The code in the template did its job when it made the page. None of it is ever visible in the output. However, you could put JavaScript code into the generated EJS page, which could validate inputs.

Question: Can a user of Tiny Survey break the application by entering an HTML command as the topic name?

> **Answer:** Another good question. There's a website hacking technique called Cross-Site Scripting (XSS), where you try to break an application by typing HTML (or other) commands. Consider the following:

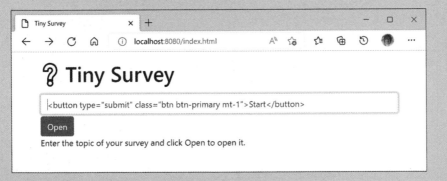

The user of the survey is trying to be sneaky. They've noticed that the `enteroptions.ejs` file just includes the topic text directly into the HTML it generates, and they fancy making another button appear on the page. The good news is that this won't work for our application.

The survey has a strange title, but we won't get extra buttons appearing on our page because the <%= operation in EJS "HTML escapes" any text before displaying it. In other words, characters that would be interpreted as commands by the browser are converted into escaped versions:

```
&lt;button type=&#34;submit&#34; class=&#34;btn btn-primary mt-1&#34;&gt;Start&lt;/
button&gt;
```

Above, you can see the text placed on the web page. You can see that the < character—which would normally start an HTML element definition—has been converted into <, as have all the other dangerous characters. In this case, the EJS framework has taken care of issues with this form of attack, but you should treat every user input as potentially hostile and make sure that it is "sanitized."

Use named route parameters

We now have a good part of the application working. A user can enter a topic and five options which are sent back to the server to create a survey. However, we do have another problem to address. The information being sent by the POST does not include the topic of the survey. How do we send the survey topic back to the server? The answer turns out to be quite simple. We can add the topic information to the URL that will receive the post when the options are submitted.

```
<form action="setoptions/<%=topic%>" method="POST">
```

Above, you can see the definition of the form that contains the options for the survey. It contains an action attribute that specifies the endpoint where the form will be submitted. The code above adds the topic name to the end of this entry point. It gets the topic name from the `topic` value supplied to the template. The form will be sent to the endpoint `"setoptions/robspizza."` We can now modify the route for this endpoint in the server code so that the topic name can be picked up and used by the program.

```
app.post('/setoptions/:topic', (request, response) => {
  let topicName = request.params.topic;
  // handle the rest of the response
})
```

Above, you can see how this works. The name of the route is now '/setop-tions/:topic'. This is called a "named route parameter." When the incoming post arrives, the Express framework splits the `topic` element off the endpoint name and copies it into a `request.params.topic` variable. The JavaScript dealing with the incoming post can now use this to build a survey object that will be held on the server.

Build a survey data object

We are working through the workflow of our Tiny Survey, viewing each step as we go. We are at the point where the user has entered the options for the survey in a form produced by the `enteroptions.ejs` page and clicked the **Start** button to post the form back to the server. The server has received the form, along with a named route parameter that gives the topic for the survey. Now we need an object to hold the survey. The object will be built from the topic and five option names.

```
app.post('/setoptions/:topic', (request, response) => {
  let topicName = request.params.topic;————————————— Get the topic of the survey
  let options = [];————————————————————————————————— Create an options array
  let optionNo = 1;————————————————————————————————— Start counting options at 1
  do {——————————————————————————————————————————————— Start of option loop
    // construct the option name
    let optionName = "option" + optionNo;——— Add the option number to the word "option"
    // fetch the text for this option from the request body
    let optionText = request.body[optionName];——— Get the option property from the body
    // If there is no text - no more options
    if (optionText == undefined) {————————————————— Exit if no option for this name
      break;
    }
    // Make an option object
    let option = new Option({ text: optionText,count:0 });
    // Store it in the array of options
    options.push(option);
    // Move on to the next option
    optionNo++;
  } while (true);
```

```
// Build a survey object
let survey = new Survey({ topic: topic, options: options });

// save it
surveys.saveSurvey(survey);

// Render the survey page
let surveyOptions = survey.getOptions();
response.render('selectoption.ejs', surveyOptions);
})
```

This is the most complicated piece of code in the application. The inputs to the code are the topic (which we got from the named route) and a request.body object that contains the options for our survey in the form of properties called option1, option2, option3, option4, and option5. The code above contains a do - while loop, which works through the properties in request.body, starting with a property called option1 and going on to try to find a property called option6 that is undefined (we only have five options) and causes the loop to exit. The code was written this way because I didn't want to fix the number of options at five in the program. Experience with people changing their minds about the number of cheeses in cheese finder has left me thinking that it is useful to be flexible about some parts of your program. Each time around the loop, a new option object is created by the following statement:

```
let option = new Option({ text: optionText, count:0 });
```

The option object is initialized with an object containing the option's text (in my case, Margherita, pepperoni, and so on) and the count of responses for that option (starting at 0). Each object is added to a list of options:

```
options.push(option);
```

In Chapter 7, we created the Option class to hold the text and option count in the survey. We import this class, along with Survey and Surveys, at the start of the tinysurvey.mjs file. The list of options is used to create a survey object containing the topic name. This is performed after the loop has finished.

```
let survey = new Survey({ topic: topic, options: options });
```

Once we have created the survey, we can store it.

```
surveys.saveSurvey(survey);
```

Scan the QR code or visit *https://www.youtube.com/watch?v=tC3sH57kHNE* for a video walk-through of this Make Something Happen.

Build a survey data object

Now, let's have a look at the process of building a data object. Put a breakpoint at line 42 in the **tinysurvey.mjs** file, start the program, and enter a new survey topic followed by the survey option. When you click **Start** on the `enteroptions` page, the program will hit the breakpoint.

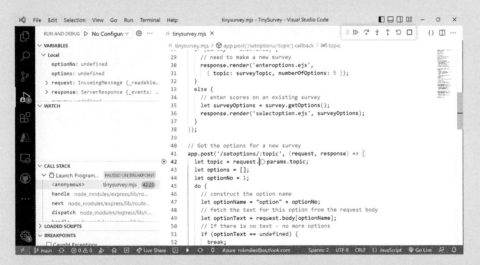

The breakpoint will be hit after you have entered the survey options and clicked the **Start** button. The **VARIABLES** view at the top-left shows the values used to create the option. You can step through the code and watch as the values are fetched from the form data and used to build a Survey object that is then stored in surveys. After stepping through the code, you can remove the breakpoint and press the **Run Program** button in the **Debug Controls** to resume program operation.

Build a select option page

We now have our survey. And we know how we can create a web application that accepts user information and stores it in an application running in the cloud. Next, we need to make a page where the users select their preferred option by clicking a radio button.

Figure 8-5 shows how the page looks. This page is displayed when creating a survey and if a user selects a survey topic that already exists.

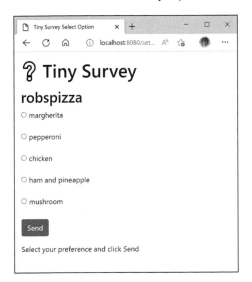

Figure 8-5 Option voting page

The page will be created from another template:

```
let surveyOptions = survey.getOptions();
response.render('selectoption.ejs', surveyOptions);
```

The statement above calls the render function to render the page from the selectoption.ejs template file. The render function is passed a surveyOptions object which contains the data needed to build the page. The surveyOptions object contains two things:

- The survey topic

- A list of the option text to be displayed

```
let surveyOptions = survey.getOptions();
```

The `tinysurvey` application can ask a survey to give it the survey options by calling the `getOptions` method from the `Survey` class. Below, you can see the code for this method. It creates an object that contains just the option information for use on the `selectoption` page.

```
getOptions() {
    let options = [];                                          Make an empty options array
    this.options.forEach(option => {                           Work through all the options
        let optionInfo = { text: option.text };     Make an object that contains the option text
        options.push(optionInfo);                              Add the object to the array
    });
    let result = { topic: this.topic, options: options };       Create the result object
    return result;                                              Return the result object
}
```

The object created by the `getOptions` method is then used by code running in the `selectoption.ejs` template shown below to create an options page that is sent to the browser.

```
<!DOCTYPE html>
<html>

<head>
    <title>Tiny Survey Select Option</title>
    <meta name="viewport" content="width=device-width, initial-scale=1.0">
    <link rel="stylesheet" href="https://cdn.jsdelivr.net/npm/bootstrap@4.3.1/dist/
css/bootstrap.min.css"
        integrity="sha384-ggOyR0iXCbMQv3Xipma34MD+dH/1fQ784/j6cY/
iJTQUOhcWr7x9JvoRxT2MZw1T" crossorigin="anonymous">
</head>

<body>
    <div class="container">
        <h1 class="mb-3 mt-3">&#10068; Tiny Survey</h1>
        <h2>
            <%=topic%>                                          Display the topic of the survey
        </h2>
        <form action="/recordselection/<%=topic%>" method="POST">
            <% options.forEach(option=> { %>                   Loop through the options
```

```
        <p>
          <input type="radio" name="selections" id="<%=option.text%>"
            value="<%=option.text%>">──────────────────── Radio button
          <label for="<%=option.text%>">
            <%=option.text%>──────────── Add the option text to the radio button
          </label>
        </p>
      <% }) %>
          <p>
            <button type="submit" class="btn btn-primary mt-1">Send</button>
          </p>
      </form>
      <p>
        Select your preference and click Send
      </p>
    </div>
  </body>

</html>
```

The `selectoption.ejs` template is like the `enteroptions.ejs` template we used to enter the survey options, except that rather than making a list of input boxes (for users to enter the options), it makes radio buttons (for users to vote). If you compare this with the `selectoption.ejs` template, there are some differences. The `selectoption` template uses a for loop to count through option numbers and create an option name for each one. The code in the `selectoption.js` template works through each option in the `options` list of the survey details using a `foreach` loop. When the Send button is clicked, the form is set to the `recordselection` endpoint in the server. The endpoint has the survey `topic` survey appended so the server's `post` handler server can use a named route to get the survey name the results are for. The code above shows the form that is created for the pizza survey. The browser groups the radio buttons because they all have the same name attribute. When one of the buttons is selected, all the others are cleared.

```
<form action="/recordselection/robspizza" method="POST">──── Named route using the topic
    <p>
      <input type="radio" name="selections" id="margherita" value="margherita">
      <label for="margherita">
        margherita
      </label>
    </p>
    <p>
```

```
        <input type="radio" name="selections" id="pepperoni" value="pepperoni">
        <label for="pepperoni">
          pepperoni
        </label>
    </p>
    <p>
        <input type="radio" name="selections" id="chicken" value="chicken">
        <label for="chicken">
          chicken
        </label>
    </p>
    <p>
        <button type="submit" class="btn btn-primary mt-1">Send</button>          Send button
    </p>
</form>
```

When the Send button is clicked, the browser sends the value of the radio button.
If the user clicks Send with the chicken button selected, the form will post the value
"chicken" to the application. The form will be posted to the /recordselection/
robspizza endpoint.

Rendering options

You might have some questions about what we have just seen.

Question: What just happened?

> **Answer:** You might be finding this hard to understand. The key to understanding what is
> happening is to go back and think about what the code has to do. The application needs
> to create a web page with a radio button for each survey option. The selectoption.ejs
> template contains the HTML definition of one radio button and a JavaScript loop that
> produces a radio button for each option. To do this, the selectoption.ejs template
> needs to know the topic of the survey (which it will display and use as a named endpoint
> for the response) and the text of each option. This information is supplied to the template
> as an object containing topic and options properties.
>
> This object is generated by calling the getOptions method on a Survey instance. This
> creates an object which contains the information to be passed into the selectoptions.
> ejs page. As we discover how more of the application pages work, we will see a pattern
> where the application creates a lump of information passed to the page to tell it what

to do. When we look at the results page (which we will see next), we will see the same pattern at work.

Question: Why don't we just pass the survey object to the `enteroptions` page?

Answer: An instance of a `Survey` object contains all the data needed by the `selectoption.ejs` template to build the page. But the code sends the result of a call of `getOptions` into the `selectoption.ejs` page instead. Why not pass the survey? This is because if I give something a reference to a survey object, they can do all kinds of things with it, including changing the counts for options or even the topic name. But if I pass a copy of the required data, there is no way this can happen. This is what I call *defensive programming*.

Question: Is it okay to use the text the user enters as attribute names in the HTML?

Answer: If you look at the code above, you will notice that the `chicken` radio button has `name` and `id` attributes that are also `chicken`. As far as HTML is concerned, these are just strings of text. They do not need to obey any particular rules for variable names in programs.

Question: What would happen if two options had the same text?

Answer: The user might create two options for "pepperoni." What would happen? You might like to try this. The program will work okay, but votes for the second option version will be counted as being for the first. A later version of the application could check for repeated option text and produce an error.

When the user clicks Send in the `selectoption` page, the form posts a result value to the `recordselection` endpoint in the application. This endpoint needs to increment the selected option's counter and display the results page.

Record survey responses

```javascript
// Got the selections for a survey
app.post('/recordselection/:topic', (request, response) => {
  let topic = request.params.topic;                              // Get the topic out of the request
  let survey = surveys.getSurveyByTopic(topic);                  // Find the survey with this topic
  if (survey == undefined) {                                     // Check if the survey exists
    response.status(404).send('<h1>Survey not found</h1>');      // Display an error if the
  }                                                              //   survey is not found
  else {
    let optionSelected = request.body.selections;                // Get the selection
    survey.incrementCount(optionSelected);                       // Increment the count for the selection
```

```
      let results = survey.getCounts();                    ─── Get the survey counts
      response.render('displayresults.ejs', results);      ─── Display the counts
   }
});
```

Above is the post route in the server that records a selection. It finds the survey, gets the survey option that has been selected, adds one to the count for that option, and renders the results page. If the survey is not found (there is no survey matching the supplied topic name), the code generates a 404 (page not found) error response. Otherwise, it updates the count and then uses the `results.ejs` template to render the results. We can step through this code and watch it run.

MAKE SOMETHING HAPPEN 41

Scan the QR code or visit *https://www.youtube.com/watch?v=0npejC0H2dM* for a video walk-through of this Make Something Happen.

Record a response

Now, let's have a look at the process of recording a response. Put a breakpoint at line 75 in the **tinysurvey.mjs** file, start the program, and enter a new survey topic, followed by the survey options. Vote for your favorite pizza topping. When you click **Send** in the `selectoption` page, the program will hit the breakpoint in the Express handler for that route.

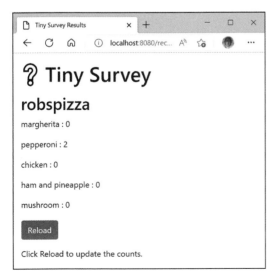

You can repeatedly click the **Step Into Function** button in the **Debug Controls** to watch the code get the survey topic, find that survey, get the selected option from the response, and then increment the counter for that response. The program running above has been stepped through to line 84 and is showing the contents of the results object which is being sent to the `displayresults` page.

Render the results

The final page that we need is the one that renders the counts for each option. The `displayresults.ejs` template does this. You can see the output that we want in **Figure 8-6**.

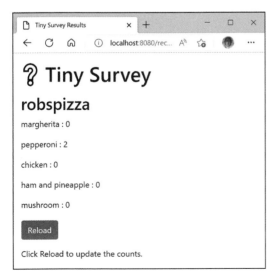

Figure 8-6   Results page

The render function that uses the template is supplied with the results object from which the counts will be obtained.

```
response.render('displayresults.ejs', results);
```

You should notice by now that all the pages that deal with the survey contents are very similar. They contain a loop that works through the options and outputs HTML elements with element properties. In this case, the properties used are the survey topic and each option's `text` and `count` properties.

```html
<!DOCTYPE html>
<html>

<head>
  <title>Tiny Survey Results</title>
  <meta name="viewport" content="width=device-width, initial-scale=1.0">
  <link rel="stylesheet" href="https://cdn.jsdelivr.net/npm/bootstrap@4.3.1/dist/
css/bootstrap.min.css"
    integrity="sha384-ggOyROiXCbMQv3Xipma34MD+dH/1fQ784/j6cY/
iJTQUOhcWr7x9JvoRxT2MZw1T"
crossorigin="anonymous">
</head>
</head>

<body>
  <div class="container">
    <h1 class="mb-3 mt-3">&#10068; Tiny Survey</h1>
    <h2 class="mb-10 mt-2">
      <%=topic%>                                          Topic of the survey
    </h2>
    <% options.forEach(option=> { %>                      Loop for each option
      <p>
        <%= option.text%> : <%= option.count %>           Option text and count value
      </p>
    <% }) %>
      <p>
        <button class="btn btn-primary mt-1" onclick="window.location.href='/
displayresults/<%=topic%>'"> Reload
        </button>
      </p>
      </form>
      <p>
```

```
        Click Reload to update the counts.
      </p>
   </div>
</body>

</html>
```

The page also contains a button that can be used to request a refresh of the count display. When this button is pressed, it must open an endpoint that will re-render the results page.

```
<button onclick="window.location.href='/displayresults/<%=topic%>'">
 Reload </button>
```

The **Reload** button above opens the `displayresults` endpoint when it is clicked. This location is supplied with the topic name, so the server can use a named route to determine the results to display.

```
// Get the results for a survey
app.get('/displayresults/:topic', (request, response) => {
  let topic = request.params.topic;                              Get the topic
  let survey = surveys.getSurveyByTopic(topic);                  Find the survey
  if (survey == undefined) {
    response.status(404).send('<h1>Survey not found</h1>');
  }
  else {
    let results = survey.getCounts();                            Get the counts
    response.render('displayresults.ejs', results);             Display them
  }
});
```

The code that handles the `displayresults` endpoint is shown above. It is similar to the code that deals with the `recordselection` endpoint, except that it doesn't update any counts.

What you have learned

In this chapter, we have created a fully functional server-based application. We now know how data is passed between the browser and the server and how to use Express to generate web pages customized by code running inside them. Now when you use web pages, you will start to see how they work. The Express framework is only one of many frameworks used to create web applications, but you now understand many of the fundamental principles underpinning how it works. Here's the usual recap, plus some points to ponder:

- You can use Bootstrap stylesheets to improve the appearance of your web pages. A page that uses Bootstrap just contains a reference to a stylesheet file which is served by Bootstrap rather than a local file.

- The node package manager (npm) program is provided as part of a Node.js installation. The company behind npm hosts a library of resources that can be incorporated into node applications.

- The resources an application uses are itemized in the dependencies section of the package.json file that describes the application. The npm program can be controlled via the terminal. The **npm init** command creates an empty package.json file, and **npm install** is used to install resources. If npm installs a resource that needs other resources to work, these are also automatically installed.

- You can create a Git repository using the git init terminal command (as long as you have installed Git on your computer). Git is integrated into Visual Studio Code. You can view files and commit changes in the **Source Control** window. You can add a gitignore file to a project to provide patterns to identify files that are not to be committed into a repository. These files are part of libraries and are not created specifically for the application.

- The Express framework can create an application server that runs under node.js. The server code assigns functions to Express "routes," which equate to endpoints the browser hits. An express route receives a request object describing the request from the server and populates a reply object with items to be sent back to the browser.

- Frameworks such as Express can host *middleware* elements that add functionality to an application. One such framework is EJS (Embedded JavaScript templates). This allows Express to render HTML files with active JavaScript components that can incorporate HTML elements into the page being generated.

- A FORM element in an HTML page contains INPUT elements into which the user can enter data values. The FORM can also contain a button to trigger a submit action by the form. If the submit method is set to POST, the form browser will send an HTTP POST to the server to deliver the values entered into the form. The server can use the urlencoded middleware to decode the information in the post and add it to the request object to be processed by the route handler for the post.

- We can use the debugger in Visual Studio Code to watch an application run and view the contents of variables.

- Within an EJS template file, the delimiters <% and %> mark the start and end of JavaScript code sections. If a template contains a JavaScript loop, the elements of HTML inside the loop are output into the page each time the loop goes around. The delimiters <%= and %> enclose JavaScript expressions. When the page is rendered, the value of the expression is placed at that point.

- The EJS call to render a template can include a reference to an object containing values used by the JavaScript running inside the template page.

- A post request from a web page can add a named route parameter to the end of the request. This allows the browser to send information to the server. The route running in the server can then extract this name. We used this in Tiny Survey so that a route could contain the survey topic.

To reinforce your understanding of this chapter, you might want to consider the following "profound questions":

Question: Do the large stylesheet files loaded from Bootstrap increase web traffic and slow down websites?

> **Answer:** Bootstrap stylesheets improve the appearance of web pages and also allow them to adapt to the device they are being displayed on. The stylesheet files are quite large, but a browser will automatically cache them on the host computer (keep local copies), so using them has very little impact on page performance and network use.

Question: What is the difference between Node.js and node package manager (npm)?

> **Answer:** Node.js is the framework that runs JavaScript code on a machine. Node package manager is a separate program that manages the packages in an application. It uses the package.json file for the application to keep track of the resources used by a particular application.

Question: How does Express middleware work?

> **Answer:** When the application starts, it binds the middleware in by calling an app.use function to specify the point where the middleware is to be used and specifies the middleware code to import.

Question: What is the difference between a route and an endpoint?

Answer: The endpoint is specified by a URL. It specifies the server's address and a path to the resource provided by the server. For example, *http://localhost:8080/index.html* is the server on port 8080 of the local machine, and the path is `index.html`. The route is the path's Express mapping (such as `index.html`) to the JavaScript function that will run to deal with the request and generate a response.

Question: What is the difference between a `GET` and a `POST`?

Answer: The HyperText Transfer Protocol (HTTP) describes commands that can be sent from the browser to the server. The `GET` command means, "please send me this page." The `POST` command means, "here is a chunk of data." A `GET` is sent when the user goes to a page. A `POST` is sent when the user submits a form.

Question: The Cheese Finder application generated a web page by adding elements to the Document Object Model. The Tiny Survey generates web pages using EJS templates. Which is better?

Answer: When we created the Cheese Finder application, we needed to make 100 buttons (one for each square on the board). We ran JavaScript inside the browser, which created HTML button elements and added them to the Document Object Model (DOM) that the browser uses to manage the page contents displayed to the user. The buttons were not downloaded from the server. The Tiny Survey application works differently. It uses JavaScript on the server inside the EJS page templates to generate HTML elements in the page sent to the browser. This is an important distinction. For Cheese Finder, the browser does the work to make the page, but for Tiny Survey, the work is done by the server. So, which is best? Using the browser (Cheese Finder) might reduce the loading on the server. Using the server (Tiny Survey) means that you can send the page to a browser that doesn't support JavaScript (although most do). It is up to the designers of the application to choose their approach. Other frameworks share the work between the browser and server in different ways.

9

Turn professional

What you will learn

You might wonder what separates a student or hobbyist program from a "professional" one. The only thing that makes "professional" code different is the fact that someone has paid money for it. This changes the relationship between the user and the author. The user is now a customer and has a right to expect a certain level of quality in the product they have purchased. The problem is that, from the outside, it is very hard to tell if that quality is present. It is only when the software fails, runs slowly, or proves to be impossible to modify that the lack of quality shows up.

In this chapter, you will learn techniques to make your applications more worthy of being paid for (or at least released to the world). You'll discover how to break applications into individual modules that are documented, tested, and contain error handling and logging. Along the way, we'll meet a new JavaScript hero in the form of the exception and discover how to use cookies to retain the state of an application in the browser. It's going to be fun.

This is the point in this section where I remind you about the glossary. I'd hate to disappoint you, so don't forget about the glossary at *https://begintocodecloud.com/glossary.html.*

Modular code

We can make the process of creating code easier by breaking a solution into separate modules. The idea behind this is that modules can be individually tested and interchanged without affecting others. The Tiny Survey application is somewhat modular in that the code that manages survey storage is in a separate file from the main program, but we can improve this by creating a helper that implements a well-defined interface between the application and its data storage needs.

The following SurveyManager class provides all the survey storage functions for the Tiny Survey application. It uses the SurveyStore classes to store the data.

```
import { Survey, Surveys } from './surveystore.mjs'

class SurveyManager{

    constructor(){                                          Constructor for the controller
        this.surveys = new Surveys();
    }

    storeSurvey(newValue){                                  Store a survey
        let survey = new Survey(newValue);
        this.surveys.saveSurvey(survey);
    }

    incrementCount(incDetails){                             Increment an option count
        let topic = incDetails.topic;
        let option = incDetails.option;
        let survey = this.surveys.getSurveyByTopic(topic);
        survey.incrementCount(option);
    }

    surveyExists(topic){                                    Check if a survey exists
        return this.surveys.getSurveyByTopic(topic) != undefined;
    }

    getCounts(topic){                                       Get the count values for a survey
        let survey = this.surveys.getSurveyByTopic(topic);
        return survey.getCounts();
    }

    getOptions(topic){                                      Get the options for a survey
```

```
        let survey = this.surveys.getSurveyByTopic(topic);
        return survey.getOptions();
    }
}
export { SurveyManager } ;
```

The `SurveyManager` class adds some new functionality. It has a `surveyExists` method that tests for the existence of a survey with a particular topic. The Tiny Survey application imports this class, creates an instance, and then uses that for all its survey storage needs. The code below is from the `tinysurvey.mjs` file:

```
import { SurveyManager } from './surveymanager.mjs';
// Create a survey manager
let surveyManager = new SurveyManager();
```

MAKE SOMETHING HAPPEN 42

Scan the QR code or visit *https://www.youtube.com/watch?v=bmai1jXC0Z0* for a video walk-through of this Make Something Happen.

Use the SurveyManager class

The starting point for this Make Something Happen is a version of Tiny Survey you can download from GitHub here:

https://github.com/Building-Apps-and-Games-in-the-Cloud/TinySurveyManager

Clone this repository to your machine and open it with Visual Studio Code. If you are unsure how to get the sample application, use the sequence described in the "Get the example application" section in Chapter 8. Just change the address of the repository that you clone. Open the application in Visual Studio Code and then open the **tinysurvey.mjs** source file.

```
    File   Edit   Selection   View   Go   Run   Terminal   Help        tinysurvey.mjs - TinySurveyManager - Visual Studio ...

    EXPLORER                 ···      JS tinysurvey.mjs ×

    ∨ OPEN EDITORS                   JS tinysurvey.mjs > ...
       ×  JS tinysurvey.mjs           1    import { SurveyManager } from './surveymanager.mjs';
    ∨ TINYSURVEY...                   2    import express from 'express';
       > node_modules                 3
       > views                        4    // Create the express application
       ◆ .gitignore                   5    const app = express();
       ⊼ LICENSE                      6
       {} package-lock.json           7    // Create a survey manager
       {} package.json                8    let surveyManager = new SurveyManager();
       JS surveymanager.mjs           9
       JS surveystore.mjs            10    const port = 8080;
       JS tinysurvey.mjs             11
                                     12    // Select ejs middleware
                                     13    app.set('view-engine', 'ejs');
                                     14
                                     15    // Select the middleware to decode incoming posts
                                     16    app.use(express.urlencoded({ extended: false }));
                                     17
                                     18    // Home page
                                     19    app.get('/index.html', (request, response) => {
                                     20      response.render('index.ejs');
                                     21    });
                                     22
    > OUTLINE                        23    // Got the survey topic
    > TIMELINE                       24    app.post('/gottopic', (request, response) => {
    > NPM SCRIPTS                    25      let topic = request.body.topic;
    > PROJECT COMPONENTS             26
    > AZURE IOT HUB                  27      let survey = surveyManager.surveyExists(topic);
                                     28
```

SurveyManager instance created and initalized

The existence of a survey with a paticular topic is checked

At the top of the file at line 8 is the statement that creates and initializes the SurveyManager instance. At line 27, you can seed the statement that checks whether a survey with a particular topic exists. If you run the application and use the browser to navigate to *localhost:8080/index.html* and enter a survey, you'll find it works like before. You can add breakpoints to watch as the different methods are called. Leave the application open so you can use it to investigate comments in the next section.

CODE ANALYSIS

Using a manager class

You might have some questions about how the manager class is used in the Tiny Survey application.

Question: What is the difference between using a manager class and just having storage classes?

> **Answer:** The previous version of Tiny Survey used a set of classes (Option, Survey, and Surveys) to store survey information. This works fine. Why are we making another class that duplicates what they are doing? The answer is that we want to separate the Tiny

Survey application code from the code used to store the data. This will make it possible to change the underlying data storage without changing any part of Tiny Survey.

Question: Why does the manager class have a `surveyExists` method?

Answer: The `Surveys` class in the survey storage provides a method called `getSurvey-ByTopic` to find a survey with a particular topic. However, an application using the `SurveyManager` class cannot access the `Surveys` storage class. The Tiny Survey application needs to know whether a survey exists and can now use this method to make this determination.

Question: Doesn't using a manager class slow the application down?

Answer: The previous version of Tiny Survey called the storage methods directly. This version calls a method in the manager class, which then calls the storage methods. This will introduce a tiny extra delay but will not affect performance in any significant way. The advantages of having a manager class are worth the performance penalty.

Comments/documentation

Proper code documentation adds a lot to your code. You might have been wondering why I've not mentioned comments just yet. That's because we haven't had much need for them until now. You don't need many comments if you use sensible variable names and a simple code structure. Otherwise, you find yourself writing statements like this:

```
totalPrice = salesPrice + handlingPrice + tax; // work out the total price
```

I think the above comment is not really needed. However, when we create a manager class, we must have comments and documentation. This is particularly the case if several people are working on the code. People using the class must be told what each method does and how to use it. There are two kinds of comments you can add to JavaScript programs:

```
// single line comment

/* Multi-line comments
   that can extend over several
   lines
*/
```

We could just sprinkle these kinds of comments over the `SurveyManager` class, but it turns out that there is a much better way of adding properly useful comments.

Scan the QR code or visit *https://www.youtube.com/watch?v=Vo_oifbnuOw* for a video walk-through of this Make Something Happen.

Working with comments

This Make Something Happen starts with a version of Tiny Survey you can download from GitHub at *https://github.com/Building-Apps-and-Games-in-the-Cloud/TinySurveyManager*. You should already have this open from the previous exercise. Open the **surveymanager. mjs** file and find line 32.

Tab to line 32

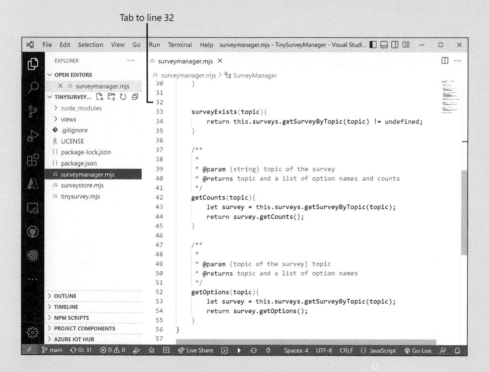

The `getCounts` and `getOptions` methods have formatted comments above them. You are going to add similar comments to the `surveyExists` method. Visual Studio code will do a lot of the work for this. Move the cursor to line 32, directly above the `surveyExists` declaration. Now type **/**** (forward slash followed by two asterisks).

```
32   /** */
33   sur abc /** */
34       JSDoc comment                                    × d;
35   }
36
```

A dialog will pop up inviting you to enter a JSDoc comment. (JSDoc comments provide interactive documentation.) Press **Enter**.

```
31
32   /**
33    *
34    * @param {  } topic
35    * @returns
36    */
37   surveyExists(topic){
38       return this.surveys.getSurveyByTopic(topic) != undefined;
39   }
```

You can now enter the comment text. The item between the braces where the cursor is presently located is where you enter the parameter type. You can also enter descriptions of the method, the topic parameter, and the return value.

```
31
32   /**
33    * Checks if a survey exists
34    * @param {string} topic topic of the survey
35    * @returns true if the survey exists in the storage
36    */
37   surveyExists(topic){
38       return this.surveys.getSurveyByTopic(topic) != undefined;
39   }
```

You can see the completed comment text in the preceding figure. The great thing about comments entered like this is that Visual Studio Code can use them to provide interactive help. To see this in action, open the **tinysurvey.mjs** file in the editor and move to line 27. Now rest the mouse cursor over the identifier **surveyExists**.

```
18   // Home page
19   app.get('/index.html', (request, response) => {
20       response.render('index.e┌───────────────────────────────────────────────┐
21   });                         │ (method) SurveyManager.surveyExists(topic:      │
22                               │ string): boolean                                │
23   // Got the survey topic     │                                                 │
24   app.post('/gottopic', (req  │ Checks if a survey exists                       │
25       let topic = request.body│ @param topic — topic of the survey              │
26                               │ @returns — true if the survey exists in the storage │
27       let survey = surveyManager.surveyExists(topic);
                                 └───────────────────────────────────────────────┘
```

Hover mouse pointer over surveyExists(topic)

Visual Studio will display a pop-up window containing the comment information you have just entered. You will get similar displays as you are editing code. This is a very good way to make "self-documenting" programs. The JSDoc comment format can be used with JSDoc3, a documentation generator that can produce websites for you. You can find out more at *https://jsdoc.app/*.

Error checking

The current implementation of the SurveyManager class has no error checking at all. The error handling is missing from the code. The methods work because they will be provided with the correct information to perform their tasks. If I'm writing a small program for my own amusement, this is fine, but if I want to incorporate the code into a program I'm going to sell or make available for others to use, there should be some error-checking in the code.

```
/**
 * Stores a survey
 * @param {Object} newValue topic string and option list
 */
storeSurvey(newValue){
    let survey = new Survey(newValue);
    this.surveys.saveSurvey(survey);
}
```

As an example of what I mean by the exclusion of error handling, consider the method above. It stores a new survey value. The newValue parameter to storeSurvey is an object that describes a survey. The goodSurveyValues variable below refers to an object containing all the information required to make a survey and could be passed into storeSurvey. However, the storeSurvey method doesn't check that the values it receives are valid.

```
let goodSurveyValues = {
  topic: "robspizza",
  options: [
    { text: "margherita", count: 0 },
    { text: "pepperoni", count: 0 },
    { text: "chicken", count: 0 },
    { text: "ham and pineapple", count: 0 },
    { text: "mushroom", count: 0 }
  ]
};
```

The badSurveyValues variable below describes a survey that has a few things wrong with it. The topic property has been entered as Topic, one of the options has a count value which is a string, and another option has no count value at all. However, the current storeSurvey method in the SurveyManager class would accept this and try to store it as a survey. We really should not be selling an application that allows things like this.

```
let badSurveyValues = {
  Topic:"bad survey",
  options: [
    { text: "margherita", count: "hello" },
    { text: 99, count: 0 },
    { text: "chicken"}
  ]
};
```

The code below uses the JavaScript in operator to test whether a new value contains topic and options properties. If these properties are missing, an error description is added to the errors string. This string will be checked at the end of the storeSurvey method. If it is empty, the survey can be stored. Otherwise, the errors string will contain a description of what is wrong with the incoming survey.

```
let errors = "";
if (!("topic" in newValue)) {
  errors = errors + "Missing topic property in storeSurvey\n";
}
if (!("options" in newValue)) {
  errors = errors + "Missing options in storeSurvey\n";
}
```

Error handling

Detecting errors is one thing, but deciding what to do when they happen is another. Two kinds of errors can happen when an application is running. There are expected errors (the user might enter an invalid username or password) and errors that shouldn't happen (the program might try to store an invalid survey).

The first kind of error should be built into the application workflow. If the user enters an invalid username or password into a login page, the application should display an appropriate message and invite the user to try again. This workflow might be expanded to allow only five user attempts before an account is locked. This depends on the application's importance and how much security effort the customer is prepared to pay for. When creating an application workflow, you must look at each step and consider what the user could do wrong. Then you add extra steps to handle this. These kinds of errors are routine errors that are to be expected.

The second kind of error is caused by a software fault or an external service failure. The workflow should ensure that a user will always enter valid surveys. These errors are outside the normal workflow of the application. These errors can best be handled by an *exception*. As the name implies, an exception is an exceptional event. Let's have a look at how exceptions are dealt with in JavaScript.

JavaScript heroes: exceptions

A good superhero always has a good escape plan. The same is true of an application. If it would not be meaningful for the application to continue, it should throw an exception object to indicate this. When attempting to store a survey with invalid contents, it is very important that this action not continue. JavaScript can abandon an action by throwing an exception. The code below is at the end of the `storeSurvey` method. It checks to see if the `errors` variable contains any messages. If it does, the `errors` variable is thrown as an exception.

```
if (errors != "") {
    throw errors;
}
```

An exception abandons the current execution flow, diverting it to a piece of code intended to handle the exception. On the next page, you can see how this works. The code creates a new `surveyManager` instance and uses it to store the survey defined in the `goodSurveyValues` variable. The code to do this is in a block following the `try` keyword. When this code runs, the survey is stored correctly.

```
let mgr = new SurveyManager();

try {
  mgr.storeSurvey(goodSurveyValues);
}
catch(error){
  console.log("Survey store failed:" + error);
}
```

Replacing the goodSurveyValues variable with the badSurveyValues variable attempts to store an invalid survey. The storeSurvey method will throw an exception, and the execution will transfer into the catch block, which will log the error on the console. The argument to the catch is the object that was thrown, which in this case is the string containing the error report.

MAKE SOMETHING HAPPEN 44

Scan the QR code or visit *https://www.youtube.com/watch?v=gfIcFt7auC4* for a video walk-through of this Make Something Happen.

Exploring exceptions

Let's take a look at how exceptions work. Start your browser and open the **index.html** file in the **Ch09-01-Exploring_Exceptions** example folder. Open the browser's **Developer Tools** and select the console view. The page's JavaScript code contains the survey management classes. You can work with them in the console. Start by creating a SurveyManager instance. Enter the following command and press **Enter**:

```
let mgr = new SurveyManager()
```

A new SurveyManager is created, and the variable mgr is set to refer to it.

```
> let mgr = new SurveyManager()
< undefined
>
```

Now that you have your survey manager, you can use it to store a survey. The web page code contains definitions of the goodSurveyValues and badSurveyValues variables. You can try to store those in the survey. Enter the following and press **Enter**:

```
mgr.storeSurvey(goodSurveyValues)
```

Storing a good survey works just fine.

```
> mgr.storeSurvey(goodSurveyValues)
< undefined
>
```

Now, let's store a bad survey and see what happens. Enter the following and press **Enter**:

```
mgr.storeSurvey(badSurveyValues)
```

This time, the storeSurvey method throws an exception.

```
> mgr.storeSurvey(badSurveyValues)
⊗ ▶ Uncaught Missing topic property in storeSurvey
   Count not a number in option margherita in storeSurvey
   Missing count in option chicken in storeSurvey
>
```

The storeSurvey call was made outside a try block, so the JavaScript engine displays an error along with the uncaught exception value. If you enclose the statement in a try block, you can get control when the exception is thrown. Enter the following and press **Enter**:

```
try { mgr.storeSurvey(badSurveyValues); } catch(error) {console.log("Ooops:"+error)}
```

This statement contains try and catch blocks. If the code inside the try block throws an exception, the code inside the catch block will execute.

```
> try { mgr.storeSurvey(badSurveyValues); } catch(error)
  {console.log("Ooops:"+error)}

  Ooops:Missing topic property in storeSurvey
  Count not a number in option margherita in storeSurvey
  Missing count in option chicken in storeSurvey
< undefined
>
```

This time, no errors are displayed because the exception has been caught. You can experiment with the error handling in the SurveyManager class by trying to store different objects of your own as surveys. You can also look at the site's source and discover just how much code you need to add to perform error testing.

Exceptions and finally

There is one last thing that you need to know about exceptions. And that is the aptly named finally block. You can add this to an exception construction to define code that is guaranteed to run regardless of what happens inside the try and catch blocks. The code below tries to store a survey. If the survey storage throws an exception, the catch block runs to deal with it. The finally block contains code that will run whatever happens inside the try and catch blocks.

The finally code will run whatever is in the catch block code. If the try–catch is running inside a function or method, and the code in the catch block contains a return, the finally code will run. If the code in the catch block throws another exception, the finally code will still run. The finally block is where we can put code that will release resources that might have been obtained in the try block.

```
try {
   mgr.storeSurvey(surveyValues);
}
catch(error){
   console.log("Survey store failed:" + error);
}
finally{
   console.log("This message is always displayed");
}
```

Using exceptions

You might have some questions about exceptions.

Question: How much code can you put in the `try` block?

> **Answer:** The `try` block can contain as much code as you like.

Question: Can exception handlers be nested?

> **Answer:** Yes. You can put a `try–catch` construction in code already running inside a `try–catch` construction. JavaScript will look for and use the "nearest" `catch` when an exception is thrown.

Question: Does the exception handler "know" where it was thrown?

> **Answer:** No. You can, of course, put information into the block of data that is thrown that will tell code in the `catch` block where the failure occurred.

Question: Is it possible to go back to the code where the exception was thrown after it was handled?

> **Answer:** No. When the exception is thrown, the execution transfers to the `catch` block (if any) and can never return.

Question: What happens if the code in the `catch` block throws an exception?

> **Answer:** If code in the `catch` block throws an exception, JavaScript will run that and look for the "nearest" `catch` block (if there is one).

Question: Does every `try–catch` construction need a `finally` block?

> **Answer:** No. You only need a `finally` block if the `try` block's code allocates resources (for example, it connects to a database or opens a file) that you want to release when the code has finished. This reduces the chances of resources being "stuck" allocated to something that will never give them back.

Question: How do we use the `try–catch` construction in an application like Tiny Survey?

> **Answer:** Good question. We could enclose the code that handles each route in a `try–catch` construction and then render an error page in the `catch` block if the code throws an exception. The code below shows how this works.

```
app.get('/index.html', (request, response) => {
  try {
    response.render('index.ejs');
  }
```

```
catch(error) {
    console.log(error);
    response.render('error.ejs');
  }
});
```

It is very unlikely that rendering the index page would throw an exception, but if it does, this would now cause the error to be logged and the error page to be displayed. However, you should never use `try-catch` to deal with an unknown error. If a piece of your code throws an exception every now and then, you should find out why the exception is thrown and fix the problem rather than use a `try-catch` to hide what is happening.

Testing

Code that is to be made available to other people should be tested first. And by testing, I don't mean running through the program a couple of times to see what happens. I'm not sure what that is called—perhaps "playing with it." Proper testing is a managed process that is part of the project. For tests to be of any use, they must be repeatable and, as much as possible, automatic. We can test the Tiny Survey application itself by writing a set of survey creation steps and then working through them. Software companies employ testers to do this, and there are also automated tools that can be used to provide simulated inputs and track the outputs. This is testing at the application level, but there is also a need for testing at the module level. We've just added a whole bunch of error handling to the SurveyManager class. It would be useful to be able to test these error handlers automatically. There are several tools available that we can add to our application to perform testing. We are going to use one called Jest. You can find out more about Jest at *https://jestjs.io/*.

Installing Jest

We can add Jest to our application in the same way we have added everything else so far: using node package manager (npm):

```
npm jest
```

Once Jest has been installed, we need to configure the application to use it for testing. This involves modifying the `package.json` file and adding a `jest.config.mjs` file to our application. We have to go through this complication because the standard version of Jest doesn't work with the `.mjs` source files we are using in our application. However, don't worry about this because the sample application for this chapter already has these settings. You can find out more about `.mjs` files in the "Require and import" section in Chapter 4.

Writing tests

Once we have Jest installed, we need to write tests for our code. The Jest framework provides functions we can use to perform individual tests. It will then run these tests and report on the results. We can start by creating a little helper function for our tests.

```
function surveyTest(newValue){
  let manager = new SurveyManager();          Create a manager
  manager.storeSurvey(newValue);          Use the manager to store the survey
}
```

The function `surveyTest` accepts an object parameter called `newValue` that defines a survey. It creates a new `SurveyManager` and uses it to store the survey. If the `newValue` contains an invalid survey description, the `storeSurvey` method will throw an exception. The test must ensure the correct exception is thrown and the exception contains the correct message. The survey description below has no options, so it should be rejected by `storeSurvey`.

```
let missingOptions = {
  topic: "robspizza"
};
```

We can create a test for this behavior using the Jest `test` function, as shown below. The first argument to the call is a string describing the test. The second argument is the function to be called to run the test. The test below uses the `expect` method, which is given a function to test—in this case, `surveyTest` with a `missingOptions` argument. After the `expect` call, we see a condition to match—in this case, a `toThrow` element, which is given the exception text that will be thrown if the test is successful.

```
test('Missing options', () => {
  expect(() =>
    surveyTest(missingOptions)).toThrow("Missing options in storeSurvey\n");
});
```

The nice thing about Jest is that if you read the code aloud, it provides a very good description of what the test will do: "Expect the surveyTest with missing options to throw 'Missing options in storeSurvey.'

Some tests use a method to perform them. The test must create a survey to test the incrementCount behavior, add one to the count for an option, and then check that the correct option value is now 1. The incrementTest function below does this, returning an empty string if it works or an error message if it fails:

```
function incrementTest() {
  let manager = new SurveyManager();
  let error = "";
  manager.storeSurvey(newSurveyValues);
  manager.incrementCount({ topic:"robspizza", option:"pepperoni"});
  let surveyOptions = manager.getCounts("robspizza");

  newSurveyValues.options.forEach(option => {
    let testOption = surveyOptions.options.find(item => item.text == option.text);
    if (testOption == undefined) {
      error = error + "option missing\n";
    }
    else {
      if (testOption.text == "pepperoni") {
        if (testOption.count != 1) {
          error = error + "count increment failed";
        }
      }
      else {
        if (testOption.count != 0) {
          error = error + "incremented wrong count";
        }
      }
    }
  });
  return error;
}
```

We can use the incrementTest function to perform a test by using a different matching function on the result of calling the test method, as shown in the code below.

```
test('Increment a count', () => {
  expect(incrementTest()).toBe("");
});
```

The `toBe` match enables a test to check for a particular result value rather than an exception. The Jest framework contains lots of different match functions. The test programs are stored in a file containing the word `test` in the filename. The tests are run from the terminal using the `npm test` command. The `npm` program opens `package.json`, finds the test command (in our case, to run Jest), and runs it.

MAKE SOMETHING HAPPEN 45

Scan the QR code or visit *https://www.youtube.com/watch?v=wIm4g9YeQdo* for a video walkthrough of this Make Something Happen.

Running tests

The starting point here is a version of Tiny Survey you can download from GitHub at *https://github.com/Building-Apps-and-Games-in-the-Cloud/TinySurveyTest*. The repository contains the application with error handling and a set of tests. Clone this repository onto your machine and open it with Visual Studio Code. If you are unsure how to get the sample application, use the sequence described in the "Get the example application" section in Chapter 8. Just change the address of the repository that you clone. Open the application in Visual Studio Code and then open the **surveymanager.test.mjs** source file.

The test file contains several tests for the `SurveyManager` class. You want to run these from the terminal, but you want to run them in the debugger, so press the debugger icon in the left-hand menu strip (the triangle with a bug) and then click the **JavaScript Debug Terminal** button.

This terminal lets you run npm and node applications in the debugger from the command line. You should do this because you might want to step through the tests. Go into the terminal window, type the following commands, and press **Enter**:

```
npm install
npm test
```

The first command installs all the libraries that are needed to run the application, including the Jest framework. The second command starts the debugger, which will load npm and run the test command. This starts Jest, which will search for JavaScript files with the word "test" in their names. These files will be opened, and the tests in them will be run. At the end, you will see a list of passed tests.

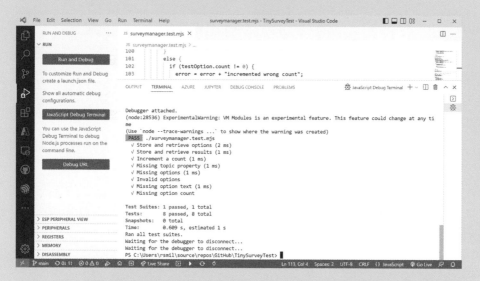

In the screenshot above, I've increased the terminal window size so you can see more of the output from the tests. There are eight tests at the moment. You might like to add some breakpoints to the tests and then re-run them so that you can watch them being performed.

Tests are hard work but very useful

The test file for the SurveyManager class is about 200 lines long. Writing it took a little while, but it was totally worth the effort. If I make any changes to how the storage works (or even implement a database-powered storage system, as we are going to in the next chapter), I can test it without doing anything other than running these tests. If you are as bored by typing in pizza toppings to test the Tiny Survey application as I am, you will appreciate how much easier automatic tests are. There is a lot more to testing and the Jest framework than has been described here, so it is worth looking at what you can do with it.

Personally, I quite like writing tests. You don't need to worry too much about efficiency since tests rarely run. It's OK to block-copy lumps of code to make new tests. (That's how I wrote most of the above.) And you get to think about how you can attack systems and make them break by creating cunning tests, which can be fun. Testing is also a really good way to ensure the functions you have created are fit for purpose. The development process for an application might include testing at a number of levels. Unit tests are performed on individual system components, integration tests are used when components are connected together, and final tests prove that the application works as a whole. There is even a development technique where you write the tests first and then fill in the code after all the tests are passed. Many programmers don't like testing, so they really appreciate someone who is good at it. That means testing might be a good way to make a name for yourself.

Logging

Logging is the final feature I think is worth mentioning here in the context of "professional" development. When something bad happens to your application, you should record this for future reference. In its simplest form, the log could just be a message written using `console.log`. You might like to add the date the event occurred. When your application is hosted in the cloud, you can view the output from the log messages. One thing you should not do is make any of your logging output visible to the user. You might think it would be useful to enable the user to see detailed error reports of your program on your application's error page. However, anyone trying to attack your site would find detailed descriptions of what has gone wrong very useful. You should restrict visible error reports to very small amounts of information.

"Professional" coding

You don't have to do everything described in this chapter when writing a program. Sometimes, I write code just to see whether other people like what it does. In that case, using the abovementioned techniques would be too much effort. However, if everyone liked my application and was willing to pay for it, I'd create a much more "professional" version. This approach is often used in the software industry. A "quick and dirty" prototype is created, and a second version addresses all the factors described above.

Store application status with cookies

In Chapter 8, we built a Tiny Survey application. The application works well, but there is room for improvement. One issue is that people can enter multiple responses to a survey. We could use the Tiny Survey application to choose a pizza topping. However, there is nothing to stop someone particularly keen on a ham and pineapple topping from repeatedly reloading the voting page and adding more and more votes for that topping. Tiny Survey should only allow one response per user.

One way to achieve this would be to use local browser storage. We first saw this in Chapter 3 in the "Storing data on the local machine" section, where we used local storage to hold the setting values for the time-travel clock. We could store a list of the survey topics a user has completed in local storage. Each time the user votes, the survey topic could be added to the list. JavaScript running in the web page could use the list to stop users from resubmitting multiple votes for the same topic. This could work, but the code must run in the browser. In the current version of Tiny Survey, all the code for our application runs in the node.js server, and it would be simpler to keep it that way. Fortunately, there is a way for a node.js server application to store data in the browser. It is called the *cookie*.

The origins of the name "cookie" are unclear. Around the time the cookie was invented, software engineers were working on what they called "magic cookies" to send data from one place to another so that the name might have come from there. It might also be that the message-passing aspect of a cookie came from fortune cookies, which are hollow biscuits containing paper messages. You can think of a cookie as a lump of data that a server can give to a browser as part of a response to a web request. The browser will give the cookie back to the server when the browser next requests a page from that server.

Cookies in Tiny Survey

We could use cookies to keep track of the surveys a user has voted in. When a user votes on a survey, the response from the server will include a survey list cookie stored by the browser. When the user visits the survey web address, the survey list cookie will be sent to the server as part of the `get` request.

Figure 9-1 shows the cookie storage in a version of Tiny Survey that uses a cookie to keep track of survey responses. You can view this information by opening the **Developer Tools** in your browser and going to the **Application** tab. You can see a cookie called `completedSurveys`, and the cookie string contains a JSON-encoded array giving the topics of two surveys, `"robspizza"` and `"robsmovies"`. The user has voted in these surveys. Code in the server uses this information to determine which surveys the user is allowed to vote in.

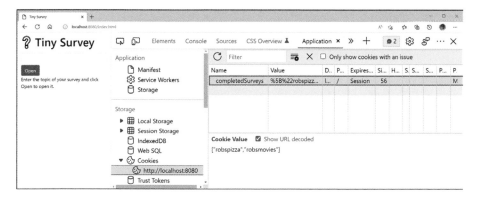

Figure 9-1   Tiny_Survey_cookies

Each web address has its own cookie storage area. The survey in **Figure 9-1** is being hosted on the local computer with the *http://localhost:8080* address. You can learn more about viewing local storage in the Make Something Happen 13, "Setting sleuthing," in Chapter 3.

Cookie middleware

When an application uses cookies, the server adds cookie data to the response sent back to the browser and responds to cookie values received as part of `get` and `post` messages from the browser. The code to implement this can be found in the cookie-parser middleware and must be installed in an application using node package manager (`npm`):

```
npm install cookie-parser
```

Once the cookie-parser library has been installed, it can be imported to the application and added to the middleware used by the application:

```
import cookieParser from 'cookie-parser';

app.use(cookieParser());
```

The cookie-parser middleware adds a cookies property to the web request object and a cookie property to the reply object.

Use cookies in Tiny Survey

Now that we know what a cookie is, we can use it in Tiny Survey. We want to stop a user from being able to vote more than once. When the user opens a survey, we need to check to see if the user has already voted in the survey and take them straight to the survey results page if they have. **Figure 9-2** shows the first page of the survey workflow. The user enters the topic they want to interact with (in this example, robspizza) and clicks the **Open** button.

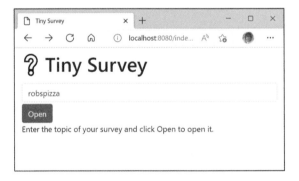

Figure 9-2   Survey start

Clicking **Open** causes the page to send a post to the gottopic route in the application running Tiny Survey. On the next page, you can see the first part of the function that deals with this post. The code checks to see if the survey storage already contains a survey with this topic. If it does, the code then checks to see if the completedSurveys list contains the topic name. If it does, the user has already completed this survey, so they are directed to the results page. If not, the user is directed to the enterOptions page to make their choice:

```
app.post('/gottopic', (request, response) => {

  let topic = request.body.topic;

  if (surveyManager.surveyExists(topic)) {
    // Need to check if the survey has already been filled in
    // by this user
    if (request.cookies.completedSurveys) {
      // Got a completed surveys cookie
      // Parse it into a list of completed surveys
      let completedSurveys = JSON.parse(request.cookies.completedSurveys);
      // Look for the current topic in the list
      if (completedSurveys.includes(topic)) {
        // This survey has already been filled in using this browser
        // Just display the results
        let results = surveyManager.getCounts(topic);
        response.render('displayresults.ejs', results);
      }
    }
    else {
      // enter scores on an existing survey
      let surveyOptions = surveyManager.getOptions(topic);
      response.render('selectoption.ejs', surveyOptions);
    }
  }
});
```

Now that we have dealt with the situation where the survey exists, it is time to handle the scenario where the user enters a topic for a survey that doesn't exist. In this situation, the user should be directed to the survey entry page to create a new survey. I thought this code would be quite simple to write, but it turned out to be more complicated than I thought. This was because a survey might not exist in the survey store but might have an entry in the completedSurveys cookie. This happens if the user fills in a survey and then restarts the Tiny Survey application, clearing the survey store. If the user re-enters a survey with the same topic, they cannot vote in the new survey because of the entry in completedSurveys. The code below deletes a survey topic from the cookie if the survey topic is not found in the storage:

```
app.post('/gottopic', (request, response) => {

  let topic = request.body.topic;
```

```
    if (surveyManager.surveyExists(topic)) {
      // Code to handle an existing survey
    else {
      // There is no existing survey - need to make a new one
      // Might need to delete the topic from the completed surveys
      if (request.cookies.completedSurveys) {
        // Get the cookie value and parse it
        let completedSurveys = JSON.parse(request.cookies.completedSurveys);
        // Check if the topic is in the completed ones
        if (completedSurveys.includes(topic)) {
          // Delete the topic from the completedSurveys array
          let topicIndex = completedSurveys.indexOf(topic);
          completedSurveys.splice(topicIndex, 1);
          // Update the stored cookie
          let completedSurveysJSON = JSON.stringify(completedSurveys);
          response.cookie("completedSurveys", completedSurveysJSON);
        }
      }
      // need to make a new survey
      response.render('enteroptions.ejs',
        { topic: topic, numberOfOptions: 5 });
    }
});
```

Figure 9-3 shows the survey page used to enter a vote. Clicking **Send** will post the selection to the recordselection route. The code in this route needs to update the count and add the survey topic to the list of completed surveys stored in the completedSurveys cookie. The incoming cookie contains a JSON string describing the array containing the survey topics list. The code converts the JSON string into a JavaScript object (the list of survey topics). It then checks to see if the list contains the current survey topic. If the topic is in the list, the user is directed to the displayresults page. This stops the user from adding more votes by refreshing the option selection page in their browser. If the completedSurveys list doesn't contain the current survey topic, the code records the vote, adds the survey topic to the list of completed surveys, and then sets the response's cookie to contain the updated survey list.

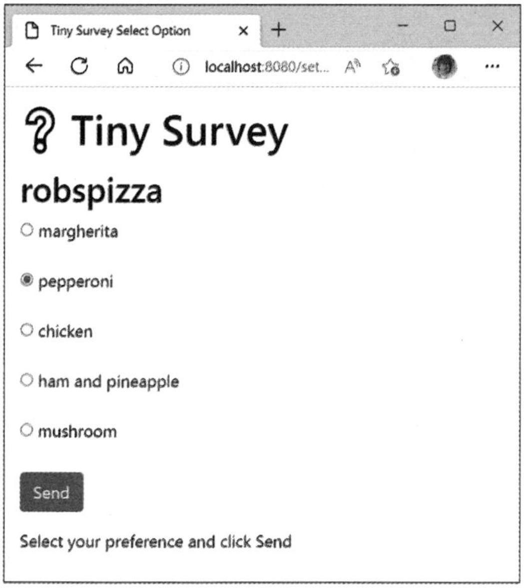

Figure 9-3   Survey select option

The code below does this. There are plenty of comments, so it repays careful study.

```
// Got the selections for a survey
app.post('/recordselection/:topic', (request, response) => {
  let topic = request.params.topic;

  if (!surveyManager.surveyExists(topic)) {
    // This is an error - display survey not found
    response.status(404).send('<h1>Survey not found</h1>');
  }
  else {
    // Start with an empty completed survey list
    let completedSurveys = [];
    if (request.cookies.completedSurveys) {
      // Got a completed surveys cookie
      completedSurveys = JSON.parse(request.cookies.completedSurveys);
    }
    // Look for the current topic in completedSurveys
    if (completedSurveys.includes(topic) == false) {
      // This survey has not been filled in at this browser
      // Get the text of the selected option
      let optionSelected = request.body.selections;
```

```
      // Build an increment description
      let incDetails = { topic: topic, option: optionSelected };
      // Increment the count
      surveyManager.incrementCount(incDetails);
      // Add the topic to the completed surveys
      completedSurveys.push(topic);
      // Make a JSON string for storage
      let completedSurveysJSON = JSON.stringify(completedSurveys);
      // store the cookie
      response.cookie("completedSurveys", completedSurveysJSON);
    }
    let results = surveyManager.getCounts(topic);
    response.render('displayresults.ejs', results);
  }
});
```

PROGRAMMER'S POINT

Sometimes, you just have to write messy code

The code to handle different combinations of survey storage and cookie state might look
messy. It would be lovely if there was a neat way of implementing this logic with just a few
lines of JavaScript. Unfortunately, there isn't. Sometimes, particularly when creating user
interfaces, you just have to write a sequence of steps to ensure that every unlikely even-
tuality is properly handled. This is one situation where lots of comments do make a huge
difference.

MAKE SOMETHING HAPPEN 46

Scan the QR code or visit *https://www.youtube.com/watch?v=dIF0ojkSHXI* for a video walk-
through of this Make Something Happen.

Investigate cookies in Tiny Survey

Your starting point is a version of Tiny Survey you can download from GitHub at *https://github.com/Building-Apps-and-Games-in-the-Cloud/TinySurveyCookies*. Clone this repository onto your machine and open it with Visual Studio Code. If you are unsure how to get the sample application, use the sequence described in the "Get the example application" section in Chapter 8. Just change the address of the cloned repository.

Set a breakpoint at line 119, as shown above. Now open your browser and navigate to *localhost:8080/index.html*, where you will find a working Tiny Survey application. Enter a new survey, add the survey options, and then vote, as shown below.

When you click **Send**, the browser will pause because it hits the breakpoint at line 119. The server is running the function for the `recordselection` route. Click **Step Into Function** in the **Debug Controls** to work through the code.

The first time the browser visits the survey page, there will be no cookies, so the code will start with an empty completedSurveys list. If you continue to step through the code, you will see the counts updated and the following three statements performed:

```
// Add the topic to the completed surveys
completedSurveys.push(topic);
// Make a JSON string for storage
let completedSurveysJSON = JSON.stringify(completedSurveys);
// store the cookie
response.cookie("completedSurveys", completedSurveysJSON);
```

The first statement adds the survey topic to the completedSurveys list. The second statement creates a JSON string that describes the list. The third statement stores the JSON string in the cookies for this site with the name completedSurveys. Step through these statements to watch them work and then press the **Continue** button in the debug controls to restart the server. Now, go back to the browser, open a new tab, and navigate to *localhost:8080/index. html*. Now, enter the same survey topic (in my case, **robspizza**) and click **Open**. You will now be directed straight to the survey results page.

Tiny Survey Results

localhost:8080/got...

Tiny Survey

robspizza

marherita : 0

pepperoni : 1

chicken : 0

ham and pineapple : 0

mushroom : 0

Reload

Click Reload to update the counts.

If you want to perform further investigations, you could put a breakpoint in the server at line 30, reload the survey index page, enter the topic, and watch as the server gets the cookie and checks for a survey topic. You can also use the browser's **Developer Tools** to view the cookie that was created, as shown in **Figure 9-1**.

CODE ANALYSIS

Using cookies

You might have some questions about cookies.

Question: How long do cookies live?

Answer: Normally, cookies are deleted when the browser program is closed. If you want cookies to hang around longer, you can give them a maximum age (maxAge) or expiry date (expire) when you create them.

```
response.cookie("completedSurveys", // cookie name
                completedSurveysJSON, // cookie string
                {maxAge:1000*60}); // age of 60 seconds
```

The above cookie would only be stored for 60 seconds. The maxAge option specifies the maximum age of the cookie in milliseconds.

```
response.cookie("completedSurveys", // cookie name
                completedSurveysJSON, // cookie string
    { expire: 24*60*60*1000 + Date.now()}); // this time tomorrow
```

The above cookie would expire a day after it was created. The expire option lets you specify a date when the cookie will be removed. The expire value is a date expressed in milliseconds.

A user could opt to remove all the cookies in their browser at any time, so it is important not to store critical application data in a cookie.

Question: Can I stop people from viewing the contents of my cookies?

Answer: No. The best way to keep cookie contents secret is to encrypt the cookie string before it is sent to the browser. We will do this in the next chapter when we store session data in cookies.

Question: Can I stop anyone from tampering with my cookies?

Answer: No. A browser could send any cookie value back to the server. However, you can "sign" the value in a cookie so any tampering would be detected. To do this, you have to give the cookie middleware a "secret" when it is created:

```
app.use(cookieParser("encryptString"));
```

The cookieParser above uses the "encryptString" string as the secret. Now, when you store a cookie, you must ask for it to be signed by adding an option:

```
response.cookie("completedSurveys", // cookie name
                completedSurveysJSON, // cookie string
                {signed:true}); // sign the cookie
```

When the cookie is created, its contents are combined with the secret string to create a validation string appended to the cookie. The same process is repeated with received cookie values. If the validation strings don't match, the cookie is invalid and will be ignored. To process your incoming signed cookies, the program uses the request's signedCookies property to get the stored cookie:

```
let completedSurveysJSON = request.signedCookies.completedSurveys;
```

Note that it is a very bad policy to put strings such as `"encryptString"` directly into your source code as I have done on the preceding page. Later, we will discover how to separate secret information from the program code.

Question: Do all browsers share the same cookies?

Answer: No. If you visit a site using Chrome and again using Edge, you will discover that the cookies stores are different.

Question: Can I manually delete cookies from my browser?

Answer: Yes. You can use the Application tab in the browser developer tools. This makes it possible for a determined person to vote more than once in Tiny Survey. They would have to delete the cookie after each vote.

Question: Can the Tiny Survey application delete cookies?

Answer: Yes. The `clearCookie` function can be called in response to clear that cookie from the browser. The function accepts the name of the cookie as a string.

```
response.clearCookie("completedSurveys");
```

The above statement removes the `completedSurveys` cookie.

Question: Which is the best cookie?

Answer: My preference is for chocolate chip, but I also like oatmeal ones a lot.

PROGRAMMER'S POINT

You should tell people you are using cookies

The Tiny Survey application only uses cookies to track the surveys a user has taken part in. It doesn't really have any privacy implications. Even so, it is considered polite (and can be legally required) to let the user know you are using cookies and perhaps even offer them the option not to use the application if they don't want to.

What you have learned

In this chapter, we have examined aspects of software construction from a professional perspective. We've learned how to break an application into separate modules to make it easier to work with. We've also seen how to create well-defined interfaces between modules and how we can generate interactive documentation by adding

JSDoc comments to the code. We've also learned the importance of error checking and how an application can use exceptions to indicate error conditions. We've worked with a test framework and built a set of unit tests for a module. Finally, we've looked at cookies and discovered how they could allow an application to retain state information in the browser. Here's a recap, plus some points to ponder.

- JavaScript applications can be broken down into modules that can be individually written and tested. A module can contain a class with methods that implement the module's behaviors.

- JavaScript code can contain comments in the JSDoc format. These can be created in Visual Studio Code by entering the **/**** sequence on the line above the item to be documented. If the item is a function or method, Visual Studio Code will create a template comment to be filled in. These comments can be used to create documentation web pages and by the Visual Studio Code editor to display information as code is entered.

- JavaScript behaviors should contain error-checking. The workflow of an application should handle user errors. JavaScript exceptions can handle other detected faults.

- A program can use the JavaScript `throw` keyword to throw an object during program execution. The `throw` ends the current sequence of execution and transfers execution to a `catch` block or ends the sequence if no `catch` block is present. The object can describe the event that caused the `throw`. For exceptions to be caught, the code must run inside a `try` block, followed by a catch block containing code to run when the exception is thrown. Exceptions can be nested; code in a `try` block can contain other `try`–`catch` constructions. When an exception is thrown, the `catch` code that runs is the code "nearest" to the `throw`. It is impossible to return to code after an exception has been thrown.

- A `try`–`catch` construction can be followed by a `finally` block containing code that runs irrespective of what happens in the `try`–`catch` construction. A `finally` block can release resources allocated in the `try` block.

- The Jest framework can be used to manage automated testing of JavaScript code. A test file can contain many tests that should each deliver a particular result. Jest provides a range of matching mechanisms to check test outputs. It will automatically run a number of tests and indicate which have passed.

- Applications should log output if they detect errors while running but not make detailed error reports publicly visible.

- A cookie is a small piece of data that an application can send to the browser as part of a response to a web request. The browser will return the cookie content as part of future requests to the same site address.

- A cookie contains name-string pairs. An application can store data values in a cookie by encoding the value as a JSON string.

- Cookies for a site are visible in a browser using the site's **Application** view in the **Developer Tools**. They can also be deleted using this interface.

- A browser will delete cookies when the browser is closed. Cookies can be given a lifetime or expiry date if they are to be held for longer. An application can also delete cookies.

To reinforce your understanding of this chapter, you might want to consider the following "profound questions":

Question: Should we always try to write "professional" code?

> **Answer:** No. But you should be aware of situations where taking on at least a few of the professional considerations described here might be a good idea.

Question: How many functions should a module provide?

> **Answer:** A module should be concerned with one purpose. You could have modules for storage, printing, user menu, and so on. If you find a module getting large, you might want to break it into submodules for different areas of functionality. While you can try to decide which modules you need and what you want them to do when you begin development, it is often hard to do this. Programmers talk about "refactoring," where they move behaviors in and out of different modules or change what they do. This should be a continuous process during development. You should not stick with a poor design just because it was the first thing you thought of.

Question: If a function detects an error, should it return an error value or throw an exception?

> **Answer:** A function can return a value that indicates whether it worked. However, a failure of the function would only be detected if the program that called it checks the returned value. However, a function that throws an exception when it detects an error will interrupt the flow of the code calling it, which is a more active form of error reporting. The worst thing a program can do is fail silently. If it crashes, at least you know it is broken. But if it fails to save data without displaying an error, that is much more of a problem because you might use it for a while before discovering the fault. Viewed in this light, throwing an exception is a good idea because there is less chance the error will be missed.

Question: Why do we need the `finally` part of a `try–catch` construction? Can't we just put code after the `try–catch` construction?

> **Answer:** This is a good question, though we need `finally`. Perhaps the code in the `catch` block throws another exception, in which case, the code following the `try–catch` construction will never get to run. Perhaps the `try–catch` construction is running inside a function, and when the `catch` block runs, it returns from that function. A `finally` block is the only way we can make sure that code is run.

Question: When should you write your tests?

Answer: Testing is not something you should consider after writing your code. It should be part of the development process. Over the years, I've discovered lots of issues with my code design while writing tests for it. Designing tests also forces you to think hard about the specification.

Question: How many tests should you write?

Answer: One of the problems with test creation is knowing when to stop. There should be at least one test for every function and one to test any failure conditions.

Question: Are cookies the only way an application can store data on a per-user basis?

Answer: You can also use local browser storage to store data, but this has to be performed by a program running in the browser itself. It is also possible for a browser and server to maintain session information in the URL used to address the site. We will investigate this in the next chapter.

Part 3
Building with cloud technologies

This part introduces techniques and tools to improve the quality of your applications. Then we move on to consider how to store application data in files and databases. Next, we discover how to create logins and implement role-based security for users of an application. Finally, we take a look at a host of exciting JavaScript-powered technologies, including creating your own servers to build a personal cloud, connecting hardware lights and buttons to servers, linking applications to Internet of Things devices, and making a fast-moving sprite-based game.

10

Store data

What you will learn

In this chapter, we will build and deploy a database-powered application. Along the way, we'll discover how JavaScript applications can interact with file stores and databases and how the asynchronous features of the language let us work with processes that might take some time to complete. We'll discover how to design and connect to database storage using the MongoDB database and Mongoose middleware. Then, we'll prepare the Tiny Survey application for deployment, creating a development environment in the process. Finally, we'll configure and deploy a working application.

File data storage

The Tiny Survey application is almost ready for deployment. However, it does have one major flaw. The present version stores the survey data in an array variable in the program. When the program stops, the variables are discarded. We need to create a version that persists the survey data. We could store the survey data in files on the server. The node.js framework provides a library of functions to interact with files. So, let's set about adding file storage to Tiny Survey. We can start by looking at how to open and write to a file.

The first thing we need to do is import the file functions. We use import to bring existing JavaScript code into our programs. You can learn all about it in Chapter 4 in the "JavaScript heroes: modules" section. The statement below uses a form of import we've not seen before. It uses a wild card character (*) to indicate that the import is to fetch all the items in the source.

```
import * as fs from 'node:fs';
```

We can now use the functions provided as part of node.js to perform file input/output. When the functions run, they will use the underlying operating system (which might be Windows, Linux, or MacOS to store the files). Let's see how we use these functions to write a file in a node.js application.

Synchronous file writing

The first file-writing function we are going to consider is called writeFileSync. This takes a string of text and writes it to a file with a particular name. The code below shows how this function could be used to store all the surveys in Tiny Survey.

```
let surveysString = JSON.stringify(this.surveys);   ── JSON encode the surveys into a string
fs.writeFileSync(this.fileName, surveysString);     ── Write the survey string to a file
console.log("File Written");                        ── Log the write as complete
```

The *synchronous* writeFileSync function accepts a filename and a string of text to write in the file. Because it's a synchronous function, the call to writeFileSync will not return until the file has been written. If there are many surveys in the system, this might take a while to complete. During that time, the server program will be frozen and unable to respond to any input.

Asynchronous file writing

A better way to write the file would be to use an asynchronous function that doesn't stop our program from running. The code below shows how to do this:

```
function writeDone(err)                          Function to run when the write is complete
{
  if(!err){
    console.log("File Written");                 Log the write as complete
  }
}
let surveysString = JSON.stringify(this.surveys);   JSON encode the surveys into a string
fs.writeFile(this.fileName, surveysString, writeDone);   Write the survey string to a file
```

The `writeFile` function works *asynchronously*. It has a third parameter, which refers to a function called when the write has finished. When the write finishes, the called function is given an argument that describes any errors that might have occurred. If the argument is `false`, that means the write worked. Above, you can see the function `writeDone`, which tests the value of `err` and displays a message if the write worked. The `writeFile` function starts the write process. Once the write process has started, the `writeFile` function returns to the caller so that the `node.js` program can continue running while the file is written. We could use this mechanism to manage the writing process, but JavaScript provides a better way of managing asynchronous operations—the `Promise`.

JavaScript heroes: the `Promise`

Promises are a great way to manage asynchronous tasks. A `Promise` is used to represent a task. If we want to use promises to manage the file input and output function calls, our program needs to import the `Promise` versions of the input/output functions, as shown below:

```
import * as fs from 'node:fs/promises';
```

Calls to interact with the file store now return `Promise` objects. What does this mean? Let's go back to my childhood for an explanation. It turns out that there were two ways that Mum could get me to tidy my bedroom. One was to stand over me and watch me do it. The other was for Mum to accept my promise that I would tidy my bedroom at some future point. Mum preferred the second arrangement because she was free to go off and ask someone else to tidy their room. When Mum stood watching me tidy my room, she was synchronized with my actions like a program using synchronous file writing. She couldn't do anything else until I'd finished tidying. If she accepted my promise, she could do other things while I was tidying. She wasn't synchronized with my actions. I was tidying my room *asynchronously* with her.

A method or function called asynchronously returns instantly with a reference to a Promise object describing the task being performed. The Promise object exposes methods that interact with the task. One of these methods is called then. The then method accepts a function to be run when the Promise is fulfilled.

The storeSurveys function below shows how we use this. This function places the survey values into a JSON string and then saves them in a file using the asynchronous writeFile function from the Promise version of the fs library. The writeFile function has been declared asynchronous, returning a Promise. The code calls the then function on the Promise to make the function display a message when the surveys have been stored.

```
storeSurveys() {
    let surveysString = JSON.stringify(this.surveys);
    fs.writeFile(this.fileName, surveysString).then(()=>console.log("File Written"));
    console.log("Started storing");
}
```

🚀 MAKE SOMETHING HAPPEN 47

Scan the QR code or visit *https://www.youtube.com/watch?v=n_L7FhslgkU* for a video walk-through of this Make Something Happen.

Saving surveys

The starting point for this Make Something Happen is a version of Tiny Survey on GitHub at *https://github.com/Building-Apps-and-Games-in-the-Cloud/TinySurveyFileStore.*

Clone this repository onto your machine and open it with Visual Studio Code. If you are unsure how to get the sample application, use the sequence described in Chapter 8 in the "Get the example application" section. Just change the address of the repository that you clone. Open the application in Visual Studio Code, open the **tinysurvey.mjs** source file, and start the program using the **Run And Debug** icon in Visual Studio Code.

Visual Studio will show the program running in the debugger. The debug console will show the `Server running` and `Surveys loaded` messages. Use the browser to navigate to *localhost:8080/index.html*, enter a survey, and select an option. Now, return to the Visual Studio Code window.

When a survey or a vote is entered, the surveys are saved by the `storeSurveys` method we saw earlier, and the messages shown above are printed. Click the red square in the **Debug Controls** to stop the program and then restart it. If you return to the browser and re-open the survey you created, you will find it has been retained. If you return to Visual Studio Code, you will find a new file in the project called **surveys.json**. Open that file in the editor.

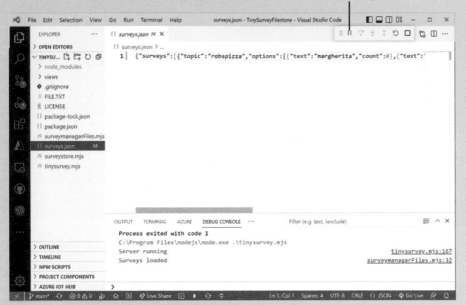

Click to stop program

This file contains the survey contents as a JSON string. The file is updated each time a new survey is entered and after an option has been selected.

CODE ANALYSIS

Survey storage with promises

You might have some questions about how asynchronous file storage works.

Question: Why does the code in the `storeSurvey` method have the messages the wrong way around?

Answer: If you understand the answer to this question, you understand how asynchronous code works in JavaScript. When the program runs, it logs the following output on the console:

```
Started storing
File Written
```

However, it looks like the program displaying these messages has the log actions reversed. See the two statements in the `storeSurveys` method on the next page:

```
fs.writeFile(filename,surveys).then(()=>console.log("File Written"));
console.log("Started storing");
```

How can the code print `Started storing` first? Remember that the function in the `then` part of the first statement runs after the `writeFile` method has been completed. Just because the code appears in the program first does not mean it runs first. The `writeFile` function has been made asynchronous, so the calling code doesn't wait for it to finish. The code above just logs a message after `writeFile` has been called, but it could go on and do other things. If you still find this confusing, consider another way of expressing what we are doing. The code below uses a variable called `writePromise` to hold the `Promise` returned by the call to `writeFile`. The `then` function is called on `write-Promise` to specify the function to be called when the `Promise` is fulfilled. If the write operation does not complete (perhaps because the storage device is full), the `promise` will not be fulfilled, and the `File Written` message will not be displayed.

Question: What happens if we change the contents of the `surveys` array before the output file has been written?

Answer: Your program will probably fail. When you make an asynchronous call, we create another sequence of program execution, which can be dangerous because we could shoot ourselves in the foot. The code below is from a very badly written data storage app. Users enter a data record, which is then saved. After the record has been saved, it is set to `null`, ready for the next use. Can you spot the bug?

```
fs.writeFile(filename,record).then(()=>console.log("File Written"));
record = null;
```

Remember that the statement following the `writeFile` call is executed before the `writeFile` function has been completed because `writeFile` is an asynchronous function that returns a `Promise` immediately after it is called. The code would delete the record storage before the file has been written. The correct way to write this code is as follows:

```
fs.writeFile(filename,record).then(()=> {
    console.log("File Written");
    record = null;
});
```

Now, the record is cleared in the `then` part of the code, which runs after `writeFile` has finished.

Question: What happens if `writeFile` never finishes?

Answer: A file operation can always fail. Perhaps a storage device is full or disconnected. In that case, the surveys would not be saved, the function specified by `then` would never be called, and the `File Written` message will not be displayed. Unfortunately, the survey program will keep on running, giving the user the impression that all is well. Later in this chapter, we will discover how to manage these conditions.

Question: Why are promises better than asynchronous callbacks?

Answer: You might look at the code for the asynchronous file storage and decide that a `Promise` doesn't make things much easier. The major difference seems to be that we can use the `then` method exposed by a `Promise` to specify a function to be called when the `Promise` is fulfilled. However, the asynchronous `writeFile` call also calls a method when the file writing is complete. The `Promise` is better because using it creates an object that represents a task. There is a lot more to the JavaScript Promise. You can fire off multiple tasks and use `Promise.all` to wait until all the tasks have been completed. You can use `Promise.race` to run multiple tasks and end when one of them finishes. (This is how you can implement timeouts on operations.)

Question: How do we make a `Promise`?

Answer: We can discover how to make a `Promise` by making a function that implements a timeout. The `makeTimeoutPromise` function below returns a `Promise` object that will be resolved a specified number of milliseconds after it has been created.

```
function makeTimeoutPromise (timeoutMillis) {
  return new Promise((resolve, reject) => {         Create a new Promise to return
    setTimeout(() => {                    Create a timeout that will call a function after a delay
      resolve('Timeout complete!');                  Call resolve when the timeout completes
    }, timeoutMillis);                                      Set the length of the timeout
  });
}
```

When a `Promise` object is created, it is supplied with a reference to the function that implements the task to be performed. The task function accepts two parameters. Both parameters are references to functions. The first function (`resolve`) is called when the task completes successfully. The second function (`reject`) is called if the task cannot be performed. The `makeTimeOutPromise` function uses the `setTimeout` function provided by JavaScript to create a timeout that will call the `resolve` function after the specified timeout. The code below calls the `makeTimeOutPromise` function and uses the `then` function on the value returned. It will log the `Timeout Complete` message that is returned by the timeout after 1,000 milliseconds (1 second).

```
makeTimeoutPromise (1000).then((message)=> {
  console.log(message);
});
```

We've seen that we can use `Promise` and `then` to create a program that appears to do two things simultaneously. The `storeSurveys` function we used in the preceding Make Something Happen appears to write a message while the `writeFile` function is writing to a file. We've seen how this can be dangerous because one sequence of execution can interfere with another, as shown earlier. Usually, we want something that will wait for an action to complete without blocking a JavaScript program from executing. To do this, we can use two more JavaScript heroes: `await` and `async`.

JavaScript heroes: await and async

We've seen how we can use the `then` part of a `Promise` to perform a "background" action while our program runs. But most of the time, we don't want to do anything while we wait for an action to complete. We can do this by using the JavaScript `await` keyword. The `loadSurveys` method below reads the surveys back into the Tiny Survey application. It uses the `fs.readFile` function to read the file's contents into a string and then uses `JSON.parse` to convert the string into an array of JavaScript objects, which can be used to construct new `Survey` instances.

```
async loadSurveys() {
    try {
        let surveysString = await fs.readFile(this.fileName);     ——— Await the readFile
        let surveyValues = JSON.parse(surveysString);             ——— Convert to a list
        let result = new Surveys();                               ——— Make an empty survey store
        surveyValues.surveys.forEach(surveyValue => {            ——— Work through the incoming surveys
            let survey = new Survey(surveyValue);                ——— Create a new survey instance
                                                                       from the incoming data
            result.saveSurvey(survey);
        });                                                      ——— Store the survey
        console.log("Surveys loaded");
        this.surveys = result;                                   ——— Set the surveys to the loaded result
    }
    catch {                                                      ——— Exception thrown if readFile fails
        console.log("Survey file not found - empty survey created");
        this.surveys = new Surveys();                            ——— Make an empty survey
        this.storeSurveys();                                     ——— Store it
    }
}
```

The call of `fs.readFile` is preceded by the `await` keyword. The `await` keyword takes the `Promise` returned by `fs.readFile` (because `fs.readFile` is an asynchronous function) and returns it to the `loadSurveys` caller. Then, it will run the rest of the load-Surveys method when the `fs.readFile` finishes. The `loadSurveys` method is defined as `async` because it returns a `Promise` object. The great thing about `await` is that it makes asynchronous code look a lot like synchronous code. We want the program to wait until `fs.readFile` has finished before it processes the contents of the stored file.

When JavaScript sees an `await`, it does some fancy footwork behind the scenes, creating a `Promise` – `then` construction, which contains the code that follows the asynchronous call. Programmers call this kind of thing *syntactic sugar*. A piece of syntactic sugar is a language feature that doesn't make anything possible you couldn't do before. It just makes something easier. Just like how adding sugar to your food doesn't always improve your diet; it just makes the food taste better. You could completely ignore the `await` keyword and write all your calls of asynchronous methods using `then`, but using `async` results in neater-looking code.

Using async in Tiny Survey

The Tiny Survey application uses a `SurveyManager` class to manage interactions with the survey storage. The `SurveyManager` loads and saves surveys and fetches survey data and options for web page display. Below is the first part of the `SurveyManager-Files` class, which uses asynchronous storage. The class has acquired an `init` method, which loads the surveys.

```
class SurveyManagerFiles {

    constructor() {
        this.fileName = "surveys.json";
    }

    async init() {
        await this.loadSurveys();
    }
    // rest of SurveyManager
}
```

CODE ANALYSIS

SurveyManagerFiles class

You might have some questions about this class.

Question: Why don't we load the surveys in the constructor for the `SurveyManagerFiles` class?

> **Answer:** The previous version of `SurveyManager` stored the surveys in a list variable created in the class's constructor. This meant that the storage was created when the manager was created. This class version has a separate `init` method that loads the surveys. It works this way because a class constructor cannot be an asynchronous function. A constructor is a method that must return an object, not a `Promise` to make an object.

Question: What happens if the `init` function never returns?

Answer: We've already noticed that operations involving files might fail or not finish. If the `promise` returned by `loadSurveys` is never resolved, the `init` function will never return because it is using an `await` on that `Promise`. The sequence of statements in the `tinysurvey.mjs` program shown below means that the web server never starts listening if the surveys are not loaded. Anyone accessing the survey website will get a "site not found" message. In the next section, we will look at better ways of managing errors like these.

```
let surveyManager = new SurveyManager();         Make the survey manager
await surveyManager.init();                       Wait for it to load the data
const port = 8080;                                     Set the server port
app.listen(port, () => {                          Start the server listening
  console.log("Server running");
})
```

Question: How do we call asynchronous functions in Express routes?

Answer: The Express framework runs code to deal with incoming web requests. We know that any function containing an `await` must be marked asynchronous. The code below shows how this is done. The method handling the `request` and `response` items is marked as asynchronous by using `async`.

```
app.post('/recordselection/:topic', async (request, response) => {
   ...
});
```

Handle file errors

So far, our code would handle a failed file open by never starting the Express server. This means browsers trying to connect to the Tiny Survey application would display "Can't reach this page" messages when the user tried to start a survey. The application should do better than this. At least it should display a message saying the site is broken. Otherwise, people might think they have typed in the wrong address. We must design some form of error handling for the Tiny Survey application to do this.

You should design your error handling at the start

We've already seen that you start your application design by considering the application's workflow. You should do something similar with errors. Before you build the program, you need to consider what could go wrong and how the code will deal with it. The previous version of Tiny Survey was completely self-contained, meaning it didn't rely on any other service that might fail. However, a version of Tiny Survey that uses a file to store surveys relies on that file, so we need to consider what the application should do if the file cannot be opened when the program starts.

We need to manage the situation where the application is active and responding to requests, but the database is unavailable. We can do this by creating a flag variable in the application, which tracks whether the database is connected, as shown below:

```
let surveysLoaded = false;
```

The initial value of the surveysLoaded flag is false. Now, we can add some code to set the flag to true when the surveys have been loaded. The code below initializes the surveyManager by calling the async method init. When the init method completes, the arrow function in the then part is called, setting the surveysLoaded flag to true and telling the application the storage is now loaded. If the application gets a request when the survey is not initialized, it can display an error page.

```
surveyManager.init().then(() => {          Arrow function runs when init has completed
  surveysLoaded = true;                    Sets the database flag to true
});
```

The code below handles the index.html route, running when a browser requests the index.html page. It checks to see if the surveys are loaded. If they are running, the index.ejs page is rendered. If not, the response's statusCode is set to 500 (which means server fault), and the error.ejs page is rendered. The status code is how a server lets a browser know whether a request was successfully handled. A status code of 200 means success, a code of 404 means the requested resource was not found, and 500 means there was something wrong at the server end.

```
// Home page
app.get('/index.html', (request, response) => {
  if (surveysLoaded) {                           Are the surveys loaded?
    response.render('index.ejs');                Render the index page if it is
  }
```

```
  else {
    response.statusCode = 500;  ———————————  Set the response status to 500
    response.render('error.ejs');  —————————  Render the error page
  }
});
```

The `error.ejs` file contains the page shown in **Figure 10-1**.

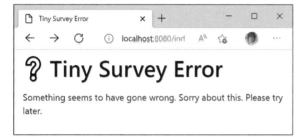

Figure 10-1   Tiny Survey errors

Create error-handling middleware

We've seen how to add code to a route handler that displays an error page if the survey data has not been loaded. We could work through the `tinysurvey.mjs` file and add the test to every single route. However, there is a much easier way to add this error handling to a route: by creating our own *middleware* to run within Express. Earlier in this book, we learned that middleware is code inserted into an application to add functionality. We've added middleware to the Tiny Survey application to render pages and process cookies. Now, we will add middleware to a route that will deal with this error condition in a route.

The code below looks much like the test we just added to the `index.html` route. However, it also looks a bit like a route handler. The `checkSurveys` function can be inserted into a route as a piece of middleware. It will be called when the route is processed. It is provided with three parameters. The first two are the `response` and the `request` objects passed into a route. The third is a reference called `next`, which refers to the next function in the middleware chain. If the surveys have been loaded, the middleware will call `next` to continue processing this path. If the surveys have not been loaded, the function sets the status code to `500` and then renders the error page. In this case, note that the `next` function is not called because the route cannot continue to the next stage. The `surveysLoaded` flag is imported from the `tinysurveys.mjs` file, and the `checkSurveys` function is exported from the file.

```
import { surveysLoaded } from '../tinysurvey.mjs';          Import the loaded flag

                                                            Create our checkSurveys
function checkSurveys(request, response, next) {             middleware function
    if (surveysLoaded) {                                    Do we have loaded surveys?
        next();                                             Call the next piece of middleware
    }
    else {                                                  Surveys not loaded
        response.statusCode = 500;                          Set the status code to server error
        response.render('error.ejs');                       Render the error page
    }
}

export { checkSurveys };
```

The code above is placed in a file called `checkstorage.mjs`, which is in a folder called `helpers` that is part of the solution. It is imported into `tinysurvey.mjs`, as shown in the code below:

```
import {checkSurveys} from './helpers/checkstorage.mjs';
```

Once the `checkSurveys` function has been imported, it can be added to a route. The code below shows how this is done. The name of the function is added to the path. When the path is followed, the `checkSurveys` middleware will run before the body of the handler function. If the `checkSurveys` middleware function doesn't make a call to `next`, the body of the path will not run at all.

```
app.get('/index.html', checkSurveys, (request, response) => {
    response.render('index.ejs');
});
```

We can add a call of `checkSurveys` to all the routes in the TinySurvey application so that none of them will work if the storage is not loaded. We can also add a chain of multiple middleware functions if we like. In Chapter 11, when we create a password-protected site, we will add the password testing element as a middleware.

🚀 **MAKE SOMETHING HAPPEN 48**

Scan the QR code or visit *https://www.youtube.com/watch?v=EpJ8_vlUeLk* for a video walk-through of this Make Something Happen.

Express error middleware

The starting point for this Make Something Happen is a version of Tiny Survey on GitHub at *https://github.com/Building-Apps-and-Games-in-the-Cloud/TinySurveyFileStoreErrorMiddleware*. Clone this repository onto your machine and open it with Visual Studio Code. If you are unsure how to get the sample application, use the sequence described in Chapter 8 in the "Get the example application" section. Just change the address of the repository that you clone. Open the application in Visual Studio Code, open the **tinysurvey.mjs** source file, and start the program. Make sure the **Debug Console** is selected in the terminal view.

Enter JavaScript statements here

Debug Console

Visual Studio will show you the program running in the debugger. Set a breakpoint at line 37, as shown in the preceding figure. Now use the browser to navigate to *localhost:8080/index.html*, enter a survey topic, and click **Start**. Now, return to the Visual Studio Code window. You will find that the server has hit the breakpoint that you set. Now, you are going to do something completely awesome: change the contents of the surveysLoaded variable using the **Debug Console** at the bottom of the Visual Studio Code window. Enter the following into the **Debug Console** and press **Enter**.

```
surveysLoaded = false
```

The **Debug Console** can be used when a program is paused at a breakpoint. It is just like the **Debug Console** you've seen in the browser's **Developer Tools**. You can execute JavaScript statements by entering them. You can change or view variable values.

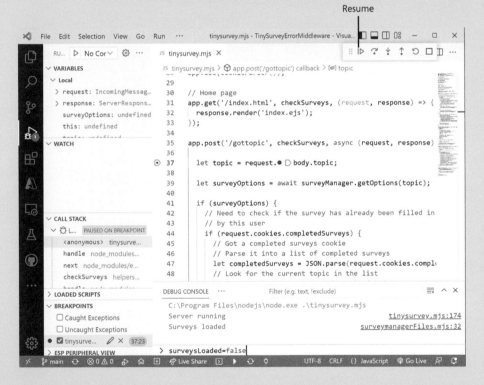

If you set surveysLoaded to false, the application thinks the surveys have not been loaded. Press the right-pointing arrow in the **Debug Controls** to resume the server. You will not see the error page just yet because the middleware will run at the start of the next route handler. Navigate to *localhost:8080/index.html* again and refresh the page in the browser to see the error page displayed.

Database storage

We can use files on the server to hold the data for the Tiny Survey application, but this is inefficient. The entire survey file is overwritten every time something changes. It would be useful if there were something we could use that would let us manipulate individual records in the survey store rather than having to write the whole file each time. It turns out that there is, and it is called a database.

JavaScript can be used with many different database engines. We are going to use one called MongoDB (*https://www.mongodb.com/home*). This is a document-oriented database. Records are stored as documents with properties that hold the data in the document. A schema defines the contents of a document. The great thing about MongoDB is that the design of a document can be changed very easily. If you discover that you need to add another item to a document (for example, we might suddenly decide we want to store the creation date of a survey), you can do this by changing the schema for the document, and everything will keep working.

Start with MongoDB

Installing the MongoDB database server on your machine creates a service that runs when your machine starts up. If you want to put your database in the cloud, there are paid hosting plans, as well as a free service you can use for small projects.

MAKE SOMETHING HAPPEN 49

Scan the QR code or visit *https://www.youtube.com/watch?v=ZBMcMCvmX-M* for a video walkthrough of this Make Something Happen.

Install MongoDB and create a database

Installing MongoDB will allow you to develop programs on your computer that use database storage. When the database is not being used, it consumes only a very small amount of memory and processor power. First, you need to open your browser and visit *https://www.mongodb.com/try/download/community*.

Select the latest **Version**, choose your **Platform**, click the Download button to get the installer, and then run it on your machine. Follow the instructions to install MongoDB. Make sure you select the option to install the MongoDB Compass application. You will be using this to manage your databases. Once installed, the MongoDB server will run in the background and wait for applications to connect to it. The server will store the database information in files on the local machine. You can interact with the server using the MongoDB Compass application installed alongside MongoDB. The application uses a network connection to interact with the database server. You can use it to view and edit the contents of database records and to create new databases. You will use it to create a database for the Tiny Survey application.

Start the **MongoDBCompass** application from your program files on your machine.

When Compass starts, it displays a dialog that lets you select the database connection you want to use. You can use Compass to manage database servers on distant machines, but we will use it to manage the databases on our machine. It should select a connection on localhost, as shown above, so just click the green **Connect** button to connect to the server on your machine.

Now we need to create a database for the Tiny Surveys application. Select the **Database** tab in the right-hand window and click the green **Create Database** button. Create a database called **tiny_surveys** containing a collection called **surveys**, as shown on the next page.

The `tiny_surveys` database and the `surveys` collection will appear in the list of databases on the left-hand side of the window.

The `tiny_surveys` database provides survey storage for the Tiny Survey program. We will use Mongoose's object modeling framework to access the database from our JavaScript code.

Mongoose and schemas

We add Mongoose to an application using `npm`, as shown below.

```
npm install mongoose
```

We can then import Mongoose into our code and use it to interact with a MongoDB database. The first thing we need to do is tell Mongoose what our data looks like. MongoDB is a *document-driven* database. A particular record in the database is a document. Multiple documents are stored in *collections*. The `tiny_surveys` database contains a single collection that contains `survey` documents. A document is described to Mongoose using a JavaScript object called a *schema*. We've already seen how a class definition tells JavaScript how to make an instance of a class. A schema object tells Mongoose how to make a MongoDB document.

Below, you can see the schema file for the Tiny Surveys application. It defines two schemas: `option` and `survey`. A `mongoose.Schema` object is initialized with an object literal that contains the property definitions. If you look at the code below, you will see that the `optionSchema` object contains `text` and `count` properties; the `text` property is a string, and the `count` property is a number. The `surveySchema` defines an object that contains a `topic` property and an array of `options`. The code below creates and exports a Mongoose model from this schema.

```javascript
import mongoose from "mongoose";                              // Import the Mongoose library

var optionSchema = mongoose.Schema({                          // Create an Option schema

    text: {                                                   // Text property
        type: String,                                         // Type of the property
        required: true                                        // Text is required
    },

    count: {                                                  // Count property
        type: Number,                                         // Type of count property
        required: true                                        // Count is required
    }
});

var surveySchema = mongoose.Schema({                          // Create a Surveys schema
    topic: {
        type: String,                                         // Survey topic
        required: true                                        // Topic is required
    },
    options: {                                                // Survey options
        type: [optionSchema],                                 // A list of options
        required: true                                        // Options are required
    }
});

let Surveys = mongoose.model('surveys', surveySchema);        // Make the model
export { Surveys as Surveys };                                // Export it
```

If we had additional documents we wanted to store in the application, we would create further schema classes and use them to create models to export.

The SurveyManagerDB class

The file store version of Tiny Survey uses a `SurveyManagerFiles` class, which stores surveys in a file. We will create a new version of this class called `SurveyManagerDB` that will use a database to store surveys. We will then change the import statement in the `tinysurveys.mjs` application to use this storage manager rather than the one created to use files. So, let's look at how we modify the storage manager to use a database rather than a file.

The code below shows the first part of the `SurveyManagerDB` class. It imports the Mongoose library and the survey database model exported by the above code. It is traditional to put schema files in their own folder (called models) in an application project. They are then imported into the application to manage the data storage for the application. The constructor for `SurveyManagerDB` does nothing. The `init` method in the class connects to the database. We could use the address of a remote server, but in this case, we are using the MongoDB server on the local machine. The `connect` method is asynchronous, so the `init` method uses `await` when calling it.

```
import mongoose from 'mongoose';                          Import the Mongoose library
import { Surveys } from './models/survey.mjs';            Import the Surveys schema

class SurveyManagerDB {

    constructor() {
    }

    async init() {
        await mongoose.connect('mongodb://localhost/tiny_surveys');   Connect to the
    }                                                                 database

    // rest of SurveyManager
}
```

We will have to create database versions of each survey management method. Each method will now interact with the database rather than the survey storage classes. Below is `storeSurvey` function. This is provided with an object containing the topic and options for storing a survey. The first time a survey is stored, the `storeSurvey` method must make a new document and save it. If a survey is already in the database, it must be updated with the contents of a new value.

```
                                                              Survey storage method
async storeSurvey(newValue) {
    let survey = await Surveys.findOne({ topic: newValue.topic });     Search for the
                                                                       survey by topic
    if (survey != null) {                                         Does the survey exist?
        await survey.updateOne(newValue);
    }                                                  If it exists, update it using the new values
    else {
        let newSurvey = new Surveys(newValue);          If it doesn't exist, make a new
        await newSurvey.save();                               Survey document
    }
}                                                            Save it in the database
```

The findOne method is used to find a single document in the collection that matches the given criteria; in this case, the document must have a topic that matches the one in the new value. If findOne cannot find a document, it returns null. A survey loaded from a collection has all the properties defined in the schema. These properties can be used directly. Below, you can see the database version of the getCounts method, which finds a survey and creates an object containing the survey topic, option names, and counts. This object will be passed to the displayresults.ejs template and used to create the results display.

```
async getCounts(topic) {
    let result;                                                Create an empty result object
    let survey = await Surveys.findOne({ topic: topic });      Find the survey to be displayed
    if (survey != null) {                                      Check if the survey was found
        let options = [];                                      Make an array of option results
        survey.options.forEach(option => {                     Loop through the options
            let countInfo = { text: option.text, count: option.count };
            options.push(countInfo);                           Make an option result
        });                                                    Add it to the list of options
        result = { topic: survey.topic, options: options };    Build the result object
    }
    else {                                                     If the survey was not found
        result = null;                                         Set result to null
    }
    return result;                                             Return the result
}
```

Scan the QR code or visit *https://www.youtube.com/watch?v=AYMMV160B0o* for a video walkthrough of this Make Something Happen.

Use a database

The starting point for this Make Something Happen is a version of Tiny Survey on GitHub at *https://github.com/Building-Apps-and-Games-in-the-Cloud/TinySurveyDatabase*. Clone this repository onto your machine and open it with Visual Studio Code. For this application to work, you must have installed MongoDB and created the database, as shown earlier.

Open the application in Visual Studio Code, open the **tinysurvey.mjs** source file, and start the program. Now, use the browser to navigate to *localhost:8080/index.html* and enter a complete survey. You should find that the application works in the same way as before. Start **MongoDB-Compass**, connect to the server, and view the **surveys** collection. You should discover that there is a document there containing a topic and options that you entered. If you are already running **MongoDBCompass**, you can choose **View > Reload Data** to refresh the display.

You can use the **MongoDBCompass** application to change the contents of documents and delete documents and even entire databases.

Testing asynchronous code

When we create asynchronous code, we must make a slight change to how our tests work. The tests themselves will call asynchronous functions, and the testing framework will call the tests asynchronously. Below is the code that calls one of the tests for the database version of Tiny Surveys

```
test('Store and retrieve options', async () => {
  const result = await optionsTest();          Await the result of the test
  expect(result).toBe("");                      Check the test result
});
```

MAKE SOMETHING HAPPEN 51

Scan the QR code or visit *https://www.youtube.com/watch?v=nTFrB1157MY* for a video walk-through of this Make Something Happen.

Test the database

If you left the application open from the previous exercise, continue with this one. Otherwise, follow the instructions in Make Something Happen 50, "Use a database," to set things up. There are some tests in the application already, so all you have to do is run them. Open the Terminal in Visual Studio Code, enter the following command, and press **Enter**:

```
npm test
```

The tests will run and pass, as shown below.

Each test runs in isolation from the next and connects and disconnects from the database as it runs. The `surveymanager` class calls the `disconnect` method (shown below) to disconnect the test from the database when the test has finished.

```
async disconnect(){
    await mongoose.disconnect();      ─── Disconnect the database connection
}
```

Tests and data storage

The previous versions of Tiny Survey stored their data in memory, so nothing persisted when they stopped running. However, the tests above interact with the live database, so running the above tests would overwrite the contents of the `Robspizza` survey. In the next section, we will look at how we can manage the use of different resources for test and deployment versions of applications.

Refactoring Tiny Survey

In Chapter 9, we identified some things that you might associate with a "professional" application. Now we are going to discover another. Professional applications should be well-structured. The Tiny Survey application has evolved from the original work-flow, and it could really be better structured. We are just about to make some significant additions to the code to allow users to log in to the service, and this would be a good point to tidy up the structure. This won't affect how the code works—or at least it shouldn't.

Create route files

First, we will separate all the routes into files to make the main program smaller and allow work to be shared in a group. Below is the route file for the application's index page. It creates an `Express.Router` instance, which implements the `get` handler for the index page. This instance is then exported from the files as `index`.

```
import express from 'express';
import { checkSurveys } from '../helpers/checkstorage.mjs';   ── Import middleware
const router = express.Router();   ───────────────────────────── Create an empty router


// Home page
router.get('/', checkSurveys, (request, response) => {   ── Set a get behavior for the router
  response.render('index.ejs');   ──────────────────── Render the index.ejs file for this route
});
export { router as index };   ──────────────────── Export the router with the name index
```

Previously, the `tinysurvey.mjs` file contained code that assigned the handler for the route to the Express application. In the refactored version, the route handler above is imported and then added to the route. The code below shows how this is done.

```
import {index} from './routes/index.mjs';   ──────────────── Import the route code
app.use('/index.html', index);   ──────────────── Connect the route to the index path
```

You can regard each route as a piece of middleware added to the Express framework that underpins the application. Note that all the route files are held in a `route` folder.

Scan the QR code or visit *https://www.youtube.com/watch?v=uMKWmKdvGwQ* for a video walkthrough of this Make Something Happen.

Look at the refactored version

The starting point here is a version of Tiny Survey you can download from GitHub at *https://github.com/Building-Apps-and-Games-in-the-Cloud/TinySurveyRefactored*. Clone this repository onto your machine and open it with Visual Studio Code. Select the Explorer view and expand all the folders in the solution. Then open the **TinySurvey.mjs** file and look at how the routes are now imported and used. If you run the application, you will discover that it works in exactly the same way. However, finding your way to different parts of the application is much easier.

```
1   import { SurveyManager } from './helpers/surveymanagerdb.mjs';
2   import express from 'express';
3   import cookieParser from 'cookie-parser';
4
5   import {index} from './routes/index.mjs';
6   import {gottopic} from './routes/gottopic.mjs';
7   import {setoptions} from './routes/setoptions.mjs';
8   import {recordselection} from './routes/recordselection.mjs';
9   import {displayresults} from './routes/displayresults.mjs';
10
11  // Create the express application
12  const app = express();
13
14  // Select the middleware to decode incoming posts
15  app.use(express.urlencoded({ extended: false }));
16
17  // Add the cookie parser middleware
18  app.use(cookieParser());
19
20  // Select ejs middleware
21  app.set('view-engine', 'ejs');
22
23  // Connect the route handlers to the routes
24  app.use('/index.html', index);
25  app.use('/', index);
26  app.use('/gottopic', gottopic);
27  app.use('/setoptions', setoptions);
```

Tiny Survey deployment

In Chapter 6, in the "Deploy an application" section, we put the Cheese Finder game into the cloud using an Azure-hosted App Service. Now, we will deploy Tiny Survey. However, before doing that, we might want to step back and consider how the development process works. You might think we just create a program and then put it in the cloud. After all, that's what we did with the Cheese Finder application. However, the Tiny Survey application is different because it uses a database to store survey information. It also has a much higher number of user interactions than Cheese Finder, and we have even built some tests for it. (Currently, these tests use the application database, which is not a good idea.) It would be useful to have a "developer mode" for when the application is being built and a "production mode" for when it is being deployed to customers. The developer mode could use a test database hosted on our local computer, and the production mode could use a database hosted in the cloud. It turns out that the designers of `node.js` and `npm` have thought of this, and the `package.json` file can be used to configure these two modes. To understand how this can work, we must first discover how environment variables are used to configure applications.

Manage environment variables

An environment variable is a value that sends information from the operating environment into the application. When we configure Azure to host our application, we will create environment variables to pass information into the application. In Chapter 6, in the "Set the port for the server" section, we used an environment variable to set the HTTP port for our Cheese Finder server. The code below is in the CheeseFinder application and tests to see if the `PORT` environment variable exists. If it does, the `port` value is set to the value in the environment variable. Otherwise, the `port` is set to `8080`. This allowed the service hosting CheeseFinder to send a port value to the application by creating an environment variable called `PORT`, which is set to the required number.

```
const port = process.env.PORT || 8080;          Set to 8080 or the PORT value

server.listen(port);                            Start listening to the port
```

Another piece of information we would like to feed into the Tiny Survey application is the connection string used for the database connection. At the moment, the database connection string is written directly into the code in the `surveymanagerdb.mjs` file, as shown below:

```
await mongoose.connect('mongodb://localhost/tiny_surveys');
```

This is the statement that connects the database to the application. The argument to the call of `connect` is a *connection string*. It is a string that defines a connection to a MongoDB database server. The present version contains a localhost address because the local machine hosts the database. When we deploy this application into the cloud, we will use the address of a database hosted on a remote server. The connection string will contain a password that will authenticate the database connection. This kind of connection string really shouldn't be in the source code of our application because we might decide to make our code open source and publish it for other people to use. If we publish our code, we also don't want to publish the address and password for our database server.

We can solve this problem by creating an environment file containing values the application can then pick up. The environment file is named `.env` and contains a set of name-value pairs. Below is an environment file for the Tiny Survey application that creates an environment variable called DATABASE-URL, which is set to the `mongodb://localhost/tiny_surveys` string.

```
DATABASE_URL=mongodb://localhost/tiny_surveys
```

We can install a library called `dotenv` for use during application development. We do this using the `npm install` command, as shown below.

```
npm install dotenv --save-dev
```

Note that the `npm install` command ends with the `--save-dev` option, which means the package will be specified in the `devDependencies` part of the `package.json` file. We don't need `dotenv` in the production code because we will configure environment variable values when we install the application on the host.

Once we have the `dotenv` library installed, we can use it in `surveymanagerdb.mjs` by importing and initializing it, as shown in the code below, which is at the top of the `surveymanagerdb.mjs` file. This code imports the `dotenv` element from the library and then calls `config` on the library to set it up.

```
import * as dotenv from 'dotenv';        ———— Get dotenv from the library
dotenv.config();                          ———— Start dotenv running
```

Once this has been set up, the program can now use values declared in the environment file, allowing us to change the database connection statement to the one below:

```
await mongoose.connect(process.env.DATABASE_URL);
```

When the program runs, the DATABASE_URL value is loaded from the environment file and used at that point in the code.

CODE ANALYSIS

Environment variables

You might have some questions about environment variables.

Question: Why are we using environment variables again?

> **Answer:** Environment variables let us send values into our application. We do this rather than modify the code when we want these values to change. When our application runs in the cloud host—for example, Azure—it will use environment variables to get setting values from the host. The .env file is a way of simulating these variables when we are developing the application.

Question: What stops the environment files from being saved in the repository whenever we check the files in with Git?

> **Answer:** We have seen that a repository can contain a .gitignore file, which contains a set of patterns matching files that are not to be stored in the repository. We first use this in Chapter 8 in the "Use gitignore" section to stop Git from saving library files in the repository. The file also contains a pattern that matches the .env file, preventing it from being stored in the repository.

Question: What happens when we load our application onto a server in the cloud?

> **Answer:** Good question. Later in this chapter, we will see how to manage environmental variables for cloud-based applications.

Question: How do we tell people what our environmental variables do?

> **Answer:** It might be a good idea to add some documentation to the project as a README.md file. See the "Create a README.md file" section later in this chapter.

Code and deploy with the nodemon package

When I start a new project, one of my first principles is to build a nice place to work. If you are going to do something many times, it makes sense to make it as easy as possible. The nodemon package can be downloaded using npm, making running and debugging your application much easier. The command below installs `nodemon` into an application as a developer dependency.

```
npm install nodemon --save-dev
```

Once `nodemon` has been installed, we can modify the `package.json` for the application to provide a way of starting it. The `package.json` file contains a `scripts` section where we can put commands that can be run from the command line. The JSON below shows how we can add script entries that we can use from the command line. There are three script entries:

- `test` uses the jest package to run the tests on the application.

- `devstart` starts `nodemon`.

- `start` starts Tiny Survey.

```
"scripts": {
  "test": "node --experimental-vm-modules node_modules/jest/bin/jest.js",
  "devstart": "nodemon tinysurvey.mjs",
  "start":"node tinysurvey.mjs"
},
```

Once these entries have been added to `package.json`, we can use commands from the terminal to trigger any of them. The command below would run the `devstart` script, starting `nodemon`.

```
npm run devstart
```

The `nodemon` package starts the application and then monitors all the source files. If any of the files change, `nodemon` will restart the application. This can be very useful when writing code because you can ensure that the program is always running with the latest source code version.

Scan the QR code or visit *https://www.youtube.com/watch?v=1UOxG_f9J0E* for a video walk-through of this Make Something Happen.

Quick development with **nodemon**

The starting point for this Make Something Happen is a version of Tiny Survey on GitHub at *https://github.com/Building-Apps-and-Games-in-the-Cloud/TinySurveyRelease*. Clone this repository onto your machine and open it with Visual Studio Code. This repository contains all the files you need to deploy TinySurvey, except the `.env` file, which gives the application the database connection. This is not stored in the public GitHub repository because we don't want to make these kinds of addresses public. Create a new file in the repository called `.env` with the contents shown below. Be sure to type them in correctly; otherwise, the application will fail when it starts.

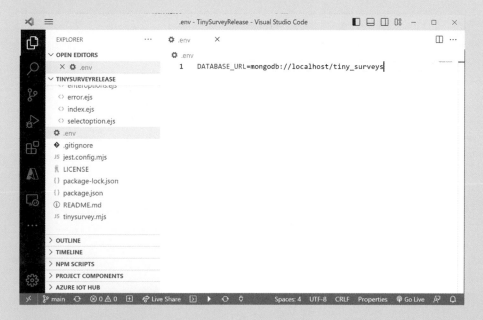

Open the file `index.mjs` in the `routes` folder. Now, select the **Run And Debug** option in the left-hand menu and click **JavaScript Debug Terminal**.

This will open a debugging terminal that attaches a debugger to any programs executed in the terminal. You add breakpoints to programs you run in the terminal. Start the program using the `npm run` command. Run the `devstart` script, as shown below, and press **Enter**.

```
npm run devstart
```

The nodemon application now watches all the application files. When you make and save a change to the `index.mjs` file (such as adding a comment), the application is automatically restarted.

Create a README.md file

If you want to tell people all about your project and how it works, you can create a README file. README files are an important part of GitHub. A repository (and even each repository folder) can contain a README file that looks like a mini-website describing the project. README files have the language extension `.md` to indicate that they are formatted using *Markdown* syntax. This is a great way to format text quickly. Markdown files can also contain images and links to other pages. Below is a tiny sample of Markdown that will tell you just about all you need to know about creating documents. For this example to work, the folder containing the README file must contain a folder named `images`, which holds the file `small-rob.jpg`. You can find the example README.md in the demonstration folder for Chapter 10 in the code samples.

```
# This is a big heading
## This is slightly smaller

This is body text.

To make another paragraph we need a line break.

Make a numbered list by starting each line with a number followed by a period (full
stop):

1. It's that
1. easy.

Make a bulleted list using stars:

* this is
* easy too

Put code into blocks by using '''
'''Javascript
function doAddition(p1, p2) {
    let result = p1 + p2;
```

```
    alert("Result:" + result);
}
'''
Links are easy too https://www.robmiles.com or with names [my blog](http://www.
robmiles.com)


Finally, you can add pictures:
![picture of rob](images/small-rob.jpg)
```

In **Figure 10-2**, you can see the Markdown as it appears in the browser. Visit
https://enterprise.github.com/downloads/en/markdown-cheatsheet.pdf to read about
the version of Markdown supported by GitHub. It is worth spending a bit of time
learning some Markdown. You can add a Markdown preview plugin to Visual Studio
Code, which makes it easy to preview your pages as you create them.

Figure 10-2   Markdown output

Scan the QR code or visit *https://www.youtube.com/watch?v=oUlkJFnwNqA* for a video walk-through of this Make Something Happen.

Deploy Tiny Survey on Azure

The Tiny Survey application needs a MongoDB database to host the survey information. You can get hosting for MongoDB databases at *mongodb.com*. You will have to create an account, but you do not have to give any payment information. Follow the process at *https://www.mongodb.com/basics/create-database*. Create the database in the shared tier to provide a small database you can use for testing. Then follow the process to create a user-name and password and use this to create the connection string for your database.

Connect to Cluster0

✓ Setup connection security ✓ Choose a connection method **Connect**

1 Select your driver and version

DRIVER	VERSION
Node.js ▾	3.6 or later ▾

2 Add your connection string into your application code

☑ Include full driver code example

```
const { MongoClient } = require('mongodb');
const uri = "mongodb+srv://dbUser:<password>@cluster0.cg3k9.mongodb.net/?
retryWrites=true&w=majority";
const client = new MongoClient(uri, { useNewUrlParser: true, useUnifiedTopology:
true });
client.connect(err => {
  const collection = client.db("test").collection("devices");
  // perform actions on the collection object
  client.close();
});
```

Replace <password> with the password for the dbUser user. Ensure any option params are URL encoded.

Having trouble connecting? View our troubleshooting documentation

Go Back   Close

The screenshot on the preceding page shows the connect instructions generated by the MongoDB Atlas web page. The `uri` variable holds the connection string. Remember to change the `<password>` placeholder to the password you have created.

Now that you have a working database, you can install Tiny Survey in the cloud and connect it to this database. Start by opening the **TinySurveyRelease** application in Visual Studio Code and following the process described in the Make Something Happen 28, "Create an Azure App service," in Chapter 6. Note that you won't be able to call the service `TinySurvey` because I've already got that name.

Don't deploy the application at the end of the process because you need to set up the connection string environment variable before you deploy it. Find the App Services collection in Azure and select the **Tiny Survey** item in the list. (You might not have as many services as I do.) Right-click **Application Settings** and select **Add New Setting** from the list that appears.

This will open a dialog to enter the name of the setting value—in this case, DATABASE_URL.

Type in the name and press **Enter**. You will be asked to enter the value for the setting, so enter the connection string you got from the MongoDB setup.

Press **Enter** to save the string in the application settings. Now, you can deploy the application. Right-click **TinySurvey** and select **Deploy To Web App**.

You will be asked to select the folder containing the application to be deployed. Select the repository folder.

A pop-up dialog will ask you to confirm the deployment. Click **Deploy**. The deployment will take a little while. At the end of the deployment, a dialog will appear at the bottom right of the Visual Studio Code window confirming the completion of the deployment.

Click **Browse Website** to view the application.

The browser will start your web application. Note that the URL shown for the above page is *tinysurvey.azurewebsites.net*, which is the Internet address for the application I uploaded. Yours will be different.

What you have learned

This has been another fun chapter. We started by considering how to read and write files. Then we learned how to manage asynchronous processes in JavaScript and made some error-handling middleware. We've built our first MongoDB database and connected a JavaScript application to id using Mongoose. Then we tidied up our code, built a proper development environment, and configured and deployed the program. Here's a recap, plus some points to ponder.

- The `fs` library in `node.js` provides file input/output to applications. The library functions all work asynchronously, returning a `promise` object describing the requested action. The code that receives the `promise` can then continue without being blocked by the call to a function, which might take some time to complete.

- A `promise` object exposes a `then` behavior which can be given a function to be called when the `promise` is resolved.

- It is frequently the case that an application wants to wait until a "promise-returning" activity completes. In this situation, the `await` keyword can be used to await the completion of a function returning a `promise`. A function or method that contains an `await` action must be marked as `async` by preceding the declaration with the keyword `async`. This is because the `await` action generates a `promise` returned to the caller of the code containing the `await`.

- It might appear that asynchronous operation allows a JavaScript application to run multiple threads of execution simultaneously. However, this is not the case. JavaScript maintains a call stack and an event list and uses them to switch rapidly between operations. Events are used to trigger new actions. For example, rather than waiting for a network transaction to finish, the underlying JavaScript code nominates an event to fire when the network transaction has finished.

- Applications can use global flag variables to indicate the application's status and change how the application responds to inputs.

- We can write our own Express middleware functions and add them to the chain of functions that process an incoming web request and generate the response. The middleware function can cut short handling a web request handler if required (for example, if a service is unavailable).

- MongoDB is a document-oriented database that holds data as a set of collections of documents. Not all the documents in a particular collection must have the same properties. This makes MongoDB more flexible than standard table-based databases. We can install a MongoDB server on our computer to manage data storage.

We can also connect an application to a database on a distant server. We can get limited MongoDB hosting from Mongo at *https://www.mongodb.com/home*.

- The Mongoose library can be added to an application using `npm`. It provides a library of functions that implement an object-oriented interface to MongoDB. An application can create *schema* objects that contain properties describing the document contents. An application can create new documents and search for and update existing ones.

- Refactoring is the process of ensuring that the structure of the code in an application is a good match to the problem being solved. It is a constant process because understanding a problem improves during development, and initial design decisions might need revisited. Refactoring also helps to make code easier to work on and imposes a navigable structure to the elements of a solution.

- The structure of an Express application can be improved by separating the routes for various endpoints into different code files. The routes become middleware items added to the Express framework underpinning the application.

- Environment variables are a means by which setting information is communicated from the operating environment into a running application. They make it easier to manage the application (there is no need to change the content of the code to use different resources), and they also make the application more secure (the source code doesn't contain any resource information).

- The `devDependencies` part of the `package.json` file for an application contains packages used when developing the program but not deployed with it.

- The `package.json` file can contain a script portion containing scripts to run when developing and testing the application.

- When developing an application, you can use the `dotenv` package and a `.env` file to create environment variables to configure an application for testing. When an application is deployed into the cloud, the process of deploying the application into the host must include setting values for the environment variables the application uses.

- When developing an application, you can use the `nodemon` package to automatically run the application each time a file in it is changed.

- An application can contain a `README.md` file that contains instructions that describe how to run and deploy the application. This file is formatted using Markdown commands which provide simple but powerful formatting commands.

- When deploying a database application as an Azure App Service, we need to create an Application Setting value containing the database connection string to be used when the application runs.

To reinforce your understanding of this chapter, you might want to consider the following "profound questions."

Question: What happens if a function contains an `await` but is not marked as `async`?

Answer: The JavaScript compiler will refuse to run such a function.

Question: What happens if my code awaits a function not marked `async`?

Answer: The JavaScript engine will just call the function as usual.

Question: What happens if a function marked `async` contains no awaits?

Answer: The function will run without a problem, but the function will not be awaited.

Question: What happens if code inside an asynchronous function throws an exception?

Answer: The exception must be caught by an exception handler wrapped around the asynchronous call. Then the exception handler for the call will run when the exception is thrown. An exception construction that encloses a number of asynchronous calls will not catch any exceptions thrown by them.

Question: What is special about a function used as middleware when processing a web transaction in Express?

Answer: The middleware function must have the correct parameters: `request` (a reference to an object describing the incoming request), `response` (a reference to an object which will describe the response), and `next` (a reference to the next middleware function in the chain of functions handling this request).

Question: How does an Express middleware function cause the processing of a request to be abandoned?

Answer: If a middleware function detects no point in continuing processing the request, it doesn't call the next middleware function in the chain.

Question: Why is a document-oriented database a good idea?

Answer: A document-oriented database doesn't insist on all the objects in a collection containing exactly the same properties. It is also possible to add new properties to documents by adding them to the schema object that describes the document contents.

Question: What is the difference between MongoDB and Mongoose?

Answer: MongoDB is a document-database technology that can be used directly. Mongoose is a framework that allows database elements to be represented by JavaScript objects.

Question: What would happen if two applications attempted to connect to the same database?

Answer: One of the great things about databases is that they were built to handle this. The database would keep working. However, if both applications start to "fight" over a particular document in the database, this might cause problems. The database will never fail in this situation, but the applications might become confused unless they have been designed to handle this.

Question: What happens if I forget to set an environment variable when deploying an application?

Answer: The value will be undefined, and the application will fail when it runs.

Question: How many free applications and databases can I have?

Answer: Both Azure and MongoDB restrict you to a single free application or database. You can use a single database with multiple applications by having each application use a different document collection.

11

Activity tracking and sessions

What you will learn

In this chapter, we will discover how to personalize the user experience of our sites. We'll start by discovering how a website can use cookies to keep track of individual visitors on a web application and connect users to the content they have created. We'll create globally unique identifiers. We'll make some Express middleware to manage user tracking and take a look at modeling techniques we can use to improve our workflow design practices. We will create a user management database and discover how to store passwords securely.

Then, we will create some security middleware for the routes on our site. Finally, we will consider how to implement role-based security to perform simple administration of the Tiny Survey application. There are quite a few things you will need to understand, but the result can be used to add security and sessions to any web application

User tracking

Our Tiny Survey application is becoming popular with users. They like how easy it is to create surveys and are pleased it doesn't allow multiple votes. But they are frustrated because once a survey has been created, it is there forever. They would like to be able to remove surveys to make new versions with different options. We chatted with them and decided that the only person who should be able to remove a survey is the person who created it. This means we need a way of identifying the person who created a particular survey.

The Tiny Survey application presently tracks when a given user has responded to a survey to prevent a user from submitting multiple votes to a survey. The tracking process uses a `completedSurveys` cookie stored on the user's machine by the browser. The cookie contains a list of the surveys a user has voted for. The Tiny Survey server sends the cookie to the browser along with each response to a web request. Each time the user browses the Tiny Survey site, the `completedSurveys` cookie is sent to the server. When a user opens a survey, the application looks for the survey topic in the cookie's list of completed surveys. If the topic is found, the user is taken to the results page. If the topic is not found, the user is taken to the voting page. You can learn more about how this works in the "Use cookies in Tiny Survey" section in Chapter 9.

Create a Globally Unique Identifier (GUID)

We will track our users by giving them a unique id value stored in a cookie by their browser. This means we need a source of unique values to use as identifiers for our users. A cryptography library built into `node.js` contains a function that can generate Globally Unique Identifiers or GUIDs. The statements below import the `randomUUID` function from the `crypto` library and then use `randomUUID` to set the variable `creatorGUID` to a random GUID.

```
import { randomUUID } from 'crypto';
let creatorGUID = randomUUID();
```

The GUID created takes the form of a random string of characters. Below, you can see a GUID that was created by the preceding code. If the code was run again, it would create a completely different GUID.

```
f7581de2-cda6-4de4-8692-0cc7b36082b1
```

The GUID doesn't identify a particular user. It doesn't tell the server that Rob Miles is visiting the site. But it makes it possible to detect when I visit the site as opposed to anyone else. But before we write any more code, we might want to consider the ethical issues raised by giving each user their own unique GUID.

User tracking ethics

The only way that Tiny Survey can identify the creator of a survey is by giving each user a unique identity and then assigning this identity to the surveys they create. This is not a hard technical problem to solve. However, it does raise ethical issues. Identity tracking could target a particular user with advertisements based on the contents of the surveys they have created or voted in. We should inform the user that we will use cookies and ask them to approve their use when visiting the Tiny Survey site for the first time. We should try to clarify what information we will store and how it will be used. To make this work, we will have to change the workflow of Tiny Survey.

Use activity diagrams to describe workflow

We have seen the idea of workflow before. We used it when creating the application workflow for Tiny Survey in Chapter 7. Until now, we have mainly used English to describe workflows. However, a diagram can be much easier to understand than text.

Figure 11-1 shows a *state diagram*, one of a family of diagram types that make up the *Unified Modeling Language (UML)*, which expresses different states the system can occupy. Visit *https://en.wikipedia.org/wiki/Unified_Modeling_Language* to learn more about UML.

This diagram shows the workflow of the original implementation of the Tiny Survey application. The large black dot at the top is the starting point. The titles of each state map onto the web pages used by the application. The lines between them give the circumstances that cause the state to change. We can use a diagram to describe workflows without writing lots of text. **Figure 11-1** shows the application checking whether a given survey exists and lets the user create a new one if there is no existing survey with the given topic.

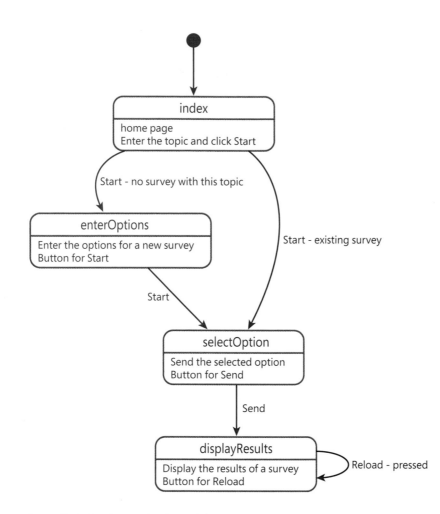

Figure 11-1 Tiny Survey simple workflow

PROGRAMMER'S POINT

Make diagrams part of your development process

Diagrams are a great way of expressing workflow. They are much easier to discuss with the users of your application than text descriptions. At this stage in the project, we are creating diagrams to show how the system will be used, not how it will be implemented. **Figure 11-1** could be used as the basis of a solution written in any computer language. I created the diagrams for this book using a web-based tool called PlantUML (*https://www.plantuml.com*), which takes simple text descriptions and draws them as diagrams. It is worth looking at the other UML diagram types that describe other parts of development. If you are working in a team, you should create standards that specify which diagram types should be used at each project stage.

Cookie approval workflow

Figure 11-2 shows the workflow for the cookie approval. If the user arrives at the index page with no tracking cookie, the `trackCheck` page is displayed. If the user doesn't want to accept a cookie, the workflow ends when they don't accept it. This part of the workflow will be added to the beginning of the application workflow.

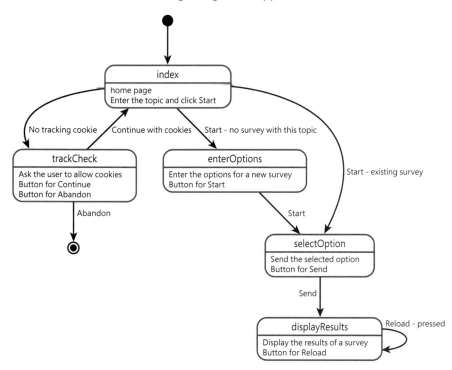

Figure 11-2 Cookie approval workflow

Figure 11-3 shows the page the application displays the first time the user visits the Tiny Survey site. The user can agree to cookies by clicking **Continue With Cookies**.

Alternatively, they can click **Abandon** if they don't want to spend any more time on the site. The page implements the test at the start of the cookie approval workflow. Let's see how we can make this work.

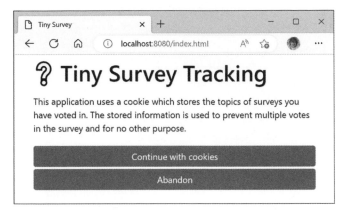

Figure 11-3 Tiny Survey tracking

Create tracking middleware

Middleware is code added to an Express application to provide additional behaviors. We've already added one piece of middleware to the Tiny Survey application. The `checkStorage` middleware has been added to every route. It displays an error page if the Tiny Survey application is not connected to its database. Find out more in the "Create error handling middleware" section in Chapter 10.

We can create some more middleware that asks the user if it is okay to create a cookie when they first visit the Tiny Survey site. The code below implements the initial page route of the Tiny Survey application. It renders the page `index.ejs` page containing the application's home page. The `checkTracking` middleware has been added to the route, as shown in the highlighted code:

```
import express from 'express';
import { checkSurveys } from '../helpers/checkstorage.mjs';
import { checkTracking } from '../helpers/trackinghelper.mjs';    Import checkTracking
                                                                        middleware

const router = express.Router();

// Home page - just render the index
router.get('/', checkTracking, checkSurveys, (request, response) => {
  response.render('index.ejs');                                    Use checkTracking
});                                                                     middleware
```

This means the checkTracking middleware function will be called when the route is used. The function is shown in the code below, which checks to see if the creatorGUID cookie exists. If it does, it calls the storeCookie function to resave the cookie so its expiry date is updated. If the cookie does not exist, the application gives the user a choice as to whether they want to continue. It does this by displaying a menu page shown previously in **Figure 11-3**. Users who click Continue With Cookies are sent to the trackingok route. If users click **Abandon**, they are sent to my blog page at *https://www.robmiles.com*.

```
function checkTracking(request, response, next) {
    // create a creator cookie if there isn't one
    let guid = request.cookies.creatorGUID;                      Get the cookie
    if (guid) {                                                  Check if the cookie exists
        // got a guid - write it back to refresh the age
        storeCreatorGUIDCookie(guid, response);        Call storeCookie to store the cookie
        next();                                             Continue to next middleware
    }
    else {
        // Not got a cookie - are we OK to track this user?
        let trackConfirm = {                                    Build a menu
            heading: "Tracking",                                Page heading
            message: "This application uses a cookie which stores "+
                     "the topics of surveys you have voted in. "+     Test describing
                     "The stored information is used to prevent "+    the page purpose
                     "multiple votes in the survey and for no other purpose.",
            menu: [                                             List of menu options
                {                                               Continue path
                    description: "Continue with cookies",
                    route: "/trackingok"                        Route for tracking OK
                },

                {                                               Abandon path
                    description: "Abandon",
                    route: "https:/www.robmiles.com"            Route for do not track
                }
            ]
        };
        response.render('menupage.ejs', trackConfirm);       Send the menu description
    }                                                          object to the template
}
```

Menu selection page

The `checkTracking` middleware uses a new page template I've added to the application. This generates pages that contain a menu. The page is called `menupage.ejs`. It receives an object describing the alternative selections and the routes to be followed. Below is the code for this EJS (Embedded JavaScript templating) page containing HTML and JavaScript. In Chapter 8, we started using EJS to build template pages in the aptly named "Use page templates with EJS" section. This `menupage.ejs` template is supplied with an object that contains a heading, a message, and a list of menu items. The object describing the tracking confirmation menu items is declared as `trackConfirm` in the `checkTracking` middleware in the `checkTracking` function in the preceding section. The `menupage.ejs` template displays the heading and message and then loops around all the items in the menu, generating a button for each. When the button is pressed, it opens the specified route.

```
<!DOCTYPE html>
<html>

<head>
  <title>Tiny Survey</title>
</head>

<body>
  <div class="container">
    <h1 class="mb-3 mt-2">&#10068; Tiny Survey <%= heading%>       ——— Display the heading
    </h1>
    <p>
      <%=message%>                                                 ——— Display the message
        <% menu.forEach( item=>{ %>                                ——— Loop round each option
          <div class="row">
            <div class="col-sm-12">
              <button class="btn btn-primary mt-1 btn-block"
                onclick="window.location.href='<%=item.route%>'">  ——— Route for the option
                <%=item.description%>                              ——— Button text
              </button>
            </div>
          </div>
        <% })%>
    </p>
  </div>
</body>

</html>
```

The trackingok route

If the user agrees to allow Tiny Survey cookies, they are directed to the `trackingok` route. This uses another piece of middleware called `addTracking` that adds a tracking cookie to a page. The code for the route is shown below with the `addTracking` middleware highlighted. When the page is loaded, the `addTracking` middleware function will be called, and a tracking cookie will be added to the site.

```
import express from 'express';
import {addTracking} from '../helpers/trackinghelper.mjs';
const router = express.Router();

// Render the home page but use the tracking middleware
router.get('/', addTracking, (request, response) => {
  response.render('index.ejs');
});


export { router as trackingok };
```

Below is the `addTracking` middleware function. It creates and stores a new `creator-GUID` value. Then it calls the next function in the middleware chain. Adding this middleware to a route will create a GUID when that route is followed. It only creates a cookie if one isn't already present.

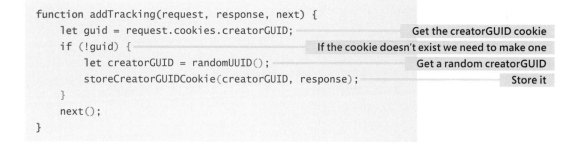

The final link in the chain is the function that stores the `creatorGUID` cookie. The `storeCreatorGUIDCookie` function refreshes an existing cookie and creates a new one. The maximum age of the cookie is set at 1,000 days.

```
function storeCreatorGUIDCookie(guid, response) {
    let cookieLifeInDays = 1000;
    let dayLengthInMillis = (24 * 60 * 60 * 1000);
    response.cookie("creatorGUID",
        guid,
        { maxAge: cookieLifeInDays * dayLengthInMillis });
}
```

MAKE SOMETHING HAPPEN 55

Scan the QR code or visit *https://www.youtube.com/watch?v=wu5CxBYRoUE* for a video walk-through of this Make Something Happen.

Checking cookies

The starting point for this Make Something Happen is a version of Tiny Survey on GitHub at *https://github.com/Building-Apps-and-Games-in-the-Cloud/TinySurveyTracker*. Clone this repository onto your machine and open it with Visual Studio Code. If you are unsure how to get the sample application, use the sequence described in the "Get the example application" section in Chapter 8. Just change the address of the cloned repository. Open the application in Visual Studio Code.

Because this repository came from GitHub, it will be missing the .env file, which contains the database server's address. You will need to create this file. Follow the instructions in Make Something Happen 53 to do this.

Next, open the **trackinghelper.mjs** source file in the **helpers** folder. Scroll down the file and click to the left of line 44 to set a breakpoint on that line. (This is the part of the code where the tracking cookie is created.) Now click the **Run And Debug** button in the left menu.

Click here to insert a breakpoint

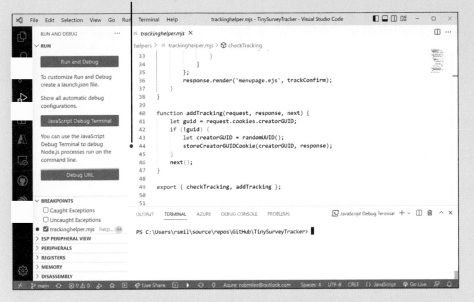

Now, click the **JavaScript Debug Terminal** button to open a debug terminal. You will use the `devstart` application to run your program to make changes and have the application automatically restart. Enter the command below into the terminal and press **Enter**.

```
npm run devstart
```

Tiny Survey is now running and waiting for connections from the browser. Start your browser and open the **Developer Tools** (press F12 in Microsoft Edge). Switch to the **Application** view in the **Developer Tools** and navigate to *localhost:8080/index.html*.

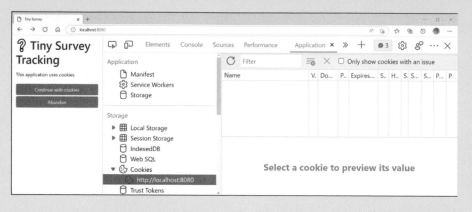

The Tiny Survey application will detect that no `creatorGUID` cookie is stored in the browser and ask if you want to continue with cookies. Click **Continue with cookies** in the browser. This will cause the application to hit the breakpoint at statement 44 of `trackingHelper.mjs`, as shown in the Visual Studio Code window. If you rest the mouse cursor over the `creator-GUID` variable, its value—the GUID—will be displayed.

GUID

```
trackinghelper.mjs ×
helpers > JS trackinghelper.mjs > ⊗ addTracking

33                    }
34                ]
35            };
36            response.render('menupage.ejs', trackConfirm);
37        }
38    }
39
40    function addTracking(request, response, next) {
41        let guid = request.cookies.creatorGUID;
42        if (!guid) {
43            let creatorGUID = rando  'e9dec46f-e7d5-48ab-a581-6ad8f69a6017'
44          ▷ storeCreatorGUIDCookie(creatorGUID, response);
45        }
46        next();
47    }
48
49    export { checkTracking, addTracking };
50
51
```

```
OUTPUT    TERMINAL    AZURE    DEBUG CONSOLE    PROBLEMS            JavaScript Debug Terminal

[nodemon] to restart at any time, enter `rs`
[nodemon] watching path(s): *.*
[nodemon] watching extensions: js,mjs,json
[nodemon] starting `node tinysurvey.mjs`
Debugger attached.
Server running
```

Above, you can see the GUID value. When you run the program, the value will be different. Use the debug controls to resume the program and return to the browser.

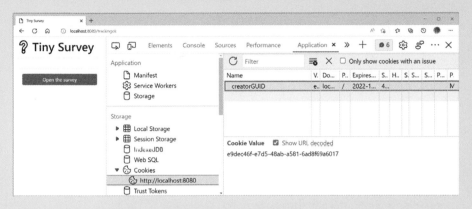

You can see that a cookie has now been added to the application containing the GUID value set by the code. You can add more breakpoints and step through more code to discover more about how the code works. You can leave this running for the next Make Something Happen.

Store survey creators

We can add the `creatorGUID` value to a stored survey to identify the user who created that survey. We do this by adding another item to the schema for the survey. Below is the modified schema for the survey. The schema defines the data item stored in the MongoDB database holding all the survey information. We first saw schema files in the "Mongoose and schemas" section in Chapter 10 when we created the original schema file for Tiny Survey storage containing the survey topic and options. The `creatorGUID` has been added to the end. All the fields have been marked as required, meaning any attempt to create a survey that doesn't contain these values will cause an exception to be thrown when the program runs.

```
// Build a survey value
var surveySchema = mongoose.Schema({
    topic: {
        type: String,
        required: true
    },
    options: {
        type: [optionSchema],
```

```
        required: true
    },
    creatorGUID: {                                        ──── Extra field to hold the creatorGUID
        type: String,                                     ──── Field is a string
        required:true                                     ──── Field is required
    }
});

// save it
await surveyManager.storeSurvey(newSurvey);
```

Now that we have somewhere to store the creatorGUID value, we must write the code to store it. The creatorGUID is added to a survey when it is created. The application creates a new survey in the setoptions path used when the user enters all the survey topics and options, as shown in the following code. The creatorGUID value in the new survey is set from the creatorGUID in the cookies, meaning every survey will have a creatorGUID property identifying the creator. The creatorGUID will be stored in the MongoDB database.

```
let newSurvey = {                                         ──── Make an object to describe the survey
    topic: topic,                                         ──── Add the topic
    options: options,                                     ──── Add the options
    creatorGUID: request.cookies.creatorGUID              ──── Add the creator
};
```

The Tiny Survey application now tracks the creator of each survey. Users are given unique identifiers that are stored as cookies in their browsers. When a user creates a survey, their unique identifier is stored along with the survey topic and options. Now we need to add the final element to make the application recognize when users open a survey they created and allow them to delete it.

Recognize survey creators

Figure 11-4 shows the complete state diagram for the Tiny Survey version we are creating. You can see the survey management element on the right side of the diagram. The survey management element is triggered when the user starts the survey and is found to be the survey owner. The survey's creatorGUID is checked when a survey topic has been entered. If it matches the user's creatorGUID of the user, the application displays a survey manager view of the survey that includes a button that can be used to delete the survey.

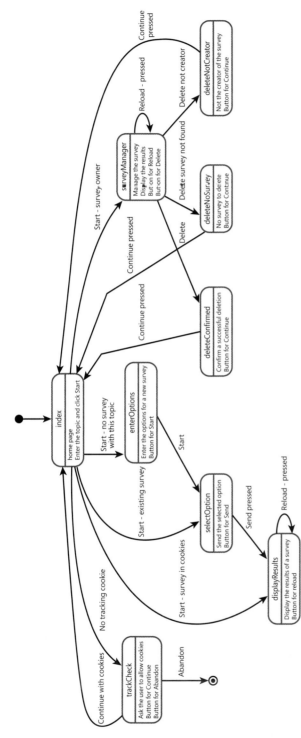

Figure 11-4 Complete state diagram

Below is the code in the `gottopic.mjs` route that does this. The `surveyOptions` returned by the `getOptions` function have been modified to include the `creatorGUID` value. The `displayresultsmanage.ejs` template is displayed if the `creatorGUID` in the survey matches the cookie's value.

```
if (surveyOptions) {
  // There is a survey with this topic
  // Need to check if this user created the survey
  if (surveyOptions.creatorGUID == request.cookies.creatorGUID) {
    // Render survey management page
    let results = await surveyManager.getCounts(topic);
    response.render('displayresultsmanage.ejs', results);
  }
}
```

If you find this code hard to understand, remember the problem we are solving. We want the application to do something different when a survey is opened by its creator. The survey contains a `creatorGUID` property that identifies the user who created it. The cookie stored by the browser that opened the survey contains a `creatorGUID` that identifies the user. If these two match, we want to render the management page. **Figure 11-5** shows the survey manager page.

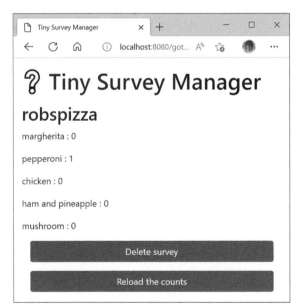

Figure 11-5 Tiny Survey Manager

It is very similar to the results display page, but it contains two buttons that can be used to delete the survey or reload the count values. If **Delete Survey** is clicked, the survey will be deleted. If **Reload The Counts** is clicked, the counts are updated. This page is defined in the `displayresultsmanage.ejs` template. The HTML for the two buttons is shown below. The buttons use a style to make them extend for the display's full width. When the **Delete Survey** button is clicked, the `deletesurvey` path is followed, with the survey topic appended to the path. When the **Reload The Counts** button is pressed, the `displayresultsmanage` path is followed, causing the page to reload with updated count values.

```
<div class="col-sm-12">
  <button class="btn btn-primary mt-1 btn-block"
   onclick="window.location.href='/deletesurvey/<%=topic%>'">        Path for delete
    Delete survey
  </button>
</div>
</p>


<p>
<div class="col-sm-12">
  <button class="btn btn-primary mt-1 btn-block"
   onclick="window.location.href='/displayresultsmanage/<%=topic%>'">   Path for reload
    Reload the counts
  </button>
</div>
```

The `deletesurvey` route is followed when the user clicks the **Delete Survey** button. The code for the route is shown below. It gets the survey options information and returns the survey's `creatorGUID`. It then makes sure that the `creatorGUID` of the stored survey matches that of the user making the request. If they don't match, an error is displayed. If they do match, the survey is deleted. If they don't match, an error is displayed. The route also displays a message if the survey is not found.

```
Router.get('/:topic', checkTracking, checkSurveys, async (request, response) => {

  let topic = request.params.topic;                          Get the survey topic

  let surveyOptions = await surveyManager.getOptions(topic);   Get the survey options

  if (surveyOptions) {                                        Do we have a survey?
    // Found the survey
    // Need to check if this person created the survey
```

```
        if (surveyOptions.creatorGUID == request.cookies.creatorGUID) {
            // This is the owner of the survey - can delete it
            await surveyManager.deleteSurvey(topic);────────────────── Call the delete function
            messageDisplay("The survey has been deleted",response);
        }
        else{
            // Not the owner - display a message
            messageDisplay("You are not the creator of this survey",response);
        }
    }
    else {
        // Survey not found
        messageDisplay("The survey was not found",response);
    }
});
```

The deletesurvey route uses the messageDisplay function, which builds and renders a menu page. The code for messageDisplay shown below creates an object that is passed into the menu page we have used before.

```
Function messageDisplay(message,response){
    let messageDescription = {
        heading: "Delete",──────────────────────── All the messages have the delete heading
        message: message,──────────────────────────── Add in the required message text
        menu: [
            {
                description: "Continue",─────────── All the messages have a continue button
                route: "/"──────────── All the messages take you back to the application index
            }
        ]
    };
    response.render('menupage.ejs', messageDescription);
}
```

The final piece of code we must look at is the function that deletes an existing survey, which is in the surveymanagerdb.mjs helper file. It uses the Mongoose connection to the database to delete the survey from the database. The connection is referred to by a variable called Surveys, which is declared in surveymanagerdb.mjs. We have used the findOne function to find a survey with a particular topic. Now, we will use the deleteOne function to delete a survey with a particular topic. The deleteOne operation might take some time, so it is an asynchronous function that returns a Promise. The code uses await to wait for the Promise to finish.

```
/**
 * Delete the survey with the given topic
 * @param {string} topic topic of the survey
 */
async deleteSurvey(topic){
    await Surveys.deleteOne(({ topic: topic }));
}
```

 **MAKE SOMETHING HAPPEN 56**

Scan the QR code or visit *https://www.youtube.com/watch?v=V9RTCB6z07w* for a video walk-through of this Make Something Happen.

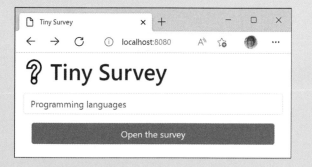

Survey management

The starting point for this Make Something Happen is the same as for the previous one. You can refer back to Make Something Happen 55 for details. Get TinyServerTracker working and connect to the index page for the site. I'm surveying programming languages for a change. Enter the topic **Programming languages**.

Click **Open The Survey** to open it. Because this is a new survey, you will now move on to setting the survey options.

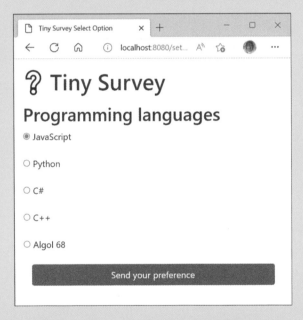

Once you have entered your options click **Start Survey** to start it.

You can now select a language option (**JavaScript**, **Python**, and so on) and then click the **Send Your Preference** button. You will be directed to the results page.

Now that you have a stored survey, you can manage it. Return to the Tiny Survey home page by entering *localhost:8080/index.html* into the browser. Enter **Programming Languages** to reopen the same survey.

The server will check the GUID value in the cookie your browser sends with the page. Because you created the survey, you are now directed to the survey management page. You can use this to delete the survey. Click **Delete Survey** to delete it; the page displays the confirmation message shown on the next page.

If you look closely at the screenshot above, you can see how the delete was triggered. The URL for the page is as shown below:

```
http://localhost:8080/deletesurvey/Programming%20languages
```

This address will send the server to the deletesurvey route. The survey topic to be deleted is given as part of the path. The Programming%20languages string is the topic name. (The %20 portion of the string is how a URL encodes a space character.) Code in the deletesurvey route will find the survey with the given topic and then delete it. You might wonder what happens if you try to delete the survey again by sending the same URL to the server a second time. Press the brower's refresh button to reload from the URL.

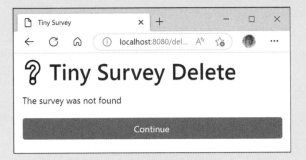

A message reading "The survey was not found" appears, meaning the application handles this correctly. If you want to investigate any behaviors in detail, you can open the source code and put breakpoints in the code to watch it run. You can find the code that implements this behavior in the file deletesurvey.mjs in the routes folder in the solution.

Tracking cookies

You might have some questions about how the cookies are used.

Question: How is a unique GUID created?

Answer: The starting point for a GUID value is the date and time. Other random elements are added to the GUID to create the unique value.

Question: Why does the program resave the cookie each time Tiny Survey is opened?

Answer: When the cookie is saved, its expiry date is updated to 1,000 days into the future. This ensures that as long as the user continues using Tiny Survey, the cookie will not expire.

Question: What happens if a user loses their `creatorGUID` cookie?

Answer: The cookie is used to identify the surveys created by a particular user. If the user buys a new computer or deletes their cookies, they will get a new cookie that is different from their original one and will not be recognized as owners of "their" surveys. It's up to us, as programmers, to decide how important this problem is. If the user is paying a large sum of money for this application and their surveys are very important to them, we could add a workflow that lets them set their own `creatorGUID` and move it from machine to machine. In the coming section "User Sessions," we'll discover how a user can log in to Tiny Survey using a username and password.

Tiny Survey improvements

The Tiny Survey program is now quite a complex piece of software. However, you may have noticed a few improvements you might like to make:

- The present version of Tiny Survey displays the management page for the creator only after the creator has reopened the survey. It would be useful to display the management page when the creator voted in the survey. How would you do this? Hint: You need to add a test that runs right after a vote has been recorded to determine which page is loaded next.

- It would be useful if the survey creator could also clear the counts back to zero. How would you implement this, and where would you put the option in the workflow? Hint: This is a bit trickier than the first improvement. You must add a new route (perhaps called `resetsurvey`) and modify the `displayresultsmanage` page. You must also add a new behavior to the `SurveyManagerDB` class (perhaps also called `resetsurvey`). However, it gets a bit easier if you remember that resetting a survey is very similar—in workflow terms—to deleting it.

If you have trouble implementing these improvements or want to compare your solution with mine, you can find my upgraded Tiny Survey on GitHub at *https://github.com/Building-Apps-and-Games-in-the-Cloud/TinySurveyUpgraded.*

User sessions

You must be familiar with registering and logging in to a website to use its services. Tiny Survey might not be the kind of application you need to log in to, but we can learn a lot by adding user logins and sessions. So, let's do that. We first need to use MongoDB to create a store for all the user information.

Store user details

The following code contains the schema for the data stored about a Tiny Survey user: the user's name, password, and email address. It also contains a list of all the surveys they have completed. This means there is no need to store a `completedSurveys` cookie in their browser to track the surveys they have taken part in. We can use an id field from the database as a `creatorGUID`, removing the need for a cookie to track the survey owner. The schema also contains a `role` property, which allows us to implement role-based security so we can have a user with an `admin` role who can update passwords. The `SurveyUsers` model is exported for use by the application.

```
import mongoose from "mongoose";

const surveyUserSchema = new mongoose.Schema(
    {
        name: {                                          Display name for the user
            type: String,
            required: true
        },
        password: {                                      Password
            type: String,
            required: true
        },
        role: {                                          User role
```

```
        type: String,
        required: true
    },
    email: {                                                    User email
        type: String,
        required: true
    },
    completedSurveys:{                                          Completed surveys
        type: [String],
        default: []
    }
});

let SurveyUsers = mongoose.model('surveyusers', surveyUserSchema);

export { SurveyUsers as SurveyUsers };
```

The Tiny Survey application code can import the SurveyUsers object and use it to interact with the document in MongoDB, which stores the information. The document will be created automatically the first time we write something into it. Now that we have defined our user storage, we can use it in the Tiny Survey application to manage the users. Let's start by looking at how we will add new behaviors to the application to do this.

Register and login workflow

Figure 11-6 shows the workflow for a simple survey with the added login and registration elements. Tiny Survey will use a cookie to track a user session. The cookie is created when the user is authenticated and contains a token providing information about the session. The token is verified when the user visits a page in the application. The user is directed to the login page if the token has expired (the session has timed out) or the cookie is missing.

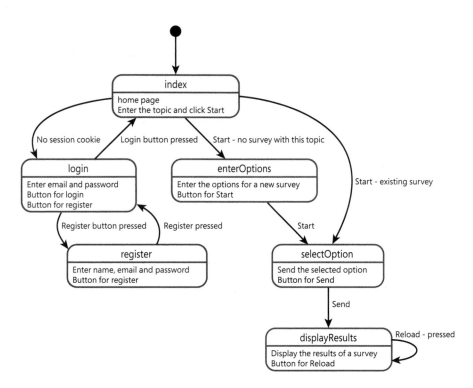

Figure 11-6 Log-in workflow

If the user doesn't have a user login, they can register. Let's start with a look at the registration page.

Register a user

Figure 11-7 shows the Tiny Survey **Register A New User** page, which contains a form with three fields: **Name**, **Email**, and **Password**. When the user clicks **Register**, the form is submitted to the `register` route, which stores the data in the `SurveyUsers` document in the database. However, before we store the user information, we need to talk about hashing.

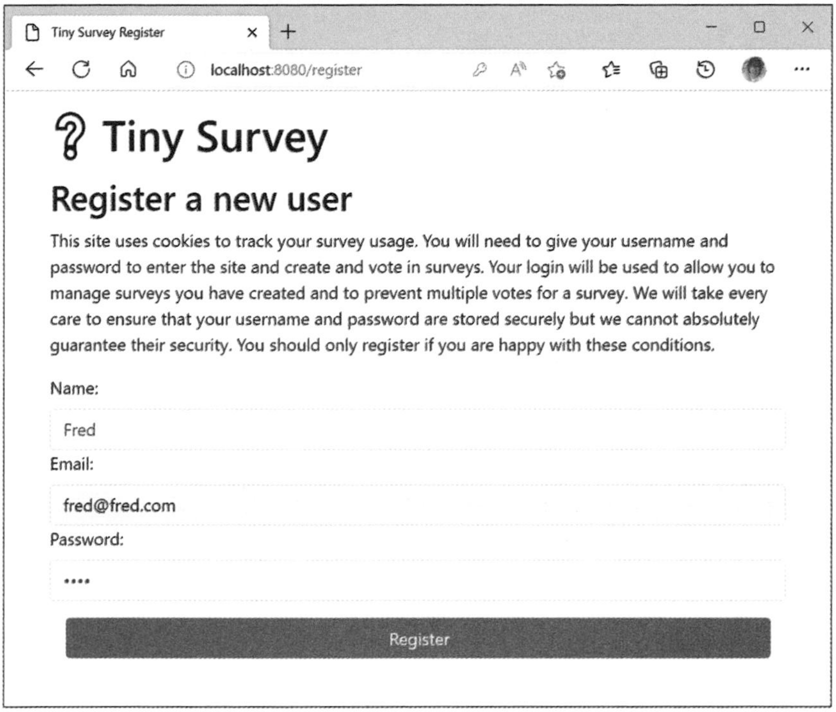

Figure 11-7 Register A New User

Hashing passwords

The password is one of the user properties that will be stored. You should never store passwords in the form they are entered. In other words, a password of "secret" should not be stored in the database as the string "secret." We prevent anyone with access to the `SurveyUsers` database from being able to view the password fields. We protect the password values from prying eyes by *hashing* them before storage. Hashing is a process that makes text unrecognizable. I think the name comes from creating a hash (a type of stew) by throwing all ingredients into a pan and then stirring them until you can't tell what's in there.

A good hash algorithm cannot be reversed; you can't take hashed text and work out the original text. The `bcrpt` library (*https://www.npmjs.com/package/bcrypt*) is used to make a hashed version of the password that is to be stored. The library is imported into the route as shown below:

```
import bcrypt from 'bcrypt';
```

The `bcrypt` library contains a function called `hash`, which can be used to hash our passwords. The `hash` function is called with two arguments: the string to be hashed and a number determining how many hashing passes will be made through the string. The more passes, the harder it is to unpick the hash. (Of course, more passes also means more time.) The Tiny Survey hash level is 10, which is a good level of security. A larger value would provide more secure hashing at the expense of using more computer power. The statement below shows how a hashed password is created. Note that this action may take some time to complete, so it is provided as an asynchronous function that must be called by using `await`.

```
const hashedPassword = await bcrypt.hash(request.body.password, 10);
```

The register route

The register route is followed when the user clicks **Register** on the registration form shown in **Figure 11-7**. The code for this route is shown below. First, a check is made to determine whether the user already exists, using the `findOne` method on the `SurveyUsers` model. The `findOne` method is supplied with an argument containing a matching pattern and returns the first matching document it finds. In this example, we want to match the email pattern in the `request` body. The body contains the email the user entered into the form; in **Figure 11-7**, the address is *fred@fred.com*. If the user is already present, an error is displayed; if the user is not present, we can create a new one.

The other values entered into the form are added to the hashed password to create a new survey user object, which is then stored in the database. The whole function is wrapped in a `try-catch` construction, and an error is displayed if an exception is thrown.

```
router.post('/', checkSurveys, async (request, response) => {
    try {
        // first try to find the user
        const existingUser = await SurveyUsers.findOne(                    Find the user
                        { email: request.body.email });

        if (existingUser) {                                               Does the user exist?
            messageDisplay("Register failed",                             Display an error if
            'User ${request.body.email} already exists', response);       we already have a
                                                                          user with this email
        }
                                                                          Hash the password
        else {
            const hashedPassword = await bcrypt.hash(request.body.password, 10);
```

```
                const user = new SurveyUsers(                          Create a user object
                    {
                        name: request.body.name,
                        password: hashedPassword,
                        role: 'user',
                        email: request.body.email
                    });
                await user.save();                                Save the user in the database
                messageDisplay("Register OK",
                    'User ${request.body.email} created',response);
        }
    }
    catch (err) {                                   Catch any exceptions and display a message
        messageDisplay("Register failed", 'Please contact support',response);
        return;
    }
})
```

CODE ANALYSIS

User registration

You might have some questions about this code.

Question: How does the hashing work?

> **Answer:** In Chapter 6, we saw how we could create pseudo-random sequences of values. Hashing uses the incoming text to create a pseudo-random sequence that is combined with the data to encode it in a way that makes it very hard to identify the original text.

Question: What does the `messageDisplay` function do?

> **Answer:** This is a helper function that accepts a heading, message, and response and then generates a message display page containing that information along with a **Continue** button, which links back to the Tiny Survey index page.

Question: What do the dollars and the curly brackets mean in the strings?

> **Answer:** This is called a *template literal*. The string must be enclosed in backticks (`) and can contain placeholders allowing you to drop expressions into the string. Each placeholder starts with a $ character and contains an expression inside braces. Placeholders are a neat way of creating formatted strings and are used to embed the email address into the message sent to the user.

Scan the QR code or visit *https://www.youtube.com/watch?v=4ykX1TT3vkY* for a video walk-through of this Make Something Happen.

Register a user

The starting point for this Make Something Happen is a version of Tiny Survey on GitHub at *https://github.com/Building-Apps-and-Games-in-the-Cloud/TinySurveyLogins*. Clone this repository to your machine and open it with Visual Studio Code.

You will have to create a `.env` file to configure the application. This file must contain five environment items. The first gives the connection to the database. The next two items are the initial admin username and password values. This username is created the first time the application runs. It is given the ability to reset user passwords. We will discuss the admin username later in the chapter. The final two items are the secret values used to create and maintain the webtokens that manage the sessions.

Use Visual Studio Code to create a `.env` file in the application containing the following lines. You can find these lines in the **README.md** file in the repository. Just copy them from that file:

```
DATABASE_URL=mongodb://localhost/tiny_surveys
INITIAL_ADMIN_USERNAME=surveyMaster@tinysurveys.com
INITIAL_ADMIN_PASSWORD=mango-chutney-diva
ACTIVE_TOKEN_SECRET=BAA95340FD3908F8571F87E30887B0E4870A4E8C4291A6498991B29661AB4
REFRESH_TOKEN_SECRET=416310A5824409FE02A5FBB8D59CB3E35E57BAA97E4B60A96EE18582DC50
```

Now start the application, open your browser, and navigate to *localhost:8080/index.html*. The Tiny Survey application will display the login page. You don't have a username yet, so click the **Register** button, as shown in **Figure 11-7**. Enter a name, username, and password and click register.

Now start the MongoDBCompass application. You first used this in the "Create a database" section of Chapter 10 when you created the Tiny Survey database. Now, you can use it to view the user you just created. Connect MongoDBCompass to the localhost database connection, open the database view, and select the **surveyusers** document.

You should see that there are two users. The first one is an admin user created automatically by Tiny Survey. (You will discover how this is used later in this chapter.) The second user is the one you just created. You can see that the `name` and `email` values are in clear text, but the `password` value is a long string of random-looking characters. This is a hashed version of the password, which I think you have probably guessed is "fred."

Now that the user and password values are stored in the database, we can use them to validate an application login. Let's do this next.

User login

Figure 11-8 shows the Tiny Server **Login** page displayed when a user visits any page in the application but doesn't have a session token cookie in their browser. The user fills in their **Email** and **Password** and clicks **Login** to start a Tiny Survey session. The email and password are entered into a form posted to the `login` route when **Login** is clicked.

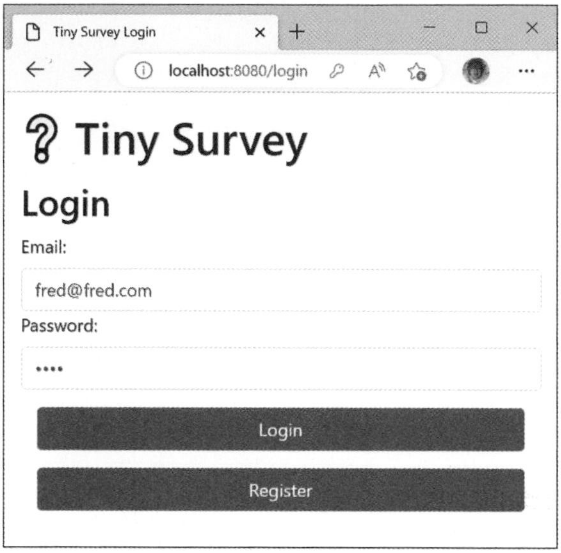

Figure 11-8 Log-in page

The code below implements the route. It starts by looking for the user. If the user is found, the `bcrypt.compare` function compares the password entered into the form with the hashed password stored in the database. If these two match, the code creates a session token, which is stored in a browser cookie. Once the cookie has been stored, the route redirects the user to the index page.

```
router.post('/', checkSurveys, async (request, response) => {
    try {
        // first find the user
        const user = await SurveyUsers.findOne({ email: request.body.email });

        if (user) {
            // we have the user - now check the password
            const validPassword = await bcrypt.compare(request.body.password,
                                                        user.password);
            if (validPassword) {
                // now make the jwt token to send back to the browser
                const accessToken = jwt.sign(
                    { id: user._id },                          Id for the token
                    process.env.ACTIVE_TOKEN_SECRET,      Encoding string for the token
                    {
                        algorithm: "HS256",              Configuration for the token
                        expiresIn: jwtExpirySeconds,
```

```
                });

            response.cookie("token", accessToken,
                            { maxAge: jwtExpirySeconds * 1000 });      Store the token
            response.redirect('/index.html');                          in a cookie
        }
        else {
            messageDisplay("Login failed", "Invalid user or password",
                            response);
        }
    }
    else {
        messageDisplay("Login failed", "Invalid user or password", response);
    }
    }
    catch (err) {
        messageDisplay("Login failed", 'Please contact support', response);
        return;
    }
})
```

Access tokens

I've used the word "token" several times in this chapter without explaining it. A token is a block of data describing a session, although I don't think that explanation helps much. You can think of it as a bit like a ticket that you need to get into an event. Each time you go into the event, the ticket is checked to ensure that it is still valid and that you can go in.

In the case of the Tiny Survey application, the ticket will be a cookie called a "token" stored in the application user's browser. The token is checked each time the user visits an application page. The best way to understand how it all works is by doing some detective work. Let's look at the token cookie to see how it works.

Scan the QR code or visit *https://www.youtube.com/watch?v=UXfTPPLGUV0* for a video walk-through of this Make Something Happen.

Investigate tokens

You start at the same point as in the previous Make Something Happen with the application at *https://github.com/Building-Apps-and-Games-in-the-Cloud/TinySurveyLogins* running, the browser open to *localhost:8080*, and the MongoDBCompass application running. You should have already created a Tiny Surveys user. Like in movies, you might also like to have some exciting hacking music running in the background. Start by logging in as the user you created and open the **Developer** view in your browser. Use the **Application** view to look at the cookies stored by the browser. You should see a cookie called **token**, which contains a large string of what looks like random text.

![Screenshot of browser developer tools showing the Tiny Survey application with the Application view open displaying the token cookie value]

We can use the debug tool provided by JSON Web Token (JWT) to look inside this token. Highlight the cookie value and copy it. Open the web page at *https://jwt.io/#debugger-io* and paste the cookie content into the left-side window.

The cookie contents will be decoded and displayed on the right-hand side. The actual payload of this token is the logged-in user's `id`. The id is a value we can get from the `SurveyUsers` database. When MongoDB creates a new document, it gives it a unique id. Tiny Surveys stores the id of a `SurveyUsers` document in the token so that it knows who is using the application. The user's `id` is the long number that starts with `639` in the payload panel above. The number you see in your token will be different. Open the MongoDB view of the database and open the `SurveyUsers` document. Now look for the entry for the user that you logged in with. You will find that the `id` on the debugging page matches the object's `id` in the database.

```
    _id: ObjectId('6396f241fa5e3f262bf92a1f')
    name: "Fred"
    password: "$2b$10$848gc495FyNuD0gdRoST/ONLajSPRRojondXkr50eZ8UTcpBjAWKe"
    role: "user"
    email: "fred@fred.com"
  > completedSurveys: Array
    __v: 0
```

This means code running on the server can pick up the current user `id` and use it to locate that user record. From this exercise, you can see that the data in a token is not protected. Anyone can paste the contents of a token cookie into the JWT debug site and look at the payload inside it. However, it turns out that the content of a cookie is not what the server is concerned about. The server is really concerned that the content of a cookie it receives has not been tampered with. The server will make a token containing a user id and then store it in a cookie from the browser. Later the server will receive the cookie back from the browser and work with that user. It should not be possible to send back a different user id to the server. This would be a way of breaking security and getting control of surveys created by someone else. To solve this problem, the server keeps a "secret" that it uses to sign the token before it is stored. The secret is held in an environment variable. The .env file holds all the environment variables. Go to Visual Studio Code and open the .env file in the Tiny Surveys project.

The ACTIVE_TOKEN_SECRET value is a long string of random text. It is used to sign the token. This string must be kept secret. Anyone with the key can create tokens that the Tiny Survey server would consider valid. We can test that the key is valid for a given token by pasting it into the debug page. Copy the active token secret out of the .env file and find the section of the page with the title "VERIFY SIGNATURE."

Paste the key into the textbox and click the "secret base64 encoded" checkbox. The page will now check that the token you have entered was encoded using that secret.

The page will now display Signature Verified. The Tiny Survey server will perform this process when it receives a token back from the browser.

You can turn off your hacker background music now. We have shown two important things:

- Tokens are stored in cookies and can contain payloads for the application to use.

- Tokens are signed when they are created and verified when they are received from the browser.

Now, let's look at the code that creates a token.

Create an access token

We are using a library called `JsonWebtoken` (*https://jwt.io/*) to create the tokens that will serve as the tickets that allow access to our application. The JWT library is imported at the start of the `login` route.

```
import jwt from 'jsonwebtoken';
```

The code below is in the `login` route we have just seen. It creates a token. The token contains the `id` of the person who is logging in. This code only runs once the username and password have been validated. It calls the `sign` function from the JWT library to create a token.

The first argument to the `sign` call is an object containing the payload to be stored in the token. In this case, it is the user `id` for the user logging in. You should never put confidential information in the token payload because, as we saw above, extracting this information from the token is very easy.

The second argument to the `sign` function is the secret that will be used to encode this token. This is held in an environment variable.

The third argument is an object containing some JWT configuration information. The first item specifies the algorithm to construct and encode the token. Tiny Survey uses HS256, representing a good compromise between performance and security. The second configuration item for Tiny Survey is the cookie's expiry time, which is held by the `jwtExpirySeconds` variable. This is how we control how long the session will be active. After the token expires, it can't be used. The session expiry for Tiny Survey is 30 seconds. Each time the user visits the site, a new token is generated, so if the user doesn't act on the site for 30 seconds, they will be automatically disconnected and have to log in again. If you think they might find this too frustrating, you can increase the value to give them more time.

```
const accessToken = jwt.sign(
    { id: user._id },                    Data to be stored in the token
    process.env.ACTIVE_TOKEN_SECRET,     GUID used to encode the token
    {
        algorithm: "HS256",              Hashing algorithm to use for the token
        expiresIn: jwtExpirySeconds,     Expiry time for the token
    });
```

Now that we have our token, we can store it in a cookie. The statement below creates a `"token"` cookie containing the `accessToken` value we just created. Note that the cookie also has an expiry date matching the token expiry. The maximum age for a cookie is expressed in milliseconds (thousandths of a second), so the value is multiplied by 1,000.

```
response.cookie("token", accessToken, { maxAge: jwtExpirySeconds * 1000 });
```

The final statement in the route uses a method we've not seen before. The `redirect` function redirects the browser to the specified address. In this case, the log-in process has finished, and the user is directed back to the application's index page. The index page will then pick up the cookie, validate it, and allow the user to work with Tiny Survey.

```
response.redirect('/index.html');
```

Authenticate tokens

We now know how to create and store user information and then use it to authenticate a login. We also know that when a user has been authenticated, the browser will store a token containing the user's `id`. The token has a limited life and has been signed with a secret held in the application, ensuring that fake tokens cannot be created.

The final piece of the authentication jigsaw is how the application uses the token to authenticate page access. That is what we are going to do now. We will create some middleware that we can add to our pages so that they can only be used when a request to them contains a valid token cookie. We know about middleware; it is code inserted into the application. We've created middleware to ask the user if cookies are okay and ensure the survey connection is valid when a page is visited.

Now, we will create a piece of middleware to validate a token when a page is visited. Below, the function `authenticateToken` gets the token and uses `JWT.verify` to verify the token contents and extract the user id payload. It then looks up the user in the database and adds a `user` property to the `response`. This means any route using the `authenticateToken` middleware will automatically be given the user information to work with. If any actions fail, the middleware returns the user to the log-in prompt. At the end of the middleware, the `next` function is called to move on to the next middleware function.

```
async function authenticateToken(request, response, next) {

  const token = request.cookies.token;                    Get the token

  // if the cookie is not set go to the login page
  if (!token) {
    response.redirect('/login');                          Go to the login page to log in
    return;
  }

  let payload;                                            Will hold the payload from the token
```

```
try {
  payload = jwt.verify(token, process.env.ACTIVE_TOKEN_SECRET);      Verify the token
} catch (e) {                                            If the validate fails, an exception is thrown
  response.redirect('/login');                             Go to login if the validation fails
  return;
}


// got the token - use the ID in the token to look up the user
const user = await SurveyUsers.findOne({ _id: payload.id });

if (user == null) {                                          If the user is not found, go to login
  response.redirect('/login');
  return;
}
|// renew the token                                          Renew the access token – see later
response.user = user;                                   Add the user property to the response object
next();                                                  Perform the next middleware item
}
```

This middleware code is stored in the helper folder and imported into the routes that want to use it. It is inserted into most of the routes in the application. However, it is not inserted into the login or register routes because those pages run before the token is created. Below, you can see how authenticateToken is inserted into a route. It is called after the checkSurveys middleware has run.

```
router.get('/:topic', checkSurveys, authenticateToken, async (request, response) =>
{
  // route code here

});
```

Session renewal

When we created a token, we noted that the token expiry was set for 30 seconds. This means the user will have to log in every 30 seconds, which they will find very frustrating. We can renew the session token each time the user visits a site page. This means that a session will time out after 30 seconds of inactivity. We can do this in the `authenticateToken` middleware. The payload of a token contains an `exp` property that gives the Unix time in seconds when the token will expire. Unix time started at 0:0:0 on January 1, 1970 (the start of the Unix Epoch) and has been counting up ever since. The code below gets the time and calculates how long before the token expires. If the time left is less than `jstRenewSeconds` (in our case, 10 seconds), a new token is created and stored.

```
const nowUnixSeconds = Math.round(Number(new Date()) / 1000);          Get time in seconds

const tokenSecondsLeft = payload.exp - nowUnixSeconds;                 Get the time left for this
                                                                       cookie in seconds

if (tokenSecondsLeft < jwtRenewSeconds) {                              Is it time to renew?
  // need to make a new token
  const accessToken = jwt.sign(                                        Make a new token
    { id: user.id },
    process.env.ACTIVE_TOKEN_SECRET,                                   Use a different secret to
    {                                                                  encode the renew token
      algorithm: "HS256",
      expiresIn: jwtExpirySeconds,
    });
                                                                       Store the cookie
  response.cookie("token", accessToken, { maxAge: jwtExpirySeconds * 1000 });
}
```

The `jwtExpirySeconds` and `jwtRenewSeconds` values have been set to demonstrate the time-out and renew behaviors without waiting too long. Making the time longer is more convenient for the user but less secure because an unattended machine will take longer to time out. You can do much more to improve the security of tokens. The additional entry in the `.env` file allows you to create a refresh behavior using a different secret from the active one.

Role-based security

Role-based security gives users different abilities based on the role that is assigned to them. It is used in Tiny Survey so that users can have their passwords reset without anyone having to manually manipulate the `SurveyUser` database document. At the start of this chapter, when creating the `SurveyUser` schema, we noted that each user has a `role` property. The `role` property is always set to the string "user" when registering a new user. However, a second role is also available to users—admin. Users with the admin role are directed to a different page when they follow the index route.

The code for this route is shown below. If the user has the `admin` role, the `adminindex` page is rendered. The page contains a form that allows the administrator to set a new password for any of the system's users.

```
import express from 'express';
import { checkSurveys } from '../helpers/checkstorage.mjs';
import { authenticateToken } from '../helpers/authenticateToken.mjs';


const router = express.Router();


// Home page - just render the index
router.get('/', checkSurveys, authenticateToken, (request, response) => {
  if(response.user.role == "admin"){
    response.render('adminindex.ejs', { name: response.user.name});    ──── Admin index
  }
  else {
    response.render('index.ejs', { name: response.user.name});         ──── User index
  }
});
```

Figure 11-9 shows the **Welcome Admin** index page, which contains a form into which the administrator can enter an updated password for the specified user. When the **Update Password** button is clicked, the `updatepassword` path is followed.

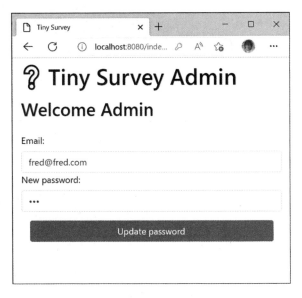

Figure 11-9 Admin index

The code for this path is shown below. It first finds the user in the database and checks to see if the user has the admin role. If so, the password is updated, encrypted, and saved to the database.

```
router.post('/', checkSurveys, authenticateToken, async (request, response) => {
    console.log("Updating a password.");

    if (response.user.role == "admin") {

        try {
            // first find the user
            const user = await SurveyUsers.findOne({ email: request.body.email });

            if (user) {
                try {
                    const hashedPassword =
                        await bcrypt.hash(request.body.password, 10);
                    user.password = hashedPassword;
                    await user.save();
                    messageDisplay("Updated OK",
                        'User ${request.body.email} updated', response);
                } catch (err) {
                    console.log("err:", err.message);
                    messageDisplay("Update failed", "Please contact support",
                                    response);
                }
            }
            else {
                messageDisplay("Update failed",
                    'User ${request.body.email} not found', response);
            }
        }
        catch (err) {
            messageDisplay("Update failed", "Please contact support", response);
            return;
        }
    }
    else {
        messageDisplay("Update failed", "User not admin", response);
    }
})

export { router as index };
```

Creating the admin user

You may be wondering where the admin user comes from. Tiny Survey uses a helper class called `userManager`. This contains an `init` function that creates an admin user if one does not exist. The `init` function in this class is called each time the application starts. You can see the code for the function below.

```
async init()
{
    const adminUser = await SurveyUsers.findOne(          Find the admin user
            { email: process.env.INITIAL_ADMIN_USERNAME });

    if (!adminUser) {                                     If there is no admin user make one
        console.log('  Admin user not registered');
        const hashedPassword =
            await bcrypt.hash(process.env.INITIAL_ADMIN_PASSWORD, 10);
        const user = new SurveyUsers(                     Create the admin user
            {
                name: "Admin",
                password: hashedPassword,
                role: 'admin',
                email: process.env.INITIAL_ADMIN_USERNAME
            });
        await user.save();                                Save the admin user
        console.log("  Admin user successfully registered");
    }
}
```

MAKE SOMETHING HAPPEN 59

Scan the QR code or visit *https://www.youtube.com/watch?v=owlNoW8Otk0* for a video walkthrough of this Make Something Happen.

Play with Tiny Survey

Now that you know how session management works, it is worth spending some time with the application. You can use the admin username and password from the preceding code to log in and change some passwords. The application behaves like lots of applications you have already used. Treat it as a place you want to visit or a murder mystery you want to solve and work through the code. You can put breakpoints in the parts you don't quite understand and watch them run. You can also use the techniques you have seen in new applications that you create.

What you have learned

This has been a fun chapter. We now know how to create reliable and secure sessions for an application. This is what we have learned.

- User tracking is achieved by storing a cookie in the user's browser. The cookie contains a unique value that identifies that user. The cookie value will be sent to the server each time the user opens a page of the application.

- User tracking has privacy implications. It is considered polite (and in some areas is required by law) to get the user's consent before tracking a user with a cookie.

- The Unified Modeling Language (UML) defines a set of diagrams that can be used to express the behavior of a system. We can use the State Diagram from UML to express the workflow through a web application. PlantUML (*https://www.plantuml.com*) provides a good way of quickly creating diagrams from the text. Note that these diagrams are not used to create or design code. They are used to express the behaviors of an application.

- If you want to perform the same action on many pages in an application, you can create middleware to do this.

- A cookie can be given a maximum age (in milliseconds) to persist in the browser.

- We can create page templates that can be used to display messages or receive options from an application user and route them to other pages.

- Properties in a MongoDB schema can be made "required," in which case an exception is thrown if an attempt is made to store an object missing those properties.

- User log-in information for an application can be stored as documents in a MongoDB database. Care should be taken to ensure that important information is stored securely. Passwords should be hashed before storage.

- Hashing is the process of taking an item and making it unrecognizable. It is not the same as encryption because it cannot be reversed. You might encrypt a message and send it to a friend, who will decrypt it to read it back. But a hashed message is rendered completely unreadable and can never be converted back to the original text. Hashing works well with passwords. The text that the user enters is hashed and compared with the hashed password stored in the system. If the two match, the user has entered a valid password.

- The `bcrypt` library can take items and hash them. It allows the user to determine how much time it takes over the hashing process.

- Sessions can be managed in Express by creating an access token stored in a cookie. The token contains payload information that is used by the application. The token is checked each time an application page is loaded. The user will be directed to the log-in page if the session is missing or expired.

- The payload in a token is not protected; it can be read back from the token. However, the token can be signed when created using a "secret string" known only to the token's creator. The token creator can check the signature when the token is received to ensure the content is valid. This is important because otherwise, a malicious user could create a token that contains invalid information.

- When a token is created, it is given an expiry time, after which it cannot be used. The receiver of a token can read this value and create a new token with a new expiry date if they want to keep the session going.

- The `jsonwebtoken` library provides a `sign` function that creates a token. The function is supplied with the payload object, the secret string used to sign the token, and a configuration object that can set the algorithm and the token's expiry time.

- The `jsonwebtoken` library provides a verify token given to the token and secret string and returns the payload object. The function throws an exception if the token is not verified.

- We can implement token validation by using a piece of middleware to check the token content and route the user to the log-in page if the token content is invalid. The middleware can also check the time left before a token expires and use this to trigger the creation of a new token if the previous one is close to expiry.

- System users can be given roles determining what behaviors they can access in an application.

To reinforce your understanding of this chapter, you might want to consider the following "profound questions."

Question: I don't understand how to design a web application. Where do I start?

Answer: The Tiny Survey design is a good thing to look at. You can use this as the basis of lots of other applications. Think of the application as a bit like a treasure hunt, where you go from location to location, getting clues telling you where to go next. In a web-based application, you go from page to page. When you arrive at a page, the route code for that page runs and decides which page to go to next. You could start by identifying pages you know the application will need, drawing them as boxes on a large piece of paper, and then working out how the user will move from one to another. You can then consider what data needs to be passed from one page to another and consider how you will do it. Look at how Tiny Survey passes the survey topic between pages. Once you have walked through your design, you can design your underlying storage schema (the things the application must store) and then create the page templates and the route code.

Question: Why are you using full-width buttons on the pages?

Answer: Good question. Up until this chapter, we have had buttons with labels. In this chapter, the buttons are larger and have the label inside them. This makes it much easier to handle changes in the screen size if you have multiple buttons.

Question: Is the user tracking in Tiny Survey really going to compromise the security of the user?

Answer: Presently, we just use the `creatorGUID` in Tiny Survey to allow the creator of a survey to manage that survey. However, once the tracking cookie is in place, there is no limit to the things that we can do with it. We can profile users based on the surveys they have created. We could add code to the Tiny Survey application that stored the voting behavior of the user by adding lists of `creatorGUID` values to each option in the survey. Then we would know exactly who had voted for what. This could all be done without adding any extra code to the application at the user's end. Whenever you allow a site to track you with a cookie, you must remember that you are trusting the operator site not to use it for invasive purposes.

Question: Do I have to learn the Unified Modeling Language?

Answer: No. You don't have to learn any of it. Use whatever drawing tool works best for you, but please do draw something, particularly if you are part of a team.

Question: How many cookies can be stored by the browser?

Answer: There is no upper limit, but most applications limit themselves to a few. It is interesting to open the **Developer Tools** and look at the cookies created by the web pages you visit.

Question: How do we recover if a user loses their `creatorGUID`?

Answer: Tiny Survey is not a serious application. But what if someone thought it was? What would happen if a user lost their `creatorGUID`? This kind of thing can happen when people use systems in ways that the creator didn't expect. Perhaps a doctor might use Tiny Survey as part of their research on many patients. Then they might buy a new computer and find themselves unable to manage their surveys. The solution to this problem lies with the Compass application supplied by MongoDB. This gives us a window into the data that lets us view `creatorGUID` values in records stored in the survey data. We could tell the doctor their `creatorGUID`, and they could set this by hand in by using the Application view in the Debug Tools in the browser.

Question: How can we stop someone masquerading as a creator?

Answer: The answer to the previous question raises the prospect of someone copying a `creatorGUID` into their browser so that they could delete surveys created by someone else. The answer to this question is that we can't stop someone from doing this, but they will only be able to do it if they know the `creatorGUID` of the person they are targeting. This is stored on their computer, and the attacker would require direct access to it.

Question: What is the difference between cookie and database access control?

Answer: A cookie is a lump of data sent from a website server and stored by the browser. The next time the browser visits that website, it will send the cookie's contents to the server as part of any HTTP requests. We used a cookie to try to prevent multiple voting in a survey. The cookie contained the topics of all the surveys the user had voted for. However, it is easy for users to change or delete cookies in their browser. The final version of Tiny Survey requires the user to log in before they can use the survey system. The information stored about a user includes a list of surveys where the user has voted. This provides a much more reliable way of tracking user activity, but it does require the user to log in and be uniquely identified before each survey session.

Question: Do I need to tell the user the application uses cookies if I use user registration to manage access to Tiny Survey?

Answer: Previous versions of Tiny Survey used cookies the browser stores to track users. The final version of Tiny Survey requires the user to log in with a password. However, although cookies are not used to track the user, they are used to maintain a login session so you should still inform the user that they are required.

Question: Why do you use the MongoDB `id` property of a user record to track the survey creator? Can you just use the `email` property instead?

Answer: Just to clarify the question: In the previous version of Tiny Survey, we added the `creatorGUID` property to all the surveys created. The `creatorGUID` was stored in a cookie in the user's browser and used to allow the survey creator to manage it. In the "log-in" version of Tiny Survey, we now use a database-created field—the `id` of a user record—to track the survey creator. The survey creator's email address will be unique, so why don't we use that? The reason is that we might decide to let the users change their email addresses in a future version of the application. If this was keyed to all their surveys, the surveys would also need to be changed. However, the `id` property provided by MongoDB is guaranteed to be unique and will never needs to be changed.

Question: How much data can you store in a token?

Answer: A token contains a payload object that can have multiple properties. It is best to keep the payload content as small as possible. Rather than storing things like images and sounds in the payload, you should store links to them.

Question: Can I add more management functions to Tiny Surveys?

Answer: Yes. It would be easy to add more elements to the admin home page. You could change usernames and even add user registration features.

Question: What happens if we lose the password for the admin user?

Answer: If the admin password gets lost, we would need to use the Compass application supplied by MongoDB to store an updated password value for the admin user. We would, of course, have to encrypt the password before storing it. Another solution would be to register a new user and then change their role property to admin.

Question: How would I implement a logout behavior?

Answer: The present version of Tiny Survey has no "logout." Sessions will time out after a while. If you want to add an explicit logout, you could create a route that deletes the token cookie, forcing the user to log in the next time they visit the site.

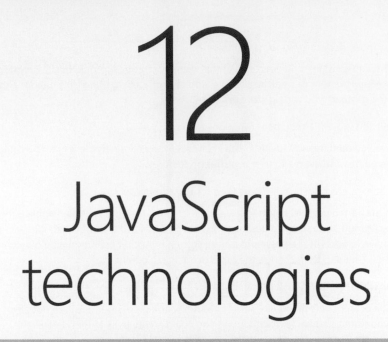

12

JavaScript technologies

What you will learn

This chapter is a bit different from the previous one. In this chapter, I want to show you some cool places you can take your JavaScript skills. The example files for this chapter contain some walkthroughs to get you started, and I'll also point you to GitHub repositories that you can download and work with. We will create our own cloud, make remote-controlled lights and locks, implement a remote button, explore how to build our own Internet of Things, and take a look at game creation. Then, I'll give you a few directions to take your JavaScript even further, from running JavaScript inside a watch to creating a JavaScript application that can tell when you are happy.

Make your own cloud

We have run our JavaScript applications in the browser, on a PC, and in the cloud. Now, we will deploy them to a much smaller device, a Raspberry Pi. This is a small but powerful computer that can run `node.js`. We can use it to host web applications (including Tiny Survey and Cheese Finder) around our local network at home. It is possible to make our hosted applications visible on the Internet, but this requires network configuration, which is beyond the scope of this book. You can start with an empty Raspberry Pi and finish with a server onto which you can deploy applications from this book.

Set up a Raspberry Pi server

The first thing we need to do is set up a Raspberry Pi to act as a server. There are several versions of Raspberry Pi available. The cheapest, the Raspberry Pi Zero, is priced at $15 USD. This would not make a great desktop PC, but it works well as a standalone server or Internet of Things (IoT) device. More expensive versions of the Pi have more power and connectivity, but all the Raspberry Pi devices have a 40-pin connector that can link to external devices. The software and data for a Raspberry Pi device are held on a microSD card. You can change the operating system and data in a Pi simply by changing the card. The instructions that follow tell you how to set up a microSD card with the Raspberry Pi operating system and then connect to it.

🚀 **MAKE SOMETHING HAPPEN 60**

Scan the QR code or visit *https://www.youtube.com/watch?v=4hVDSYNy6ks* for a video walk-through of this Make Something Happen.

Build a server

You will need a Raspberry Pi, a blank micro-SD card, and a micro-SD card reader to perform this activity. Plug the SD card reader into your computer, insert the SD card into the reader, and open the site at *https://www.raspberrypi.com/software/.* Download and install the Raspberry Pi imager program from that site. You will use this to put the operating system onto the card. Start the imaging software. It may ask you to confirm that you want to change the settings on your machine; if so, confirm this is what you want to do.

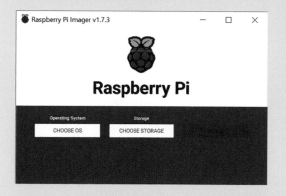

Now, click the **CHOOSE OS** button to select the operating system you want to use.

Pick the first option, **Raspberry Pi OS (32-Bit)** and click **CHOOSE STORAGE** to select the SD card you want to write.

My system has two external drives, so I must make sure I'm using the correct one—the 8.0 GB drive. If you see more than one drive, you should know which is the SD card. One way to do this is to remove the SD card, run the installer, and note the drives shown. Then exit the installer, plug in the SD card, and run the installer again. The card that appears is the one you want to use.

Now that you have selected the source and destination, you can configure the operating system that is about to be written. This is very useful because you can access and use the Pi as soon as it has been booted. Click the gear wheel at the bottom right of the Installer window to open the **Advanced Options** dialog.

The hostname is the first thing you must set. This will allow you to find the Pi on your local network when it starts running. Give your machine a name and make a note of it; I've called mine **iotmaster**. Set a username and password for the Pi, and make sure you note these as well. Make sure to choose the **Enable SSH** and **Use Password Authentication** settings. Finally, you can enter your network WiFi credentials (**Set Username And Password** and **Configure Wireless LAN**). The newly built Pi will automatically connect to your network when it starts up. You can set other options, but these are the most important. Click **SAVE** to save them. Now, click **WRITE** to write the image. The installer will ask you to confirm the action before it begins writing the operating system to the card. It will download the operating system if required. Once the SD card has been written, you can insert it into your Raspberry Pi and power it up. Give it a few minutes to get started and connect to it from your PC. Open a PowerShell command prompt (right-click the Windows button and select PowerShell from the menu that appears) and enter the following command. Replace the word **hostname** with the name you gave your machine.

```
ssh hostname.local -l pi
```

The `ssh` command tries to open a secure shell connection to a host. The host should reply as shown below.

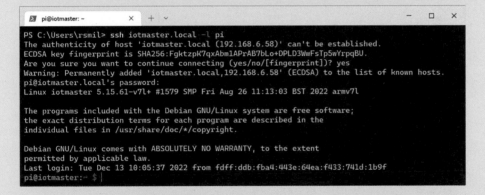

The first time you contact the Pi, the Secure Shell Protocol (SSH) program will ask you to verify the authenticity of the connection. You can see this at the top of the above screenshot. Just reply yes when asked if you want to continue connecting. You will now be connected to your Pi, as shown above. If the Pi does not respond, ensure that it is powered up, that the hostname you entered matches the one it was created with, and that the Pi is connected to the same network as your PC. Leave the machine and the terminal program open for the next activity.

Installing node

Now that we have a working Raspberry Pi, we can connect to it and put it to work. The Raspberry Pi computer can run a graphical user interface. You can connect a keyboard, mouse, and monitor and use it as a fully-fledged computer. You can even install Visual Studio Code on the machine to develop programs. However, you will probably find that your main computer will give you a better experience, as the Raspberry Pi is not quite fast enough to complete with a laptop or a desktop PC. We will control our Pi using the terminal interface. In Chapter 4, in the "Install node" section, we used the terminal to work with node. You can also use those commands on the Pi, although the prompt is slightly different. You will notice that some commands we enter have the word sudo in front of them. This "supervisor do" abbreviation means that the command should be given supervisor permissions when running.

MAKE SOMETHING HAPPEN 61

Scan the QR code or visit *https://www.youtube.com/watch?v=E4Wvir0Vg3Y* for a video walk-through of this Make Something Happen.

Install node

Now that you have your Pi running and connected, you are going to install node so that you can run JavaScript. This involves typing a couple of commands. The first command gets the latest version of node onto your machine; the second installs it.

```
sudo curl -fsSL https://deb.nodesource.com/setup_16.x | sudo bash -
sudo apt-get install -y nodejs
```

Both commands generate quite a bit of output. When they have finished, you can enter the command to start node.

node

```
pi@iotmaster: ~                    ×    +  ∨                    —  □  ×

0 upgraded, 1 newly installed, 0 to remove and 0 not upgraded.
Need to get 24.2 MB of archives.
After this operation, 120 MB of additional disk space will be used.
Get:1 https://deb.nodesource.com/node_16.x bullseye/main armhf nodejs armhf 16.18.1-deb-1nodes
ource1 [24.2 MB]
Fetched 24.2 MB in 6s (3,874 kB/s)
Selecting previously unselected package nodejs.
(Reading database ... 106329 files and directories currently installed.)
Preparing to unpack .../nodejs_16.18.1-deb-1nodesource1_armhf.deb ...
Unpacking nodejs (16.18.1-deb-1nodesource1) ...
Setting up nodejs (16.18.1-deb-1nodesource1) ...
Processing triggers for man-db (2.9.4-2) ...
pi@iotmaster:~ $ node
Welcome to Node.js v16.18.1.
Type ".help" for more information.
>
```

Congratulations, you now have a server to host your applications. You can use the command .exit to leave node and return to the command prompt.

Host an application

Now that we have node on our computer, we need to get the application code. We can use the Git program to do this. We worked with Git via the command line in Chapter 8 when we created the Tiny Survey Project. Now we are going to use Git to load a repository from GitHub. The Pi has the Git program pre-installed, so we can just use it from the command prompt.

🚀 **MAKE SOMETHING HAPPEN 62**

Scan the QR code or visit *https://www.youtube.com/watch?v=cPEk2CP3oCs* for a video walk-through of this Make Something Happen.

Host an application

You are going to use Git to download repositories from GitHub onto the Pi. Before you do this, you need to install the Git application. Enter the following command:

```
sudo apt-get install -y git
```

You will see the Git program installed. Now you can clone a repository onto your Pi. The command below copies a version of TinySurvey onto your machine. Enter it on a single line.

```
git clone https://github.com/Building-Apps-and-Games-in-the-Cloud/TinySurveyFilestore
```

The Git program creates a folder that contains all the files in the repository. View the contents using the cd (change directory) and ls (list files) commands. Enter each command below and press **Enter** after each.

```
cd TinySurveyFilestore/
ls
```

You can see all the files that have been fetched from GitHub. However, at the moment, the application is missing all the libraries. You must use npm to install these for you. Type in the following command and press **Enter**.

```
npm install
```

Once the library files have been downloaded, you can run the TinySurvey application using node.js.

```
node tinysurvey.mjs
```

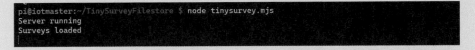

Now, you can open the browser on your computer and visit the site hosted by the Pi. This version of Tiny Survey will be running behind port 8080, so you need to add 8080 to the command, as shown below. Note that I called my server `iotmaster`; you will have to enter the name of your server in the URL instead:

```
http://iotmaster.local:8080/index.html
```

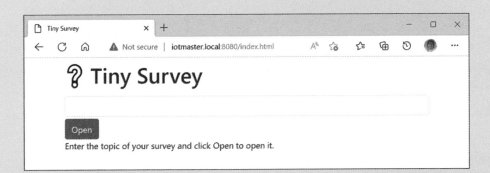

You are now running Tiny Survey on a machine you have just built. Congratulations! You can try downloading other repositories from GitHub and running them. Press **CTRL+C** to interrupt a running site and get back to the command prompt.

Use MongoDB on your server

The MongoDB database is not running on our Raspberry Pi, so any applications that try to connect to a local database will fail. To run MongoDB on your Pi, you must install a 64-bit version of the operating system. You can find a nice description of how to do it by visiting

https://www.mongodb.com/developer/products/mongodb/mongodb-on-raspberry-pi/

Shut down the server

The last thing we will do in this section is to learn how to shut down the server. While it is usually okay to just turn off the power to stop a Raspberry Pi, you should really follow a proper shutdown sequence to make sure that the operating system has the chance to close any open files and resources.

MAKE SOMETHING HAPPEN 63

Scan the QR code or visit *https://www.youtube.com/watch?v=hlyCRdN8NRc* for a video walk-through of this Make Something Happen.

Shut down the server

Start by using **CTRL+C** to stop the running server. Now enter the following command:

```
sudo shutdown -h now
```

The server will stop, and your shell connection will eventually time out.

Running a server

This has been the briefest of introductions to creating your own server. The Raspberry Pi uses a version of Linux as its operating system. If you want to practice running and configuring Linux, you can run Linux on your Windows PC using the Windows Subsystem for Linux. Visit *https://learn.microsoft.com/en-us/windows/wsl/install* to find out more.

Control hardware from a server

The Raspberry Pi we used to create a server can also be connected to hardware via the device's General-Purpose Input/Output (GPIO) pin connector. This is the row of exposed pins on the top. These connections can be used in a variety of ways. We will use an output pin to control an LED and as an input to read a button. The Raspberry Pi does not have the power to drive large lights and motors from its outputs, but the signals can control relays and other circuits. A Raspberry Pi can also read signals with variable levels (analog) and digital (on/off) signals produced by the switch we will use.

Browser-controlled light

We are going to start by creating a browser-controlled light. The lamp can be turned on and off by clicking buttons on a web page hosted by Raspberry Pi. We have made web pages containing buttons before, but now we will create a route on the server that turns the lights on and off. The page shown in **Figure 12-1** contains two buttons.

Figure 12-1 Light controller

The HTML elements for the buttons are shown below. When they are clicked, they navigate to the `setLightState` route with a route parameter that is either `on` or `off`.

```
<button onclick="window.location.href='/setLightState/on'">
    Light On
</button>
<button onclick="window.location.href='/setLightState/off'">
    Light Off
</button>
```

When the button is clicked, the browser loads a page from the setLightState. The setLightState route handler reads the route parameter and calls a function to turn a LED connected to the Raspberry Pi on or off. The code for the route is shown below. The lightControl object contains methods to turn the light on or off.

```
router.get('/:state', (request, response) => {

  let state = request.params.state;

  if (state == "on"){
    lightControl.on();
  }

  if (state == "off"){
    lightControl.off();
  }
  response.redirect('/index.html');
});
```

The lightControl object is an instance of the OutGPIO class that talks to the Raspberry Pi hardware. The OutGPIO class is shown below. It uses a library called onoff, which contains a class called Gpio providing access to the Raspberry Pi hardware. The onoff library must be installed using npm to be used in this program.

```
import * as onoff from 'onoff'; //include onoff to interact with the GPIO
class OutGPIO {
    constructor() {
    }

    init() {
        console.log("Initialising OutGPIO");
        if (onoff.Gpio.accessible) {                    Do we have hardware access?
            this.gpio = new onoff.Gpio(4, 'out');       Make a Gpio instance
        }
```

```
        }

    on() {
        console.log("OutGPIO on");
        if (onoff.Gpio.accessible) {
            this.gpio.writeSync(1);                         Set the output high
        }
    }

    off() {
        if (onoff.Gpio.accessible) {
            this.gpio.writeSync(0);                         Set the output low
        }
        console.log("OutGPIO off");
    }
}
```

The OutGPIO class contains on and off methods to control an external device, setting the output level to on (high) or off (low).

Output hardware

The led we are going to control via the web page hosted on the Raspberry Pi is connected to the General-Purpose Input/Output (GPIO) pin connector on the Pi. **Figure 12-2** shows how an LED connects to a Raspberry Pi pin. The pin we are using is called GPIO 4. Each pin is represented by a number, but this doesn't relate to the pin numbers on the connector itself. You can find a complete description of the pins and what they can be used for here:

https://www.raspberrypi.com/documentation/computers/raspberry-pi.html

The 330-ohm resistor is added to limit the current flow through the LED. Without it, we may damage both the Raspberry Pi and the LED. When our program writes 1 to the output port, the Pi sets the voltage on the output pin to 3.3 volts. This causes a current to flow through the LED and the resistor to the ground, making the LED light up.

Figure 12-3 shows the circuit in physical form. The object on the right is called a *breadboard* and has holes into which we can push wires and component connections. The holes are connected horizontally underneath by metal strips, so if we arrange the components as shown in **Figure 12-3**, we create the circuit shown in **Figure 12-2**.

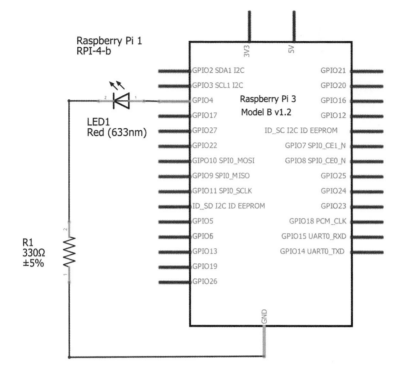

Figure 12-2 Raspberry Pi LED output circuit

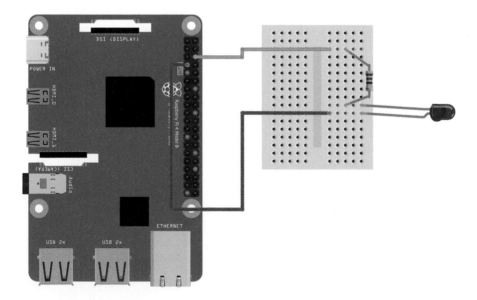

Figure 12-3 Raspberry Pi LED output breadboard

Scan the QR code or visit *https://www.youtube.com/watch?v=cJzLNNkgVmU* for a video walkthrough of this Make Something Happen.

Control an output

You will need a Raspberry Pi and the hardware shown in **Figure 12-3**. The code is on GitHub at *https://github.com/Building-Apps-and-Games-in-the-Cloud/RemoteLight*. Use Git to clone the software onto your Pi and then start it. Then use a browser on your PC to navigate to the page hosted by the Pi (shown in **Figure 12-1**)and press the **Light On** button. You should see the LED go on and off.

The code at *https://github.com/Building-Apps-and-Games-in-the-Cloud/RemoteLock* could be used to create a remote-controlled lock. It asks for a password. If the password is entered correctly, the program pulses the output for 1 second to trigger a latch to unlock. You will need to look inside the program files for the application to determine the password.

Remote button

We now know how to make a Raspberry Pi application that can host a web page that allows remote users to control the state of an output from the Pi. Next, we will make an application that reads the button state of a button connected to the server and sends this state to users viewing a web page hosted by the Pi. We could use this to start a race. Everyone in the race could visit the page, and when the button connected to the server was pressed, their browsers would tell them the race had started.

Figure 12-4 shows the display produced by the application. The UP message indicates the button is not pressed. When the button is pressed, the display changes to DOWN. Many people could view this page and see the button change to DOWN when it is pressed on the server.

Figure 12-4 Server button

Input hardware

We will use a button to provide the input to the Raspberry Pi running the server application. The button contains a switch that is closed when the button is pressed. We can connect this to a pin on the Raspberry Pi and then use Gpio instance from the onoff library to read the input state.

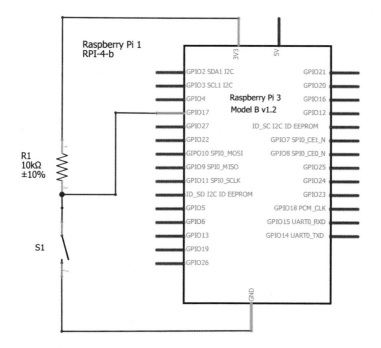

Figure 12-5 Raspberry Pi button input circuit

We connect the button to a Raspberry Pi using the circuit shown in **Figure 12-5**. The button uses GPIO17. When the button is not pressed, the 10k resistor (which is connected to the 3.3-volt supply) lifts the input to 1. When the button is pressed, the switch connects the input to the ground, causing the input to drop to 0.

Figure 12-6 shows how the circuit would be constructed on a breadboard. The software uses the same Gpio object from the onoff library as the output example. A Gpio instance can be configured as an input when it is created. The statement below creates an object that represents GPIO pin 17. The input must trigger an action when the input changes from low to high and when the input changes from high to low. This behavior is selected with the both configuration option.

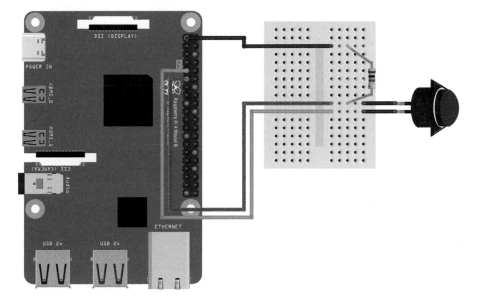

Figure 12-6 Raspberry Pi button input breadboard

The input also has a debounceTimeout filter implemented inside the port object to reduce repeated triggering if the switch generates signal noise as it is opened and closed.

```
this.gpio = new onoff.Gpio(17, 'in', 'both',{debounceTimeout:10});
```

The application could read the input port to determine whether the button has been pressed, but this is not what we want. We would like to call a function when the signal changes state. The Gpio class provides a watch method that specifies a function to be called when the input signal changes state. The code below shows how this is used inside the inGPIO object to provide input signals to the application. The function receives value and error parameters if an error is displayed. Otherwise, the new value is checked against the previous one. If there is a change, the callback method is called to deliver the updated value to the application.

```
this.gpio.watch((error,value) => {
    if(error){                                              ──── Check for an error
        console.log('GPIO ${this.GPIONumber} error ${error}');
    }
    else {                                                  ──── Got a valid input
        // Make sure the value has changed
        if(this.oldValue==undefined){                       ──── First signal change
            console.log('    Sending:${value}');
            // send the result to the callback
            this.callback(value);                           ──── Call the callback function
        }
        else {                                              ──── See if the signal has changed
            if(this.oldValue != value){
                console.log('    Sending:${value}');
                // send the result to the callback
                this.callback(value);                       ──── Call the callback function
            }
        }
        this.oldValue = value;                              ──── Update the old value
    }
})
```

CODE ANALYSIS

The watch function

You may have some questions about what is happening here.

Question: What does the watch function do again?

Answer: Our server needs to know when the input signal changes from 0 to 1 or vice versa. The watch function lets our program say: "When you get a change on the input, call this function." The function in the code above is an arrow function that ensures we have had a genuine change in state. If a genuine state change occurs, a callback function is called.

Question: What do you mean by a "genuine" change in state?

Answer: The function called by watch should only be called when the value of the input signal changes. However, when I tested the code with a very noisy switch, I discovered that sometimes the program would get multiple triggers for a value at the same level. I've implemented a filter that remembers the previous state in the variable oldValue and only responds to changes. This is a nice example of using software to compensate for hardware issues.

Question: What does the callback function do?

> **Answer:** The callback function is how the input function sends a message to the application to tell it that the input state has changed. Below is the constructor for the InGPIO class. It is supplied with the pin number to use and a function to be called when the input changes state. These values are stored in the object.

```
constructor(GPIONumber, callback) {
    this.GPIONumber = GPIONumber;
    this.callback = callback;
}
```

> The code below shows how an InGPIO instance is created. The application uses pin 17, and the sendButtonState function is called when the input changes state.

```
let buttonGPIO = new InGPIO(17, sendButtonState);
```

Use WebSockets to send values from a server

Until now, every action an application performs has been in response to a request from the browser. The browser sends a message, and the server returns a response. However, with the button-connected server, this will not work. If the button changes, the server must send a message back to the browser. One way to do this would be for application users to refresh the page repeatedly. We could create a page for the button state viewer that regularly updates the button state display by using an interval timer like the one used in the ticking clock program from Chapter 3. However, there is a better way of doing this by using *WebSockets*.

Make a WebSocket

A WebSocket is a direct connection between code running in the browser and code running in the server. You can think of it as a pipe between the two. Code in the server can push values to the pipe so they will appear in the browser and vice versa.

Server WebSocket

The server will send a message to the browser when the button changes state. We are going to use the WS WebSocket library (*https://github.com/websockets/ws*). We need to install this into the server application, as shown below:

```
npm install ws
```

Once the library has been imported, we can use it in the application. The statement below imports the library.

```
import { WebSocketServer } from 'ws';
```

Now that we have the library, we can create a WebSocket server. The code is slightly complicated because web sockets use an HTTP connection as the transport, and we also want to use Express to host the pages. The code below creates an `app` server for Express (just like in previous applications) and then uses that to create an HTTP server and WebSocket server.

```
const app = express();                                    Make the express application
const httpServer= http.createServer(app);     Create an HTTP server from the express connection
const webSocketServer= new WebSocketServer({ httpServer});     Create a WebSocketServer
                                                                from the http connection
```

Now that we have our server, we can add behaviors to it. We do this by specifying events and then creating functions that respond to those events. One event occurs when a browser client connects to the WebSocket hosted by the server. The code below responds to a connection request and adds the connection to a list of connections. It also specifies functions to run when the socket sends a message and when a socket is closed. The server doesn't need to respond to incoming messages, so these are just printed on the console. When a socket closes, it is removed from the list.

```
let sockets = [];                                         List of connected sockets
webSocketServer.on('connection', (socket) => {            Runs when a client connects
    console.log("connected");
    sockets.push(socket);                                 Add the socket to the list
    socket.on('message', (message) => {                   Runs when the socket sends
        console.log('Received ${message}');                 a message to the server
    });
    socket.on('close', function () {                      Runs when the socket closes
        sockets = sockets.filter(s => s !== socket);
    });
});
```

Send messages from the server

In the "Remote button" section earlier in this chapter, we saw how the application could connect a function to GPIO pin, which runs when the pin changes state. The code below shows how the sendButtonState function is attached to GPIO pin 17.

```
let buttonGPIO = new InGPIO(17, sendButtonState);
```

Now we can fill in the sendButtonState function, which sends a message to all the connected sockets. The function works through all the connected sockets and calls the send method on each socket. The parameter to the send method is the state that was received from the GPIO pin.

```
function sendButtonState(state) {
    sockets.forEach(s => s.send(state));
}
```

Browser WebSocket code

The final part of the remote button application is the code that runs in the browser to create the WebSocket connection and then update the page when a message is received from the server. The WebSocket code is already built into the JavaScript environment in the browser, so we can just create a WebSocket, as shown in the statement below. When the socket is created, it is given the host's address. In this case, the button server is running on a machine on the local network called iotmaster.local and is using port 8080.

```
let socket = new WebSocket('ws://iotmaster.local:8080');
```

Note that the statement above connects to the iotmaster server. You must change this address if you gave your server a different name. Once the socket has been created, we can specify a function to run when a message is received. The code below shows how this is done. The socket's onmessage property specifies a function to be called when a message is received from the socket. We're using an arrow function that finds the buttonBanner object and then sets the text in the object to UP or DOWN.

```
socket.onmessage = (msg) => {
    let element = document.getElementById("buttonBanner");
    if(msg.data==1){
```

```
        element.innerText = "UP";
    }
    else {
        element.innerText = "DOWN";
    }
};
```

🚀 **MAKE SOMETHING HAPPEN 65**

Scan the QR code or visit *https://www.youtube.com/watch?v=jU8KVNrLxOo* for a video walk-through of this Make Something Happen.

Monitor a button

To perform this activity, you will need a Raspberry Pi and the hardware shown in Figure 12-3. Visit *https://github.com/Building-Apps-and-Games-in-the-Cloud/RemoteButton* to get the code for the application. Use Git to clone the software onto your Pi and start it. Then use the browser on your PC to navigate to the page hosted by the Pi and press the button connected to the Pi. The message on the web page will update.

We can use WebSockets to link the browser and the server directly. We could make a version of Tiny Survey, which updated the scores in real time as new values were entered. But what if we just wanted to send messages from one system to another? In that case, we can use a network mechanism called MQTT. Let's take a look at that.

Use MQTT

IBM developed MQTT (Message Queue Telemetry Transport) as a system management tool. It uses a "publish and subscribe" mechanism, which allows connected devices to communicate. The MQTT broker maintains a list of "topics." A device connected to the broker can subscribe to topics and publish messages to a topic.

Figure 12-7 shows a button, light, and an MQTT broker attached to a network. The broker maintains a list of topics. Any device on the network can publish a message to any topic and subscribe to any topic to receive messages from it. When a device publishes to a particular topic, all the devices that have subscribed to that topic will receive the published data. In **Figure 12-7**, the light has subscribed to the `data/button001` topic. Pressing the button could publish a message turning the light `on`. Many devices can subscribe to the same topic, so we could use one button to turn on many lights. Also, any device can publish to a particular topic, so we could have many buttons controlling the same light. To make life even more interesting, we can use wildcards in topics, so a system could subscribe to the data topic and receive all the messages published to that topic. Each message contains the sender's identity and the data packet.

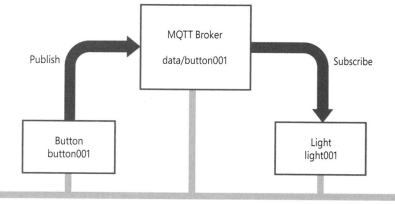

Figure 12-7 Button, light, and MQTT broker

The MQTT broker is an application that runs on a server connected to the network. When a device starts, it connects to the broker. Some brokers are open, meaning any device can connect, publish, and subscribe to any topic. Others require a device to authenticate to the broker with a username and password. You can run an MQTT broker on any machine, including the Raspberry Pi. The broker can run on the same machine hosting a `node.js` site. The Mosquitto broker is a good one to use. You can find it at *https://mosquitto.org/*. The Azure IoT Hub will also work as an MQTT broker.

MQTT installations can use secure sockets for their traffic to protect them from network eavesdroppers.

MQTT in a `node.js` application

The MQTT library from `mqtt` is used to connect a `node.js` application to an MQTT broker. This is installed in the usual way, as shown below:

```
npm install mqtt
```

Once the MQTT library has been installed, an application can connect to an MQTT broker using the `connect` function. The code below shows how a device can connect to an MQTT broker. It uses an open MQTT broker provided by HiveMQ (*https://www.hivemq.com/*). We can use this for testing and demonstration, but it is completely open. Anyone can publish, and anyone can subscribe to topics. The connection below uses the lowest quality of service (level 0) for sending simple commands.

```
import * as mqtt from "mqtt"                                    Import the library
let mqttClient = mqtt.connect("mqtt://broker.hivemq.com");      Call connect
```

Publish a message

Once a client connection has been created, the application can send messages to topics on the MQTT server. The code below sends the "Hello world" message to the topic "data." It is not possible to discover who, if anyone, received the message. The message doesn't go to anyone if no devices are subscribed to the "data" topic. If hundreds of devices are listening, they will all receive the "Hello world" string.

```
mqttClient.publish("data","Hello world");
```

Subscribe to a topic

The first step in receiving messages from MQTT is to subscribe to a topic. The statement below tells the `mqttClient` to subscribe to the data topic. If you want a device to subscribe to multiple topics, they can just perform several calls to subscribe with the required topic names.

```
mqttClient.subscribe( "data", { qos: 1 });
```

Quality of service

When you subscribe to a topic, you also set the "quality of service" of the connection. There are three levels of service. At level 0, a device will send a signal message to the broker. It might get through, or it might not. At level 1, a device will send multiple messages to the broker until it is told that the message has gotten through. This provides guaranteed delivery, but topic subscribers may get multiple copies of the message. Level 2 provides a guaranteed delivery, which subscribers receive exactly once. The higher the level, the more complex the protocol between the device and the broker. You should decide how much you care about messages getting lost and pick the appropriate service quality. It might not matter if one of many sensor readings gets lost, but you might want to ensure that important messages are received.

Get messages from a topic

The following code causes a JavaScript function to run when an incoming message is received on one of the topics subscribed to by the `mqttClient`. The following function prints the message and topic on the console.

```
this.mqttClient.on("message", (topic, message) =>
  console.log('Received ${message} on ${topic}'));
```

MAKE SOMETHING HAPPEN 66

Scan the QR code or visit *https://www.youtube.com/watch?v=2gDZdh_hdi0* for a video walk-through of this Make Something Happen.

Create an MQTT-controlled lamp

You will need a Raspberry Pi and the hardware shown in **Figures 12-3** and **12-6**. The code is on GitHub at *https://github.com/Building-Apps-and-Games-in-the-Cloud/MQTTLamp*. Use Git to clone the software onto your Pi. The program does not implement a website. Instead, it is run from the terminal. It sends on and off messages to the MQTT data topic and turns the LED on and off in response to incoming messages on the data topic. We can interact with the lamp by visiting the page *http://www.hivemq.com/demos/websocket-client/* and connecting to the HiveMQ server. Then we can publish the messages on or off to control the lamp

You could use this as the basis for a set of connected lights that listen on different topics. It uses the open MQTT broker at *mqtt://broker.hivemq.com*.

We have just scratched the surface with MQTT in this section. An MQTT broker connection can be password protected, and data can be sent using secure sockets to protect from eavesdropping. But it can also be used as a very simple and cheap way of connecting devices. The code above will run on the Raspberry Pi Zero. In the next section, we will discover just how far you can take JavaScript and MQTT.

Create an Internet of Things network

I created the "Connected Little Boxes" project to connect devices using MQTT to move messages between devices. Each message contains a JSON-formatted command that enables one device to control another. You could use it to connect a light to a button so that the light comes on when pressed or display a temperature value from a distant sensor. The project now supports a range of devices, including buttons, servos, rotary encoders, printers, environmental sensors, and text displays. I've also created a server application to manage devices and send messages to them. The Connected Little Box devices don't run JavaScript. Instead, they are controlled by an embedded C++ program, which manages the sensors and outputs connected to the box and sends and receives JSON-encoded messages over MQTT.

Create your own IoT devices

The Connected Little Boxes site at *https://www.connectedlittleboxes.com* is shown in **Figure 12-8**. Here you can find out about the project and even create your own device. Just plug an ESP32 or ESP8266 microcontroller into your computer and click **Get Started** on the page to install the Connected Little Boxes software on the device and configure it for your home WiFi. I suggest the WEMOS D1 mini device if you want an ESP8266 or the WEMOS D1 ESP32 if you want the ESP32. The ESP32 device has more power and can connect to hosts (including Azure IoT Hub) using secure sockets. These devices are found from suppliers such as Ali Express (*https://www.aliexpress.com/*). A device can control various peripherals, including LEDs, printers, environmental sensors, displays, buttons, and rotary encoders. A single device can control multiple peripherals.

Figure 12-9 shows several Connected Little Boxes, including pixel rings, text displays, passive infrared (PIR) sensors, buttons, rotary encoders, and servos. There are also designs for a thermal printer and light chains of NeoPixels. All the devices run the same software, which is configured for each application.

Figure 12-8 Connected Little Boxes site

Figure 12-9 Connected Little Boxes

Manage devices using the Connected Little Boxes server

You can use a server application to manage a Connected Little Boxes installation. Much of the code in the server uses techniques we have seen in this book. The server application uses log-in and session management. The user and device details are stored in MongoDB documents. When a user logs in, they can manage and control their devices. A user can display a list of the devices and then select a device to manage.

Figure 12-10 shows the configuration page for a device. Devices can be tagged and given friendly names.

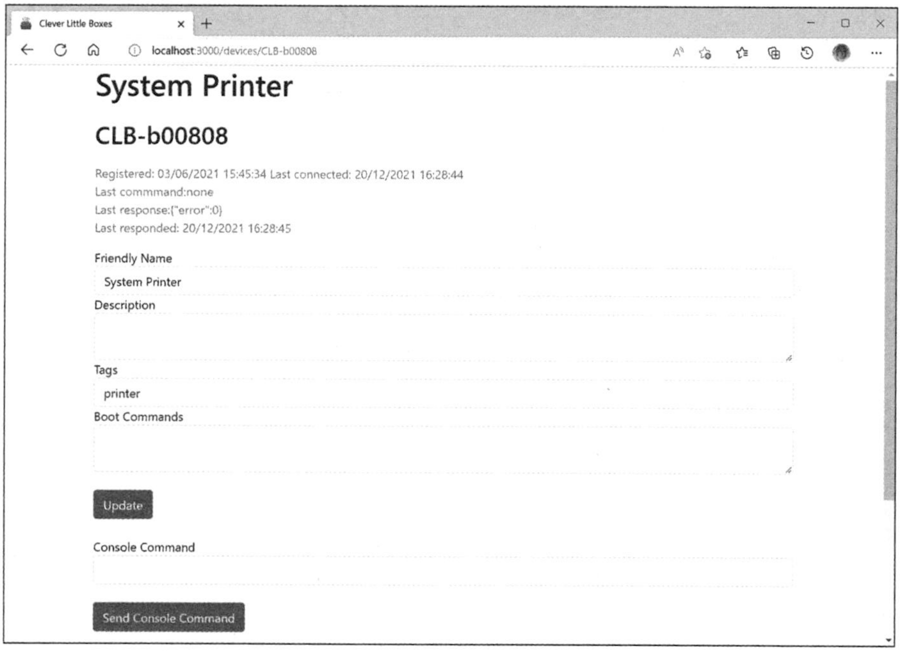

Figure 12-10 Device configuration page

The software, circuit, and box designs are available from GitHub at the Connected Little Boxes organization site at *https://github.com/connected-little-boxes*. There are repositories for the boxes and the server used to manage and control them. There are also designs for the circuits a 3D printable boxes for all the devices. We don't have the space to go into too much detail, but if you want to build a network of connected devices, there is much to explore.

Create a game using Phazer

In my *Begin to Code with JavaScript* book, we created a game called Cracker Chase using the HTML canvas element. In the game, you steered the cheese to catch crackers while being chased by tomatoes. We created a sprite engine and a simple physics model to make the game work. However, you should use a framework such as Phazer (https://phaser.io/) to create a game that runs inside a browser. Phazer provides sprite animation, a physics engine, particle effects, and scene management. You can use it to create arcade-quality 2D games that will run inside the browser. The games are hosted on an HTTP or Express site serving the game files.

Serving static files from Express

Until now, all the files we have served from an Express server have been EJS files containing HTML document templates. However, sometimes you want to serve out HTML files and other resources such as images and sounds. The statement below shows how to do this. It creates a static route. All the files to be shared out are in the public folder. Once this static route has been added to the server middleware, Express will look in the server's public folder for any HTML or resource files requested by the browser. If a matching file is found, it is returned to the browser.

```
app.use (express.static('public'));
```

The static folder can contain folders so that you can separate the files. You can also create multiple static routes, and the express server will look at each one in turn. For the CrackerChase game, the public folder contains the `index.html` file for the game itself and all the asset folders holding the images and sounds used by the game. We don't have the space for a detailed description of how Phazer works in this book, but I have created a Phazer version of Cracker Chase for you to explore. It uses the built-in Phazer physics engine, which controls the movement of the sprites and detects collisions. There are many other examples to explore and many tutorials you can follow to learn more.

Scan the QR code or visit *https://www.youtube.com/watch?v=b_aL4hz0GqY* for a video walk-through of this Make Something Happen.

Play Cracker Chase

You can find the code for the Phazer Cracker Chase game is on GitHub at *https://github.com/Building-Apps-and-Games-in-the-Cloud/CrackerChase*. Use Git to clone the software onto your PC. Then start it running and visit *http://localhost:8080* to play the game.

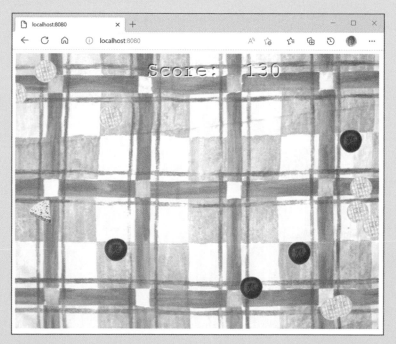

As I made the Phazer version of Cracker Chase, I found many features I wanted to explore. You can make sprites collide and bounce off each other. You can give them mass and angular velocity so they can rotate. You can create animated sprites using sprite sheets. You can create fixed elements for things like platform games. It is a very powerful system.

Further development

Here are some other technologies that you might find interesting as you expand your knowledge of JavaScript. There are further links to the topics in the code examples for this chapter.

Typescript

As we have learned JavaScript, we've noticed some aspects of the language design make creating applications harder than it needs to be. JavaScript is perhaps a bit too relaxed about how types can be combined and changed. As the name implies, Typescript (*https://www.typescriptlang.org/*) adds type management to JavaScript and a compilation process that detects errors that would be hard to spot in JavaScript code. A compiled Typescript program is a JavaScript program, so you can use Typescript anywhere you can use JavaScript. If you want to create safer and easier-to-manage code and learn how a language can use types to make code better and safer, you should take a look at TypeScript.

React

We've seen how the Express framework creates a user interface. This is a good stepping stone to learning React (*https://reactjs.org/*). React lets you make stateful user interface components that automatically update only required elements when the user interacts with the application.

Electron

The Electron framework (*https://www.electronjs.org/*) creates free-standing applications powered by JavaScript. We know that we can run JavaScript applications by installing the `node.js` framework on a PC, but Electron builds on this to allow you to create cross-platform applications that can be installed and just run like any other application. The Visual Studio Code application we have used since Chapter 1 is a

JavaScript program running on our PC using Electron. If you want to create free-standing applications powered by JavaScript, you should look at this.

Graphql

We've seen how our applications interact with databases by sending them queries and then working with the data that comes back. We used this in the Tiny Survey application when we worked with stored surveys. The Grapql framework (*https://graphql.org/*) makes working with your data stores easy.

Socket.io

The socket.io (*https://socket.io/*) framework builds on WebSockets to provide a powerful platform that you can use to create connected applications. It provides user identification and session management. You can use it to create multiplayer games or any distributed application. It will save you a lot of effort and is well worth a look.

ml5.js

You can use machine learning to create applications that can recognize objects, read your facial expression, identify the pose you are striking, compose music, and do many other things. You can use the ml5.js (*https://ml5js.org/*) library to connect to a JavaScript implementation of TensorFlow, a very popular machine-learning tool. You can get a great introduction to machine learning in JavaScript in the Coding Train videos starting at *https://www.youtube.com/watch?v=26uABexmOX4*.

Espruino

If you want to run JavaScript code on a tiny device—or even a watch—you should look at Espruino products (*http://www.espruino.com/*). They can be programmed in JavaScript directly from your browser over Bluetooth. They can talk to other Bluetooth devices as well as external peripherals.

What you have learned

This has been a fun chapter. We now know how to create reliable and secure sessions for an application. This is what we have learned.

- You can install node.js on a small machine such as the Raspberry Pi and use it to host JavaScript applications in your own "mini cloud."

- A node.js application running on a Raspberry Pi can interact with hardware connected to the Pi. This allows clients to connect via a browser to interact with the hardware on the server. We can use this to create a light that can be controlled by the browser and a button on the server that can be used to send a signal to users browsing the website.

- A JavaScript application can use the WebSockets framework to pass data to and from the browser and the server. Either the browser or the server can initiate a WebSocket connection. The data in the connection can be passed over an HTTP connection. This allows a server application to send a message to the browser without the browser making a request. We used it to send a message to connected users when a button connected to the server hardware was pressed.

- Message Queue Telemetry Transport (MQTT) is a way that devices with small amounts of computing power (for example, microcontrollers) can communicate with themselves and with servers. MQTT uses a publish-and-subscribe service hosted by an MQTT broker. Devices can connect to the broker and subscribe to topics and publish messages to topics. When the broker receives a publish request for a given topic, it will publish the message data to all the devices subscribed to that topic. This makes it very easy for two devices to communicate. One subscribes to a topic, and the other publishes messages to it. Topic names can be arranged in a hierarchy, and a device can subscribe to a point in that hierarchy and receive all the messages for all the topics below that point. For example, a device could subscribe to the **sensors** topics and receive all the messages to topics such as **sensors/kitchen** and **sensors/garage**. Each message contains the full topic name and the data.

- The JavaScript MQTT library can be installed in a node.js application, allowing a program to publish and subscribe.

- You can run an MQTT broker on a Raspberry Pi device. A good one to use is the Mosquitto broker. You can also use Azure IoT Hub as an MQTT broker. MQTT connections can be authenticated by a username and password and sent using a secure sockets connection.

- The Phazer framework makes it easy to create games using JavaScript. It contains lots of elements specifically for game creation.

- An express application can serve static files (act as an HTTP server) for pages and resources that are not to be generated by templates.

And now, for the last time in the book, you might want to consider the following "profound questions" to reinforce your understanding of this chapter.

Question: Can I run JavaScript on any computer?

Answer: JavaScript programs are interpreted. The source of a JavaScript program is fed into a program that works out what each statement does and then performs that statement. This is in contrast with a compiled language such as C++. A compiled C++ program is a sequence of instructions directly performed by the hardware of the target device. For a device to run JavaScript programs, it must be powerful enough to run the JavaScript interpreter. The processor inside a Raspberry Pi can run the JavaScript interpreter, but the one in an Arduino device (a popular computer for embedded applications) is not powerful enough.

Question: How do I make a Raspberry Pi server run my JavaScript when it starts up?

Answer: This is a good question. We have seen how we can start a `node` and turn a Raspberry Pi into an application server. We might like this to happen each time the Pi is turned on. The simplest way is to edit `rc.local` in the `/etc` folder. This contains commands that are to be obeyed when the Pi boots up. Add the command to start your program to this file, and it will be started when the machine boots. This will work, but if your application crashes, you must turn the Pi off and on again to restart it. A better way is to use a tool called `systemd`, an operating system component used to stop and start services. You can tell the system to restart your program if it crashes.

Question: How much hardware can I connect to a Raspberry Pi?

Answer: A Raspberry Pi has a 40-pin connector that exposes many interface pins. You can't use all of them, but you can certainly use up to 20 or so. A Raspberry Pi can supply enough power for LEDs and small peripherals, but if you want to control motors, you may have to add circuits and power supplies that can deliver more power than the pins on the Pi.

Question: I'm running Visual Studio Code on my Pi, and it is very slow. Can I fix this?

Answer: By turning off some of the optimizations, you can make Visual Studio Code run much better on a Raspberry Pi. Open it up, use **CTRL+SHIFT+P** to open the command window, and type **Preferences: Configure Runtime Arguments**. This opens a configuration file containing the **disable-hardware-acceleration** property, which is normally commented out. Remove the comments so the line "lights up." Quit Visual Studio and restart it. Now, you should find the user interface properly usable.

Question: What kind of data can I send down a WebSockets connection?

Answer: You can send any kind of data you like. In this chapter, we sent simple text commands, but you could send JSON that describes complex objects. The difficulty with WebSockets is organizing all of the connections on the server side. Take a look at the socket.io framework, which helps a lot.

Question: What kind of devices can I connect using MQTT?

Answer: You can connect very low-power devices to an MQTT network. There are MQTT client libraries for a variety of different languages and platforms. I suggest the Paho client as a good starting point. See *https://www.eclipse.org/paho/*.

Question: What happens if an MQTT device fails?

Answer: MQTT was originally created for sending system management messages between computers. An MQTT device sends the broker regular "I'm still alive" messages. It can set a "last wishes" behavior, causing the broker to send a message automatically if it hasn't heard anything from an MQTT device. This allows other devices to be informed when an MQTT device fails.

Question: Can I make 3D games with Phazer?

Answer: The Phazer framework is primarily 2D, although some 3D physic engines work with it. If you are just starting out with game development, my strong advice is to start with 2D to keep things simple.

Question: What else can I do with JavaScript?

Answer: Almost anything. There are libraries for a huge range of different applications. My strongest advice is to search for these when you have a bright idea and want to start building it. There is a good chance that an existing library or tool will help you build your solution. Make sure to search GitHub before you start writing lots of code. And remember to have fun.

Index

U

UML (Unified Modeling Language), 439, 483

undefined value (JavaScript), 15

unit tests, 373

urlencoded middleware, 322

URLs (universal resource locators), 153, 209

user communication in Node.js, 131

user engagement, 95

user input, 88-95

user sessions

    access tokens, 469-473

        authenticating, 475-476

        creating, 473-475

    logging in users, 467-469

    logging out users, 485

    registering users, 462-467

        messageDisplay function, 465

        password hashing, 463-465

        register route, 464

        template literals, 465

    renewing, 476-477

    role-based security, 477-480, 485

    storing details, 460-461

    workflow, 461-462

user stories, 268

user tracking, 438. *See also* cookies

    activity diagrams in workflow, 439-440

    checkTracking middleware, 442-445

    cookie approval workflow, 441-442

    cookie checking, 446-449

    ethics of, 439

    GUIDs, 438-439, 459

    security and, 483

    storing survey creator GUID, 449-450

    survey management, 450-458

UTC (Coordinated Universal Time), in random number generation, 234-235

V

validation

    with classes (JavaScript), 275-280

    of input, 334

varDemo function, 103

variables (JavaScript)

    in debugging, 28-30

    declaring in modules, 144

    global, 74-79

    local, security, 99

    scope, 99-106, 121

    setting, 22

var keyword, 99-106, 121

varScopeDemo function, 101

version management with Git, 311-315

viewing settings values, 97-98

virtual documents, 56

visibility of variables, 99-106, 121

Visual Studio Code

    installing, 51-53

    Live Server extension, 54-55

    performance optimization, 521

    stopping Go Live servers, 62

W

watch function, 503-505

web, 4

    Internet versus, 39

    cloud service providers and, 5-7

web browsers. *See* browsers

Web Content Accessibility Guidelines, 180

web pages. *See also* HTML (Hypertext Markup Language)

    buttons on, 73

    creating elements with JavaScript, 106-107

        button responses, 112-114

        event listeners, 117-118

        with loops, 107-111

        random number generation, 112

    editing, 59-61

    embedding JavaScript in, 62

    events on, 69-72

    hosting. *See* web servers

    JavaScript interaction, 63-69

    JavaScript modules in, 139-144

    loading, 57

    as logical documents, 56-57

    storing data on local machines, 95-98

    stuck functions (JavaScript) on, 85

    user input, 88-95

web servers, 4-6

    Cheese Finder game code, 197-198, 201-205

    cookies, 374-385

    creating, 145-146

    debugging, 147-150, 199-201

    endpoints, creating, 190-191

    fault analysis, 219

    file serving from, 153-159

    host addresses, setting, 245-246

    HTML file delivery, 191-194

    JavaScript on, 9

    player observation, 252

    port numbers, setting, 244-245

    protocols, 189-190

X–Y–Z